Psychiatry/ Neurology

PreTest® Self-Assessment and Review

D1378575

Psychiatry/ Neurology

PreTest® Self-Assessment and Review

Second Edition

Edited by

Joseph H. Friedman, M.D.
Chief, Department of Neurology
Roger Williams Medical Center

Associate Professor of Clinical Neurosciences
Brown University
Providence, Rhode Island

James D. Duffy, M.D.
Chief of the Program in Neuropsychiatry
Butler Hospital

Assistant Professor, Department of Psychiatry and Human Behavior
Brown University
Providence, Rhode Island

McGraw-Hill, Inc.
Health Professions Division
PreTest Series

New York   St. Louis   San Francisco
Auckland   Bogotá   Caracas   Lisbon   London
Madrid   Mexico   Milan   Montreal   New Delhi   Paris
San Juan   Singapore   Sydney   Tokyo   Toronto

123456789MALMAL998765432

ISBN 0-07-051983-8

The editors were Gail Gavert and Bruce MacGregor.
The production supervisors were Clara B. Stanley and Gyl A. Favours.
This book was set in Times Roman by Maryland Composition Co., Inc.
Malloy Lithographers, Inc., was printer and binder.

Library of Congress Cataloging-in-Publication Data

Psychiatry/neurology : PreTest self-assessment and review.—2nd ed.
  / edited by Joseph H. Friedman, James D. Duffy.
        p. cm.
     Rev. ed. of: Psychiatry/neurology / William DeMyer, Marian K.
DeMyer. c1982.
     Includes bibliographical references.
     ISBN 0-07-051983-8
     1. Psychiatry—Examinations, questions, etc. 2. Neurology—
Examinations, questions, etc. 3. Neuropsychiatry—Examinations,
questions, etc. I. Friedman, Joseph H. II. Duffy, James D.
III. DeMyer, William, Psychiatry/neurology.
     [DNLM: 1. Neurology—examination questions. 2. Psychiatry—
examination questions. WM 18 P9748]
RC457.P774 1992
616.8′0076—dc20
DNLM/DLC
for Library of Congress   91-25469
                                                                              CIP

Contents

Preface

This text contains 750 questions and answers to test neurologists and psychiatrists preparing for Part I of their specialty Board examinations. Part I of the American Board of Psychiatry and Neurology tests the basic sciences pertinent to clinical practice. Part I does not purport to test clinical skills as such, which are tested on Part II. Candidates must pass Part I to become eligible to take Part II.

When taking Part I of the Board examination, the neurology candidates will answer approximately 270 questions in neurology and 90 in psychiatry, for a total of 360 questions. Psychiatry candidates will answer 250 questions in psychiatry and 90 in neurology, for a total of 340 questions. The actual proportion of questions devoted to each basic science in this text approximates the proportion that will appear on the Board examination.

The questions in this text are arranged according to subject matter. In this way candidates can readily score themselves in each field to determine the adequacy of their preparation. On the actual Board examination the questions will be arranged randomly rather than by subject matter. Within any given field in this text, as well as on the Board examination, the sequence of questions is meaningless. Do not look for any order or meaning in the sequence of questions.

We wish to thank Drs. Harry W. Fischer, Leena Ketonen, Mary Ambler, Mehdi Abedi, and Julie Armada for providing illustrations. We are particularly indebted to Dr. Haruo Okazaki for generously providing illustrations for the chapter on neuropathology.

Joseph H. Friedman, M.D.
James D. Duffy, M.D.

Introduction

Psychiatry/Neurology: PreTest Self-Assessment and Review, 2/e, has been designed to provide physicians with a comprehensive, relevant, and convenient instrument for self-evaluation and review within the broad areas of psychiatry and neurology. Although it should be particularly helpful to residents preparing for the American Board of Psychiatry and Neurology certification examination, it should also be useful for physicians in practice who are simply interested in maintaining a high level of competence in psychiatry or neurology. Study of this self-assessment and review book should help to (1) identify areas of relative weakness; (2) confirm areas of expertise; (3) assess knowledge of the sciences fundamental to psychiatry and neurology; (4) assess clinical judgment and problem-solving skills; and (5) introduce recent developments in psychiatry and neurology.

This book consists of 750 multiple-choice questions that parallel the format and degree of difficulty of the questions on the above-mentioned Board examinations. The questions in each chapter are followed by answers, paragraph-length explanations, and specific page references to either textbooks or journal articles. The bibliography at the end of this book is divided into neurology and psychiatry sections.

We have assumed that the time available to the reader is limited; as a result, this book can be used profitably a chapter at a time. By allowing no more than two and a half minutes to answer each question, you can simulate the time constraints of the actual Board examinations. When you finish answering all the questions in a chapter, spend as much time as necessary verifying answers and carefully reading the accompanying explanations. If after reading the explanations for a given chapter, you feel a need for a more extensive and definitive discussion, consult the references listed.

Based on our testing experience, examinees on most medical examinations who answer half the questions correctly would score around the 50th or 60th percentile. A score of 65 percent would place the examinee above the 80th percentile, while a score of 30 percent would rank him or her below the 15th percentile. In other words, if you answer fewer than 30 percent of the questions correctly, you are relatively weak in that area. A score of 50 percent would be approximately average, and 70 percent or higher would be honors.

We have used three basic question types in accordance with the format of the American Board of Psychiatry and Neurology certification and recertification examinations. Considerable editorial time has been spent trying to ensure that each question is clearly stated and discriminates between those physicians who are well prepared in a subject and those who are less knowledgeable.

This book is a teaching device that provides readers with the opportunity to objectively evaluate and update their clinical expertise, their ability to interpret data, and their ability to diagnose and solve clinical problems. We hope that you will find this book interesting, relevant, and challenging. The authors, as well as the PreTest staff, would be very happy to receive your comments and suggestions.

Psychiatry/ Neurology

PreTest® Self-Assessment and Review

NEUROLOGY

Neuroanatomy

DIRECTIONS: Each question below contains five suggested responses. Select the **one best** response to each question.

1. The red nucleus receives afferent projections from two major sources. These are

   (A) the oculomotor nucleus and the deep cerebellar nuclei
   (B) the thalamus and the deep cerebellar nuclei
   (C) the thalamus and the rubrospinal tract
   (D) the deep cerebellar nuclei and the cerebral cortex
   (E) the cerebellar cortex and the cerebral cortex

2. The optic tract ends primarily in the lateral geniculate body. Fibers also terminate in which one of the following structures?

   (A) Pretectal area
   (B) Medial geniculate body
   (C) Inferior colliculus
   (D) Red nucleus
   (E) Onuf's nucleus

3. The taste buds on the anterior two-thirds of the tongue receive their innervation from cranial nerve

   (A) V
   (B) VII
   (C) IX
   (D) X
   (E) XII

4. The cortical efferent pathway for volitional horizontal eye movements is best described by which of the following statements?

   (A) The pathway does not decussate
   (B) The pathway has equal numbers of decussating and nondecussating fibers
   (C) The pathway decussates in the supraoptic commissure of Meynert
   (D) The pathway decussates between the midcollicular and midpontine levels
   (E) The pathway runs down to the medulla and returns to the pons without decussating

5. The term *thalamic fasciculus* is most closely synonymous with

   (A) field H of Forel
   (B) field H_1 of Forel
   (C) field H_2 of Forel
   (D) all three fields of Forel
   (E) none of the above

6. A mass in the jugular foramen would cause all the following EXCEPT

   (A) hoarseness
   (B) Horner's syndrome
   (C) dysphagia
   (D) weakness of the sternomastoid muscle
   (E) deviation of the soft palate to the opposite side

7. Use of horseradish peroxidase as a technique for identifying neuroanatomic pathways depends on

    (A) retrograde transport along axons
    (B) destruction of myelin sheaths
    (C) Wallerian degeneration
    (D) inhibition of oxidative metabolism
    (E) inhibition of protein synthesis

8. Hemiballismus is typically associated with infarctions of the

    (A) ipsilateral subthalamic nucleus
    (B) contralateral subthalamic nucleus
    (C) ipsilateral pars reticulata of the substantia nigra
    (D) contralateral pars reticulata of the substantia nigra
    (E) red nucleus

9. The ansa lenticularis is correctly described by which of the following statements?

    (A) It is a nucleus between the internal and external segments of the globus pallidus
    (B) It connects the subthalamic nucleus to the putamen
    (C) It starts in the medial globus pallidus and eventually joins the thalamic fasciculus, terminating in the thalamus
    (D) It connects the putamen to the globus pallidus
    (E) It is a fiber bundle originating in the medial thalamus and terminating in the pars reticulata of the substantia nigra

10. Which one of the following statements concerning the cavernous sinus is true?

    (A) It is an irregular network of veins adjacent to the internal carotid artery and cranial nerves III, IV, V, and VI
    (B) It drains the rectus sinus
    (C) It is an arteriovenous structure
    (D) It drains directly into the internal jugular vein
    (E) It is distinct on each side and does not communicate with its partner

11. Assuming that the other cranial nerves remain intact, interruption of the IIIrd nerve causes the eyeball to be rotated

    (A) medially and up
    (B) medially and down
    (C) laterally and up
    (D) laterally and down
    (E) upward in the midline

12. A patient complains of diplopia only when looking up and to the right. The diplopia most probably represents weakness of

    (A) the right superior rectus or left inferior oblique muscle
    (B) the right superior oblique or left inferior rectus muscle
    (C) the right lateral rectus or left medial rectus muscle
    (D) the right inferior oblique or left superior rectus muscle
    (E) none of the above

13. A patient feels a sudden pop in his back while shoveling. The next day he awakens with severe pain and numbness of the big toe on the right foot. It is most likely that the patient has a herniated intervertebral disk at the interspace of

    (A) L3–L4
    (B) L4–L5
    (C) L5–S1
    (D) S1–S2
    (E) S2–S3

14. The two cranial nerves that differ radically from the typical histology of peripheral nerves are

    (A) I and II
    (B) III and IV
    (C) V and VI
    (D) VII and VIII
    (E) IX and XII

15. All the following statements concerning cranial nerve VII are true EXCEPT

    (A) lesions proximal to the geniculate ganglion cause weakness of muscles of facial expression, hyperacusis, impaired taste, and impaired tearing
    (B) lesions distal to the geniculate ganglion cause hyperacusis and may cause taste loss but no problem with tearing
    (C) a partial lesion of the VIIth nerve at the stylohyoid foramen may cause only facial weakness
    (D) aberrantly regenerating parasympathetic fibers following a VIIth nerve injury proximal to the geniculate ganglion are the cause of crocodile tears
    (E) patients with Bell's palsy often experience numbness because there are facial cutaneous sensory areas supplied by the facial nerve

16. All the following statements concerning the inferior olive (oliva) are true EXCEPT

    (A) uncrossed olivocerebellar fibers form the largest part of the inferior cerebellar peduncle
    (B) it projects widely through the cerebellar cortex
    (C) it projects to the deep cerebellar nuclei
    (D) afferents to it arise from the cerebral cortex
    (E) afferents to it arise from the red nucleus

17. The intermediolateral nucleus of the spinal cord

    (A) receives input from dorsal root ganglia
    (B) modulates proprioceptive input
    (C) sends out preganglionic sympathetic fibers
    (D) receives unmyelinated pain fibers
    (E) is the origin for gamma motor neurons

DIRECTIONS: Each question below contains four suggested responses of which **one or more** is correct. Select

A	if	**1, 2, and 3**	are correct
B	if	**1 and 3**	are correct
C	if	**2 and 4**	are correct
D	if	**4**	is correct
E	if	**1, 2, 3, and 4**	are correct

18. The IVth cranial nerve may correctly be described as

    (1) being the only cranial nerve to attach to the dorsal aspect of the brainstem
    (2) having the smallest diameter of all the cranial motor nerves
    (3) undergoing complete internal decussation
    (4) containing no myelinated fibers

19. A lesion that occupies the shaded area in the figure shown below would cause which of the following signs?

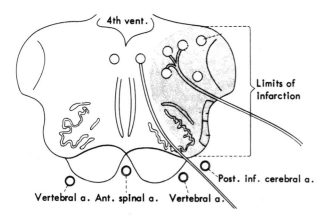

Used with permission of Macmillan Publishing Company, from *Medical Neurology* (p 546), by Gilroy J and Meyer JS, © 1975.

    (1) Contralateral loss of the corneal reflex
    (2) Contralateral paralysis of the arm and leg, sparing the facial movements
    (3) Contralateral dystaxia
    (4) Contralateral loss of pain and temperature of body and extremities

20. Regarding the figure shown below, correct statements include which of the following?

    (1) Large neurons appear in the plexiform layer
    (2) Purkinje cells are seen at the upper margin of the granular layer
    (3) The external granular layer is evident at the bottom of the photograph
    (4) This section could be from the posterior lobe of the cerebellum

21. The spinal cord is supplied by which of the following arteries?

    (1) Recurrent artery of Heubner
    (2) Artery of Adamkiewicz
    (3) Posterior inferior cerebellar artery
    (4) Vertebral arteries

22. The term *corpus striatum* includes the

    (1) caudate nucleus
    (2) globus pallidus
    (3) putamen
    (4) claustrum

23. A lesion of the nerve shown by the arrow in the figure below would produce which of the following clinical signs?

Adapted from Adams and Victor, ed 4, Fig 46-6, with permission.

    (1) Absence of the quadriceps muscle stretch reflex
    (2) Atrophy of the posterior muscles of the calf
    (3) Reduction in the circumference of the thigh
    (4) Loss of sensation over the posterior aspect of the thigh

24. Major, well-established components of the thalamic fasciculus include the

    (1) medial lemniscus
    (2) dentatorubrothalamic tract
    (3) pallidal efferent fibers
    (4) corticothalamic fibers

25. Electron microscopy characteristically shows which of the following structural features at synapses?

    (1) Small, round vesicles
    (2) Endoplasmic reticulum
    (3) Electron-dense material along the pre- and postsynaptic membranes
    (4) No mitochondria

26. Horner's syndrome may be caused by

    (1) infarctions in the distribution of the posterior inferior cerebellar artery
    (2) compressive spinal cord lesions at C7–T1
    (3) intrinsic spinal cord lesions in the upper thoracic segments
    (4) an ipsilateral hypothalamic lesion

27. The deep cerebellar nuclei may be characterized by which of the following statements?

    (1) They receive inhibitory input from the cerebellar cortex
    (2) They receive excitatory input from pontine nuclei
    (3) They provide a major feedback system to the cerebellar cortex
    (4) They provide most of the cerebellar outflow via the superior cerebellar cortex

28. Pallidothalamic fibers terminate in significant numbers on which of the following nuclei?

    (1) Ventralis posterolateralis
    (2) Ventralis lateralis
    (3) Medialis dorsalis
    (4) Ventralis anterior

DIRECTIONS: Each group of questions below consists of lettered headings followed by a set of numbered items. For each numbered item select the **one** lettered heading with which it is **most** closely associated. Each lettered heading may be used **once, more than once, or not at all.**

Questions 29–33

For each of the descriptions of cortical connections or projections listed below, select the thalamic nucleus to which it most closely relates.

(A) Lateral geniculate body
(B) Nucleus medialis dorsalis
(C) Nucleus pulvinaris
(D) Nucleus anterior and lateralis dorsalis
(E) Nucleus ventralis lateralis

29. Projects visual impulses to the calcarine cortex

30. Connects with frontal lobe anterior to the motor cortex (prefrontal cortex)

31. Projects to the nonstriate areas (eulaminate isocortex) of the parieto-occipito-temporal lobes

32. Projects to the motor cortex

33. Connects with the limbic cortex of the cingulate gyrus

Questions 34–37

For each of the statements listed below, select the region of the hypothalamus most closely involved.

(A) Ventromedial nucleus in tuberal region
(B) Supraoptic nuclei
(C) Posterior hypothalamus
(D) Preoptic region
(E) Arcuate nucleus

34. This area is concerned with water balance

35. Body heat is increased by this region when core temperature declines

36. Destruction of this area bilaterally results in hyperphagia

37. This region is important in controlling release of gonadotropic hormones from the pituitary

Questions 38–42

For each lesion listed below, match the visual field defect (if any) to which it is most closely related.

(A) Partial contralateral superior homonymous quadrantanopia
(B) Superior altitudinal hemianopia of both eyes
(C) Partial contralateral inferior homonymous quadrantanopia
(D) Complete contralateral homonymous hemianopia without macular sparing
(E) No visual field defect

38. Complete destruction of the calcarine cortex of one occipital lobe

39. Destruction of the anterior part of the temporal lobe

40. Bilateral destruction of the inferior bank of the calcarine fissure

41. Unilateral destruction of the inferior part of the parietal lobe

42. Destruction of the splenium of the corpus callosum

Neuroanatomy

Answers

1. **The answer is D.** (*Carpenter, ed 3. p 186.*) The red nucleus is a prominent midbrain structure. It contains, in addition to neurons, myelinated fibers to the superior cerebellar peduncle and the oculomotor nerve. Its major input arises from the deep contralateral cerebellar nuclei after crossing in the caudal midbrain. The cerebral cortex projection arises from the precentral and premotor cortex.

2. **The answer is A.** (*Carpenter, ed 3. p 258.*) The optic tract projects to the pretectal area, where the consensual pupillary reflex arc is located, and to the superior colliculus. The superior colliculus is important in visual tracking and voluntary eye movements. In many animals an additional connection to the suprachiasmatic nucleus in the thalamus has been detailed. This connection is undoubtedly important in circadian rhythmicity.

3. **The answer is B.** (*Adams RD, ed 4. pp 187–188.*) The VIIth cranial nerve innervates the taste buds on the anterior two-thirds of the tongue. The IXth and Xth cranial nerves innervate the remaining taste buds. The major clinical indication for testing of taste is the suspected presence of a VIIth nerve lesion. Testing of taste of the posterior part of the tongue and pillars innervated by the IXth and Xth nerve lacks practical clinical value. The testing of taste is an unsatisfactory method for evaluation of brainstem function. No discrete brainstem lesions that abolish taste regularly occur, and the actual central pathway in humans remains in some doubt.

4. **The answer is D.** (*Adams RD, ed 4. p 208.*) Although the exact corticobulbar pathway for horizontal conjugate eye movement has yet to be precisely identified, it is thought to decussate somewhere between the midcollicular level of the midbrain and midpontine levels. Interruption of the fibers at pontine levels after decussation impairs lateral conjugate gaze ipsilateral to the lesion. Interruption of the fibers rostral to the decussation impairs gaze contralateral to the lesion. The decussation of the optomotor fibers occurs in the tegmentum. These fibers do not interrupt the other cortical efferent fibers that occupy the basis.

5. **The answer is B.** (*Carpenter, ed 3. p 307.*) Field H_1 of Forel is the lamina of myelinated fibers between the zona incerta and the thalamus. This lamina of fibers is also termed the *thalamic fasciculus*. It receives fibers from fields H and H_2, but is most nearly synonymous with field H_1. This field conveys sensory fibers from the lemnisical systems and motor fibers of cerebellar and pallidal origin. Therefore, it is not a unitary tract with a single unitary function. The thalamic fasciculus forms a shell of myelinated fibers around the ventral surface of the thalamus and becomes continuous with the shell of myelinated fibers around the lateral aspect of the thalamus, known as the *external medullary lamina*. The myelinated capsule extends continuously across the dorsum of the thalamus, where it

7

is designated the *striatum zonale*. The medial border of the thalamus, which forms the boundary of the third ventricle, contains few myelinated fibers. Thus the thalamus is surrounded by myelinated fibers that form a capsule ventrally, laterally, and dorsally, but not medially.

6. **The answer is B.**   (*Adams RD, ed 4. p 1085.*)   Cranial nerves IX, X, and XI exit the skull via the jugular foramen. Lesions of the IXth and Xth nerves cause unilateral vocal cord weakness, dysfunction of swallowing, and soft palate weakness. The XIth nerve innervates the sternomastoid and the upper trapezius. Horner's syndrome is caused by interruption of the sympathetic fibers between the hypothalamus and the upper thoracic cord and then between the cord and the face along the carotid artery.

7. **The answer is A.**   (*McGeer, ed 2. p 34.*)   Use of horseradish peroxidase to exhibit neuroanatomic connections depends on retrograde transport of the material along axons. Horseradish peroxidase, a glycoprotein of relatively low molecular weight (43,000 daltons), enters axons or axonal endings by pinocytosis after injection into the central nervous system. The axon then transports the material to the perikaryon, where it can be displayed by the appropriate chemical reactions, thus identifying the cell of origin of the axon. If given intravenously, horseradish peroxidase passes the muscle capillaries but fails to penetrate the blood-brain barrier. If it did penetrate the barrier, horseradish would lack usefulness as a tracer because the perikarya would take it up indiscriminately. This technique supplements the older techniques of tracing axonal pathways by degeneration methods, but it is impractical for use in the human brain because it requires direct injections and sacrifice of the animal.

8. **The answer is B.**   (*Adams RD, ed 4. pp 63, 66. Carpenter, ed 3. p 317.*)   *Ballismus* refers to flinging, throwing, or kicking movements caused by involuntary contractions of proximal muscles. This is often considered a proximal form of chorea. In the primate, surgical lesions of the subthalamic nucleus (nucleus of Luys) produce contralateral hemiballismus. Because the ballismus is abolished if further lesions are made in the ipsilateral globus pallidus, the fascicularis lenticularis or the ventral lateral thalamic nuclei, it is thought that the subthalamic nucleus exerts an inhibitory influence on the globus pallidus and the ventral thalamus. In humans hemiballismus usually arises from lesions of the subthalamic nucleus but may rarely arise from other basal ganglia structures or the thalamus.

9. **The answer is C.**   (*Carpenter, ed 3. pp 307–308.*)   The term *ansa* designates a looplike structure. In this case it is a fiber bundle that originates in the lateral portion of the medial segment of the globus pallidus. It sweeps around the posterior limb of the internal capsule, enters field H of Forel, and then enters the thalamic fasciculus, which terminates in the rostral ventral thalamic nuclei.

10. **The answer is A.**   (*Carpenter, ed 3. p 412.*)   The cavernous sinus is an irregular network of veins that encases the internal carotid artery and cranial nerves III, IV, V, and VI. The two sinuses communicate with each other via the basilar venous plexus and then drain into the petrosal sinuses. Blood then enters the transverse sinus and the internal jugular vein.

11. **The answer is D.**   (*Adams RD, ed 4. p 213.*)   After interruption of the IIIrd nerve (with the other cranial nerves intact), the eyeball turns out and slightly down. This position is dictated by the unopposed pull of both the intact lateral rectus, which turns the eyeball out, and the intact superior oblique, which turns the eyeball down as one of its actions and also intorts it. The eyeball is actively pulled into the down and out position by these intact muscles because the ocular muscles, unlike all other skeletal muscles, maintain some tonus even when the eye is not moving. Thus, the tone in these two muscles, unopposed by the paralyzed antagonistic muscles, actively deviates the eye in their direction of action.

12. The answer is A. (*Adams RD, ed 4. pp 213–215.*) A patient who has diplopia on looking up and to one side most likely has weakness of either the superior rectus muscle of the abducting eye or the inferior oblique muscle of the adducting eye. With the eye abducted, the superior rectus muscle elevates the eye. With the eye adducted, the inferior oblique muscle elevates the eye. These muscles of the two eyes are yoked together by a central regulating mechanism. A patient who has weakness of the medial or lateral recti would experience diplopia on lateral gaze, not just when looking laterally and up. If a patient with a superior rectus palsy looks laterally and up with that eye, the superior rectus muscle is the only elevator, and the muscle has its strongest action as an elevator with the eye in that position. If that eye looks medially and up, the action of the superior rectus muscle converts to adduction and intorsion. Under these circumstances, the inferior oblique muscle of that eye becomes the strongest and only elevator muscle, when the eye rotates medially and up.

13. The answer is B. (*Rowland, ed 8. pp 400–404.*) A patient with pain and numbness radiating into the right great toe most likely has an L4–L5 intervertebral disk herniation. Herniation of a lumbar disk is likely to affect the nerve root of the next lower segment. Thus an L4–L5 herniation affects L5 and an L5–S1 herniation affects S1. The L5 root innervates the large toe and dorsum of the foot in most persons, and the S1 root innervates the lateral aspect of the foot and small toe. Compression of the roots causes sensory complaints in the corresponding regions of the foot. The sacral vertebrae fuse into a single mass and lack intervertebral disks.

14. The answer is A. (*Carpenter, ed 3. pp 255–258, 323–324.*) Cranial nerves I and II do not have a histologic pattern like that of the other cranial nerves. Cranial nerve I contains only small, unmyelinated afferent axons. Cranial nerve II, rather than being a peripheral nerve, is part of the central nervous system and has oligodendroglia rather than Schwann cell myelin. Thus, nerves I and II fail to display the same pathologic reactions as the nerves with the typical peripheral histologic structure. The olfactory neurons arise from the ectodermal olfactory epithelium. The nerve cell bodies lie in the nasal mucosa. Their tiny, unmyelinated axons perforate the cribriform plate to synapse on the olfactory bulb. These axons may have the slowest conduction velocity of any nerves in the body. The so-called optic nerves represent the stalk of diverticuli that grow out from the ventral part of the diencephalon to produce the retina. Axons from the ganglion cell layer of the retina grow back through this stalk, constituting the optic nerve; but the stalk begins as central, rather than peripheral, nervous system and remains histologically as central nervous system.

15. The answer is E. (*Carpenter, ed 3. pp 149–153.*) The VIIth nerve contains some innervation from the spinal trigeminal tract (Vth nerve), which supplies the external auditory meatus and a patch in the retroauricular region. When herpes zoster causes a VIIth nerve paresis, vesicles are evident either behind the ear or on the external ear, not on the face. This is called the *Ramsey-Hunt syndrome.* The VIIth nerve exits the stylohyoid foramen and includes fibers from the superior salivatory nucleus and the nucleus fasciculus solitarius. Nerves from the geniculate ganglion supply taste to the anterior two-thirds of the tongue and terminate in the gustatory nucleus. Preganglionic neurons in the salivatory nucleus supply the chorda tympani, the lacrimal glands, and the submandibular and sublingual salivary glands.

16. The answer is A. (*Carpenter, ed 3. p 111.*) The inferior olive is the most prominent structure in the medulla and has the appearance of a folded bag. It is a major source of input to the cerebellum and constitutes the single largest portion of the contralateral inferior cerebellar peduncle. It projects widely through the cerebellar cortex and to the deep cerebellar nuclei and receives input from the cerebral cortex, red nucleus, periaqueductal gray, and the central tegmental tract.

17. The answer is C. (*Carpenter, ed 3. p 67.*) The intermediolateral nucleus is found in the thoracic and lumbar portions of the spinal cord, where it sends out preganglionic sympathetic fibers. These leave the cord via the ventral roots and synapse in the sympathetic ganglia, which then send fibers to the non-nervous-system end organ. Parasympathetic regions of the spinal cord lie in the cervical and sacral regions.

18. **The answer is A (1, 2, 3).** (*Carpenter, ed 3. p 173.*)   The IVth cranial nerve is the only nerve to exit from the dorsal surface of the brainstem. It has the smallest diameter of any cranial nerve. It undergoes a complete internal decussation before exiting at the junction of the superior medullary velum with the inferior colliculus. It conveys myelinated motor axons to the superior oblique muscle. After exiting from the dorsal aspect of the brainstem, the IVth nerve runs through the lateral wall of the cavernous sinus before entering the orbit through the superior orbital fissure. Interruption of the IVth cranial nerve at any site along its course causes paralysis of only one ocular rotatory muscle. The superior oblique muscle is the only muscle that the nerve supplies. The patient has diplopia on looking downward and inward with the affected eye. Patients sometimes compensate by keeping their head tilted, causing a pseudotorticollis.

19. **The answer is D (4).** (*Adams RD, ed 4. pp 634–638.*)   The shaded area in the figure accompanying the question shows the area usually involved in the lateral medullary syndrome of Wallenberg. This area receives its blood supply from the posterior inferior cerebellar artery (PICA) and is most often affected by an infarct. The occlusive arterial lesion is frequently in the vertebral artery rather than the PICA. The lesion may be limited to the lateral medullary area or to the cerebellar hemisphere, which the PICA also irrigates with blood, or it may involve both the medulla and cerebellum. The signs of a lesion usually include contralateral loss of pain and temperature sensation due to interruption of the crossed spinothalamic tract, and loss of pain and temperature sensation on the ipsilateral face from interruption of the descending root of the Vth cranial nerve. The corneal reflex may be reduced ipsilaterally, but more often it remains intact. Involvement of the spinocerebellar tracts or cerebellar hemispheres results in ipsilateral ataxia. An ipsilateral Horner's syndrome indicates that the descending fibers for the thoracolumbar autonomic system run through the lateral reticular formation of the medulla, the site of the infarct. Affected patients also usually have vertigo, sometimes nystagmus, and frequently nausea and vomiting. Such patients lack paralysis and pyramidal signs because the pyramids do not receive their blood supply from the PICA. Consciousness is preserved if the lesion is confined to the medulla.

20. **The answer is C (2, 4).** (*Carpenter, ed 3. pp 199–203.*)   This photomicrograph is of normal cerebellar cortex. The histology of the cerebellar cortex, unlike that of the cerebral hemisphere cortex, is uniform throughout, so that this particular section could represent any part of the cerebellar cortex. The cortex consists of three layers, which are—from the outside in—the molecular, Purkinje cell, and granular cell layers. The most striking features of the cerebellar cortex are the densely packed cells in the granular cell layer and the large Purkinje cells at the upper margin of this layer with their long processes extending perpendicularly to the surface of the cortex. The plexiform and external granular layers exist in the cerebral cortex, which has six layers, not three.

21. **The answer is C (2, 4).** (*Carpenter, ed 3. pp 392–394.*)   The spinal cord is supplied in the rostral region by branches of the vertebral arteries and radicular arteries. The paired anterior spinal arteries, one from each of the vertebral arteries, join to form a single, midline anterior spinal artery, which is also supplied by the segmental arteries. The anterior spinal artery branches into anterior radicular arteries. The posterior aspect of the cord is supplied by paired posterior radicular arteries that derive from segmental arteries. The artery of Adamkiewicz is the largest anterior radicular artery and generally travels with a lower thoracic or upper lumbar spinal root. The PICA supplies the medulla and cerebellum. The recurrent artery of Heubner supplies portions of the basal ganglia.

22. **The answer is A (1, 2, 3).** (*Carpenter, ed 3. p 34.*)   By definition, the corpus striatum includes the caudate, putamen, and globus pallidus. The caudate and putamen form a single nucleus that is partially cleft as the internal capsule slices through the striatum to divide it into two separate parts.

The caudate and putamen do retain their original continuity around the anteroventral edge of the anterior limb of the internal capsule. The interdigitation of the white capsular fibers with the edges of the adjacent gray caudate putamen gives a striated appearance—thus, the name *striatum*. The term *neostriatum* refers specifically to the putamen and caudate, which in lower animals is a single structure.

23. **The answer is B (1, 3).** (*Adams RD, ed 4. pp 1070–1071.*) In the figure accompanying the question, the arrow indicates the femoral nerve, a major branch of the lumbosacral plexus. The femoral nerve arises from lumbar roots 2, 3, and 4. It supplies motor fibers to the quadriceps femoris muscle, composed of the rectus femoris, vastus lateralis, vastus medialis, and vastus intermedius muscles. These muscles occupy the anterior compartment of the thigh and extend the leg at the knee. A lesion of the femoral nerve would cause weakness of knee extension and atrophy of the quadriceps muscles, with a reduction in the circumference of the thigh and absence of the stretch reflex of the quadriceps femoris muscle. An affected patient would lose sensation over the anteromedial aspect of the thigh. The lateral femoral cutaneous nerve mediates sensation on the anterolateral aspect of the thigh. One of the commonest causes of femoral neuropathy is diabetes mellitus.

24. **The answer is A (1, 2, 3).** (*Carpenter, ed 3. pp 308–309.*) The thalamic fasciculus consists of the lamina of myelinated fibers that runs along the ventral or inferior aspect of the thalamus, between it and the zona incerta. It conveys those axons that synapse in the thalamus from the lemnisci, dentatorubral system, and globus pallidus. It lacks corticothalamic axons, which approach the thalamus from other directions via the thalamic peduncles, rather than the thalamic fasciculus. Thus, the thalamic fasciculus serves to connect the thalamus with infracortical structures rather than with the cerebral cortex. A synonym for the thalamic fasciculus is field H_1 of Forel.

25. **The answer is B (1, 3).** (*Cooper, ed 5. pp 10–12.*) Electron microscopy shows that synapses contain small, round structures called *synaptic vesicles* that are presumed to contain neurotransmitters. Synapses have electron-dense materials called *synaptic bars* along the membrane of the pre- and postsynaptic cell. The synapses contain many mitochondria, but as a rule they show few microtubules. Microtubules are numerous along the axon and in the perikaryon and dendrites. Endoplasmic reticulum is abundant in the perikaryon but lacking in the axon and synapse.

26. **The answer is E (all).** (*Adams RD, ed 4. pp 435–436. Gilman S, ed 7. pp 185–186.*) Horner's syndrome consists of the triad of ptosis, miosis, and facial anhidrosis, although not all three are present with partial lesions. It results from interruption of sympathetic innervation to the face and eye. The fibers originate in the hypothalamus and descend ipsilaterally through the brainstem tegmentum to the intermediolateral columns of the eighth cervical segment and upper three thoracic segments. They then exit the cord and travel with the common and then internal carotid artery. Interruption of the pathway at any point, such as in the medulla with a Wallenberg stroke (PICA syndrome) or cord lesions at the level of the intermediolateral columns, can cause the syndrome.

27. **The answer is E (all).** (*Carpenter, ed 3. pp 208–211.*) The four deep cerebellar nuclei—the dentate, emboliform, globose, and fastigial—receive afferent innervation from the cerebellar cortex as well as from the rest of the brain, primarily from pontine nuclei. Cerebellar input flows through the inferior and middle cerebellar peduncles, whereas cerebellar output travels primarily from the dentate, emboliform, and globose nuclei via the superior cerebellar peduncle. There is an intricate connection in both directions between the cerebellar cortex and the deep nuclei. Since the cerebellar cortex provides only inhibitory projections and the deep nuclei have been found to be active, it has been assumed that the pontine projections to the deep nuclei are excitatory in nature.

28. **The answer is C (2, 4).** (*Carpenter, ed 3. pp 308–309.*) The pallidothalamic fibers project to the ventral intermediate and anterior parts of the thalamus, where they end in nucleus ventralis lateralis

and nucleus ventralis anterior. These connections help to bring the thalamus into the extrapyramidal motor circuits. The most posterior nucleus of the ventral tier is a sensory relay nucleus. The pallido-thalamic fibers loop under the internal capsule as the ansa lenticularis or run directly across the capsule as the fasciculus lenticularis. The fibers of the two fasciculi curve upward into the thalamus by joining the thalamic fasciculus, from which they enter the ventral tier of thalamic nuclei. These ventral tier nuclei then distribute to the motor cortex of the frontal lobe to form a link between the pyramidal and extrapyramidal circuits.

29–33. The answers are: 29-A, 30-B, 31-C, 32-E, 33-D. (*Carpenter, ed 3. pp 228–253.*) The thalamic nuclei have particular connections with the cerebral cortex. The calcarine cortex of the occipital lobe receives the projections from the lateral geniculate body. The medial and lateral geniculate bodies constitute the metathalamus. The nucleus ventralis posterior is the other major specific sensory relay nucleus of the thalamus. It relays somatic sensation to the parietal cortex.

The frontal lobe anterior to the motor cortex (the prefrontal cortex) has strong thalamocortical and corticothalamic connections with nucleus medialis dorsalis. The psychosurgical operation called *prefrontal lobotomy* severs these connections. Bilateral damage to these connections results in apathy and indifference to pain. At one time, such surgery was in vogue for a variety of psychiatric disorders, including schizophrenia. Its use is now limited to some patients with intractable pain or obsessive-compulsive neuroses and selected patients who are unresponsive to less radical therapies.

The nonstriate (eulaminate isocortical) areas of the parieto-occipito-temporal lobes have connections with the nucleus pulvinaris. This nucleus belongs to the dorsal tier of thalamic nuclei that lack a direct sensory relay function. Nucleus pulvinaris belongs with the association nuclei of the thalamus, which include the nucleus medialis dorsalis and the nucleus lateralis posterior. These nuclei connect with the parts of the cerebral cortex not directly devoted to the sensorimotor systems.

The motor cortex receives projections from the nucleus ventralis lateralis and the nucleus ventralis anterior. The nucleus ventralis lateralis constitutes the thalamic relay nucleus for the efferent system issuing from the cerebellum via the dentatorubrothalamic pathway. Along with the nucleus ventralis anterior, it also has connections with the globus pallidus. Thus these nuclei, which occupy anterior positions in the ventral tier of thalamic nuclei, have a prominent role in linking the extrapyramidal with the pyramidal circuits.

The limbic cortex has connections with the nucleus ventralis anterior and the nucleus lateralis dorsalis. The nucleus ventralis anterior projects to the anterior cingulate cortex, area 24 of Brodmann, while the nucleus lateralis dorsalis projects to the posterior cingulate cortex, area 23 of Brodmann. Thus, these are limbic nuclei of the thalamus.

34–37. The answers are: 34-B, 35-C, 36-A, 37-D. (*Carpenter, ed 3. pp 284–285.*) The hypothalamus is important in exerting control over a large number of behavior-related functions, such as autonomic functions, sexual and reproductive functions, sleep cycles, appetite, water and electrolyte balance, and rage. The anterior hypothalamus is important in cooling the body and responds to temperature increases; the posterior aspect does the opposite. Bilateral destruction of the anterior regions results in hyperthermia; bilateral destruction of the posterior regions results in poikilothermia. The supraoptic nucleus secretes vasopressin, which is important in water balance. Decreased vasopressin release results in diabetes insipidus. The ventromedial nucleus is important in satiety and anger. Its destruction results in increased eating due to the loss of satiety. The preoptic area is one region, including the amygdaloid complex, that is important in controlling ovulation.

38–42. The answers are: 38-D, 39-A, 40-B, 41-C, 42-E. (*Adams RD, ed 4. pp 202–204.*) Complete destruction of the calcarine cortex of one occipital lobe causes a complete contralateral homonymous hemianopia without macular sparing. This cortex receives the pathway originating in the temporal half of the ipsilateral eye and nasal half of the contralateral eye.

Destruction of the anterior part of the temporal lobe destroys the portion of the geniculocalcarine tract that loops around the temporal ventricle (Meyer's loop). These fibers convey the pathway originating in the inferior temporal quadrant of the ipsilateral retina and the inferior nasal quadrant of the contralateral retina, causing a contralateral superior field defect. The quadrantic field defect is usually incomplete but fairly homonymous.

Bilateral destruction of the inferior bank of the calcarine fissure causes a superior altitudinal visual field defect in both eyes. The inferior bank of each calcarine fissure receives the pathway that originates in the inferior temporal quadrant of the ipsilateral retina and the inferior nasal quadrant of the contralateral retina. Joining the two superior quadrantic field defects gives a superior altitudinal hemianopia.

Destruction of the inferior part of the parietal lobe causes a partial contralateral inferior homonymous quadrantanopia. The lesion destroys the superior fibers of the geniculocalcarine radiation. These fibers mediate the inferior homonymous fields contralaterally.

Interruption of the corpus callosum fails to cause a visual field defect per se. The lesion might, however, also encroach on the calcarine cortex located posterior to the splenium of the corpus callosum and cause a field defect in this way. A lesion extending laterally from the corpus callosum, such as a butterfly glioblastoma, would be very unlikely to cause a field defect because the geniculocalcarine tract, which conveys optic impulses, passes lateral to the wall of the lateral ventricle, separating it a considerable distance from the splenium.

Neuropathology

DIRECTIONS: Each question below contains five suggested responses. Select the **one best** response to each question.

43. All the following disorders are associated with neurofibrillary tangles EXCEPT

    (A) postencephalitic parkinsonism
    (B) progressive supranuclear palsy
    (C) dementia pugilistica
    (D) Down's syndrome
    (E) Shy-Drager syndrome

44. Progressive multifocal leukoencephalopathy (PML) is caused by

    (A) a human polyoma virus called the JC virus
    (B) a paraneoplastic autoimmune process
    (C) a slow virus related to the kuru prion
    (D) an as-yet-unknown mechanism
    (E) HIV

45. The most common intracranial mass lesion in the American adult with AIDS is due to

    (A) CNS lymphoma
    (B) Kaposi's sarcoma
    (C) staphylococcal abscess
    (D) polymicrobial abscess
    (E) toxoplasmosis

46. Brain abscesses in association with congenital heart disease usually are

    (A) solitary
    (B) polymicrobial
    (C) frontal in location
    (D) occipital in location
    (E) cerebellar in location

47. In tuberous sclerosis, the periventricular nodules characteristically occur in which of the following locations?

    (A) The frontal horns
    (B) The occipital horns
    (C) The ventricular roof
    (D) Mainly in the third ventricle
    (E) Along the thalamocaudate seam

48. An alcoholic patient shows severe dystaxia of gait with little involvement of the arms and no dysarthria or nystagmus. These findings result from which of the following lesions?

    (A) Degeneration of the spinocerebellar tracts
    (B) Degeneration of the flocculonodular lobe
    (C) Atrophy of the anterior vermis
    (D) Diffuse Purkinje cell loss in the entire cerebellum
    (E) Diffuse granule cell loss in the entire cerebellum

49. A muscle biopsy of a patient suspected of having polymyositis shows moderate amounts of inflammatory cells, recent necrosis, some regenerative changes in the fibers, and also some grouped atrophy of muscle fibers suggesting denervation atrophy. In this context, the significance of the denervation atrophy is that it

    (A) invalidates the diagnosis of polymyositis
    (B) establishes neurogenic atrophy as the correct diagnosis
    (C) suggests that the patient has two diseases
    (D) suggests that the patient has a toxic neuropathy
    (E) suggests a vasculitis of the vasa nervorum

50. Tropical spastic paraparesis has been associated with which one of the following etiologies?

    (A) Chick peas (*Lathyrus sativus*)
    (B) Human T-cell leukemia virus type I (HTLV-I)
    (C) Canine distemper virus
    (D) Machine oil ingestion
    (E) An inherited enzyme deficiency

51. The pathogenesis of arthrogryposis multiplex congenita is best described as being

    (A) overwhelmingly acknowledged as an expression of myelodysplasia
    (B) overwhelmingly acknowledged as myopathic
    (C) related to a defect in connective tissue
    (D) a congenital peripheral neuropathy
    (E) a symptom complex of varied causes

52. A muscle biopsy of a patient affected by the Kearns-Sayre syndrome of ophthalmoplegia with retinitis pigmentosa is likely to show

    (A) giant mitochondria with excessive quantities of lipids
    (B) dense central portions of muscle fibers that stain positively with the periodic acid-Schiff reaction
    (C) bacillus-like rods in the muscle fibers
    (D) ragged red type I fibers in the Gomori stain
    (E) central nuclei

53. An AIDS patient with an encephalitis but no mass lesions has unilaterally impaired vision. The fundus shows a white exudate with surrounding hemorrhage and edema. The most likely cause is

    (A) cytomegalovirus (CMV)
    (B) metastatic Kaposi's sarcoma
    (C) lymphoma
    (D) human immunodeficiency virus (HIV)
    (E) cryptococcus

54. All the following statements about the neurologic complications of subacute infective endocarditis are true EXCEPT

    (A) mycotic aneurysms tend to occur distally rather than proximally as with berry aneurysms
    (B) acute encephalopathy is common
    (C) aseptic meningitis is common
    (D) brain abscesses are common
    (E) seizures are common

55. The following low-power photomicrograph shows dilated vessels with thrombosis. Which one of the following correctly identifies the abnormality?

From Okazaki, 1989; with permission.

(A) Old infarct with partial revascularization
(B) Glioblastoma multiforme
(C) Hemangioblastoma
(D) Metastatic hypernephroma
(E) Arteriovenous malformation

56. The baby whose brain is shown below would most likely have

(A) been a twin
(B) had AIDS
(C) had polycystic kidneys
(D) had a myelomeningocele
(E) had any one of a number of in utero viral infections

57. A patient known to drink large quantities of beer was admitted to the hospital within weeks of starting a diuretic. His sodium level on admission was 105 meq/L. After a good initial response to rapid correction of his electrolytes, he began to develop progressive quadriparesis. The photomicrograph reveals the lesion. Which of the following is the correct diagnosis?

From Okazaki, 1989; with permission.

(A) Marchiafava-Bignami syndrome
(B) Wernicke-Korsakoff syndrome
(C) Central pontine myelinolysis
(D) Multiple sclerosis
(E) Syringomyelia

58. The lesion depicted below is a preventable disease. Choose the one correct treatment that would have made this disorder extremely unlikely.

From Okazaki, 1989; with permission.

(A) Thiamine
(B) Vitamin B_{12}
(C) Vitamin B_6
(D) Vitamin E
(E) Penicillin

59. The brain of a teen-ager shown below is best described as illustrating

(A) respirator brain
(B) hemiatrophy
(C) Alexander's disease
(D) metastatic cancer
(E) progressive multifocal leukoencephalopathy (PML)

60. A 30-year-old woman presents with weight loss, poor concentration, and depression developing over a month and a mildly unsteady but difficult to characterize gait disorder. The lesions below illustrate her diagnosis. The correct diagnosis is

From Okazaki, 1989; with permission.

(A) multiple sclerosis
(B) Epstein-Barr encephalitis
(C) progressive multifocal leukoencephalopathy (PML)
(D) Lyme encephalitis
(E) acquired immunodeficiency syndrome (AIDS)

61. An AIDS patient develops a progressive hemiparesis affecting her leg more than her arm. There is a mild dementia as well. The CT scan of the brain with contrast reveals no abnormality. The photograph below shows the lesion. The correct diagnosis is

From Okazaki, 1989; with permission.

(A) toxoplasmosis
(B) tuberculosis
(C) multiple metastases from Kaposi's sarcoma
(D) progressive multifocal leukoencephalopathy (PML)
(E) Creutzfeldt-Jakob disease

62. This tumor occurs in several histologic types but is of glial origin. The figure shows the epithelial type. It has a predilection for the ventricles but does not always have an intraventricular portion. Which of the following is the correct identification?

From Okazaki, 1989; with permission.

(A) Astrocytoma
(B) Ependymoma
(C) Chordoma
(D) Lymphoma
(E) Metastatic germ cell tumor

63. The photomicrograph below depicts which of the following nutritional disorders?

From Okazaki, 1989; with permission.

(A) Subacute combined degeneration
(B) Pyridoxine deficiency
(C) Wernicke's encephalopathy
(D) Lathyrism
(E) Lead encephalopathy

64. This mass was found in an elderly man who had suffered focal motor seizures for at least 5 years. Which abnormality is the correct description of the figure?

From Okazaki, 1989; with permission.

(A) Meningioma
(B) Arteriovenous malformation
(C) Vascularized lining of a chronic subdural hematoma
(D) Cavernous hemangioma
(E) Capillary venous malformation

65. The two figures are sections from different parts of the same neoplasm. Which is the correct diagnosis?

From Okazaki, 1989; with permission.

(A)   Astrocytoma grade II
(B)   Glioblastoma
(C)   Metastatic Kaposi's sarcoma
(D)   Medulloblastoma
(E)   Craniopharyngioma

DIRECTIONS: Each question below contains four suggested responses of which **one or more** is correct. Select

A	if	**1, 2, and 3**	are correct
B	if	**1 and 3**	are correct
C	if	**2 and 4**	are correct
D	if	**4**	is correct
E	if	**1, 2, 3, and 4**	are correct

66. The electron photomicrograph of peripheral nerve below exhibits

(1) an absence of myelinated fibers
(2) numerous inflammatory cells
(3) active Wallerian degeneration
(4) onion-bulb formation

67. A patient with cardiac arrest resulting in brain death is maintained on a respirator for 72 h. At autopsy, the brain would typically show which of the following?

(1) Collapse of the ventricles with extreme swelling
(2) Extreme firmness of the white matter to palpation
(3) Universal necrosis of neurons
(4) Thrombosis of most or all large cerebral arteries

68. In neurofibromatosis there is an increased association with which of the following tumors?

(1) Optic nerve gliomas
(2) Acoustic neuromas
(3) Trigeminal neuromas
(4) Ependymomas

69. Focal slowing of nerve conduction velocity at sites of chronic nerve entrapment, with normal conduction velocities distally, is related histologically to which of the following pathologic changes?

(1) Lymphocytic infiltration
(2) Nerve trunk edema
(3) Atrophy of the endoneurium
(4) Segmental demyelination

70. True statements concerning cerebral amyloid angiopathy include

(1) it spares the basal ganglia
(2) it is unrelated to systemic amyloidosis
(3) it is a recognized cause of lobar hemorrhages
(4) it is uncommon in older patients

71. Lipochrome (lipofuscin) may be characterized as

    (1) being an intracellular pigment that resists degradation
    (2) accumulating in many types of aging neurons
    (3) accumulating in the neurons of infants with Batten-Mayou disease
    (4) having an association with brain enlargement (megalencephaly)

72. In the periodic paralyses, one might observe which of the following during a paralytic attack?

    (1) Hypokalemia
    (2) Normokalemia
    (3) Hyperkalemia
    (4) Vacuolar myopathy on biopsy

73. Types of meningitis that occur with markedly increased frequency in American patients with AIDS include

    (1) pneumococcus
    (2) tuberculosis
    (3) pneumocystis
    (4) cryptococcus

74. Neuropathies with predominantly Schwann cell degeneration rather than primary axonal degeneration include

    (1) acute idiopathic polyneuritis (Landry-Guillain-Barré syndrome)
    (2) most cases of Charcot-Marie-Tooth peroneal muscular atrophy
    (3) diphtheria
    (4) uremic neuropathy

DIRECTIONS: Each group of questions below consists of lettered headings followed by a set of numbered items. For each numbered item select the **one** lettered heading with which it is **most** closely associated. Each lettered heading may be used **once, more than once, or not at all.**

Questions 75–77

For each diagnosis listed below, select the figure to which it is most closely related.

A

B

C

D

    E None of the above

75. Normal muscle

76. Neurogenic atrophy in an adult

77. Muscular dystrophy

Questions 78–82

For each pattern of demyelination or dysmyelination described below, select the disease to which it is most closely related.

    (A)   Pelizaeus-Merzbacher disease (aplasia axialis congenita)
    (B)   Sudanophilic leukodystrophy
    (C)   Metachromatic leukodystrophy
    (D)   Krabbe's globoid cell leukodystrophy
    (E)   Adrenoleukodystrophy

78.   The absence of myelin affects the parieto-occipital region most prominently but does extend into the frontal regions, often somewhat asymmetrically. The lesion shows three zones, visible on cut section and by CT scan

79.   Typically, the brain shows more or less symmetrical tigroid patches of myelinated fibers against an unmyelinated background of white matter. No enzymatic deficiencies are known

80.   The centrum ovale shows diffuse demyelination tending to affect the periventricular region maximally and sparing the arcuate fibers. No enzymatic abnormalities are recognized

81.   The brain and peripheral nerves contain an excess of sulfatides that stain brown with basic dyes

82.   The brain shows a disfuse demyelination, and the peripheral nerves show a segmental demyelination. Microscopic sections of cerebral white matter show accumulations of large spherical cells, many of which contain more than one nucleus

Neuropathology

Answers

43. The answer is E. (*Adams JH, ed 4. pp 117, 708.*) Neurofibrillary tangles (NFTs) are most commonly associated with Alzheimer's disease but are characteristic of other disorders as well. The NFTs of progressive supranuclear palsy are composed of paired straight filaments, which are different from the paired helical filaments found in the other disorders. The NFTs are associated with neuronal dropout and sometimes astrocytic gliosis in each of the disorders. The etiology of the NFTs in these varied disorders is unknown. The Shy-Drager syndrome is one of the "multisystem atrophies," which include striatonigral degeneration and olivopontocerebellar atrophy. Their pathology is characterized primarily by neuronal loss and gliosis in brainstem, basal ganglia, and cerebellar structures. In Shy-Drager syndrome there is involvement of autonomic structures as well.

44. The answer is A. (*Adams RD, ed 4. p 609.*) Progressive multifocal leukoencephalopathy (PML) occurs almost only in the context of a severe immunodeficiency state. Initially described in patients with lymphoma, it also has been recognized in other immunocompromised hosts, such as transplant recipients, patients with leukemia, and most recently in AIDS patients. It is caused by the human polyoma, JC virus, although a few cases have been caused by the SV 40 virus. It is untreatable and causes death in 2 to 20 months.

45. The answer is E. (*McArthur, Medicine 66:407–437, 1987.*) In general, the most common cause of intracranial masses in American adult patients with AIDS is cerebral toxoplasmosis. In other areas, tuberculosis is a more common pathogen. Diagnosis of toxoplasmosis is based on biopsy; serologic studies are usually not helpful since a high percentage of adults are serologically positive for the infection. Although all the other listed pathogens cause intrabrain masses, they are less common than toxoplasmosis.

46. The answer is A. (*Adams RD, ed 4. p 567.*) Brain abscesses associated with congenital heart disease usually are solitary. The number and distribution of brain abscesses provide some clue as to the cause. Therefore, knowledge of distributional patterns becomes important. Abscesses from mastoiditis or sinusitis tend to be adjacent to the site of infection. Thus, a frontal lobe abscess would be unlikely to have originated in the mastoid. Such an abscess would most likely be blood-borne and the clinician should suspect the lungs or heart as the organ of origin. Many chronic lung conditions serve as a source of brain abscesses. Lung abscesses themselves and bronchiectasis, for example, may provide the primary source of an infected embolus that could travel to the brain. In most cases a single organism is responsible for the infection.

47. The answer is E. (*Adams RD, ed 4. p 984. Okazaki, ed 2. pp 260–261.*) The periventricular nodules of tuberous sclerosis characteristically occur along the thalamocaudate seam (sulcus terminalis).

This characteristic distribution helps to distinguish these nodules from other periventricular lesions. Their profusion along the sulcus terminalis leads to a "dripped wax" effect resembling congealed wax drippings. The lesions also regularly occur in the cortex and may even be located in the white matter. The nodules of tuberous sclerosis consist of peculiar neural cells that are difficult to classify as either neuronal or glial. Some nodules may undergo malignant transformation, but most are hamartomatous with a potentiality for growth that is similar to the surrounding normal tissue.

48. **The answer is C.** (*Adams RD, ed 4. p 837. Okazaki, ed 2. p 193.*)   A particular syndrome characterized by unsteadiness of gait, little or no dystaxia on formal testing of the legs, and sparing of the arms, eyes, and speech is related to degeneration of the anterior and superior parts of the vermis and adjacent parts of the anterior lobe. All neurons of this region are affected, the Purkinje neurons perhaps more so than others. This syndrome is the closest approximation to an anterior lobe syndrome in humans. The clinical appearance is similar to that of the cerebellar aspect of the Wernicke-Korsakoff syndrome. Adams and Victor maintain that alcoholic cerebellar degeneration is probably the same process as the ataxia of Wernicke-Korsakoff syndrome.

49. **The answer is E.** (*Adams RD, ed 4. pp 952–953.*)   Some denervation atrophy occurs fairly often in muscles of patients who have polymyositis. Thus, this finding neither invalidates the diagnosis nor suggests a second disease process. Presumably, it indicates inflammatory involvement of the vasa nervorum of the peripheral nerves, with infarction and subsequent denervation atrophy of parts of the muscle. A muscle biopsy in and of itself is insufficient for the diagnosis of a neuromuscular disease. Some dystrophic muscle shows a considerable inflammatory component but absence of denervation atrophy. The biopsy should be integrated with the full range of clinical data to achieve a final diagnosis.

50. **The answer is B.** (*Rowland, ed 8. pp 695–696.*)   Tropical spastic paraparesis is a subacute disease restricted to tropical regions around the world. It has been associated with antibodies to the retrovirus HTLV-I (note that HTLV-III is the AIDS virus, also labeled as HIV-1) in about 80 percent of cases throughout the world. However, exposure to HTLV-I does not imply the presence of neurologic disease and the virus has not been shown to be causal as of this time. Clinically the illness is usually of subacute onset with corticospinal tract, posterior column, and bladder dysfunction and thus resembles a spinal cord form of multiple sclerosis.

51. **The answer is E.** (*Adams RD, ed 4. p 1142.*)   Arthrogryposis multiplex congenita refers to the condition of an infant born with more than one joint in a fixed position. Thus, it is a descriptive clinical term instead of a true diagnosis. Arthrogryposis is a symptom complex of varied causes rather than a disease entity with a specific, universally acknowledged pathogenesis. Any mechanism that interferes with mobility during intrauterine development may produce the clinical picture of multiple fixed joints. Oligohydramnios, which hampers intrauterine motility, or prolonged paralysis of the fetus by curare-like drugs may cause the syndrome in experimental animals. The pathogenetic mechanisms may involve hypoplasia or destruction of ventral horn neurons, destruction of nerves, and disease of muscle or connective tissue. Children born with their legs fixed in flexion and adduction are likely to have the myopathic variety of the arthrogryptotic syndrome.

52. **The answer is D.** (*Adams RD, ed 4. p 1144.*)   The muscle biopsy of a patient affected by the Kearns-Sayre syndrome of ophthalmoplegia, retinitis pigmentosa, and heart block shows ragged red type I fibers in the Gomori stain of muscle. These ragged red fibers are typical of mitochondrial myopathies. The syndrome may include retardation, hearing loss, and cerebellar and vestibular dysfunction. The other biopsy findings mentioned in the question occur in one of the various congenital myopathies, several of which may also affect the ocular or cranial nerve muscles. In central core disease, the central parts of the fibers stain positively with the periodic acid-Schiff reaction for carbohydrates. In nemaline myopathy, bacillus-like rods occur in the muscle fibers. The muscle

biopsy shows central nuclei in centronuclear myopathy. These various biopsy findings are virtually diagnostic of the disease in question.

53. **The answer is A.** (*Mandell, ed 3. p 1079.*) CMV is present in most AIDS patients and is transmitted in routes similar to those of HIV. It has a predilection for the retina, often involving one first rather than the two simultaneously. While toxoplasmosis also involves the retina, the coexistent encephalitis makes CMV a more likely pathogen. CMV can be cultured from blood or urine in over 80 percent of cases. Twenty-five percent of patients dying with CMV retinitis also have CMV in the brain.

54. **The answer is D.** (*Jones, Brain 112:1295–1315, 1989. Pruitt, Medicine 57:329–343, 1978.*) Brain abscesses are uncommon with endocarditis, especially in the subacute forms, and tend to be microscopic. Mycotic aneurysms may occur anywhere but tend to occur in distal parts of the vascular tree so that many aneurysmal ruptures result in intraparenchymal hemorrhages. Seizures are relatively common, presumably because of microemboli to the cortex. Acute encephalopathy and aseptic meningitis, with a granulocytic or lymphocytic pleocytosis, are common. Both are probably due to multiple microemboli. CSF may or may not grow the bacterial pathogen even when a granulocytic pleocytosis is present.

55. **The answer is E.** (*Okazaki, ed 2. pp 76–82.*) An arteriovenous malformation (AVM) is a tangled collection of thick-walled abnormal blood vessels that are structurally between veins and arteries. These malformations occur predominantly in the cerebrum (90 percent) and half occur in the middle section of the brain. As in the photomicrograph, they tend to have a wedgelike appearance with the wider base in the cortex. Neurologic damage and seizures occur on the basis of ischemia, compression, and hemorrhage; the last is proportional to the size of the AVM. Treatment of the AVM is somewhat controversial.

56. **The answer is A.** (*Adams JH, ed 4. pp 474–476.*) Multicystic encephalopathy is a poorly understood entity that occurs in twins. The severity varies so that its presence is not necessarily incompatible with life. The brain is usually small but has a normal gyral pattern with multiple cysts that are relatively symmetric in distribution. The cortex is thin to the point of being a fine membrane in some regions. The cause of the problem is unknown. The distribution of the lesions tends to be outside the vertebral arterial tree but is not in the distribution of a single blood vessel.

57. **The answer is C.** (*Okazaki, ed 2. p 194.*) Central pontine myelinolysis (CPM) is a severe disorder affecting the pons primarily, but also the striatum, thalamus, internal capsule, and cerebellum. It is a demyelinating disorder with relative preservation of axons and neurons that has been strongly associated with rapid correction of severe hyponatremia of multiple causes. That CPM does not occur routinely with rapid correction of sodium level argues against this as the sole causal factor.

58. **The answer is E.** (*Okazaki, ed 2. p 130.*) The lesion depicted is tabes dorsalis, one of the forms of tertiary syphilis. Obviously this could have been prevented by earlier treatment with penicillin or another appropriate antibiotic. It is characterized pathologically by the degeneration of the dorsal roots and posterior columns with preservation of the dorsal ganglia. Tabes dorsalis is clinically characterized by the loss of posterior column function manifest primarily by a loss of position sense (as demonstrated in the Romberg test). This disorder occurs many years after the primary infection.

59. **The answer is B.** (*Poirier, ed 3. pp 207–208.*) A teen-ager's brain should have small ventricles and very tight sulci. The brain presented shows an obvious asymmetry but no other abnormality. The age of the patient clearly indicates that the "full" side is the normal side and the other side is atrophic. This generally occurs as the result of a perinatal brain insult that is often difficult to identify but is often ascribed to vascular occlusion or obstetric trauma. Respirator brain and Alexander's

disease are diffuse processes affecting both sides. Progressive multifocal leukoencephalopathy does not cause a significant change in brain size.

60. **The answer is E.**   (*Okazaki, ed 2. p 141.*)   The figures reveal multinucleated giant cells (left) and a microglial nodule (right). These are pericapillary in distribution and are typical of the lesions seen in AIDS encephalopathy (AIDS-dementia complex). The history is not uncommon for the onset of the AIDS-dementia complex, which is a result of the HIV virus itself rather than of a secondary infection. Clinically one cannot easily distinguish this from cytomegalovirus encephalitis. There is widespread demyelination and there may be vacuolar degeneration as well, particularly in the white matter of the spinal cord.

61. **The answer is D.**   (*Okazaki, ed 2. p 140. Poirier, ed 3. p 120.*)   Progressive multifocal leukoencephalopathy (PML) is one of the many secondary infections that occur in AIDS patients. First described in patients with lymphomas and later in other severely immunocompromised hosts, it now may be most commonly seen in AIDS patients. It is the result of infection with a papovavirus, the JC virus (not the agent of Creutzfeldt-Jakob disease, which is itself a slow virus, or prion). This disorder causes large, confluent areas of demyelination that are usually asymmetric and have a predilection for the subcortical hemispheric white matter. On histology there are discrete areas of inflammation with giant astrocytes, abnormal oligodendroglia with viral particles, and macrophages.

62. **The answer is B.**   (*Okazaki, ed 2. pp 224–225. Poirier, ed 3. pp 27–29.*)   Ependymomas usually occur in children and have a predilection for the fourth ventricle. They are of glial origin, and of gliomas in the spinal cord, ependymomas form the majority and tend to occur in the caudal portion. The tumors tend to be highly cellular and may form tubules and perivascular pseudorosettes. In this photomicrograph the tumor has formed true rosettes.

63. **The answer is C.**   (*Okazaki, ed 2. pp 191–192.*)   This figure is a high-power view of the mamillary body, the site most often involved in Wernicke's encephalopathy, a deficiency of thiamine occurring in the context of an inherited transketolase deficiency. The major lesions occur in the periventricular gray around the third and fourth ventricles and aqueduct of Sylvius. The capillaries are prominent both in number and in size, and petechial hemorrhages are very common. Neurons themselves are relatively well preserved although some degenerative changes do occur. Myelinated axons are more affected.

64. **The answer is A.**   (*Okazaki, ed 2. pp 224–225. Poirier, ed 3. pp 27–29.*)   The figure shows a meningioma with characteristic epithelial-like cells clustered in tightly wrapped whorls around a hyalinized, calcified center called a *psammoma body*. Meningiomas occur in two major histologic types: the endotheliomatous type, composed of cells having an epithelial appearance, and the fibroblastic type, which looks similar to fibrous tissue. Both may have psammoma bodies, although they are more common in the endotheliomatous type. In cases where the psammoma bodies are profuse, the tumor is often called a *psammomatous meningioma*.

65. **The answer is B.**   (*Okazaki, ed 2. pp 204–219.*)   It is common to find different pathologies in different parts of a glioblastoma multiforme. Different regions often have different degrees of mitoses and cellular abnormalities. With immature cell types, special staining with glial fibrillary acidic protein may be required to demonstrate the glial origin of the cells.

66. **The answer is D (4).**   (*Poirier, ed 3. pp 240–241.*)   The electron photomicrograph is a cross-section of an onion-bulb formation of a peripheral nerve. These occur with repeated bouts of segmental demyelination and remyelination. When extensive, as occurs in many hereditary neuropathies such as Charcot-Marie-Tooth and Dejerine-Sottas, these cause hypertrophic changes that may be clini-

cally evident. The endoneurium has a loose appearance and contains increased amounts of collagen. There is an increase in the concentric whorling of the Schwann cells around the axon sheath.

67. **The answer is B (1, 3).**   (*Okazaki, ed 2. pp 61–62.*)   The so-called respirator brain typically shows extreme swelling of the gray and white matter accompanied by collapse of the cerebral ventricles. Although in some instances the tissue feels fairly firm, typically it is very soft. Usually, the brain shows transforaminal and transtentorial herniation. Microscopically, the brain shows universal death of all neurons. The endothelial cells swell tremendously, occluding the smaller vessels. While the veins and venous sinuses typically contain thrombi, the larger arteries usually remain patent. The necrosis of tissue and absence of blood flow may or may not involve the spinal cord. Thus, in patients with a dead brain, some spinal reflexes may remain—although of course these patients will lack evidence of reflexes mediated through the brainstem.

68. **The answer is A (1, 2, 3).**   (*Adams RD, ed 4. pp 985–987.*)   Von Recklinghausen's disease, neurofibromatosis, is a common disorder that has a wide clinical spectrum. It appears to be autosomal dominant in its inheritance pattern but many patients have no identified affected ancestor, which suggests either subclinical disease or frequent mutations. The skin is the most commonly affected site, but the central and peripheral nervous system, the skeleton, and multiple organs may all be affected. In the central nervous system the occurrence of bilateral acoustic neuromas or neuromas appearing at a young age is a strong clue to the diagnosis. Trigeminal neuromas, nerve root ganglioneuromas, and optic gliomas also occur. There is an increased incidence of malignant degeneration of central tumors leading to gliomas in 2 to 5 percent of cases.

69. **The answer is D (4).**   (*Adams RD, ed 4. pp 1023–1024.*)   Focal slowing of conduction velocity at entrapment sites, with preserved distal conduction, is related to segmental or local demyelination of the nerve. The preservation of the distal axons and their myelin sheaths accounts for the preserved conduction velocity. The nerve trunk edema and lymphocytic infiltration that may be seen in various peripheral neuropathies are not the usual lesions at entrapment sites. The endoneurium undergoes proliferation and thickening rather than atrophy. Surgical treatment by decompression or transposition of the nerve trunk may allow restoration of function, regeneration of the myelin sheaths, and an increase in conduction velocity across the lesion site.

70. **The answer is A (1, 2, 3).**   (*Okazaki, ed 2. p 170.*)   Primary cerebral amyloid angiopathy is a common finding in older patients. It is almost always seen in conjunction with senile plaques. Medium-sized cortical vessels frequently develop aneurysms leading to intraparenchymal hemorrhages (lobar hemorrhages). The deep gray structures of the basal ganglia are unaffected by the disorder. Cerebral amyloid is completely unrelated to either primary or secondary systemic amyloid.

71. **The answer is A (1, 2, 3).**   (*Adams RD, ed 4. pp 809–810. Okazaki, ed 2. p 14.*)   Lipochrome is a pigment that accumulates in aging neurons. In light microscopy, it appears as a yellowish-brown, amorphous mass. It accumulates near the axon hillock of many neurons and has a predilection for pyramidal cells of the cortex, ventral motor neurons, and the olivary and dentate nuclei. In some dementias, lipochrome may fill much of the cytoplasm of neurons. Although lipochrome is rarely evident in the neurons of infants and young children, it is the most conspicuous intracellular lesion in Batten-Mayou disease (ceroid lipofuscinosis). In spite of this lipochrome accumulation in the neurons in Batten-Mayou disease, brains affected by this disorder are atrophic and lower in weight than normal. This finding stands in contrast to certain other degenerative diseases, such as the mucopolysaccharidoses, in which the intracellular product causes brain enlargement, i.e. a metabolic megalencephaly.

72. **The answer is E (all).**   (*Poirier, ed 3. p 227.*)   The periodic paralyses are rare, autosomal dominantly inherited disorders. In some families the attacks occur with hypo-, hyper- or normokalemia. Severe

hypokalemia of any etiology, such as with diuretic use or acute tubular necrosis, will cause generalized weakness that may be severe and is not to be confused with these hereditary syndromes. Muscle biopsy reveals rounded vacuoles that may be PAS-positive or clear.

73. **The answer is C (2, 4).** (*McArthur, Medicine 66:407–437, 1987.*)   Adult patients with AIDS suffer from infection from multiple opportunistic organisms. The HIV virus itself is a common cause of aseptic meningitis, but among nonviral causes cryptococcus is the most common. CNS tuberculosis is increased among patients with AIDS, but pneumococcus and the other pathogens common in normal hosts are not significantly more common in patients with AIDS. Pneumocystis does not invade the CNS.

74. **The answer is A (1, 2, 3).** (*Adams RD, ed 4. p 1024.*)   Acute idiopathic polyneuritis, most cases of peroneal muscular atrophy, diphtheria, infantile metachromatic leukodystrophy, and Krabbe's disease produce segmental demyelination. The loss of myelin accounts for the extremely low nerve conduction velocities that characterize these conditions. The advent of nerve biopsy, usually performed on the sural nerve (a purely sensory nerve), has served to clarify the pathogenesis of a variety of neuropathies predominantly affecting either myelin sheaths or axons. Some neuropathies predominantly affect distal parts of axons with the demyelination secondary to Wallerian degeneration of the axon. In these conditions, such as uremia and nutritional deficiency states, the nerve conductions may or may not be slow and are therefore not helpful indices.

75–77. **The answers are: 75-C, 76-A, 77-D.** (*Adams JH, ed 4. pp 1026–1034, 1052–1056, 1064–1076.*)   Figure C shows normal muscle. All muscle fibers have a uniform coloration and show faint stippling, indicating minimal ice crystal artifact. The fibers have a fairly uniform size. The outline of each fiber has a gently polyhedral or polygonal shape in the trichrome-stained frozen section. The nuclei are all subsarcolemmic in location. Very little endomysial connective tissue is present, but the perimysium is evident and contains blood vessels. Inflammatory cells are absent. A segment of normal peripheral nerve appears at the left of the section.

Figure A shows neurogenic atrophy in an adult. The muscle fibers stain fairly uniformly. The large fibers have the usual polyhedral outline, and their nuclei maintain a subsarcolemmic location. Inflammatory cells are absent. The abnormal feature consists of groups of collapsed profiles of atrophic muscle fibers. These appear in clusters and may show some rounding of their nuclei, which do not appear flattened against the sarcolemma as in the normal fibers. This pattern indicates a neurogenic atrophy in mature muscle. It contrasts with figure B, which shows the typical pattern of neurogenic atrophy in a child. In this case, the child exhibits Werdnig-Hoffmann disease, and the customary feature of neurogenic atrophy in infants is the rounding of the atrophic fibers rather than the polyhedral flattening as seen in figure A.

Figure D shows muscular dystrophy. The diagnostic features consist of some variation in fiber size with enlargement of some fibers and rounding of the contour. The increased space between the individual muscle fibers indicates an accompanying fibrosis. Later, much more necrosis and inflammation may occur with fatty replacement. The serum creatine phosphokinase (CPK) will be highest during the early stages of dystrophy. Histochemical stains in dystrophy will show a poor differentiation of fiber types. Although the microscopist can suspect Duchenne's muscular dystrophy from the section, the same features may occur in other dystrophies. Thus, the final diagnosis of the type of dystrophy depends on a blending of the total clinical information and genetic history with the physical findings and the muscle biopsy.

78–82. **The answers are: 78-E, 79-A, 80-B, 81-C, 82-D.** (*Adams JH, ed 4. pp 369–376, 526–531. Poirier, ed 3. pp 133–138.*)   The demyelinating diseases are a heterogeneous group of disorders, often genetic in origin, in which the pattern of myelin deficiency differs from one disease to another—often differing so much as to constitute a decisive diagnostic feature. However, the pathologic distribution of the demyelination is only one feature in the nosology of the disease.

In adrenoleukodystrophy, a sex-linked recessive disorder and the commonest form of leukodystrophy in males, the loss of myelin predominantly affects the parieto-occipital regions of the brain but does extend frontally. The demyelination shows three zones. The central zone exhibits little or no myelin and appears quiescent histologically, showing only glial scarring. The second zone contains some surviving myelin and preserved axons and displays a prominent perivascular inflammatory reaction. The most peripheral of the three zones shows scattered demyelination with axonal preservation and the presence of numerous para-amino-salicylic acid (PAS)-positive and sudanophilic macrophages. In adrenoleukodystrophy, the localization of the most intense inflammation in the second zone differs from multiple sclerosis, which exhibits the most intense inflammation at the periphery of the lesion. Clinically, the male child with adrenoleukodystrophy usually appears normal at birth and in early infancy and begins to show neurologic retrogression between 3 and 12 years of age. The bronze skin, reflecting the adrenal insufficiency, provides a clinical clue to the type of neurologic disorder present.

In Pelizaeus-Merzbacher disease, a sex-linked recessive disorder, the brain classically shows patches of myelinated fibers scattered through otherwise amyelinated white matter; but some brains that are genetically and clinically associated with this disorder lack myelin entirely. Thus, the classic pathologic finding of tigroid patches of myelin constitutes only one link in the chain of diagnostic evidence for identifying the disease. The absence of myelin probably represents a failure of myelin formation rather than demyelination as such. Pelizaeus-Merzbacher disease is manifested in the neonatal period by oscillating eye movements. Cases of so-called adult-onset Pelizaeus-Merzbacher disease, which at autopsy show tigroid patches of preserved myelinated fibers, probably have little relation to the classic entity; nor does Cockayne's syndrome, which shows similar preserved myelin patches.

In sudanophilic leukodystrophy, the demyelination affects the centrum ovale diffusely but tends to concentrate in the periventricular zone and to spare the arcuate fibers. The arcuate fibers consist of the short association fibers of a hemisphere that connect one area of cortex with the neighboring areas. These short association fibers curve around the depth of the gyri, from which they receive the name *arcuate*. The arcuate fibers are preserved in some other types of leukodystrophy, such as globoid cell leukodystrophy. In sudanophilic leukodystrophy, the myelin degeneration products stain orthochromatically with dyes and, as implied in the name *sudanophilic,* the degeneration products have an affinity for sudan black. The sudanophilia by itself fails to constitute a pathognomonic feature. The sudanophilic material has a high content of esterified cholesterol. Similar sudanophilic degradation products of myelin occur in a variety of disorders ranging from phenylketonuria to head injuries.

In metachromatic leukodystrophy, a metabolic product accumulates in the central and peripheral nervous systems. This substance appears brownish in cresyl violet or thionin stains, which ordinarily produce a blue color. The prefix *meta-* indicates this alteration in tinctorial reaction. The basic defect usually is a deficiency in the lysosomal enzyme arylsulfatase A. In other cases, multiple sulfatases are deficient. The metabolic substance that accumulates in the tissues consists of sulfatides, which are sulfuric acid esters of cerebrosides. The discovery of the fact that the metachromatic substance consisted of a lipid led to the renaming of metachromatic leukodystrophy as sulfatide lipidosis, placing it with the disorders of lipid metabolism rather than with the demyelinating diseases. The disease typically manifests in infants or children and has a sex-linked recessive inheritance pattern.

In Krabbe's globoid cell leukodystrophy, demyelination affects the central and peripheral nervous systems. Affected patients have a defect in galactocerebroside β-galactosidase. The outstanding pathologic feature is the presence of globoid cell macrophages that appear as clumps in the white matter and often have multiple nuclei. The macrophages and Schwann cells contain abnormal tubules on electron-microscopic sections. Globoid leukodystrophy follows a recessive inheritance pattern. It usually manifests by neurologic retrogression in the young infant, and the patient is usually dead by 4 years of age.

Neurophysiology

DIRECTIONS: Each question below contains five suggested responses. Select the **one best** response to each question.

83. Stimulation of the supplementary motor area produces movements that are

    (A) more discrete and isolated than those produced in area 4
    (B) more consistently contralateral than those produced in area 4
    (C) complex and bilateral, involving trunk and legs
    (D) restricted to the face and hand
    (E) restricted to release of sphincters

84. Cerebellar dysfunction is most severe when the lesion involves the

    (A) spinocerebellar tracts
    (B) frontopontine tract
    (C) temporopontine tract
    (D) pontocerebellar tract
    (E) superior cerebellar peduncle

85. The troponin-tropomyosin system has which of the following actions?

    (A) It excites the myosin to contract
    (B) It inhibits the contractile protein actin
    (C) It unites with excess magnesium ions
    (D) It splits adenosine triphosphate (ATP)
    (E) None of the above

86. In most persons, interruption of the corpus callosum is likely to cause apraxia of the

    (A) right and left extremities
    (B) right extremities only
    (C) left extremities only
    (D) arms only
    (E) legs only (gait apraxia)

87. In the neuropathies that primarily affect axons, as contrasted to those that primarily cause Schwann cell degeneration, the nerve conduction velocity is usually

    (A) 10 to 15 meters per second (m/s)
    (B) 35 to 40 m/s
    (C) 50 to 80 m/s
    (D) more than 80 m/s
    (E) too variable to have diagnostic significance

88. A patient with a spinal cord lesion at level T10 who attempts to sit up from a supine position will exhibit an umbilicus that

    (A) migrates downward (caudad)
    (B) migrates upward (rostrad)
    (C) migrates laterally
    (D) is protrusive
    (E) does not move

89. The duration of posthyperventilation apnea in patients with diffuse bilateral cerebral disease is

    (A) prolonged because of release of the brainstem inhibitory center from cerebral suppression
    (B) prolonged because of loss of the drive to breathe that comes from an intact cerebrum
    (C) reduced because of oversensitivity of the carotid bodies to oxygen saturation
    (D) reduced because of hippocampal lesions
    (E) the same as in normal subjects

90. If an EMG was performed on a patient with asterixis whose arms were raised in front with the hands extended, one would expect to see which one of the following?

    (A) A brief contraction in the extensors of the hand
    (B) Simultaneous contractions in the extensors and flexors of the hand
    (C) A brief silence in the extensors of the hand
    (D) Irregular contractions and silences in the extensors and flexors of the hand
    (E) None of the above

91. A hypertensive patient with the acute onset of Broca's aphasia (predominantly expressive with poverty of speech) and a right central facial palsy also shows a tendency for deviation of the eyes to the left. The most probable cause of the eye deviation is

    (A) a separate destructive lesion in the right frontal eye field
    (B) an extension of the lesion into the left frontal eye field
    (C) an interruption of corticobulbar fibers at the brainstem level
    (D) a lesion of the left occipital lobe
    (E) a lesion of the right occipital lobe

92. The sternocleidomastoid muscle acts to turn the head

    (A) contralaterally, tilt it contralaterally, and flex it
    (B) contralaterally, tilt it ipsilaterally, and protrude it
    (C) contralaterally, tilt it contralaterally, and retract it
    (D) ipsilaterally, tilt it ipsilaterally, and extend it
    (E) ipsilaterally, tilt it ipsilaterally, and protrude it

93. After interruption of the right Vth nerve, a patient's mandible responds in which of the following ways?

    (A) It deviates to the left when opened
    (B) It deviates to the right when opened
    (C) It opens in the midline
    (D) It cannot be opened
    (E) It shows an overbite when closed

94. The tonic neck reflex consists of

    (A) extending the ipsilateral arm and leg and flexing the contralateral arm and leg
    (B) extending the contralateral arm and leg and flexing the ipsilateral arm and leg
    (C) extending the ipsilateral arm and contralateral leg
    (D) extending the contralateral arm and ipsilateral leg
    (E) displaying none of the above reflexes

95. After caloric-induced nystagmus, volitional visual fixation has which of the following effects on nystagmus?

    (A) It augments the nystagmus
    (B) It inhibits the nystagmus
    (C) It increases the slow component
    (D) It increases the fast component
    (E) None of the above

96. The accommodation, or "near reflex," of the eyes consists of

    (A) pupillodilation, convergence, and lens thickening
    (B) pupillodilation, intorsion, and lens thickening
    (C) pupilloconstriction, divergence, and lens thickening
    (D) pupilloconstriction, convergence, and lens thickening
    (E) pupilloconstriction, extorsion, and ptosis

97. The percentage of the corticospinal tract that arises from Brodmann's area 4, the primary motor area, is approximately

    (A) 15
    (B) 30
    (C) 50
    (D) 75
    (E) almost 100

DIRECTIONS: Each question below contains four suggested responses of which **one or more** is correct. Select

A	if	**1, 2, and 3**	are correct
B	if	**1 and 3**	are correct
C	if	**2 and 4**	are correct
D	if	**4**	is correct
E	if	**1, 2, 3, and 4**	are correct

98. Contraction myoedema (slow waves of contraction that ripple over the muscle during a postural change) is very likely to be associated with

    (1) complaints of stiffness and tightness in the muscles
    (2) percussion myoedema
    (3) slow relaxation after voluntary contraction of muscles
    (4) delayed relaxation of muscles involved in stretch reflexes

99. Relaxation of muscle depends on

    (1) union of troponin-tropomyosin with calcium
    (2) enzymatic hydrolysis of the actin-myosin complex
    (3) union of magnesium with the myosin
    (4) calcium uptake by the sarcoplasmic reticulum

100. Characteristics of conduction aphasia include which of the following?

    (1) Fluent paraphasia with retention of prosody
    (2) Retention of comprehension and awareness of word errors
    (3) Striking inability to repeat words or nonsense syllables
    (4) Interruption of the arcuate fasciculus and overlying cortex

101. Cardiac rhythm disturbances thought to arise as a result of a cerebral infarct include which of the following?

    (1) Atrial fibrillation
    (2) Premature ventricular contractions
    (3) Bradycardia
    (4) Heart block

102. Sleep paralysis is associated with which of the following characteristics?

    (1) It occurs most commonly during transition to or from sleep
    (2) It is initially associated with a strong feeling of fear
    (3) It disappears when a person is called or touched
    (4) It is associated with a shift of potassium into muscle

103. A temporary increase in muscle strength on repetitive contractions may be seen with some frequency in

    (1) myotonic dystrophy
    (2) McArdle's phosphorylase deficiency
    (3) myasthenia gravis
    (4) small cell carcinoma of the lung

104. Stimulation of autonomic neurons in the sacral cord segments 2 through 4 should produce which of the following?

    (1) Detrussor muscle contraction
    (2) Catecholamine production
    (3) Acetylcholine production
    (4) Detrussor muscle relaxation

105. True statements regarding gamma motoneurons include that they

    (1) innervate intrafusal muscle fibers
    (2) are subject to descending pathway inhibition
    (3) are smaller than alpha motoneurons
    (4) innervate extrafusal muscle fibers

SUMMARY OF DIRECTIONS				
A	B	C	D	E
1, 2, 3 only	1, 3 only	2, 4 only	4 only	All are correct

106. During sleep most movement disorders either improve considerably or resolve completely. Which of the following movement abnormalities will usually persist during sleep?

    (1) The chorea of Huntington's disease
    (2) The tics of Gilles de la Tourette syndrome
    (3) The tremor of Parkinson's disease
    (4) Palatal myoclonus

107. Carotid sinus stimulation may result in syncope as a consequence of

    (1) reflex bradycardia
    (2) reflex hypotension, a depressor response
    (3) a central mechanism without bradycardia or hypotension
    (4) reflex sympathetic vasoconstriction of cerebral vessels

108. Conditions that may produce or enhance fasciculations include

    (1) severe dehydration
    (2) organophosphate poisoning
    (3) exercise in untrained persons
    (4) hypocalcemia

109. In benign positional vertigo the Hallpike maneuver will induce which of the following?

    (1) Torsional (rotary) nystagmus
    (2) Nystagmus that lasts usually less than 15 s
    (3) Vertigo that habituates rapidly
    (4) Reversal of nystagmus and vertigo on sitting up

110. Patients with Broca's aphasia frequently exhibit

    (1) a contralateral central type of facial palsy
    (2) dysgraphia with either the right or left hand
    (3) some degree of loss of speech comprehension
    (4) jargon speech and neologisms

111. The myasthenic syndrome of Eaton-Lambert differs from myasthenia gravis by showing

    (1) a predilection for proximal muscles of the limbs and girdles
    (2) a decremental response in the EMG after repetitive nerve stimulation
    (3) an association with carcinoma
    (4) uniformly better response to anticholinesterase medication

112. In the early evaluation of a patient with suspected Guillain-Barré syndrome, which of the following electrophysiologic tests would be likely to reveal an abnormality?

    (1) Repetitive nerve stimulation
    (2) H reflex
    (3) Central conduction velocity
    (4) F wave

113. During rapid eye movement (REM) sleep in a normal person, which of the following will occur?

    (1) There is hypotonia
    (2) Vital signs become irregular
    (3) The subject is easily roused
    (4) The EEG shows normal awake activity posteriorly

114. An homonymous altitudinal hemianopia (a defect of the upper or lower field that involves both sides) may be due to lesions of

    (1) the lateral geniculate body
    (2) the retina
    (3) the visual association area
    (4) the posterior cerebral artery

DIRECTIONS: Each group of questions below consists of lettered headings followed by a set of numbered items. For each numbered item select the **one** lettered heading with which it is **most** closely associated. Each lettered heading may be used **once, more than once, or not at all.**

Questions 115–118

For each ocular movement listed below, choose the ocular rotatory muscle that is most closely involved.

(A) Superior oblique muscle
(B) Superior rectus muscle
(C) Inferior rectus muscle
(D) Inferior oblique muscle
(E) Medial rectus muscle

115. Elevation of the eye (with the eye abducted)

116. Intorsion of the eye (with the eye abducted)

117. Depression of the eye (with the eye adducted)

118. Elevation of the eye (with the eye adducted)

Questions 119–122

A comatose patient whose head is elevated at 30 degrees has eyes at midline. Fifty milliliters of ice water is instilled into the left ear. Correlate the diagnoses below with the associated eye findings.

(A) Eyes remain midline
(B) Right eye adducts, left eye does not move
(C) Left eye abducts, right eye does not move
(D) Both eyes move to the left
(E) Conjugate bobbing occurs

119. Lesion in the right medial longitudinal fasciculus (MLF)

120. Left abducens palsy

121. Brain death

122. Bihemispheric disease sparing the brainstem

Neurophysiology

Answers

83. **The answer is C.** (*Kandel, ed 2. pp 494–496.*) The supplementary motor area produces complex, frequently bilateral movements of the axial muscles and legs, although a full somatotopic representation does exist. The most discrete contralateral movements come from area 4. Isolated sphincter movements cannot be obtained from the supplementary area. The role of the supplementary area in brain function remains to be determined. It may be responsible for some return of voluntary function after pyramidal tract destruction because it has bilateral projections. Blood flow studies show an increased activity of the supplementary motor area during complex volitional movements, and aphasia has been reported after infarction of the region.

84. **The answer is E.** (*Adams RD, ed 4. p 73.*) Lesions of the afferent systems to the cerebellum cause relatively little clinical dysfunction. For example, a high cervical cordotomy that is performed to relieve pain and involves sectioning of the entire ventral spinocerebellar tract on one side results in little, or merely transient, dysfunction. Some damage may occur to the cerebellar cortex or white matter, with little clinical defect. The most severe signs of cerebellar dysfunction are due to lesions of the efferent system (such as destruction of the superior cerebellar peduncle), or with large, severely destructive lesions of the cerebellar cortex and deep white matter. As with lesions elsewhere, the clinical expression of the lesion will vary with the age of the person when the lesion occurs, the size of the lesion, and the rate of tissue destruction.

85. **The answer is B.** (*Adams RD, ed 4. pp 1010–1012.*) The troponin-tropomyosin system inhibits the contractile protein actin and prevents its union with myosin. The latter event leads to muscular contraction. After depolarization (induced by the action potential) spreads to the interior of the muscle fiber, calcium is released from the sarcoplasmic reticulum, where it is stored. Calcium binds to the troponin-tropomyosin protein that inhibits the combination of actin and myosin. The interaction of actin and myosin leads to the rapid release of energy by splitting of ATP, a reaction that provides the energy for contraction. Muscle relaxation, which is an active process, occurs when calcium reunites with the sarcoplasmic reticulum.

86. **The answer is C.** (*Chusid, ed 19. p 32.*) Interruption of the corpus callosum is likely to cause apraxia of only the left extremities. The theory is that the locus for motor schema (or the ideation for movement) is located in the left hemisphere of right-handed persons, presumably in the left posterior parasylvian area. Interruption of the corpus callosum would disrupt the transfer of information from this locus in the left hemisphere to the right. Since the right hemisphere directs movement of the left extremities, the defect would be expressed in the left extremities. Since the connections through the deep white matter between the left posterior parasylvian region and the left motor cortex

remain intact, apraxia of the right extremities, which are controlled by the left motor cortex, would be absent.

87. **The answer is B.** (*Adams RD, ed 4. pp 1023–1024.*)   In the primary neuropathies with "dying-back" (retrograde) or Wallerian (orthograde) degeneration, the conduction velocity is usually in the range of 35 to 40 m/s and thus only slightly reduced from normal. Those nerve fibers that remain conduct at approximately their normal rate. In the neuropathies that cause primarily Schwann cell degeneration, the conduction velocity is profoundly reduced, often to the range of 10 to 15 m/s. This fact is in keeping with the supposition that one role of the myelin sheath is to increase conduction velocity. Both toxic-metabolic neuropathies and heredofamilial neuropathies may be associated with primarily axonal or myelin sheath degeneration.

88. **The answer is B.** (*Chusid, ed 19. p 101.*)   When a patient with a spinal cord lesion at level T10 attempts to sit up, the umbilicus migrates upward (rostrally). This is called *Beevor's sign.* The T8 and T9 spinal cord segments innervate the abdominal muscles rostral to the umbilicus and the T11 and T12 segments innervate the muscles caudal to the umbilicus. The intact upper abdominal muscles acting unopposed by the paralyzed lower muscles pull the umbilicus rostrally, which appears after a T10 lesion. In other words, the umbilicus migrates in the direction of pull of the intact muscles. Normally, the pull exerted by the upper and lower abdominal muscles is equal and opposite, leaving the umbilicus centered.

89. **The answer is B.** (*Plum, ed 3. p 33.*)   The duration of posthyperventilation apnea after a patient completes five rapid voluntary deep inhalations and exhalations is less than 10 s in normal subjects and is prolonged in subjects with diffuse cerebral disease. The reduction in CO_2 results in the apnea. The prolongation of posthyperventilation apnea in patients with bilateral cerebral disease illustrates the fact that part of the drive to breathe comes from an intact, functioning cerebrum. Loss of cerebral function from bilateral cerebral disease reduces the drive to breathe, not only after hyperventilation but also in obtundation or even in sleep, contributing to sleep apnea.

90. **The answer is C.** (*Adams RD, ed 4. p 82.*)   Asterixis is frequently called *negative myoclonus.* It is evaluated by having the patient extend a limb, usually the arms with the hands extended. When pronounced it may be seen proximally as well as distally in the arms and the legs. During prolonged muscle contraction there is a brief period of electrical silence during which the muscle relaxes. When the hands are extended, this sudden silence causes the hands to flap. It is often not understood that to evaluate asterixis the patient must be conscious, as the muscle contractions must be voluntary.

91. **The answer is B.** (*Adams RD, ed 4. p 210. Kandel, ed 2. pp 582–583.*)   Deviation of the eyes to the left due to a cortical lesion and in association with Broca's aphasia and a central facial palsy suggests extension of the lesion into the adjacent frontal eye fields. Destruction of this region eliminates the vector acting to turn the eyes (and head) to the right. The right frontal center, intact and acting unopposed by its destroyed mate, turns the eyes to the left. Lesions in the other locations listed in the question could affect eye turning, but parsimony favors a single lesion rather than multiple ones.

92. **The answer is B.** (*Chusid, ed 19. p 130.*)   The sternocleidomastoid muscle acts to turn the head contralaterally, tilt it ipsilaterally, and protrude it. One can readily confirm the role of the muscle by palpating it during these actions. The usual clinical test for the action of the muscle is to test contralateral head rotation, but the muscle's strength in the other maneuvers is also easily tested and its action easily observed. Knowledge of its other actions sometimes helps in the analysis of hysterical paralysis. In involuntary movement disorders with spasmodic torticollis, the overaction of the sternocleidomastoid muscle frequently causes head tilt as well as rotation. However, the other neck muscles also frequently are involved in head turning and head tilting. Hence, surgical section

of the sternocleidomastoid alone fails in the treatment of spasmodic torticollis. The head may continue to tilt and turn in the absence of this muscle.

93. **The answer is B.**   (*Chusid, ed 19. p 121.*)   After interruption of the right Vth nerve, the affected patient's mandible deviates to the right. A patient with unilateral paralysis of the lateral pterygoid muscle will show ipsilateral deviation of the mandibular tip on opening the jaw and weakness of jaw movement contralaterally. The action of the lateral pterygoid is to protrude the mandible, depress its tip, and move it to the opposite side. These actions depend on the origin and insertion of the pterygoid muscles and the manner of suspension of the mandible. When a patient with a unilateral Vth nerve lesion and lateral pterygoid paralysis opens the jaw, the opposite, intact pterygoid protrudes the mandible to the weak side.

94. **The answer is A.**   (*Adams RD, ed 4. pp 471–472.*)   An infant whose head is turned to one side extends the ipsilateral arm and leg and flexes the contralateral arm and leg. While normal infants in the age range of 2 to 4 months will spend considerable amounts of time in the tonic neck reflex (TNR) posture and will, to some degree, exhibit the TNR when the examiner turns the infant's head, the normal infant readily struggles out of it and the response fatigues. This reflex may be briefly obtained in 60 percent of normal infants 1 to 2 months old and then becomes less common. In older children it is generally a sign of abnormality. Abnormality is evidenced by a machinelike response that persists. Such an infant has some disturbance in cerebral control of movement and generally will have some form of cerebral palsy. The TNR also may appear in infants with degenerative diseases of the cerebrum.

95. **The answer is B.**   (*Adams RD, ed 4. p 217.*)   Deliberate visual fixation inhibits caloric or vestibular nystagmus. The cortical influence thus overrides the vestibular mechanisms. A dancer uses this phenomenon to inhibit vestibular symptoms induced by a series of spins or pivots. The dancer deliberately fixes the eyes on some stationary point, then retains fixation as long as possible while the body turns. Then the dancer snaps the head around to resume fixation as long as possible, while the body turns independently of the head. Thus, during most of the turn, the eyes and head remain fixed while the body turns. Both the inhibitory effect of visual fixation and the brief time occupied by turning the head reduce the vestibular stimulation. Therefore, one can best elicit vestibular nystagmus using Frenzel glasses to inhibit fixation. Brainstem and cerebellar nystagmus are elicited better through fixation.

96. **The answer is D.**   (*Adams RD, ed 4. p 206.*)   To accommodate for near vision requires the eyes to converge, the lens to thicken, and the pupils to constrict. Convergence aims the visual axis of each eye at the near target. Thickening of the lens increases its ability to focus the more divergent rays from the near object on the retina, and pupilloconstriction narrows the aperture that admits light rays to the retina, producing a pinhole camera effect. The nervous system coordinates these three actions into a single reflex. However, as a person reaches the fifth decade, loss of lens elasticity prevents the normal thickening that should occur to accommodate for near vision. The affected person then complains of blurred vision for near objects, a condition called *presbyopia*.

97. **The answer is B.**   (*Carpenter, ed 3. p 378.*)   The corticospinal tract is thought to have about 31 percent of its fibers originate in area 4, about 40 percent in the parietal lobe, and about 29 percent in the premotor area (Brodmann's area 6), which is immediately rostral to the primary motor area. Impulses in the corticospinal tract cause contractions of isolated muscles and are important in control of voluntary skilled motor activities. Although the giant Betz cells in the motor strip are a histologic hallmark of this area, the total contribution of Betz cells to the corticospinal tract is only about 3 percent.

98. The answer is E (all). (*Adams RD, ed 4. p 1095.*) Contraction myoedema and percussion myoedema, stiffness of muscles, and slow relaxation of muscles all occur together in hypothyroidism, in association with complaints of weakness. These findings, in association with the classic symptoms of dry skin and husky voice, establish a diagnosis of hypothyroid myopathy. The physical findings in hypothyroidism separate hypothyroid myopathy from conditions involved in the differential diagnosis of muscular diseases such as dystrophy, polymyositis, and the myotonias.

99. The answer is D (4). (*Adams RD, ed 4. pp 1010–1012.*) Muscle relaxation is an active metabolic process that requires the union of calcium with the sarcoplasmic reticulum. Deficiency of calcium or of the energy mechanisms that bind it to the sarcoplasmic reticulum interferes with muscular relaxation. Contraction of muscle—as seen in certain disorders with exercise intolerance—may reflect a disturbance in the metabolism of the ionic binding required for muscle relaxation. This process, like contraction itself, is ATP-dependent.

100. The answer is E (all). (*Adams RD, ed 4. pp 385–386.*) The characteristics of conduction aphasia include fluent paraphasia with retention of prosody, retention of comprehension, awareness of word errors, striking inability to repeat words or nonsense syllables, and a lesion that usually interrupts the arcuate fasciculus. Wernicke proposed a major center for the reception of language in the posterior superior temporal region and a center for expression in the posterior inferior frontal region. Separation of these two regions by interruption of the intervening cortex of the supramarginal gyrus and inferior parietal lobule and of the interconnecting white matter, predominantly the arcuate fasciculus, produces conduction aphasia. The arcuate fasciculus is a large bundle of fibers, which, as the name implies, arc around the sylvian fissure from the temporal lobe to the frontal lobe. A major distinction between conduction aphasia and Wernicke's aphasia is that the ability to comprehend speech and to recognize word errors is lost in Wernicke's aphasia and retained in conduction aphasia.

101. The answer is C (2, 4). (*Meyers, Stroke 13:838–842, 1982.*) Cardiac arrhythmias are relatively common in the setting of an acute cerebral infarct and are thought to be mediated by increased sympathetic output. Observed rhythms have been premature ventricular contractions and all three types of heart block. Cardiac necrosis with elevated CPK has also been noted. Atrial fibrillation is often a cause of stroke rather than an outcome. Bradyarrhythmias are not believed to be induced by strokes.

102. The answer is A (1, 2, 3). (*Adams RD, ed 4. pp 310–311.*) Sleep paralysis occurs most commonly in the narcolepsy tetrad. It appears during the transition phases of wakefulness-to-sleep and of sleep-to-wakefulness. At the onset it frequently creates fear in the subject, but with repeated episodes the patient learns to deal with the problem. Sleep paralysis is most frequent when a patient is falling asleep and may be accompanied by dreams, the so-called hypnagogic hallucinations. The striking feature of sleep paralysis is its instantaneous disappearance when the patient is touched or hears a sound. This fact indicates that the disorder is related to a disturbance in the central nevous system rather than to a sudden potassium shift in muscle, which would be too slow to explain so rapid an arousal from sleep paralysis. However, patients with periodic paralysis who have a disturbance in potassium balance also may experience very severe fright and anxiety because of a similar feeling of helplessness during their muscular paralysis.

103. The answer is D (4). (*Adams RD, ed 4. p 1094.*) A paradoxical increase in the strength of muscular contraction may occur in patients with small cell carcinoma of the lung. Affected patients complain of weakness that increases with use; but they may show a temporary increase in strength, measurable both clinically and by electromyography. This feature helps to distinguish the myasthenic state of affected patients from true myasthenia gravis, in which continuous use of a muscle reduces its strength.

104. The answer is B (1, 3). (*Gilman S, ed 7. p 187.*)   The parasympathetic system is cholinergic and arises from cranial nerve nuclei and the sacral cord. Its role in bladder function and sexual function is crucial. The parasympathetics from S2, S3, and S4 innervate the detrussor, and parasympathetic activity causes the detrussor to contract. Parasympathetic activity also relaxes the bladder neck, which allows the contracting bladder muscles to force the urine into the urethra.

105. The answer is A (1, 2, 3). (*Gilman S, ed 7. pp 24–25.*)   Intrafusal muscle fibers are those muscle fibers within the muscle spindle. Extrafusal fibers are those outside, in the bulk of the muscle. Alpha motoneurons are large in size and control extrafusal contraction. Beta motoneurons innervate both types of muscle fibers and are important in controlling spindles. Gamma motoneurons are small and innervate the intrafusal muscles only. They control spindle length and thus the response of the sensory nerves to muscle stretch.

106. The answer is D (4). (*Adams RD, ed 4. p 83.*)   It is uncommon for movements to persist during sleep. If one sees the bed of a patient with Huntington's disease in the morning, it will be markedly disturbed, but this is the result of movements before and after sleep. During sleep virtually all tremors, tics, and choreic movements resolve regardless of the etiology. Palatal myoclonus and epilepsia partialis continua do not change during sleep, which separates them from the other disorders. In the dystonic disorders, the associated tremor resolves during sleep but the sustained abnormal muscle contractions may persist or resolve, so that observation during sleep in a dystonic patient is a relatively useless exercise.

107. The answer is A (1, 2, 3). (*Adams RD, ed 4. p 295.*)   Carotid sinus stimulation may cause reflex bradycardia, arterial hypotension without bradycardia, and a central type of response possibly due to cerebral ischemia or to some unrecognized mechanism. Carotid sinus stimulation does not produce syncope as a result of sympathetic vasoconstriction of cerebral vessels. In a patient suspected of carotid sinus syncope, all three mechanisms or combinations of mechanisms should be considered, and the patient properly monitored for each by ECG, EEG, and blood pressure recordings. Carotid sinus stimulation should be performed only under conditions in which possible cardiorespiratory arrest can be properly managed. It should be avoided in patients who are elderly, have heart disease, or are at risk for cerebrovascular accidents.

108. The answer is E (all). (*Adams RD, ed 4. pp 1099–1100.*)   Conditions that produce fasciculations range from exercise to organophosphate poisoning. Exercise in untrained persons and severe dehydration are intrinsic causes of the membrane instability that results in the motor unit discharges constituting the fasciculations. Organophosphates are extrinsic anticholinesterase agents that increase the amount of acetylcholine. Low calcium blood levels likewise increase membrane instability. These nonneurologic causes of fasciculations need to be distinguished from the primarily neurologic disorders associated with fasciculations. Benign fasciculations, which are fasciculations appearing in otherwise healthy persons, also must be differentiated from fasciculations due to neuronal disease. In patients with benign fasciculations, there is no known evidence of toxic-metabolic disorder, atrophy or weakness, or EMG indications of denervation.

109. The answer is E (all). (*Adams RD, ed 4. pp 241–242.*)   The Hallpike maneuver consists of lying a patient supine from a seated position with the head tilted backwards by 30 degrees and then rotated to one side by 30 degrees. With vestibular dysfunction the patient develops vertigo after a few seconds along with a rotatory nystagmus that is proportional to the severity of the vertiginous symptoms. The rotation is due to simultaneous contractions of vertical and horizontal eye muscles and typically involves the twelve o'clock point of the eye beating toward the floor. This phenomenon fatigues after a few trials, but while changing positions, the nystagmus and symptoms reverse directions as the patient reverses positions.

110. The answer is A (1, 2, 3). (*Adams RD, ed 4. pp 382–383.*)   While the cardinal feature of Broca's aphasia is sparse, telegraphic speech consisting of nouns and verbs with few prepositions, articles, or conjugations, patients with this disorder also frequently show a contralateral facial palsy of central type, dysgraphia, and some degree of loss of speech comprehension. Jargon speech or neologisms, which characterize Wernicke's aphasia, are absent. The lesion of Broca's aphasia typically involves the posterior inferior part of the frontal lobe. Since the motor area for the face is adjacent, it is frequently affected by the lesion, resulting in a contralateral central type of facial palsy.

111. The answer is B (1, 3). (*Adams RD, ed 4. pp 1159–1160.*)   The Eaton-Lambert syndrome differs from myasthenia gravis by showing a predilection for proximal limb and girdle muscles and an association with carcinoma. It is not, however, always associated with carcinoma. The Eaton-Lambert syndrome shows an incremental response in the EMG after repetitive nerve stimulation, whereas myasthenia shows a decremental response. The muscle weakness of the Eaton-Lambert syndrome responds poorly to anticholinesterase medication. The syndrome may appear in advance of any overt signs of the primary neoplasm. Its presence should initiate a screening examination for an occult neoplasm. Unlike those with myasthenia gravis, patients rarely have eye involvement, often get stronger with repetitive movements, and often have other complaints, such as dry mouth.

112. The answer is C (2, 4). (*Adams RD, ed 4. p 1037.*)   Acute idiopathic polyneuritis, the Guillain-Barré syndrome (GBS), is an ascending sensorimotor neuropathy that affects people of all ages. It follows viral illnesses in a majority of cases and causes a progressive problem starting in the feet with numbness, tingling, and, to a more profound degree, weakness. Deep tendon reflexes are lost early on. The pathologic process is quite patchy but has a predilection for ventral and dorsal roots and is demyelinating in nature. Nerve conduction studies show slowing of conduction velocity due to the demyelination, but the patchy nature of the process makes distal conduction velocities unreliable. F and H responses test the motor and sensory nerves along their entire course and are therefore the tests most likely to reveal an abnormality early on. EMG is useless early in the course and central conduction velocity would probably be normal.

113. The answer is A (1, 2, 3). (*Adams RD, ed 4. p 203.*)   Normal subjects have fairly regular sleep cycles with periods of 90 to 100 min during which they cycle from stages 1 through 4 into REM sleep, where dreaming occurs. During REM sleep, the EEG shows a light (stage 2) sleep pattern, except for prominent eye movements, and the subject becomes hypotonic. Vital signs become somewhat irregular and the pupils change in size. During REM subjects are easily roused, whereas it is difficult to rouse subjects during stages 3 and 4.

114. The answer is D (4). (*Adams RD, ed 4. p 203.*)   Altitudinal defects in one eye are due to retinal disease. The retinal vessels travel vertically so that proximal ischemia will infarct the upper or lower halves of the retina, or both. To have a homonymous deficit the lesion must be in the brain. To have visual losses homonymously in both fields means the brain lesion must be bihemispheric so that isolated lesions of the occipital cortex caused by posterior cerebral artery ischemia are the only explanation.

115–118. The answers are: 115-B, 116-A, 117-A, 118-D. (*Adams RD, ed 4. pp 213–214.*)   With the eye abducted, the most effective elevator is the superior rectus muscle, and the most effective intorter is the superior oblique muscle. With the eye adducted, the most effective depressor is the superior oblique muscle, and the most effective elevator is the inferior oblique muscle. All of these muscles change their actions depending on the position of the eye.

A distinction has to be made between the strongest and most effective action of an ocular rotatory muscle and all of its possible actions. In testing the main, or most effective, action of muscle, this action should be isolated from the secondary or tertiary actions of the muscle. The muscle has some help in its secondary and tertiary actions, allowing for some compensation by other muscles; but the eyeball can be rotated into a position that calls for the sole or principal action of the muscle. This position provides the best and most exclusive test of the integrity of the muscle.

To test the integrity of the left inferior rectus muscle, for example, a physician asks a patient to look down and to the left. The outward rotation of the eye by the lateral rectus muscle places the eyeball in such a position that the only muscle that will turn the eye down is the inferior rectus muscle. With the eye in the primary position or medially rotated, some of the depressant action of the inferior rectus muscle is dissipated, either in adduction or intorsion—actions that it shares with other muscles. To understand these secondary and tertiary actions, the origin and insertion of the muscles must be known. In addition, the line of pull of each muscle must be analyzed in terms of vectors, whereupon the relationship of the vectors to the axes of the eyes can be understood.

119–122. The answers are: 119-C, 120-B, 121-A, 122-D. (*Adams RD, ed 4. p 283.*) In the patient with intact consciousness, a small amount of cold water in the left ear causes the eyes to beat to the right. The mnemonic is "COWS" for cold-opposite, warm-same, in which the direction is that of the fast component of the nystagmus. In normal subjects the eyes remain midline because of tonic firing from various structures, including the vestibular nuclei. With cold stimulation the affected nerve has a reduction in its firing rate, which causes the eyes to *slowly* deviate to the affected side. The fast phase, which is compensatory, is to the opposite side. Warm stimulation induces the opposite nystagmus. In a patient with a fully functional brainstem, ice water in the left ear causes both eyes to move conjugately to the left. If an MLF lesion is present on the right, ice water in the left ear will cause the left eye to deviate left as is normal, but the right eye will not cross the midline to the left. With a left abducens palsy the left eye will not cross the midline to the left, but the right will adduct normally. In brain death there is no reflex, so the eyes remain midline.

One can simply summarize the findings by thinking of the ice water in the left ear as being equivalent to a command to look to the left in an awake patient—then all the above signs become obvious.

Neurochemistry

DIRECTIONS: Each question below contains five suggested responses. Select the **one best** response to each question.

123. To achieve release of acetylcholine from a nerve ending, which of the following is necessary?

(A) Sodium influx
(B) Potassium efflux
(C) Sodium influx and potassium efflux
(D) Calcium influx
(E) Sodium efflux and potassium influx

124. The biochemical abnormality that is shared by the inborn errors of the urea cycle and that has neurologic manifestations is which of the following?

(A) A great increase in urea excretion
(B) Large amounts of prehepatic bilirubin in the blood
(C) High blood ammonia levels
(D) High serum uric acid levels
(E) Deficiency of brain carbamoyl-phosphate synthetase

125. Within hours after ligation of a sympathetic nerve, an accumulation of excessive catecholamine would be found in the

(A) dendrites
(B) perikaryon
(C) axon proximal to the ligature
(D) axon distal to the ligature
(E) synaptic terminals

126. Of the following tests, the most reliable for the diagnosis of hepatic coma is

(A) venous serum ammonia
(B) arterial serum ammonia
(C) CSF ammonia
(D) CSF glutamine
(E) CSF pH

127. In Duchenne's pseudohypertrophic muscular dystrophy, the serum CPK value is

(A) roughly constant throughout the course of the disease
(B) greatly elevated prior to overt, clinically apparent weakness
(C) greatly elevated only in later stages of the disease
(D) increased as the weakness becomes severe
(E) unrelated to the stage of the disease

128. The rate of transport of metabolic substances from the perikaryon to the periphery in peripheral nerves is estimated to be in the range of

(A) 1 mm to 1 m/day
(B) 1 to 10 m/day
(C) 1 m/min
(D) 10 to 100 m/min
(E) 45 to 60 m/s

129. An 8-year-old child experiences several episodes of extreme irritability, unsteadiness of gait, and a skin rash in response to sunlight. His parents are second cousins. The single most important diagnostic test would be

(A) an EEG with photic stimulation
(B) a CT scan
(C) a urinary amino acid screen
(D) a serum lipid profile
(E) a liver biopsy

130. The most important mechanism for inactivating or terminating the action of catecholamine neurotransmitter released at the synaptic cleft is thought to be

(A) irreversible binding of the catecholamine with the postsynaptic membrane
(B) energy-dependent reuptake of the transmitter by the presynaptic neuron
(C) inherent instability of the neurotransmitter
(D) addition of sulphate radical by sulphatases
(E) isomerization from the D to the L form

131. After release into the synaptic cleft, acetylcholine is removed mainly by

(A) passive diffusion into the interstitial fluid and CSF
(B) engulfment into the postsynaptic membrane by pinocytosis
(C) return to the presynaptic ending by passive diffusion
(D) enzymatic hydrolysis with presynaptic uptake of choline
(E) long-term binding to the presynaptic surface

132. Striatal dopamine is located in highest concentration in the

(A) perikarya of striatal neurons
(B) glia
(C) dendrites
(D) synapses
(E) perivascular space

133. The "second messenger" theory of the mechanism of action of neurotransmitters (and other signaling substances such as hormones) suggests that the primary messenger substance

(A) releases a second substance into the synaptic cleft
(B) releases a second substance that inactivates the degradative enzymes for the neurotransmitter
(C) activates the enzyme-controlled metabolism of cyclic nucleotides
(D) blocks the energy-dependent expulsion of sodium
(E) acts on the DNA to alter the encoded genetic constitution of the cell

134. Abetalipoproteinemia (Bassen-Kornzweig syndrome) results in

(A) deficiency of vitamin E
(B) increased high-density lipoproteins
(C) decreased levels of vitamins B_6 and B_{12}
(D) increased serum levels of lecithin
(E) abnormally increased levels of vitamins A and K

135. The problem in identifying glutamic acid as a neurotransmitter is that

(A) none of the enzymes that could act on it can be isolated from the nervous system
(B) it fails to pass the blood-brain barrier
(C) it may also have a significant role in intermediary metabolism
(D) it cannot be demonstrated in the CNS
(E) it cannot be shown by iontophoresis to have any effect on neuronal polarization

136. The rate-limiting enzyme for catecholamine synthesis is

(A) dopa decarboxylase
(B) phenylalanine hydroxylase
(C) tyrosine hydroxylase
(D) aromatic amino acid decarboxylase
(E) dopamine β-hydroxylase

DIRECTIONS: Each question below contains four suggested responses of which **one or more** is correct. Select

A	if	**1, 2, and 3**	are correct
B	if	**1 and 3**	are correct
C	if	**2 and 4**	are correct
D	if	**4**	is correct
E	if	**1, 2, 3, and 4**	are correct

137. Correct statements about the metabolism of acetylcholine include which of the following?

    (1) An active uptake system returns acetylcholine to the interior of the presynaptic neuron
    (2) The cholinergic neurons manufacture both the acetyl group and the choline group
    (3) The rate-limiting factor is the availability of acetyl groups
    (4) Acetylcholinesterase hydrolyzes acetylcholine to acetic acid and choline

138. "Classic neurotransmitters" are removed from the synaptic cleft by which of the following?

    (1) Diffusion
    (2) Reuptake
    (3) Enzymatic degradation
    (4) Irreversible binding with the receptor

139. Glutamate functions in the brain as

    (1) a putative excitatory neurotransmitter
    (2) a precursor of γ-aminobutyric acid
    (3) an ammonia scavenger in detoxification
    (4) an energy source in coupled phosphorylation

140. Major differences between serotonin and catecholamine metabolism include no apparent

    (1) feedback inhibition of serotonin synthesis
    (2) active uptake mechanism for serotonin
    (3) activation of a secondary messenger by serotonin as contrasted to catecholamines
    (4) depletion of serotonin by reserpine

141. Neurologic diseases that may be associated with red or brown urine include

    (1) McArdle's disease
    (2) porphyria
    (3) alcoholic myopathy
    (4) polymyositis

142. The neurosecretory granules isolated from catecholaminergic neurons of the peripheral and central nervous system are characterized by

    (1) having a high concentration of dopamine or norepinephrine
    (2) having the complete system of enzymes for synthesis of catecholamines
    (3) containing high concentrations of ATP and ATPase
    (4) lacking a distinct membrane under electron microscopy

143. Correct statements concerning serotonin, norepinephrine, and histamine include which of the following?

    (1) The metabolic pathway to each begins with an essential amino acid
    (2) The precursor undergoes decarboxylation
    (3) Monoamine oxidase is involved in their inactivation or degradation
    (4) Each of the substances has a potent vasoactive effect

	SUMMARY OF DIRECTIONS			
A	B	C	D	E
1, 2, 3 only	1, 3 only	2, 4 only	4 only	All are correct

144. Acetylcholine fulfills criteria for a neuro-transmitter at

(1) neuromuscular junctions on skeletal muscle
(2) motor neuron collaterals to Renshaw cells
(3) preganglionic endings in the paravertebral ganglia of the autonomic system
(4) Purkinje cell synapses on the midline cerebellar nuclei

145. Characteristics of monoamine oxidase (MAO) include which of the following?

(1) It converts catecholamines to their corresponding aldehydes by oxidative deamination
(2) It exists only in a single unique form specific for catecholamines
(3) It is located in high concentration in mitochondria
(4) It is the rate-limiting enzyme in the catecholamine metabolic pathway

146. In its metabolic pathway, γ-aminobutyric acid (GABA) may be described as

(1) being derived from glucose and glutamic acid
(2) undergoing transamination and subsequently entering the Krebs cycle
(3) undergoing a rapid increase in concentration in postmortem tissues
(4) producing many derivatives that could act as neuromodulators or neurotransmitters

147. In regard to its distribution, γ-aminobutyric acid may correctly be described as

(1) being confined to the CNS
(2) being present in much higher concentrations in the ventral than dorsal horns
(3) having a very low concentration in white matter
(4) having a very low concentration in the basal ganglia and substantia nigra

148. Central cholinergic pathways are thought to include which of the following?

(1) Collaterals from the ventral horn motor neurons to the Renshaw cells
(2) Afferents to the hippocampus from the septum and diagonal band
(3) Cranial nerves IX, XI, and XII
(4) Projections from the majority of the raphe nuclei

149. Neurotransmitters found in very high concentrations in the striatum include

(1) dopamine
(2) norepinephrine
(3) serotonin
(4) glycine

150. Evidence that glycine may be a neurotransmitter is reflected in which of the following statements?

(1) It hyperpolarizes the postsynaptic membrane in spinal motor neurons
(2) Its inhibitory action is blocked by strychnine but not by other amino acid receptor blockers
(3) Stimulation of dorsal spinal cord roots produces glycine release in the cord
(4) Anoxia of the lumbar spinal cord produces a marked decline both in spinal interneurons and in glycine concentrations

151. True statements concerning neurofibrillary tangles include

    (1) they increase with age
    (2) they lie outside the neuron
    (3) on electron microscopy they are paired
    (4) they contain little protein

152. In one animal model of multiple sclerosis, experimental allergic encephalitis, true statements include which of the following?

    (1) It is caused by attenuated virus
    (2) Myelin basic protein can trigger the demyelinating lesions
    (3) The illness can be transferred from one animal to another via cell free plasma
    (4) The illness can be transferred from one animal to another via T cells

DIRECTIONS: Each group of questions below consists of lettered headings followed by a set of numbered items. For each numbered item select the **one** lettered heading with which it is **most** closely associated. Each lettered heading may be used **once, more than once, or not at all.**

Questions 153–156

For each procedure or operation described below, choose the neurotransmitter that it would deplete.

    (A) Glycine in the spinal cord
    (B) Dopamine and norepinephrine in the central and peripheral nervous system
    (C) Acetylcholine
    (D) Glutamic acid
    (E) Serotonin from the cerebral cortex

153. Destruction of the granule cells in the cerebellum

154. Destruction of interneurons (by controlled hypoxia)

155. Administration of 6-hydroxydopamine

156. Destruction of the nucleus basalis of Meynert

Questions 157–160

For each of the neurotransmitters listed below, choose the precursor with which it is most closely associated.

    (A) Tyrosine
    (B) Tryptophan
    (C) Glutamic acid
    (D) Glucose or citrate
    (E) Alanine

157. Acetyl group of acetylcholine

158. Serotonin

159. Dopamine

160. γ-Aminobutyric acid (GABA)

Questions 161–164

For each of the statements listed below, match the peptide that best fits the description.

    (A) Endorphins
    (B) Cholecystokinin (CCK)
    (C) Substance P
    (D) Neurotensin
    (E) Vasopressin

161. Putative pain transmitter found in high concentration in the dorsal horn neurons of the substantia gelatinosa

162. A nonapeptide synthesized in the supraoptic nucleus that causes thirst when released into the bloodstream

163. A peptide hormone that often colocalizes with dopamine in the upper brainstem

164. Generic term for a large class of neuropeptides with morphinelike activity

Questions 165–168

Match the disorder with the biochemical defect.

    (A) Abnormal amino acid transport
    (B) Disorder of phenylalanine hydroxylase
    (C) Lack of hypoxanthine-guanine phosphoribosyltransferase
    (D) Deficient activity of cystathionine reductase
    (E) Deficiency of hexosaminidase B

165. Blond, blue-eyed child with early vomiting followed by delayed development, then seizures

166. Childhood strokes and ectopic lens

167. Renal tubular acidosis, rickets, retardation, and myopathy

168. Retardation, choreoathetosis, and self-mutilation

Neurochemistry

Answers

123. The answer is D. (*Kandel, ed 2. pp 120–125.*) Using an experimental preparation that blocked sodium channels, Katz and Miledi demonstrated that electrical depolarization still resulted in acetylcholine release proportional to the magnitude of the depolarization. Blocking both sodium and potassium channels produced a similar result. Thus, although sodium influx and potassium efflux are necessary for a normal action potential, they are not required to release neurotransmitters. Calcium is required, however, and the quantity of neurotransmitter released depends on the amount of calcium influx that occurs during depolarization.

124. The answer is C. (*Rowland, ed 8. p 534.*) A biochemical abnormality that is shared by the inborn errors of the urea cycle is an increase in the blood ammonia level. The formation of urea via the urea cycle is both the only known metabolic pathway for urea synthesis in humans and the major pathway for ammonia detoxification. Patients with an inborn error of the urea cycle have a deficiency of one of the five enzymes that lead to the biosynthesis of urea. When urea fails to be produced because of a block along the pathway of urea production, ammonia will accumulate in the body tissues and fluids. Ammonia accumulation leads to vomiting, lethargy, convulsions, hypotonia, coma, and mental retardation. Exacerbations may be related to the ingestion of large amounts of dietary protein. Although hepatomegaly may occur, there is no evidence of jaundice. The best single screening test for a urea cycle disorder is a determination of blood ammonia level. The specific defect is subsequently identified by the abnormal pattern of amino acid excretion in the urine and direct demonstration of the particular enzyme defect by biochemical assay of the patient's cells.

125. The answer is C. (*Cooper, ed 5. p 248.*) After a ligature is placed around a sympathetic nerve, catecholamines accumulate just proximal to the ligature. The accumulation begins shortly after the ligature is placed. This observation supports the supposition that the neurotransmitter substance is manufactured in the perikaryon and transported down the axon to the terminals for storage and release. The idea that a substance originates in the central nervous system and undergoes transportation distally is an ancient theory in the history of medicine. We no longer speak of this substance as "animal spirits" but as neurohumors. Ramón y Cajal was one of the first scientists to demonstrate the distention of nerves proximal to a ligature, but he lacked the biochemical tools to demonstrate the nature of the accumulated substance.

126. The answer is D. (*Plum, ed 3. pp 222–225.*) In hepatic encephalopathy and coma there is usually an elevation of liver enzymes, a respiratory alkalosis, and an elevation of serum ammonia levels due to failure of the liver to clear the ammonia. Liver enzymes are frequently normal in advanced liver failure. CSF glutamine is probaly the most sensitive test. Blood ammonia does not penetrate the blood-brain barrier but is rapidly metabolized to glutamine.

127. The answer is B. (*Rowland, ed 8. pp 711–712.*) In pseudohypertrophic muscular dystrophy, the serum CPK value is greatly elevated prior to overt clinical manifestations. It remains high during the early clinical course and drops later as the muscle mass is reduced. Thus, the CPK determinations help in early diagnosis of the disease in infants, prior to clinical signs of the weakness. High CPK values also are present in the fetus, and CPK measurement of fetal blood levels can lead to a prenatal diagnosis. CPK exists in at least three isoenzymes—from muscle, heart, and brain. Muscle CPK blood levels are elevated in Duchenne's dystrophy, as is the cardiac isoenzyme. Normally the serum contains no brain CPK.

128. The answer is A. (*Cooper, ed 5. pp 247–249.*) The rate of axoplasmic transport of substances is variously estimated as 1 mm to 1 m/day. Interestingly, the rate of regeneration of axons is in the range of 1 to 5 mm/day, which approximates the rate of slow axoplasmic flow. Whether axoplasmic flow increases or decreases during regeneration remains in dispute. The rate of transport of metabolic substances down the axon (1 mm to 1 m/day) contrasts with the rate of propagation of the nerve impulse, which is in the range of 45 to 60 m/s. This vastly greater rate of impulse propagation underscores its electrical nature in contrast with axoplasmic flow, which involves the movement of ions, molecules, or even macromolecules.

129. The answer is C. (*Rowland, ed 8. pp 497–498.*) The combination of intermittent episodes of unsteady gait (ataxia), emotionality, and a photosensitive skin rash in a patient coming from a consanguineous mating suggests Hartnup disease. This disease is a recessively inherited error of metabolism characterized by a deficiency in the gastrointestinal and renal transport of tryptophan and certain other monoaminomonocarboxylic amino acids. The critical diagnostic test for Hartnup disease is the demonstration of the pattern of excessive excretion of monoaminomonocarboxylic acids in the urine. The direct selection of this single, simple urine screening test eliminates the need for further laboratory testing.

130. The answer is B. (*Cooper, ed 5. pp 245–247.*) Probably the most important mode of inactivation of catecholamine neurotransmitter at the synaptic cleft is an energy-dependent reuptake of the substance into the presynaptic neuron. Whatever the mechanism, apparently it is efficient because little of a catecholamine such as norepinephrine overflows into the circulation, in spite of strong stimulation of sympathetic nerves. While degradation by monoamine oxidase (MAO) or catechol-*O*-methyltransferase (COMT) accounts for much of the inactivation of released catecholamine neurotransmitter, the inhibition of these enzymes fails to potentiate the effect of nerve stimulation. In favor of the importance of active reuptake is the fact that a sympathetic neuron can concentrate catecholamines from surrounding media by a ratio as great as 10,000 to 1.

131. The answer is D. (*Cooper, ed 5. pp 185–188.*) The removal and inactivation of acetylcholine after its release appears to be mainly dependent on enzymatic hydrolysis. The choline part of the molecule is then actively transported back into the presynaptic cell by an energy-dependent mechanism. The availability of choline appears to be the limiting factor in acetylcholine synthesis, and this mechanism of active return of choline may be a mechanism for conservation of a rate-limiting metabolite. In some instances, the entire neurotransmitter molecule is taken up by the presynaptic ending and presumably can be recycled many times without undergoing degradation or resynthesis.

132. The answer is D. (*Adams RD, ed 4. pp 58–59.*) Fractionation of the striatum with subsequent chemical analysis shows the highest concentrations of dopamine in the synaptosomal fraction. This observation indicates that the striatum, rather than producing its own dopamine, receives it from elsewhere via axonal transport. Its accumulation in the synaptosomes suggests that it plays a neurotransmitter role. The nigrostriatal pathway apparently provides the majority of dopaminergic synapses for the striatum. Interruption of this pathway or degeneration of the substantia nigra is associated with a severe decrease in the dopamine content of the striatum.

133. **The answer is C.** (*McGeer, ed 2. pp 165–168.*) Just how the primary chemical messenger—whether neurotransmitter or hormone—activates the target cell to do its job of secreting, contracting, or firing an impulse is one of the fundamental questions of cell biology. Current theory suggests that the combination of the neurotransmitter with its receptor activates nucleotide cyclase and sets into play a series of enzymatically dependent events that provide the energy for the subsequent actions of the target cell. A whole series of ''Koch's postulates'' has been developed to justify the recognition of a second messenger mechanism, just as they have been developed to justify recognition of a particular substance as a primary neurotransmitter.

134. **The answer is A.** (*Rowland, ed 8. pp 547–549.*) Abetalipoproteinemia is a rare disorder of children that was one of the first hereditary ataxias described. The child is unable to synthesize the apoprotein of beta-lipoprotein, which results in a decrease in plasma levels of chylomicrons, low-density lipoproteins, very low-density lipoproteins, cholesterol, triglycerides, lecithin, cephalin, and sphingomyelin. Fat-soluble vitamins A, E, and K are markedly reduced because of fat malabsorption. The clinical syndrome consists of progressive ataxia, areflexia, weakness, retinitis pigmentosa, impaired proprioception, and ophthalmoparesis. Acanthocytes account for over 50 percent of the red blood cells seen on a peripheral blood smear. The neuropathology is widespread and includes segmental demyelination in peripheral nerves, demyelination in spinal cord posterior columns, and loss of neurons in the cerebellar cortex and anterior horns of the spinal cord. The neuropathologic explanation for the ophthalmoparesis is still unknown.

135. **The answer is C.** (*Cooper, ed 5. pp 161–170.*) Glutamic acid can be demonstrated to have excitatory effects on crustacean muscle and mammalian neurons. It and the enzymes that metabolize it can be isolated from nervous tissue. The main problem in identifying glutamic acid as a neurotransmitter is that it has a role in intermediary metabolism, which gives it a much more ubiquitous distribution in comparison to other putative neurotransmitters like dopamine, which can be localized to specific neurons and specific tracts.

136. **The answer is C.** (*Cooper, ed 5. pp 203–205.*) The term *catecholamine* refers to compounds composed of a benzene ring with two adjacent hydroxyl moieties (the catechol nucleus) plus an amine group. The term refers to dopamine, epinephrine, and norepinephrine. The synthesis of catecholamines starts with tyrosine or with phenylalanine, which is converted to tyrosine and then metabolized to L-dopa, dopamine, norepinephrine, and epinephrine in that order. The rate-limiting enzyme is tyrosine hydroxylase, which converts L-dopa to dopamine. It is this fact that allows L-dopa to be successful in treating Parkinson's disease; that is, the rate-limiting synthesis step has been bypassed.

137. **The answer is D (4).** (*Cooper, ed 5. pp 175–188.*) In the metabolism of acetylcholine, the rate-limiting factor is the availability of choline, which apparently is manufactured mostly in the liver and transported to the neurons. Acetylcholinesterase hydrolyzes acetylcholine to acetic acid and choline. An active transport mechanism returns choline, but not the entire acetylcholine molecule, to the neuron. One stumbling block in acetylcholine research has been the lack of a drug that specifically blocks the uptake of choline.

138. **The answer is A (1, 2, 3).** (*Kandel, ed 2. p 172.*) Neurotransmitters are quickly removed from the postsynaptic cleft. The most common mechanism is reuptake by the presynaptic neuron, but enzymatic degradation also occurs. Diffusion occurs to some degree in all transmitter systems.

Acetylcholine is one neurotransmitter that is primarily degraded enzymatically. Neuropeptides, unlike the classic neurotransmitters, generally remain for long periods of time in the synaptic cleft and the mechanism for their removal is not understood.

139. The answer is E (all). (*Cooper, ed 5. pp 78, 161–170.*)   Glutamate has numerous roles in the CNS. It is a putative excitatory neurotransmitter, a precursor of γ-aminobutyric acid, and an ammonia scavenger and is involved in energy metabolism. It also is a structural amino acid for protein synthesis. Glutamine and other putative amino acid neurotransmitters can be derived from glucose, and glutamate is involved in many other metabolic reactions including proline, glutathione, and *N*-acetylaspartate production.

140. The answer is B (1, 3). (*Cooper, ed 5. pp 322, 330.*)   Although serotonin and catecholamine metabolism share many features, serotonin synthesis differs in its apparent freedom from feedback inhibition. There is strong evidence for activation of a secondary messenger by catecholamines, as has been demonstrated in the effect of stimulation of the nucleus locus ceruleus on the Purkinje cells. Reserpine depletes both catecholamines and serotonin, which has confounded the correlation between neurohumoral levels and behavior.

141. The answer is E (all). (*Rowland, ed 8. pp 724–726.*)   A number of neurologic diseases may produce reddish brown discoloration of the urine. The color results from hemoglobin or myoglobin pigments. The pigmented urine in most instances of neuromuscular disease results from necrotic or injured muscle, which liberates myoglobin, or from the biosynthesis of heme. The liberated pigment damages the kidney and leads to renal failure. Renal failure poses a threat to survival in many neuromuscular diseases that might not, in themselves, be fatal, including McArdle's disease, porphyria, alcoholic myopathy, and polymyositis.

142. The answer is B (1, 3). (*Cooper, ed 5. pp 32–33, 237.*)   Subcellular particles called *neurosecretory granules* isolated from catecholaminergic neurons have high concentrations of dopamine or norepinephrine and of ATP and ATPase. The ATP may bind the norepinephrine within the granules by means of a salt linkage. The granules lack the complete enzyme systems for the synthesis of the catecholamines. Electron microscopy shows that the granules have a dense core and a well-developed outer membrane. The very structure of these neurosecretory granules raises questions as to whether they could fuse with the presynaptic membrane and release their neurotransmitter contents rapidly enough to account for synaptic transmission. An alternate theory is that they form a long-term storage system rather than the immediately mobile neurotransmitter that responds so quickly to the arrival of the nerve impulse.

143. The answer is E (all). (*Cooper, ed 5. pp 243, 316–321, 340–345.*)   The metabolic pathway to serotonin begins with tryptophan, to norepinephrine with phenylalanine or tyrosine, and to histamine with histidine. Tryptophan, phenylalanine, and histidine all are essential amino acids. Each of the amino acids undergoes decarboxylation. Monoamine oxidase may be involved in the activation or degradation of serotonin, norepinephrine, and histamine. All three substances produce vasoactive agents. Tryptophan produces tryptamine and tyramine, and phenylalanine produces norepinephrine and epinephrine, all of which are vasopressors (as is serotonin), whereas histamine is a vasodilator.

144. The answer is A (1, 2, 3). (*Cooper, ed 5. pp 190–192.*)   Acetylcholine fulfills criteria for a neurotransmitter at neuromuscular junctions on skeletal muscles, motor neuron collaterals to Renshaw cells, and preganglionic endings in the paravertebral ganglia. It also is the presumptive neurotransmitter in the postganglionic parasympathetic terminals. Cholinergic transmission also may occur in the hippocampus from the diagonal band and septum, thus from rhinencephalic structures at the base of the forebrain. The habenulointerpeduncular tract also may be cholinergic. Other suggested cholinergic systems include the ascending reticular activating system, the primary afferents in auditory and visual systems, and some dorsal root fibers. The subject of cholinergic transmission in the cerebral cortex remains unsettled. In almost all known instances, acetylcholine acts as an excitatory transmitter, although evidence for inhibitory transmission exists for some sites. The Purkinje cells strongly inhibit the midline nuclei, and the transmitter is thought to be γ-aminobutyric acid (GABA).

145. The answer is B (1, 3). (*Cooper, ed 5. pp 242–244.*) Monoamine oxidase (MAO) converts catecholamines to their corresponding aldehydes by oxidative deamination. It exists in more than one form and lacks specificity for catecholamines, acting on a number of other substances including serotonin, tryptamine, and tyramine. It is generally regarded as existing in highest concentration in the mitochondria. It is not a rate-limiting enzyme in the catecholamine pathways. In spite of the presumed role of MAO in inactiving various biogenic amines that could serve as neurotransmitters, the action of these transmitters appears to be unaffected by the inactivation of MAO.

146. The answer is E (all). (*Cooper, ed 5. pp 125–127, 135.*) γ-Aminobutyric acid (GABA) has an amino acid precursor, glutamic acid, but also can be derived from glucose. GABA undergoes transamination and then may enter the Krebs cycle. A striking fact about GABA is that it can produce a large number of compounds that may have neuromodulator or neurotransmitter actions. It can produce compounds that have anesthetic action or that may depress or excite some neurons. Thus, the metabolic derivatives of GABA are under intensive study at this time. One problem in assessing GABA levels or the effects of chemical manipulations on the GABA content of the CNS is that GABA undergoes a very rapid rise in concentration in post-mortem tissues, which may result from activation of glutamic acid decarboxylase at death.

147. The answer is A (1, 2, 3). (*Cooper, ed 5. pp 125–126.*) γ-Aminobutyric acid (GABA) and its synthesizing enzyme glutamic acid decarboxylase are confined to the CNS, including the retina, which is embryologically derived from the CNS. GABA is found in much higher concentrations in the gray matter than in the white matter, in keeping with its presumed role as a neurotransmitter. It is found in high concentrations in the ventral horns, where inhibitory effects do occur, rather than in the dorsal horns, where excitatory neurotransmitters predominate. A GABA pathway is believed to run from the striatum to the pallidum and substantia nigra; the synthesizing enzyme for GABA (glutamic acid decarboxylase) and its degradative enzyme (GABA-transaminase) are in high concentration in these regions.

148. The answer is A (1, 2, 3). (*Cooper, ed 5. pp 190–192. McGeer, ed 2. pp 245–252.*) Although technical difficulties prevent the establishment of acetylcholine as a neurotransmitter in central pathways as firmly as in the peripheral nervous system, some central pathways are thought to be cholinergic. The most likely pathways include Renshaw collaterals from the ventral horn motor neurons, hippocampal afferents from the diagonal band and septum, the habenulointerpenduncular tract, the ascending reticular activating system, and cranial nerves containing voluntary motor fibers (III through VII, IX, XI, and XII). Several other central cholinergic pathways are suggested. On the other hand, many central pathways lack evidence of being cholinergic; many, such as the raphe nuclei, which appears to be serotonergic, have other putative neurotransmitters.

149. The answer is B (1, 3). (*McGeer, ed 2. pp 228, 285, 329–337.*) The striatum contains several putative neurotransmitters in high concentration, including dopamine, serotonin, acetylcholine, γ-aminobutyric acid (GABA), and polypeptides. It contains low amounts of norepinephrine and glycine. The high concentrations of dopamine and serotonin and low amounts of norepinephrine are thought to reflect the density of innervation of the striatum by the various tegmental nuclei. In particular, the low concentration of norepinephrine reflects only a slight innervation of the striatum by the norepinephrinergic pathways arising in such tegmental nuclei as the locus ceruleus.

150. The answer is E (all).   (*Cooper, ed 5. pp 159–160. McGeer, ed 2. pp 230–231.*)   Glycine has been determined to fulfill the requirements for a neurotransmitter in the spinal cord and is a candidate neurotransmitter at other sites as well, including the retina, cerebellar Golgi cells, brainstem afferents to dopaminergic cells in the substantia nigra, and others. It hyperpolarizes the membrane of spinal motor neurons, which causes a fall in membrane resistance and a rise in chloride ion permeability. Its action is blocked by strychnine but not bicuculline, a GABA blocker. The localization of glycine follows the localization of strychnine binding, which again suggests a neurotransmitter role. Glycine is localized primarily to the ventral and dorsal gray in the spinal cord in interneurons. When the thoracic aorta is clamped, the resultant ischemia/anoxia preferentially destroys most spinal interneurons and brings with it a similar drop in glycine concentration. In a perfused cord preparation, stimulation of the dorsal roots brings about glycine release.

151. The answer is B (1, 3).   (*Siegel, ed 4. p 533.*)   Neurofibrillary tangles (NFT) are seen in Alzheimer's disease and several other neurodegenerative disorders such as Down's syndrome, progressive supranuclear palsy (PSP), and dementia pugilistica, but they also appear with increasing frequency in aging. They are composed of protein primarily and are seen in various parts of the neuron. NFTs form paired filaments that are helical, except in PSP, where they are straight.

152. The answer is C (2, 4).   (*Siegel, ed 4. pp 703–704.*)   There are acute, chronic, and chronic relapsing forms of experimental allergic encephalitis (EAE). The acute form occurs with the injection of myelin basic protein (MBP) and Freund's adjuvant. This leads to widespread demyelination in the brain. This disorder is transferred via T cells from animal to animal and not by a serum-borne substance. The chronic form is brought on by the addition of other myelin chemicals to MBP. The relapsing form occurs with the addition of non-MBP components of myelin or after the transfer of certain T cell clones from an animal with the acute form.

153–156. The answers are: 153-D, 154-A, 155-B, 156-C.   (*Cooper, ed 5. pp 159, 162, 198, 210.*)   By certain manipulations, the experimenter can deplete the nervous system of specific substances presumed to be neurotransmitters. Controlled hypoxia causes a selective necrosis of interneurons in the spinal cord. The glycine content of the spinal gray matter is reduced, offering one line of evidence that glycine may be the transmitter that mediates the inhibitory effect of these neurons.

The intravenous administration of 6-hydroxydopamine causes a chemical sympathectomy in the peripheral nervous system. When given by intraventricular injections or when applied directly in the central nervous system, the drug causes a fairly specific destruction of catecholamine-containing neurons.

The nucleus basalis of Meynert is the principal source of cholinergic input to the cortex. It is affected in Alzheimer's disease.

A virus that selectively destroys granule cells in the cerebellum has been found. This results in a 95 percent loss of granular cells and a decrease in cerebellar glutamate.

157–160. The answers are: 157-D, 158-B, 159-A, 160-C.   (*Cooper, ed 5. pp 128, 175, 218, 318.*)   The precursor of the acetyl group of acetylcholine is glucose or citrate; of serotonin, tryptophan; of dopamine, tyrosine; and of γ-aminobutyric acid (GABA), glutamic acid. These precursor substances, occurring in the diet, undergo several metabolic transformations to gain activity as neurotransmitters. With some further slight metabolic transformation, the neurotransmitter loses its capacity to excite or inhibit the postsynaptic neuron. The elaborate metabolic pathway involved insures that only the exact substance rather than a substance that happens to enter the blood, will affect the function of the neurons.

The precursors of acetylcholine differ from the other precursors in this group. The precursors of serotonin, dopamine, and GABA are all amino acids. The acetyl group of acetylcholine is readily available from the catabolism of glucose. The choline that comes from the diet is the rate-limiting moiety of acetylcholine synthesis. Choline is taken up for recycling by the presynaptic ending, after the splitting of acetylcholine by cholinesterase at the synapse.

The recycling of one moiety of a transmitter, choline, appears to be unusual. The biogenic amines are transformed by undergoing methylations or hydroxylations. In the case of amino acid–related transmitters, inactivation may ultimately involve deamination. Serotonin is inactivated by both oxidation and deamination. The end product of this process is 5-hydroxy-indoleacetic acid. The carboxyl group of the acetic acid replaces the amino grouping on the terminal carbon of the aliphatic portion of the molecule.

161–164. The answers are: 161-C, 162-E, 163-B, 164-A. (*Cooper, ed 5. pp 361–364, 370, 381–382.*) The neuropeptides derive from precursor molecules (prohormones) which themselves are biologically inactive. Although they are secreted from neurons, they have not been shown to meet all criteria for neurotransmitters. They often coexist with documented neurotransmitters and appear to modify their actions. CCK, for example, is found in the same neurons as dopamine in the ventral tegmental area. Substance P is present in many scattered brain areas but is concentrated in the substantia gelatinosa of the spinal cord and is thought to mediate pain. While it is a potent depolarizing substance in the cord, it has such a long duration of action that it has not been fully accepted as a transmitter. Vasopressin and oxytocin are similar peptides found in the hypothalamic supraoptic and paraventricular nuclei. Vasopressin is a potent antidiuretic hormone that increases distal tubular reabsorption in the kidney. In animals and humans it also acts to improve immediate memory and attention. *Endorphin* is a generic term for a variety of peptides with morphinelike activity. There are now three major classes: the promelanocortin-derived peptides, the proenkephalin-derived peptides, and the prodynorphin-derived peptides.

165–168. The answers are: 165-B, 166-D, 167-A, 168-C. (*Rowland, ed 8. pp 491–493, 496–497, 499–500.*) Phenylketonuria is caused by a deficiency of phenylalanine hydroxylase, which is normally found in organs outside of the brain. As a result of this, the normal hydroxylation of phenylalanine to tyrosine does not take place. If not recognized, a normal diet will lead to accumulations of large amounts of phenylalanine. In the brain there is a delay of maturation, defective myelination, and decreased pigmentation of the substantia nigra. Affected children have deficient pigmentation. They are irritable and vomit early on before showing delayed milestones. By 18 months seizures are common.

Homocystinuria is the most common disorder of metabolism of sulfur-containing amino acids. In most cases, cystathionine synthetase is lacking. The enzyme synthesizes the catabolism of cystathionine from homocysteine and serine. As a result, increased levels of homocysteine and methionine accumulate. Patients have strokes in the first year or two of life and invariably have ectopic lenses.

There are a few different disorders of amino acid transport. The oculocerebrorenal syndrome of Lowe is sex-linked recessive. Patients have elevated lysine levels in urine. The kidney defect is an aminoaciduria with renal tubular acidosis and rickets. Neurologically there is severe retardation and growth delay.

Lesch-Nyhan syndrome is a disorder of purine metabolism due to a lack of hypoxanthine-guanine phosphoribosyltransferase. This leads to increased purine metabolism with a build-up of uric acid that may simulate gout. The neurologic syndrome that differentiates it from most other disorders is the uniform presence of self-mutilation. Severe dementia, spasticity, and choreoathetosis start in the first year.

Neuropharmacology

DIRECTIONS: Each question below contains five suggested responses. Select the **one best** response to each question.

169. A postganglionic Horner's syndrome can be distinguished from a preganglionic or central one using which one of the following drugs?

    (A) Cocaine
    (B) Atropine
    (C) Hydroxyamphetamine
    (D) Pilocarpine
    (E) Timolol

170. A patient lacking available history is brought in off the street with delirium; pupillodilatation; dry, flushed skin and mucous membranes; peculiar myoclonus-like twitchings; tachycardia; and fever. The clinical condition appears to be deteriorating during a period of 45 min of observation. The drug of choice for treatment would be which of the following?

    (A) Edrophonium
    (B) Thiamine
    (C) Phenobarbital
    (D) Physostigmine
    (E) Metocurine iodide (Metubine)

171. To dilate the pupil without paralyzing accommodation, the examiner would use a drug that

    (A) blocks parasympathetic endings
    (B) blocks sympathetic endings
    (C) stimulates parasympathetic endings
    (D) stimulates sympathetic endings
    (E) does none of the above

172. A patient with a history of drug abuse is brought to an emergency room with obtundation, a respiratory rate of 7 breaths per minute, and pinpoint pupils, but no other frank neurologic signs. A glucose test-tape shows a normal blood glucose level. The patient is intubated. The most appropriate management of this patient would involve which of the following measures?

    (A) Immediate CT scan
    (B) Administration of pure oxygen
    (C) Intravenous bolus of 50% glucose
    (D) Administration of intravenous naloxone
    (E) Immediate lumbar puncture

60

173. Local anesthetic agents like procaine are thought to act by

    (A) inhibiting cyclic AMP
    (B) inhibiting the oxidative enzymes of the mitochondria in the perikaryon and synaptic endings
    (C) blocking pyridoxal-dependent enzymes of the catecholamine metabolic pathway
    (D) blocking the voltage-dependent transient rise in membrane permeability to sodium
    (E) completing depolarization

174. Of the several drugs that have value in the relief of spasticity, the one that acts directly on skeletal muscle is

    (A) diazepam (Valium)
    (B) dantrolene
    (C) mephenesin
    (D) cyclobenzaprine
    (E) methocarbamol

175. Which of the following statements regarding botulinum toxin (botulin) A is true?

    (A) It is the treatment of choice for blepharospasm and hemifacial spasm
    (B) It is not helpful in torticollis
    (C) It weakens muscles by blocking the motor end plate
    (D) It acts by uncoupling myofibrils
    (E) It interrupts acetylcholine synthesis

176. The most widely accepted theory to explain tachyphylaxis by sympathomimetic drugs is which of the following?

    (A) Irreversible binding of the neurotransmitter at the receptor site
    (B) Stimulation of degradative enzymes
    (C) Increased flushing of intercellular fluid through the synapse
    (D) Displacement of neurotransmitter from the presynaptic terminals
    (E) Release of dopamine β-hydroxylase

177. In a patient suspected of having ocular myasthenia, no improvement in the ptosis or ocular palsy and no subjective complaints or objective signs of cholinergic stimulation appeared after initial injection of 2 mg of edrophonium followed by 1 mg every 30 s for a total dose of 10 mg. The most appropriate management of this patient is to

    (A) conclude that the patient does not have myasthenia gravis and discontinue testing
    (B) perform the same test using neostigmine
    (C) perform a curare test
    (D) perform a Jolly test (look for decremental response after repetitive nerve stimulation)
    (E) administer additional edrophonium until improvement occurs or signs or symptoms of cholinergic overactivity appear

178. Tardive dyskinesia most commonly involves the

    (A) neck
    (B) mouth and tongue
    (C) arms and hands
    (D) legs and feet
    (E) eyelids

179. The primary mechanism of the anticonvulsant action of phenytoin (Dilantin) is currently thought to be which of the following?

    (A) Increasing the amount of γ-aminobutyric acid in the cortex
    (B) Binding with glutamic acid receptor sites at synapses
    (C) Depolarization of all neuronal membranes
    (D) Blockage of sodium channels in resting membranes
    (E) Stimulation of acetylcholinesterase

180. Malignant hyperthermia is correctly characterized by which of the following statements?

    (A) It can be induced by antipsychotic drugs
    (B) It can be precipitated by halothane
    (C) It is best treated with a paralyzing agent like succinylcholine
    (D) It responds to intravenous diazepam
    (E) It is rarely familial

181. The antipsychotic drug LEAST likely to cause anticholinergic side effects is

    (A) chlorpromazine (Thorazine)
    (B) clozapine (Clozaril)
    (C) haloperidol
    (D) amitriptyline
    (E) carbamazepine

182. An unknown middle-aged man is brought to the emergency room in status epilepticus. An intravenous line has been inserted and blood samples have been obtained. The first step in treating this patient should be the administration of

    (A) diazepam 5 mg IV
    (B) phenobarbital 130 mg IV
    (C) glucose 50 g with thiamine 100 mg IV
    (D) thiamine 100 mg IV
    (E) paraldehyde 50 mg IV

183. A manic-depressive patient recently started on lithium treatment begins to show diarrhea, ataxia, fasciculations, tremor, overactive muscle stretch reflexes, and seizures. The blood lithium level is 1.5 meq/L. The best interpretation of these findings is that the

    (A) correct diagnosis of delirium tremens was overlooked
    (B) symptoms and lithium blood level are compatible with lithium intoxication
    (C) patient has acute hyperthyroidism
    (D) lithium has precipitated a catecholaminergic crisis
    (E) patient must have received a stimulant medication and should have a toxicology screening

184. MPTP is a toxin that causes parkinsonism in humans. All the following statements about MPTP are true EXCEPT that it

    (A) must be converted in glial cells to MPP+ to become toxic
    (B) is prevented from becoming toxic if monoamine oxidase (MAO) B is blocked
    (C) destroys striatal as well as nigral neurons
    (D) primarily affects dopaminergic neurons
    (E) produces an opiate "high"

185. A striking difference in the response of the nigrostriatal system to mechanical or pharmacologic interruption of impulse flow, as contrasted to the other catecholaminergic systems, is that the interruption results in

    (A) increased storage of dopamine in the axonal terminals and increased production
    (B) great increase in acetylcholine in the striatum
    (C) immediate switch to serotonin neurotransmission
    (D) no change in the production or storage of dopamine because of steady-state kinetics of the system
    (E) extreme depletion of dopamine in the striatum

186. Infantile spasms are most likely to respond to which one of the following medications?

    (A) Valproic acid
    (B) Carbamazepine
    (C) Clonazepam
    (D) ACTH
    (E) Bromide

187. An overdose of which one of the following drugs can cause fixed and unequal pupils?

    (A) Phenobarbital
    (B) Glutethimide
    (C) Amphetamine
    (D) Lithium
    (E) Imipramine

188. Deprenyl (selegiline; Eldepryl) may be characterized by which of the following statements?

    (A) It has been demonstrated to slow the progression of disability in Parkinson's disease
    (B) It is a potentially dangerous drug because it blocks the enzyme monoamine oxidase
    (C) It has a major symptomatic effect in otherwise untreated patients with Parkinson's disease
    (D) It improves memory function in Parkinson's disease
    (E) It is useful in Parkinson's disease because of its antidepressant effects

189. Which one of the following statements concerning the pharmacokinetics of phenytoin is true?

    (A) Brain concentration equals the protein-bound concentration in the blood
    (B) Only small amounts bind to plasma protein
    (C) In the therapeutic range, the plasma half-life increases with the concentration
    (D) At low plasma concentrations, the drug has a longer half-life than at high concentrations
    (E) There is little variability in the plasma half-life

190. Meperidine (Demerol) may have a fatal interaction with

    (A) lithium
    (B) benztropine
    (C) tricyclic antidepressants
    (D) monoamine oxidase antidepressants
    (E) phenytoin

191. Chronic use of which one of the following drugs may lead to auditory hallucinations in an otherwise clear sensorium?

    (A) Levodopa
    (B) Phenobarbital
    (C) Cocaine
    (D) Ethanol
    (E) Alprazolam

192. Which one of the following drugs causes a syndrome of visual hallucinations in an otherwise clear sensorium?

    (A) Amphetamine
    (B) Methanol
    (C) Ethanol
    (D) Cocaine
    (E) Levodopa

193. A patient with leukemia is admitted with mild confusion, a lower motor neuron facial palsy on one side, and biceps weakness on the contralateral side. His brain CT scan is normal but spinal fluid reveals a lymphocytic pleocytosis with a mildly low glucose and mildly elevated protein. No leukemic cells are seen initially, but fungal and bacterial cultures are negative. Which drug is most likely to be beneficial?

    (A) Methotrexate
    (B) Dexamethasone
    (C) Amphotericin
    (D) Isoniazid
    (E) Cisplatin

DIRECTIONS: Each question below contains four suggested responses of which **one or more** is correct. Select

A	if	**1, 2, and 3**	are correct
B	if	**1 and 3**	are correct
C	if	**2 and 4**	are correct
D	if	**4**	is correct
E	if	**1, 2, 3, and 4**	are correct

194. Dexamethasone has been proved to be effective in reducing the edema associated with which of the following conditions?

    (1) Cerebral infarction
    (2) Glioma
    (3) Cerebral trauma
    (4) Abscess

195. Pseudotumor cerebri has been linked to which of the following medications?

    (1) Ferrous sulfate
    (2) Tetracycline
    (3) Pyridoxine
    (4) Vitamin A

196. Manipulations that increase the action of tyrosine hydroxylase in catecholaminergic neurons include which of the following?

    (1) Administration of monoamine oxidase inhibitors
    (2) Administration of tyramine
    (3) Administration of 6-hydroxydopamine or α-methyl-ρ-tyrosine (AMPT)
    (4) Increased activity of the catecholaminergic neurons

197. Petit mal (three cycles per second spike and wave) seizures can be treated with which of the following medications?

    (1) Valproic acid
    (2) Phenobarbital
    (3) Ethosuximide
    (4) Phenytoin

198. Which of the following statements would apply to the pharmacology of tardive dyskinesia?

    (1) It is thought to result from hypersensitivity of cholinergic receptors
    (2) It may resolve when the offending agent is stopped
    (3) The dyskinesia will worsen within days of increasing the offending drug
    (4) It may be masked by antidopaminergic drugs

199. Clozapine, which is classified as an "atypical neuroleptic,"

    (1) has few adverse effects
    (2) may induce parkinsonism
    (3) has been linked to tardive dyskinesia
    (4) is an effective antipsychotic drug

200. Anticholinesterase drugs commonly cause which of the following?

    (1) Increased gut motility
    (2) Increased salivation
    (3) Increased muscle strength in patients with myasthenia
    (4) Mydriasis

201. The actions of cocaine include which of the following?

    (1) It potentiates sympathetic activity
    (2) It blocks reuptake of catecholamines at nerve terminals
    (3) It blocks nerve impulses with local application
    (4) It desensitizes the emesis center in the brain

202. Plasmapheresis is useful in treating

   (1) myasthenia gravis
   (2) lupus cerebritis
   (3) Guillian-Barré syndrome
   (4) paraneoplastic peripheral neuropathies

203. Adverse effects of carbamazepine (Tegretol) in therapeutic levels include

   (1) aplastic anemia
   (2) peripheral neuropathy
   (3) hyponatremia
   (4) hyperactivity

204. Medications useful in the treatment of Parkinson's disease include which of the following?

   (1) Benztropine
   (2) Amantadine
   (3) Pergolide
   (4) Amitriptyline

205. True statements concerning the use of ergot alkaloids in the treatment of migraine include

   (1) excessive use may lead to rebound migraines
   (2) excessive use may cause retroperitoneal fibrosis
   (3) they are most useful during the aura
   (4) they are useful in prophylaxis

Neuropharmacology

Answers

169. **The answer is C.** (*Glaser, ed 2. p 479.*)   Postganglionic lesions of the sympathetic chain produce denervation supersensitivity of the iris so that the pupil dilates more than normal to a sympathetic stimulus. Since it blocks the reuptake of norepinephrine, cocaine is not helpful in localizing a Horner's syndrome. Atropine will dilate all pupils that respond to cholinergic stimuli. Pilocarpine constricts both pupils. Timolol is a beta blocker that will not alter the pupil size. Hydroxyamphetamine 1% causes a release of sympathetic stores in the neuron innervating the pupil. If the lesion is postganglionic, the nerves to the iris are damaged and will have little or no norepinephrine to release, whereas the norepinephrine supply is normal if the lesion is preganglionic. Hydroxyamphetamine will therefore cause a marked dilatation in a preganglionic Horner's syndrome and little response in a postganglionic lesion.

170. **The answer is D.** (*Gilman AG, ed 8. pp 157–158.*)   The combination of delirium, pupillodilatation, dryness of skin and mucous membranes, tachycardia, and fever exhibited by the patient presented in the question suggests cholinergic (muscarinic) blockade, which most commonly would be due to ingestion of atropinelike drugs, including the tricyclic antidepressants. The drug of choice both for therapy and as a diagnostic aid is physostigmine, a potent peripheral and central anticholinesterase. Physostigmine, like many other anticholinesterases, penetrates the blood-brain barrier to counteract the central effects of the cholinergic blocking agents. It must be administered cautiously and the patient monitored in an intensive care unit (ICU) because of the tendency of this drug to cause cardiac arrhythmias and hypotension. Phenothiazines, which have cholinergic blocking action, would only worsen the patient's condition. Phenobarbital would further impair the patient's sensorium. A preferable anticonvulsant would be diazepam. Edrophonium would have muscarinic and cholinergic effects peripherally, but not centrally, and would act for too short a period of time. Metocurine iodide (Metubine) would block the nicotinic action of acetylcholine on skeletal muscle (which would not prove beneficial) and thiamine would be ineffective, although not harmful.

171. **The answer is D.** (*Gilman AG, ed 8. p 162.*)   To dilate the pupil without paralyzing accommodation requires a drug that stimulates sympathetic endings on the pupillodilator muscle, the only muscle of the eyeball innervated by the sympathetic nervous system. The parasympathetic nervous system innervates two muscles—the ciliary muscle, required to adjust the lens thickness in accommodation, and the pupilloconstrictor muscle. A parasympathetic blocking agent would result in pupillodilatation, but it would paralyze the ciliary muscle and prevent lens thickening during accommodation. A drug that paralyzes the ciliary muscle is called a *cycloplegic*. During the action of the cycloplegic the patient will have blurred vision because of the lack of ability to control lens thickness and because of the large pupil that permits the light rays to traverse the periphery of the lens.

Short-acting mydriatics in common use are anticholinergic. When mydriasis alone is desired, weak solutions of cyclopentolate or tropicamide are used in combination with a sympathomimetic drug.

172. The answer is D. (*Gilman AG, ed 8. pp 500, 501, 516.*) The clinical picture of the patient described in the question suggests morphine intoxication. A dose of intravenous naloxone provides the critical immediate diagnostic test by reversing the respiratory depression and pupilloconstriction. The result becomes apparent within a few minutes, and the test may be repeated two or three times. If a response fails to occur, the diagnosis of morphine intoxication becomes doubtful. In a patient without morphine intoxication, naloxone would have no observable effect. In the event of a negative response to the test, one might then consider a CT scan or lumbar puncture. Administration of glucose would not be helpful since the glucose test-tape shows normal blood glucose level (which also excludes diabetic coma). Although respiratory assistance is indicated, it would be unwise to administer pure oxygen. In the presence of morphine intoxication, the breathing response to CO_2 is relatively depressed; thus, the patient depends upon the hypoxia as a stimulus to breathe. Under this circumstance, pure oxygen, by removing the effective stimulus to breathe, may further impair ventilation.

173. The answer is D. (*Gilman AG, ed 8. pp 312–313.*) Local anesthetics such as procaine appear to act by blocking the voltage-dependent transient rise in membrane permeability to sodium that accompanies the nerve impulse. As sodium exits from the cell during passage of the nerve impulse, the membrane shows an increasing conductance to sodium that is voltage-dependent. The anesthetic agent binds within the sodium channel in such a way as to block the inward flow of sodium with the passage of the impulse. The action appears to take place on the inner surface of the neuron membrane and raises the threshold for neuronal excitability. At higher concentrations potassium channels are also blocked.

174. The answer is B. (*Gilman AG, ed 8. pp 480–481.*) Most of the drugs that have value in the treatment of spasticity work mainly through the central nervous system. Mephenesin and methocarbamol depress spinal polysynaptic reflexes. However, not all agents that depress polysynaptic reflexes reduce spasticity. Other centrally acting drugs that are active against spasticity may have different actions. Baclofen, although chemically related to GABA, hyperpolarizes primary afferent terminals rather than depolarizing them as does GABA. Cyclobenzaprine, chemically related to the tricyclic antidepressants, also acts centrally but by an unknown mechanism. Only dantrolene appears to have its primary action on muscle, where it may reduce the amount of calcium released from the sarcoplasmic reticulum. Although dantrolene reduces reflex muscle contractions more than volitional muscle contractions, its tendency to cause weakness limits its value.

175. The answer is A. (*Jankovic, N Engl J Med 324:1186–1194, 1991.*) Botulinum toxin A (Botox) is one of seven toxins produced by *Clostridium botulinum*. It produces weakness by blocking nerve release of acetylcholine and thus providing functional motor denervation of the injected muscles. It has proved extremely effective in the treatment of hemifacial spasm and blepharospasm and has been approved by the FDA for use in these conditions as well as for the treatment of strabismus. While Botox is also effective in other forms of dystonia, such as torticollis, it has not yet been approved for use in these other conditions (as of 1991).

176. The answer is D. (*Gilman AG, ed 8. p 105.*) *Tachyphylaxis* refers to the decreasing effect of repeated doses or repeated infusions of a drug. The usual explanation is that those drugs displaying tachyphylaxis act indirectly by releasing some of the natural neurotransmitter stored at the presynaptic nerve endings. Because only a limited amount of neurotransmitter is available for release, the repeated administration of the drug fails to produce any further release. The amount available for release by the drug is judged to be quite small because nerve stimulation will produce the expected response even though repeated drug administration becomes ineffective. The administration of the appropriate sympathomimetic drug also will elicit the response, which shows that the receptors remain functional.

177. The answer is E. (*Gilman AG, ed 8. p 145.*)   Edrophonium should be given to a suspected myasthenic person until either some improvement occurs in the muscle function being assessed, or some symptoms or signs of cholinergic overactivity become apparent. In a pharmacologic test of this type, the clinician titrates the drug rather than giving a predetermined amount of medication based on milligrams per kilogram of body weight. The medication is given until an end point is reached. Signs of either an improvement in the disease or of overdose constitute the end point. A common mistake in testing for myasthenia is to give too little medication. Some myasthenic patients have a tremendous tolerance for anticholinesterase medications. Unless the medication is pushed to tolerance, the pharmacologic test may fail to identify these patients. Under some conditions, it might be wise to try any of the other procedures mentioned—a neostigmine, curare, or Jolly test—but an adequate edrophonium test should be completed first.

178. The answer is B. (*Rowland, ed 8. p 574.*)   Chronic use of dopamine blocking drugs frequently leads to an often irreversible movement disorder, tardive (late onset) dyskinesia. There is no definite duration known for a threshold risk, but most authorities use a 3-month exposure as a guideline for published reports on the syndrome. While there are many forms of tardive dyskinesia, the most common is a choreoathetoid movement disorder involving the oral-buccal-lingual area, with such movements as writhing tongue, chewing, lateral jaw movements, and lip puckering. Other body areas are less frequently involved.

179. The answer is D. (*Gilman AG, ed 8. pp 440–441.*)   Although anticonvulsants may have several actions, phenytoin (Dilantin) is thought to restrict the flow of sodium ions across resting neuronal membranes as well as membranes undergoing electrically or chemically induced depolarization. It thus tends to suppress repetitive firing of neurons. Tetrodotoxin and saxitoxin appear to act in the same way. Phenytoin will even block the sodium channels held open by veratroidine. Electrically, phenytoin does tend to cause *hyper*polarization of neuronal membranes rather than depolarization. There is no satisfactory evidence that phenytoin has any primary action either on the enzymes that produce or degrade neurotransmitters or in blocking neurotransmitter function by binding with receptors.

180. The answer is B. (*Gilman AG, ed 8. p 176.*)   Malignant hyperthermia (MH) is distinguished clinically from malignant neuroleptic syndrome by its pharmacologic characteristics. MH is often familial, although this history is often lacking because family members with the predisposition may not have been exposed. It is precipitated by halothane, succinylcholine, and occasionally other general anesthetics or neuromuscular blockers. It is treated with dantrolene sodium, ventilation, and careful attention to acidosis from muscle contraction and renal function, which can be damaged by the myoglobin released from damaged muscles. MH may not occur on first exposure to the anesthetic.

181. The answer is C. (*Gilman AG, ed 8. p 392.*)   Haloperidol is an antipsychotic that has few anticholinergic side effects. As a result of this and its safety profile for blood pressure and cardiac rhythm, it is one of the most widely used antipsychotic agents. Both chlorpromazine and clozapine have anticholinergic effects in addition to their causing hypotension, which sometimes limits their use. Amitriptyline and carbamazepine are not antipsychotic agents. Amitriptyline is a tricyclic antidepressant with potent anticholinergic effects.

182. The answer is C. (*Rowland, ed 8. pp 802–803.*)   In an unknown patient with status epilepticus, an infusion of glucose should be given first in case the patient has hypoglycemia as the etiology. Since a glucose infusion can precipitate Wernicke's encephalopathy in a patient with a massive thiamine deficiency, thiamine should be given concurrently. If this fails to break the seizures, then a benzodiazepine such as diazepam should be given. Persistent seizures will cause irreversible brain damage even if the patient is adequately ventilated and not acidotic, so immediate seizure control is crucial. It is important to have drawn all necessary blood samples before the infusion, if at all possible, to assess the etiology of the seizures.

183. The answer is B. (*Adams RD, ed 4. p 203.*) The appearance of diarrhea, ataxia, fasciculations, overactive muscle stretch reflexes, and seizures in a patient who has been started on lithium therapy is entirely compatible with lithium toxicity. Since the usual therapeutic range for lithium is between 0.8 and 1.2 meq/L, the observed value of 1.5 meq/L would support a diagnosis of lithium toxicity. Moreover, since the patient recently began treatment, this blood level probably represents a fairly rapid climb of the lithium level. Such sudden changes are more likely to cause symptoms than very gradual changes. To invoke a coexistent disorder in this patient would violate the principle of diagnostic parsimony. Many of the symptoms of lithium overdosage imitate other states like delirium tremens, barbiturate withdrawal, or a thyroid storm—all of which may be associated with signs of overactivity of the nervous system in the form of tremors, increased stretch reflexes, and seizures. A thyroid crisis would be unlikely in this patient because the effect of lithium is to reduce thyroid function.

184. The answer is C. (*Langston, Adv Neurol 9:485–507, 1986.*) MPTP was discovered by an unfortunate accident followed by diligent detective work. It is a synthetic drug derived from meperidine and was sold to intravenous narcotics abusers without knowledge of its neurotoxicity. MPTP destroys nigral dopaminergic neurons in animals and in the one human autopsied. In older animals it affects the locus ceruleus, a noradrenergic set of neurons, as well. The drug is itself nontoxic but is taken into glial cells where it is metabolized to MPP+. This then exits the glial cell and poisons the nigral neurons. MAO-B is required in this toxification process. Blocking MAO-B with inhibitors such as pargyline or deprenyl prevents MPTP from becoming toxic.

185. The answer is A. (*Cooper, ed 5. pp 274–276.*) Usually, when a neuronal pathway ceases to function or becomes less active, the synthesis and metabolism of the neurotransmitter are reduced accordingly. The nigrostriatal dopaminergic pathway seems to be anomalous in this regard. When impulse flow in this pathway is interrupted by mechanical or pharmacologic lesions, the amount of dopamine in the axonal terminals in the striatum increases, and the activity of the rate-limiting enzyme tyrosine hydroxylase also increases. Just how this increased enzyme activity occurs is unclear. Similar increases in the activity of tyrosine hydroxylase fail to occur in central norepinephrinergic pathways when they are quiescent. In fact, the norepinephrinergic pathways respond in the opposite way.

186. The answer is D. (*Rowland, ed 8. p 798.*) Infantile spasms are more likely to respond to ACTH (20 to 40 units daily) than to standard anticonvulsants. Drugs useful in myoclonus, such as clonazepam and valproic acid, may also be helpful. The ketogenic diet is another important approach to therapy.

187. The answer is B. (*Plum, ed 3. pp 243–245.*) Glutethimide intoxication can produce an unusual neurologic picture including midposition pupils that may be unreactive and unequal. Overwhelmingly high doses of barbiturates may also produce unreactive pupils but this is very uncommon. Glutethimide also produces a prolonged and fluctuating level of coma. Persistent noxious stimulation may transiently increase the patient's level of consciousness or responsiveness. The fixed and unequal pupils that may occur in glutethimide poisoning may mislead the examiner into diagnosing a structural lesion in the midbrain as the etiology of the coma.

188. The answer is A. (*Parkinson Study Group, N Engl J Med 321:1364–1371, 1989.*) Deprenyl (selegiline; Eldepryl) is a nonreversible inhibitor of the enzyme monoamine oxidase B (MAO-B). There are two forms of MAO. The A form is found in the gut and is important in metabolizing tyramine. Blockade of the A form, which occurs with the monoamine oxidase inhibiting antidepressants, subjects patients to tyramine-induced hypertensive crises. Blockage of the B form occurs in the brain and is quite safe. The DATATOP study, which followed 800 patients with Parkinson's disease, half treated and half not, showed that deprenyl slows progression of disability in PD without producing a significant symptomatic improvement in motor function, depression, or intellectual or memory function. It is not known, however, if the drug actually slows disease progression.

189. **The answer is C.** (*Gilman AG, ed 8. p 441.*) The pharmacokinetics of phenytoin must be understood to use the drug properly. It has a plasma half-life of 6 to 24 h in the subtherapeutic range, which is due to first-order (exponential) elimination characteristics. Above about 10 mg/mL the elimination becomes dose-dependent, so that half-life increases with the plasma concentration. Most of the drug is bound to albumin and the rest is free. The free fraction equilibrates with the brain level of the drug so that the free drug level is a more accurate indicator of therapeutic range than is the total plasma concentration. When increasing doses in a patient, one must be careful of the increasing half-life or toxicity will occur.

190. **The answer is D.** (*Gilman AG, ed 8. p 507.*) Meperidine may cause respiratory depression or severe agitation with delirium, seizures, and high fevers when used in combination with a monoamine oxidase antidepressant. This reaction is associated with the MAO inhibiting drugs that block both forms of MAO and has yet to be associated with deprenyl, a drug that blocks only the B form of MAO. The interaction of meperidine and MAO inhibitors is potentially lethal. Interestingly, the same interaction has not been noted with other opiates.

191. **The answer is D.** (*Adams RD, ed 4. pp 878–879.*) Some chronic alcoholics develop a syndrome of auditory hallucinosis. The sounds are usually voices that say bad things about the subject. Initially the voices are thought to be real, and the subject behaves appropriately for that delusion. Generally the hallucinations resolve and the subject returns to normal, but occasional alcoholics develop a chronic state in which they continue to suffer from the auditory hallucinations. In general the subject then is able to separate the false sounds from the real.

192. **The answer is E.** (*Gilman AG, ed 8. p 470.*) Levodopa has a large number of adverse behavioral effects, including confusion, delusions, paranoia, depression, mania, and psychoses. One of the more common psychiatric side effects is a syndrome of visual hallucinations—usually nonthreatening people, often children, who visit. These visions never make any sounds and are often perceived as illusions after a very brief period. Recognition of their illusory nature, however, does not prevent their recurrence. This is partly a dose-related phenomenon and is often due to the concomitant use of other antiparkinson drugs as well. Ethanol causes visual hallucinations only in the context of delirium tremens. Amphetamine may induce a schizophrenic-like psychosis, but hallucinations occur in an altered mental state. Methanol and cocaine do not cause visual hallucinations.

193. **The answer is A.** (*Gilman AG, ed 8. p 1226.*) The combination of altered mentation, multifocal lower motor neuron abnormalities, and a lymphocytic pleocytosis is classic for carcinomatous meningitis. The lack of malignant cells in the CSF is not uncommon and repeated studies may be required to identify the cancerous cells. The only medication of any use in treating this condition is intrathecal methotrexate, which may cause a chemical meningitis and increases the risk of white matter degeneration with radiation.

194. **The answer is C (2, 4).** (*Gilman AG, ed 8. p 1457.*) Steroids have been shown to be effective in reducing vasogenic edema, that is, the brain edema caused by abnormally permeable blood vessels. This condition occurs with inflammation around abscesses and also around neoplasms. Steroids have no demonstrated efficacy in brain swelling caused by cytotoxic edema, which is caused by

cell swelling and cell death. They have been studied in both stroke and trauma without the demonstration of benefit. This is in contrast, however, to a recent study that shows significant benefit in the early use of large steroid boluses following severe injury to the spinal cord.

195. **The answer is C (2, 4).** (*Adams RD, ed 4. pp 509–511.*) Pseudotumor cerebri, by definition, is a syndrome due to increased intracranial pressure without apparent cause. Its clinical presentation typically is progressive headache or blurred vision and dizziness. It generally occurs in obese young women. The elevated intracranial pressure results in papilledema, which, if severe and chronic, may lead to progressive visual loss. Sixth nerve palsies may also occur. While the syndrome has been occasionally associated with steroid withdrawal and various endocrine abnormalities, there is a clear association with excessive doses of vitamin A and tetracycline.

196. **The answer is D (4).** (*Cooper, ed 5. pp 224–231.*) Tyrosine hydroxylase converts tyrosine to dihydroxyphenylalanine on its way to norepinephrine and epinephrine. The activity of tyrosine hydroxylase undergoes a homeostatic adjustment to the need for catecholaminergic neurotransmitter, but pharmacologic manipulation can also alter its activity. Increased neuronal activity requires more neurotransmitter and activates or increases the action of the synthetic enzymes like tyrosine hydroxylase that produce the transmitter. Administration of an MAO inhibitor will increase the amount of intraneuronal catecholamine, resulting in a feedback inhibition of tyrosine hydroxylase. Administration of tyramine increases the amount of intracellular catecholamine and also produces a feedback inhibition of catecholamine synthesis. Administration of 6-hydroxydopamine selectively kills catecholaminergic neurons and thus results in an absence of their contained enzymes, including tyrosine hydroxylase. Many drugs, like α-methyl-ρ-tyrosine and other amino acid analogues, will inhibit tyrosine hydroxylase, and some may find clinical application for that reason.

197. **The answer is B (1, 3).** (*Adams RD, ed 4. p 269.*) Petit mal seizures respond equally well to valproic acid and ethosuximide. These seizures do not respond to antiepileptic drugs useful in other forms of epilepsy such as phenytoin, phenobarbital, and carbamazepine. When petit mal seizures are also associated with tonic clonic activity, then valproic acid is the drug of choice, because it is effective in both seizure types.

198. **The answer is C (2, 4).** (*Rowland, ed 8. p 574.*) Tardive dyskinesia (TD) is thought to be related to dopamine receptor supersensitivity that occurs as a result of chronic receptor blockade. This occurs with typical antipsychotic drugs as well as antiemetics such as prochlorperazine (Compazine) and gastric motility enhancers such as metoclopramide (Reglan). TD can be masked by increasing the dopamine blockade or by depleting dopamine (with drugs such as reserpine). Anticholinergics will often worsen TD. A general rule is that drugs that improve parkinsonism worsen TD (such as anticholinergics) and drugs that worsen parkinsonism (such as antipsychotics) improve the signs of TD.

199. **The answer is D (4).** (*Balldessarini, N Engl J Med 324:746–754, 1991.*) Clozapine is classified as an "atypical neuroleptic" because of certain properties that it lacks. Although it is equally or more effective as an antipsychotic than typical neuroleptics and does block dopamine receptors, it does not cause parkinsonism and has yet to be linked to a case of tardive dyskinesia. It does, however, have a host of potential side effects, which include somnolence, seizures, hypotension, hyperthermia, tachycardia, hypersalivation, and a 1 percent incidence of granulocytopenia.

200. **The answer is A (1, 2, 3).** (*Gilman AG, ed 8. pp 137–138.*) Anticholinesterase drugs such as physostigmine are useful in the treatment of myasthenia gravis. They act by inhibiting the breakdown of acetylcholine and thus potentiating its effect, which causes adverse effects that are generally predictable based on the effects of acetylcholine. In the eye they cause miosis. There is increased motility in the gut along with increased gastric acid production.

201. The answer is A (1, 2, 3). (*Gilman AG, ed 8. p 319.*) Cocaine has systemic activity that is due to its blockage of the catecholamine reuptake mechanism. It thus acts to increase the activity of the sympathetic autonomic system, with such effects as increased heart rate and blood pressure and mydriasis. When applied locally it inhibits initiation and conduction of nerve impulses, thus accounting for its properties as a local anesthetic. Its main therapeutic uses are as an anesthetic in the eye and the nasal and sinus passages. It does not inhibit the vomit center and actually induces emesis in some.

202. The answer is B (1, 3). (*Adams RD, ed 4. pp 1039, 1159.*) Plasmapheresis is a process in which plasma is exchanged for albumin. In two separate studies, plasmapheresis has been shown to be helpful in treating Guillain-Barré syndrome if instituted within 2 weeks of onset of the disease. It is recommended for patients with respiratory or gait failure. It has been used effectively in treating myasthenia gravis for several years; however, its role is less well defined in this very unpredictable disease. Although it is thought to act by reducing concentrations of a toxic substance, improvement in myasthenia does not parallel changes in anti-acetylcholine-receptor antibody.

203. The answer is B (1, 3). (*Gilman AG, ed 8. p 448.*) Carbamazepine initially may cause drowsiness and clumsiness, but these problems usually resolve fairly quickly. Although the drug had been thought to be dangerous because of its effects on bone marrow, a mild depression of the white blood count occurs in 10 percent of patients and generally resolves without drug discontinuation. Only 2 percent of patients require drug discontinuation because of persistent leukopenia. Aplastic anemia is rare, with an estimated incidence of one per 200,000. Another complication is the syndrome of inappropriate ADH secretion, which results in hyponatremia.

204. The answer is E (all). (*Rowland, ed 8. pp 666–667.*) Although the mainstay of therapy for Parkinson's disease (PD) is levodopa, other agents are often useful adjuncts. Anticholinergics such as benztropine are helpful with tremor and rigidity. Amantadine appears to have an effect on increasing dopamine release. Dopamine agonists such as bromocriptine and pergolide act directly on the striatum and bypass the degenerated nigral neurons. Tricyclic antidepressants are often useful, especially amitriptyline, because of the antidepressant (depression is a common PD problem), anticholinergic, and soporific effects (sleep disturbance is also common in PD).

205. The answer is B (1, 3). (*Gilman AG, ed 8. pp 940–947.*) Ergot alkaloids are effective in the treatment of individual migraine attacks, particularly when used very early in the episode. They are particularly useful during the aura. The mechanism of action is still not clear, although ergot alkaloids had been previously thought to act via vasoconstriction. They are not sedating and are not analgesic, hence the antimigraine properties are quite specific. Long-term or excessive use leads to an increasing requirement for benefit and to rebound migraines on withdrawal. Thus they are not useful for prophylaxis. Unlike methysergide, ergots do not cause connective tissue problems.

Neuroradiology

DIRECTIONS: Each question below contains five suggested responses. Select the **one best** response to each question.

206. In the radiograph below, the most likely interpretation is

(A) normal angiogram
(B) hydrocephalus
(C) avascular anterior mass
(D) anterior cerebral aneurysm
(E) upward displacement of the first segment of the anterior cerebral artery

207. In AIDS patients with toxoplasmosis, the most common area affected is

(A) the cortex
(B) the inferior surface of the frontal lobes
(C) the subependymal regions
(D) the basal ganglia
(E) any supratentorial location

208. The single most sensitive test for the demonstration of abnormalities associated with multiple sclerosis is

(A) spinal fluid analysis
(B) evoked response testing (all modalities combined)
(C) CT of the brain with a double dose of contrast and 4-h delayed scan
(D) MRI of the brain with and without enhancement
(E) positron emission tomography (PET) scan

209. The following brain CT scans (left is unenhanced, right enhanced) of a middle-aged man from central Africa is most consistent with which of the following?

(A)   Glioblastoma
(B)   Tuberculoma
(C)   Cysticercosis
(D)   *Echinococcus* infection
(E)   Lymphoma

210. The CT scan of a teen-aged child below indicates which of the following disorders?

(A) Arnold-Chiari malformation
(B) Cystic astrocytoma
(C) Dandy-Walker syndrome
(D) Lissencephaly (agyria)
(E) Enlarged cisterna magna

211. A patient's unenhanced CT scan was normal and the enhanced CT scan is below. The most likely diagnosis is

(A) anterior communicating artery aneurysm
(B) granuloma
(C) calcification
(D) cysticercosis
(E) old myelogram dye

212. The following unenhanced CT scan in a 54-year-old patient would be consistent with which of the following metabolic derangements?

(A) Low serum calcium
(B) Elevated serum calcium
(C) Low serum copper
(D) High serum ceruloplasmin
(E) Cyanide intoxication

213. The most sensitive test for distinguishing radiation necrosis from recurrence of brain tumor is

(A) MRI without gadolinium
(B) MRI with gadolinium contrast
(C) CT with double-dose contrast and delayed scanning
(D) radioisotope scan
(E) PET scan

214. In the radiograph below the most likely diagnosis is

(A) multiple mycotic aneurysms
(B) cerebellar cyst
(C) sagittal sinus thrombosis
(D) normal venous study
(E) normal arterial study

215. On the radiograph below the most likely diagnosis is

216. In the radiograph below, the patient most likely suffers from

(A) pontine glioma
(B) cervical cord disk herniation
(C) cervical spondylosis
(D) syringomyelia
(E) normal

(A) neurofibromatosis
(B) tuberous sclerosis
(C) Paget's disease
(D) polycystic kidney disease
(E) Hand-Schüller-Christian disease

217. A patient with back pain has the MRI shown below. What neurologic problem is likely?

(A) Urinary incontinence
(B) Urinary retention
(C) Proximal leg weakness
(D) Distal leg weakness
(E) Paraplegia

218. The most sensitive test for diagnosing the presence of subarachnoid blood following rupture of a berry aneurysm is

(A) CT scan without contrast
(B) CT scan with contrast
(C) spinal tap
(D) MRI of brain without contrast
(E) MRI of brain with contrast

219. In the radiograph below, the most likely diagnosis is

(A) intramedullary metastasis
(B) epidural hematoma
(C) astrocytoma
(D) disk herniation
(E) meningioma

220. In the unenhanced CT scan below, the most likely diagnosis is

221. In the radiograph below, the most likely diagnosis is

(A) metastatic disease
(B) polycystic kidney disease
(C) hypoparathyroidism
(D) tuberculosis
(E) tuberous sclerosis

(A) middle cerebral artery infarct
(B) head trauma
(C) cysticercosis
(D) herpes simplex encephalitis
(E) Creutzfeldt-Jakob disease

222. A patient who has the MRI below is most likely to have which of the following neurologic abnormalities?

223. A patient with AIDS has the MRI below. All the following are diagnostic considerations EXCEPT

(A) Light-near pupillary dissociation and upgaze paresis
(B) Gait ataxia
(C) Bitemporal field cuts
(D) Binasal field cuts
(E) Alien hand syndrome

(A) lymphoma
(B) Kaposi's sarcoma
(C) toxoplasmosis
(D) progressive multifocal leukoencephalopathy (PML)
(E) tuberculosis

224.   In the CT scans below, the left is unenhanced and the right is enhanced. The most likely diagnosis is

    (A)   abscess
    (B)   mycotic aneurysm
    (C)   glioma
    (D)   metastatic melanoma
    (E)   orbital roof meningioma

225.   Which one of the following types of tumors usually produces blastic lesions seen on plain x-ray?

    (A)   Breast
    (B)   Lung
    (C)   Kidney
    (D)   Prostate
    (E)   Melanoma

226.   An isolated tumor growing from the clivus would most likely be

    (A)   eosinophilic granuloma
    (B)   osteosarcoma
    (C)   chordoma
    (D)   osteoma
    (E)   Wegener's granulomatosis

227. Fibromuscular dysplasia is a disease primarily of renal arteries that may also affect the cerebral arteries. The most common cerebrovascular angiographic abnormality is

(A) circle of Willis aneurysms
(B) carotid bifurcation stenosis
(C) vein of Galen malformations
(D) "string of beads" sign in the vertebral arteries
(E) "string of beads" sign in an internal carotid artery

DIRECTIONS: Each question below contains four suggested responses of which **one or more** is correct. Select

A	if	**1, 2, and 3**	are correct
B	if	**1 and 3**	are correct
C	if	**2 and 4**	are correct
D	if	**4**	is correct
E	if	**1, 2, 3, and 4**	are correct

228. In the first 24 h of an ischemic stroke, which of the following imaging studies would be likely to reveal an abnormality?

(1)   CT with and without contrast
(2)   T1 MRI
(3)   CT with double-dose contrast after 1 h
(4)   T2 MRI

---

229. A 6-year-old American child develops headaches and ataxia. The CT scan with and without contrast are shown below. Other sections show no other abnormalities. The most likely diagnoses include which of the following?

(1)   Medulloblastoma
(2)   Meningioma
(3)   Astrocytoma
(4)   Metastatic tumor

DIRECTIONS: Each group of questions below consists of lettered headings followed by a set of numbered items. For each numbered item select the **one** lettered heading with which it is **most** closely associated. Each lettered heading may be used **once, more than once, or not at all.**

Questions 230–233

Match the structures with the appropriate letter labels on this coronal section through a normal brain.

Adapted from Fisher and Ketonen, Fig. 2-43, with permission.

230. Head of caudate nucleus

231. Globus pallidus

232. Substantia nigra

233. Red nucleus

Questions 234–238

For each cranial nerve listed below, choose the skull aperture through which it passes.

    (A) Foramen magnum
    (B) Superior orbital fissure
    (C) Jugular foramen
    (D) Stylomastoid foramen
    (E) Foramen lacerum

234. Xth cranial nerve

235. IIIrd cranial nerve

236. Ophthalmic division of the Vth cranial nerve

237. VIth cranial nerve

238. IXth cranial nerve

Neuroradiology

Answers

206. The answer is D. (*Joynt, pp 85–108.*) This angiogram shows an outpouching at the junction of the anterior cerebral and anterior communicating arteries. On a single projection, the exact location is difficult to identify, but the balloon-shaped structure is evident. In general it is important to have multiple views, both to identify the existence of the aneurysm and to localize its neck. The most common location for aneurysms is at the junction of these two vessels.

207. The answer is D. (*Mandell, ed 3. pp 1059–1092.*) Toxoplasmosis abscesses are the most common intracranial masses found in AIDS patients. Although they may appear as solitary ring enhancing lesions on contrast-enhanced CT scans, magnetic resonance imaging (MRI) generally reveals multiple lesions. These include lesions in the basal ganglia in almost all patients. Unfortunately, since there are many other potential causes for multiple intracranial lesions, one sometimes has to treat patients blindly because CSF toxoplasmosis serologies are not very useful.

208. The answer is D. (*Joynt, p 40.*) MRI of the brain is the most sensitive test for identifying abnormalities in multiple sclerosis. There are several problems, however, associated with the use of MRI. The findings can be nonspecific and may be difficult to distinguish from ischemic disease. Some patients with clinically definite multiple sclerosis have normal brain studies, either due to disease confinement to the spinal cord or to a certain degree of test insensitivity. Finally, there is little correlation between the lesions seen on MRI and the neurologic examination or prognosis. Patients with optic neuritis as their only clinical abnormality seem to be at no greater risk of developing clinical multiple sclerosis if their initial MRI was positive over those whose MRI was negative.

209. The answer is A. (*Adams RD, ed 4. pp 524–525.*) While a central African man must be considered at high risk for parasitic infections of the brain such as cysticercosis and infection with *Echinococcus,* tuberculomas, and AIDS-related diseases, this CT is most consistent with a diagnosis of glioblastoma. These tumors usually are hypodense on the unenhanced CT and usually, but not always, enhance with contrast. Unlike metastases and abscesses such as those of TB, they often have an irregular shape and are almost always solitary. CNS lymphoma is typically periventricular in location and generally enhances diffusely. The two parasitic infections usually show multiple, round cysts on CT; cysticercosis also often has a central calcified region corresponding to the scolex of the worm.

210. The answer is C. (*Adams RD, ed 4. pp 975–979.*) The Dandy-Walker syndrome is caused by a developmental aberration in which the midline cerebellum fails to develop normally. This causes a huge cyst in place of the fourth ventricle. Other abnormalities of midline structures occur, including enlargement of the other ventricles and anomalies of the corpus callosum. The four Arnold-Chiari malformations are tonsillar herniation of the cerebellum, downward displacement of the medulla and fourth ventricle into the cervical canal, cervical meningomyelocele with cerebellar herniation, and cerebellar hypoplasia. Lissencephaly (agyria, or "smooth brain") refers to a small brain without sulci and gyri. An astrocytoma, although typically in the posterior fossa in a child, has a round shape and should show a rim of solid tissue. Similarly, an enlarged cisterna magna would not produce a midline indentation in a pattern similar to the fourth ventricle.

211.   **The answer is A.**   (*Joynt, pp 85–108.*)   The enhanced CT scan shows an aneurysmal outpouching at the junction of the right anterior cerebral and anterior communicating arteries. In the plane of the section one can see the left middle cerebral and posterior cerebral arteries as well as the right anterior and posterior cerebral arteries. The equal brightness of the aneurysm and the anterior cerebral arteries suggests that the aneurysm is not thrombosed. The obvious communication between the structures suggests the diagnosis. While the other diagnostic entities could give a similar appearance on a contrast-enhanced CT, all the other answers would have a similar appearance on the unenhanced scan.

212.   **The answer is A.**   (*Adams RD, ed 4. pp 803–805.*)   Hypoparathyroidism results in low levels of serum calcium. In about half of cases there is deposition of calcium in the small blood vessels of the basal ganglia and the dentate nuclei of the cerebellum. While calcifications in these areas may occur on an idiopathic basis without deranged calcium metabolism, the occurrence of this type of CT scan abnormality in the setting of dementia, parkinsonism, chorea, or seizures should raise the question of hypoparathyroidism. A low serum calcium and parathormone level make the diagnosis. Hyperparathyroidism with elevated calcium and Wilson's disease with low serum copper levels do not alter the brain CT scan. Cyanide poisoning on rare occasions has been reported to induce basal ganglia infarcts and a parkinsonian syndrome but does not cause calcifications.

213.   **The answer is E.**   (*Report of the Therapeutics and Technology Assessment Subcommittee, Neurology 48:163–167, 1991.*)   Distinguishing tumor recurrence from radiation necrosis is a difficult and important task in patients who have had gross removal of a primary or metastatic tumor followed by radiation therapy (RT). The time course for both can be the same and both produce identical clinical deficits. Unfortunately CT and MRI cannot distinguish the two entities with or without contrast, and radioisotope scans are of no additional benefit. PET scan however can reliably distinguish the two as brain regions of RT necrosis have little or no metabolic activity whereas recurrent tumors are hypermetabolic.

214.   **The answer is C.**   (*Joynt, pp 131–134.*)   The venous angiogram shown reveals a sudden cutoff anteriorly of the superior sagittal sinus, which indicates a thrombosis. It is important to notify the radiologist of this potential diagnosis in advance as most angiograms are performed to evaluate arterial rather than venous disease and less attention may be paid to this part of the study. Although anteriography had been the required test to make this diagnosis in the past, MRI now has superseded this. The clinical presentations for this disorder include pseudotumor cerebri and stroke syndromes, primarily involving the parasagittal regions of the brain. It occurs in the coagulopathic states where venous thrombosis is increased, such as sickle cell disease, polycythemia, and the postpartum state.

215.   **The answer is D.**   (*Adams RD, ed 4. pp 748–751.*)   This sagittal MRI of the cervical cord and brainstem nicely illustrates the power of the technique for revealing syrinxes, which can otherwise be very difficult to visualize. There is a slitlike dark section seen in this radiograph that extends above and below the C3 vertebral body. In this case a cervical myelogram would probably not have revealed any abnormality as the cord does not appear widened. The clinical presentation of

syringomyelia is quite broad, but the classic central cord findings of diminished pain and temperature sense with intact light touch should always point to its diagnosis. Most cases are associated with Arnold-Chiari type I malformations, and occasional cases are the result of cord tumors.

216. The answer is A. (*Adams RD, ed 4. pp 985–987. Joynt, p 97.*) The CT scan shows two large masses that emanate from the internal auditory canal. The differential diagnosis of the lesions would include meningiomas, metastatic tumors, and giant aneurysms. However, the symmetry of their location would argue strongly for an underlying illness such as neurofibromatosis type 2, which has a marked increased incidence of bilateral acoustic neuromas. This has been linked to a gene abnormality on chromosome 22. Patients would present with progressive deafness.

217. The answer is C. (*Joynt, p 289.*) The MRI shows severe destruction of the L2 vertebral body caused by multiple myeloma. The level of the lesion is below the caudal end of the spinal cord in most patients and in this particular case the cord's tip can be seen ending at the level of L1. Therefore one should not expect a cauda equina syndrome with urinary incontinence due to bladder atonicity, but rather a syndrome of root compression of L2 or L3. The patient is therefore most likely to have weakness in hip and quadriceps muscles and a diminished knee jerk.

218. The answer is C. (*Joynt, pp 31, 77–84.*) The diagnosis of subarachnoid hemorrhage is one of the few areas in which MRI is not of significant value. The CT scan without contrast is clearly a better test and is the first diagnostic test that should be performed. It confirms the diagnosis in most cases, showing blood outside the brain, but it is also sensitive to the presence of blood in the ventricles and parenchyma. Occasionally it will reveal the aneurysm as well. The CT scan is helpful in predicting vasospasm, as the location and size of the blood clot is useful for this. However, if the blood volume is small and dispersed, the CT will not visualize it. It is thought that a spinal tap will yield the diagnosis in virtually all cases if a few hours elapses between the ictus and the tap in order to allow the blood time to diffuse into the lumbar sac.

219. The answer is E. (*Joynt, p 277.*) This myelogram is clearly of the thoracic region, as the ribs are easily seen. The large segment that blocks the dye is clearly not at disk level, which eliminates the diagnosis of disk herniation. Since there is not a complete blockage of the canal, the upper and lower limits of the lesion are seen. One can see the cord pushed to the right (in the radiograph on the left), away from the thecal sac, which implies an intradural but extramedullary lesion. Intradural extramedullary lesions are most likely neurofibromas or meningiomas.

220. The answer is E. (*Adams RD, ed 4. pp 982–985.*) The CT shows calcifications extending into the lateral ventricles, a classic radiologic sign for tuberous sclerosis. The lateral ventricles contain masses that look like candle drippings. When these calcify, the CT looks like the one shown. Patients with this inherited disorder are at increased risk for malignant degeneration of their abnormal glial cells and develop large cell astrocytomas that tend to occur near the lateral ventricle.

221. The answer is D. (*Adams RD, ed 4. pp 603–604.*) The CT shows a large, hypodense region in the left frontal and temporal lobes. The abnormality spares large areas of cortex in both these lobes. In addition the lesion extends medially into the anterior cerebral territory as well as laterally into the middle cerebral artery territory, yet spares parts of both. There is effacement of the gyral pattern on the left, which indicates that the pathology is acute. Head trauma is an unlikely cause of such a large lesion because no blood is evident. CMV does not usually cause CT abnormalities and cysticercosis causes relatively round, discrete lesions often with a central calcified scolex. Herpes simplex enters the brain via the inferior surface of the frontal and temporal lobes and typically causes a necrotizing encephalitis affecting the frontal and temporal lobe.

222. The answer is A. (*Rowland, ed 8. p 316.*)   This MRI shows a large pineal region mass. The differential diagnosis for tumors in this area includes pinealoma, dysgerminoma, glioma, and meningioma. Clinically one would expect a Parinaud's syndrome: light-near pupillary dissociation, upgaze paralysis, and convergence or retraction nystagmus.

223. The answer is D. (*Rowland, ed 8. p 141.*)   There is a large mass in the right basal ganglia. While this is most likely to be toxoplasmosis, other possibilities include any of the causes of masses in AIDS patients. These include all the other entities except PML, which causes white matter disease and has no mass effect.

224. The answer is E. (*Joynt, pp 100–104.*)   The unenhanced CT shows a large right frontal mass that is clearly seen without contrast enhancement. The stippled nature and the density in one area suggest this represents calcification rather than blood. The enhanced study shows that the mass enhances diffusely. These findings are most consistent with a meningioma. Lower planes of section would reveal an attachment to the meninges not seen here. An abscess would not enhance diffusely. Mycotic aneurysms are intraparenchymal but do not become this large. Gliomas generally do not calcify. Melanoma does tend to bleed but is usually smaller and not solitary.

225. The answer is D. (*Joynt, p 195.*)   Prostate carcinoma is the only common cancer that usually produces blastic lesions. Other metastases such as those of lung and breast may produce a mixed picture of lytic and blastic lesions or, less commonly, blastic alone. Kidney metastases are almost always lytic. It should be noted that blastic lesions weaken the involved bone even though new bone is laid down.

226. The answer is C. (*Joynt, p 193.*)   Chordomas are notochordal in origin and characteristically arise in the sacrococcygeal spine, the skull, or the vertebral spine in descending order. In the skull they originate in the clivus, where they cause bone destruction, but they may extend in any direction and cause CNS dysfunction. Eosinophilic granuloma most commonly involves the outer skull. Osteosarcoma does not arise from the skull. Osteomas generally occur in the sinuses. Wegener's granulomatosis primarily involves sinuses and extends from there.

227. The answer is E. (*Joynt, p 66.*)   Originally described as a renal arterial disease, fibromuscular dysplasia also may affect the cerebral arterial tree. While often associated with cerebral aneurysms, the most common cerebrovascular abnormality occurs in the internal carotid artery. Several areas of dilatation alternating with areas of stenosis cause a "beaded string" appearance. Two-thirds of cases have bilateral involvement. One-third of cases have aneurysms. The common carotid and the carotid bifurcation are spared in this disease. Clinical manifestations include TIA, CVA, and subarachnoid hemorrhage.

228. The answer is C (2, 4). (*Joynt, pp 19–24.*)   In the first 24 h of an ischemic stroke the CT scan is usually negative. It often takes 24 h or longer for the decreased attenuation on unenhanced CT and the irregular enhancement on contrast CT to appear. T1 MRI is usually negative in the very early stage of stroke and reveals decreasing signal and increasing distinctness of the lesion over time. The T2 MRI tends to be positive early and to produce a bright signal (T1 produces a dark image of the lesion) that initially has indistinct margins due to the irregularity of the edema surrounding the early infarct.

229. The answer is B (1, 3). (*Joynt, pp 86–99.*)   Childhood brain tumors, both primary and metastatic, tend to occur in the posterior fossa. This is true for metastatic brain abscesses as well. Therefore, the location of this mass and the secondary hydrocephalus are not unexpected. The most common childhood brain tumors are primary, with medulloblastomas and astrocytomas most common. Meningiomas do not occur in children and metastatic disease is rare.

230–233. The answers are: 230-A, 231-B, 232-D, 233-C. (*Fischer, p 97.*)   The head of the caudate creates the comma shape in the frontal horns of the lateral ventricles. The other basal ganglia structures are generally seen in the usual CT planes of sections that do not include portions of the midbrain. In the coronal sections one gets an appreciation of the proximity of the substantia nigra to the putamen and globus pallidus and of the substantia nigra to the red nucleus. The red nucleus and the substantia nigra are located at midbrain levels. The globus pallidus is separated into external and internal segments; the external segment is contiguous with the putamen. Together the putamen and globus pallidus make up the lentiform nucleus, so called because of its lenslike shape.

234–238. The answers are: 234-C, 235-B, 236-B, 237-B, 238-C. (*Adams RD, ed 4. pp 211, 1077, 1079. Carpenter, ed 3. p 153.*)   All the cranial nerves pass through apertures in the base of the skull. Some apertures transmit more than one nerve. Characteristic syndromes occur when a lesion affects the conjunction of nerves at particular sites of exit from the skull.

Cranial nerves III, IV, VI, and the ophthalmic division of V run through the superior orbital fissure. The VIth cranial nerve runs through Dorello's canal at the medial tip of the petrous part of the temporal bone, in company with the inferior petrosal sinus. Both nerve and vessel then enter the cavernous sinus. Inflammation of the petrous bone involves the VIth nerve at the canal of Dorello and the nearby Vth nerve, producing Gradenigo's syndrome.

The IXth, Xth, and XIth cranial nerves all run through the jugular foramen in the posterior fossa. A lesion at this site, such as a tumor of the glomus jugulare, involves all three nerves (syndrome of Vernet).

In contrast to these apertures that transmit multiple cranial nerves, other apertures such as the optic canal and the hypoglossal canal transmit only one cranial nerve. The arteries traverse the apertures as follows: carotid arteries through the foramen lacerum, ophthalmic arteries through the optic canal, vertebral arteries through the foramen magnum, and the middle meningeal arteries through the foramen spinosum.

Ophthalmology, ENT, CSF, Microbiology, Endocrinology, and Immunology

DIRECTIONS: Each question below contains five suggested responses. Select the **one best** response to each question.

239. Which of the following statements is true of Leigh's disease (subacute necrotizing encephalitis)?

   (A) The biochemical abnormality is a deficiency of thiamine
   (B) A biochemical abnormality of the pyruvate dehydrogenase complex is thought to result in Wernicke syndrome–type lesions, except for sparing of mamillary bodies
   (C) A biochemical abnormality leads to extensive cerebral demyelination
   (D) The pathologic lesions of spongiform degeneration, focal necrosis, and vascular proliferation affect the brainstem and cortex equally
   (E) The brainstem abnormality that causes respiratory dysfunction results in hypoxic brain changes such as the loss of neurons in Sommer's sector

240. The fast—or kickback—phase of caloric or optokinetic nystagmus is thought to depend on

   (A) efferent brainstem connections from the frontal eye fields
   (B) ascending connections from the proprioceptors in the neck
   (C) integrity of the cerebellar vermis
   (D) impulses originating in the retina
   (E) the dorsal longitudinal fasciculus

241. A long, narrow head would be the result of premature closure of which of the following sutures?

   (A) Sagittal
   (B) Coronal
   (C) Metopic
   (D) Basilar synchondrosis
   (E) None of the above

242. A patient with a polyneuropathy that has developed over several weeks has anemia, white transverse bands across the nails, jaundice, and brownish cutaneous pigmentation. The most likely explanation is

   (A) porphyria
   (B) lead poisoning
   (C) arsenic poisoning
   (D) INH (isoniazid) neuropathy
   (E) a paraneoplastic syndrome

243. Patients with carbon dioxide narcosis from respiratory failure in the setting of chronic obstructive pulmonary disease (COPD) commonly exhibit

(A) seizures
(B) ophthalmoparesis
(C) asterixis or myoclonus
(D) increased sensitivity to pain
(E) respiratory rates increased from baseline

244. Which of the following findings concerning nystagmus would point to a lesion in the labyrinth rather than in the brainstem or cerebellum?

(A) Rotary nystagmus that does not change direction with direction of gaze; vertigo proportional to severity of nystagmus
(B) Horizontal nystagmus that changes direction with direction of gaze; nystagmus more severe than symptoms
(C) Horizontal nystagmus in primary position worse on gaze to one side but that changes directions; no vertigo
(D) Severe vertiginous symptoms, with anxiety but no nystagmus on Hallpike maneuvers
(E) Horizontal nystagmus that changes direction with direction of gaze; short latency to onset with Hallpike maneuver; lack of fatigue with Hallpike maneuver

245. An enlarged head with normal ventricles (macrocephaly) is commonly seen in children as a result of all the following conditions EXCEPT

(A) Tay-Sachs disease
(B) Alexander's disease
(C) spongy degeneration of infancy (Canavan-van Bogaert-Bertrand disease)
(D) subdural hematomas
(E) Menke's disease

246. The EMG finding that is most characteristic of chronic denervation and most reliably distinguishes it from other neuromuscular diseases is

(A) fibrillations
(B) giant polyphasic motor units
(C) low-amplitude motor units
(D) electrical silence during rest
(E) myotonia

247. A full interference pattern with low-amplitude potentials in the EMG is most characteristic of

(A) McArdle's disease
(B) muscular dystrophy
(C) myasthenia gravis
(D) acute denervation
(E) chronic denervation

248. All the following statements about neurologic manifestations of Lyme disease are true EXCEPT

(A) most patients have a history of erythema chronicum migrans (ECM)
(B) facial weakness is an early occurrence (within 2 months of the appearance of the lesion)
(C) most patients have a history of arthritis
(D) the second most common cranial neuropathy is of the VIIIth nerve
(E) nerve conduction studies are usually normal in Lyme neuropathy

249. The most common cranial neuropathy seen in Lyme disease is

(A) an Argyll Robertson pupillary defect
(B) facial weakness
(C) facial numbness
(D) acoustic nerve dysfunction
(E) VIth nerve palsies

250. The gene for Huntington's disease has been localized to chromosome

(A) 4
(B) 9
(C) 15
(D) 21
(E) 23

251. The typical hemorrhages that occur in the retina secondary to acute increased intracranial pressure occupy the

    (A) choroid
    (B) nerve fiber layer
    (C) subhyaloid space
    (D) vitreous body
    (E) anterior chamber

252. The site of a restricted lesion that would selectively impair vertical gaze is the

    (A) collicular plate
    (B) cerebellar vermis
    (C) region dorsomedial to the red nuclei
    (D) bioccipital region
    (E) internal capsule

253. A patient presents with a fever, painful ear, facial pain, facial weakness, and a VIth nerve palsy. The most likely explanation is

    (A) acoustic neuroma with hemorrhage
    (B) basilar aneurysmal rupture
    (C) inflammation of the apex of the petrous pyramid
    (D) vasculitis
    (E) external otitis

254. A patient has difficulty seeing to the left with the left eye and to a lesser degree to the right with the right eye. Visual acuity and the remainder of the neurologic examination are normal. The most likely diagnosis is

    (A) lesion of the optic chiasm
    (B) lesion of the left lateral geniculate body
    (C) lesion of both optic nerves
    (D) vascular retinal disease
    (E) psychogenic disorder

255. In most normal persons, at maximum lateral gaze the limbus of the *ab*ducting eye reaches

    (A) almost exactly to the apex of the external canthus
    (B) 1 mm short of the external canthus angle
    (C) 1 mm beyond the external canthus angle
    (D) one-half of the distance from cornea to canthus
    (E) none of the above positions

256. A patient has diplopia on left lateral gaze. Examination shows slight weakness of abduction of the left eye, but the right eye hyperadducts when the patient looks to the left. In this case, hyperadduction of the right eye is best explained by

    (A) a lesion of the ipsilateral medial longitudinal fasciculus
    (B) a supranuclear palsy of gaze from interruption of frontobulbar pathways
    (C) preexisting ocular malalignment
    (D) Hering's law of equal supranuclear innervation of yoke muscles
    (E) a hysterical or malingering patient

257. To test for the integrity of the IVth cranial nerve in a patient with a IIIrd nerve palsy, the examiner asks the patient to look in which of the following directions?

    (A) To the side opposite the IIIrd nerve palsy and down
    (B) To the side ipsilateral to the IIIrd nerve palsy and up
    (C) To the midline and up
    (D) To the midline
    (E) Upward

Questions 258–260

A previously well patient has been experiencing a gradual onset of weakness for 2 days, with some vague tingling in the extremities but no incontinence. He has generalized flaccid muscle weakness—perhaps worse proximally. Ocular movements, speaking, and swallowing are normal, but facial movements are questionably weak. On percussing the tendons, the examiner elicits no response. Sensory examination discloses questionable loss of vibratory sensation in the toes. Serum electrolytes (meq/L) are Na^+ 137, K^+ 3.4, Cl^- 100, Ca^{2+} 7; CPK is normal.

258. The most likely diagnosis is

   (A) electrolyte imbalance
   (B) acute myelitis
   (C) acute polymyositis
   (D) acute polyradiculitis (Landry-Guillain-Barré syndrome)
   (E) familial periodic paralysis

259. On the third day of illness of the patient described, a lumbar puncture is performed. Analysis of the CSF discloses these findings: WBCs 5/mm³; glucose 65 mg/dL; protein 35 mg/dL; immunoelectrophoretic profile normal. The best interpretation of these results is which of the following?

   (A) They argue most strongly for acute myelitis
   (B) They are most compatible with electrolyte imbalance
   (C) They argue against polymyositis
   (D) They exclude the Landry-Guillain-Barré syndrome
   (E) They are compatible with acute myelitis, electrolyte imbalance, polymyositis, and Landry-Guillain-Barré syndrome

260. The previously mentioned patient continued to have flaccid paralysis for a number of weeks and showed some slight recovery after 3 months but then began to complain of headache and some blurred vision. Examination disclosed mild papilledema. The significance of this new finding is that it

   (A) probably represents a new disease
   (B) implies the presence of a brain tumor rather than a neuromuscular disease
   (C) suggests impending renal failure
   (D) raises the question of lead poisoning and lead neuropathy
   (E) probably reflects chronically elevated CSF protein levels

261. Patients affected with the medial longitudinal fasciculus (MLF) syndrome, when attempting to look to one side, display

   (A) nystagmus of the adducting eye and paresis of the abducting eye, with normal convergence during accommodation
   (B) nystagmus of the abducting eye with paresis of the adducting eye, and adductor paresis during accommodation
   (C) nystagmus of the abducting eye with paresis of the adducting eye, but adduction of the eyes during accommodation
   (D) nystagmus of both adducting and abducting eyes, with paresis of vertical movements
   (E) paresis of the abducting and adducting eyes, but adduction of the eyes during accommodation

262. Neurologic complications of adult myxedema include all the following EXCEPT

   (A) decreased CSF protein
   (B) facial weakness
   (C) vertigo
   (D) hearing loss
   (E) delirium

263. An abnormal IgM spike found on a serum protein electrophoresis that is not associated with a plasma cell dyscrasia would most likely be associated with which one of the following neurologic syndromes?

    (A) Peripheral neuropathy
    (B) Cerebellar degeneration
    (C) Limbic encephalitis
    (D) Optic neuritis
    (E) Guillain-Barré syndrome

264. Opsoclonus in children and infants is mainly associated with

    (A) small cell carcinoma of the lung
    (B) Sydenham's chorea
    (C) neuroblastoma
    (D) Wilms' tumor
    (E) acute lymphocytic leukemia

265. The true vestibular component of caloric nystagmus is

    (A) the slow deviation phase
    (B) the quick kickback phase
    (C) both quick and slow horizontal phases
    (D) the vertical quick phase only
    (E) both quick and slow vertical phases

266. Downbeat nystagmus localizes the lesion to

    (A) the labyrinth
    (B) the anterior vermis
    (C) a variety of locations within the brainstem
    (D) the cervicomedullary junction
    (E) none of the above

267. In performing a cold caloric irrigation of the ear of a patient sitting upright, an examiner should position the patient by

    (A) leaving the patient's head vertical
    (B) inclining the patient's head 60 degrees backward
    (C) inclining the patient's head 30 degrees forward
    (D) tilting the patient's head to the side of the irrigation
    (E) bending the patient's trunk forward

DIRECTIONS: Each question below contains four suggested responses of which **one or more** is correct. Select

A	if	**1, 2, and 3**	are correct
B	if	**1 and 3**	are correct
C	if	**2 and 4**	are correct
D	if	**4**	is correct
E	if	**1, 2, 3, and 4**	are correct

268. Lead poisoning in children may cause

    (1) ataxia
    (2) hemiplegia
    (3) seizures
    (4) lethargy

269. True statements regarding syphilis in an HIV-positive patient include which of the following?

    (1) The delay between primary infection and neurologic involvement is reduced
    (2) The CSF VDRL test may be negative
    (3) Strokes due to meningovascular involvement are extremely rare
    (4) Intravenous rather than intramuscular penicillin is the treatment of choice

270. Diagnostic features that distinguish nonparalytic (concomitant) heterotropia from paralytic heterotropia include which of the following?

    (1) The angle of the ocular malalignment remains the same during all directions of movement when both eyes are used
    (2) Each eye shows a full range of movements when the other is covered
    (3) Opacity of the media or severe refractive error may be present in one eye
    (4) The patient complains of diplopia

271. Clinical characteristics of Adie's pupil include

    (1) anisocoria
    (2) irregular pupillary margin
    (3) slow constriction and dilation
    (4) frequent association with hyperactive stretch reflexes

272. An examiner places strong positive lenses (Frenzel lenses) over a patient's eyes to inspect for positional or caloric-induced nystagmus in order to

    (1) produce pupilloconstriction
    (2) occlude visual fixation
    (3) prevent vertigo
    (4) magnify the eye movements

273. Ragged red fibers are associated with which of the following?

    (1) Myoclonus and ataxia
    (2) Cardiac arrhythmias
    (3) Diplopia
    (4) Paroxysmal ataxia

274. Hyperthyroidism is frequently accompanied by which of the following motor system syndromes?

    (1) Myasthenia gravis
    (2) Periodic weakness with hypokalemia
    (3) Ophthalmoplegia
    (4) Enlarged, firm muscles

275. Correct statements concerning the syndrome of progressive ophthalmoplegia include which of the following?

    (1) Historically, opinions have differed concerning its classification as a myopathic or a neurogenic disease
    (2) It is frequently associated with retinitis pigmentosa
    (3) It is characterized by ptosis and weakness of eye closing as well as by ophthalmoplegia
    (4) Affected patients frequently present with diplopia

SUMMARY OF DIRECTIONS

A	B	C	D	E
1, 2, 3 only	1, 3 only	2, 4 only	4 only	All are correct

276. Which of the following will cause xanthochromia?

    (1) Jaundice
    (2) Elevated CSF protein
    (3) Hypercarotenemia
    (4) Rifampin

277. Causes of optic neuritis include which of the following?

    (1) Postviral syndrome
    (2) Herpes zoster
    (3) Syphilis
    (4) Viral infections

278. With closed head injuries, commonly affected brain sites include

    (1) frontal
    (2) brainstem
    (3) temporal
    (4) occipital

279. True statements concerning primary central nervous system lymphomas include

    (1) they diffusely enhance with contrast
    (2) they almost always are surrounded by significant edema
    (3) they are usually periventricular
    (4) the contrast enhancement is exquisitely sensitive to steroid but the tumor itself rarely shrinks

280. Myotonia may be identified by which of the following features?

    (1) It increases with increasing contractions of the muscle
    (2) It is demonstrable by percussion
    (3) It is electrically silent in EMG
    (4) It occurs after a single strong contraction

281. Diabetes is associated with which of the following neurologic problems?

    (1) Bell's palsy
    (2) Subacute proximal leg weakness
    (3) Impotence
    (4) Complete third nerve palsy

DIRECTIONS: Each group of questions below consists of lettered headings followed by a set of numbered items. For each numbered item select the **one** lettered heading with which it is **most** closely associated. Each lettered heading may be used **once, more than once, or not at all.**

Questions 282–285

For each of the disorders listed below, choose the inheritance pattern with which it is most closely associated.

(A) Autosomal dominant
(B) Autosomal recessive
(C) Sex-linked recessive
(D) Hereditary influence without following a strict mendelian pattern
(E) No clear evidence of a hereditary predisposition

282. Duchenne's muscular dystrophy

283. Myotonic dystrophy

284. Pelizaeus-Merzbacher disease

285. Myelomeningocele

Questions 286–289

Match the following.

(A) Polymyositis
(B) Trichinosis
(C) Carnitine palmitoyl transferase (CPT) deficiency
(D) Limb girdle dystrophy
(E) Myotonic dystrophy

286. This muscle disorder usually begins in the third decade and is associated with a peculiar facial appearance due to masseter atrophy, ptosis, and frontal baldness

287. This disorder affects women more than men and generally begins in middle age with subacute, painless, symmetric, proximal weakness

288. Patients with this disorder usually have extraocular muscle and tongue involvement

289. This disorder, primarily of males, causes recurrent episodes of myoglobinuria

Questions 290–293

For each disorder listed below, choose the chromosomal condition with which it is most closely associated.

(A) 5 Deletion
(B) Trisomy 21
(C) Trisomy 13
(D) XXY
(E) No deletion or error of chromosome number is found

290. Holoprosencephaly/arhinencephalia

291. Cri du chat (cat's cry syndrome)

292. Neurofibromatosis

293. Klinefelter's syndrome

Ophthalmology, ENT, CSF, Microbiology, Endocrinology, and Immunology

---

Answers

239. The answer is B. (*Adams RD, ed 4. pp 786–787.*) Leigh's disease is an autosomal recessive disorder that generally has its onset in the first few years of life. It has a variable clinical presentation dependent in part on the age of onset. One of the characteristic features that occurs in some children is a markedly abnormal respiratory pattern. Although multiple biochemical abnormalities have been found, none has yet been proved to be universally present. It is generally agreed that the central problem occurs in the pyruvate dehydrogenase complex. The pathologic features are similar to those of Wernicke's disease except for sparing of the mamillary bodies. Spongiform degeneration, necrosis, vascular proliferation, and gliosis occur in the thalamus, brainstem, and spinal cord.

240. The answer is A. (*Adams RD, ed 4. p 218.*) The fast—or kickback—phase of caloric nystagmus depends in large part on the integrity of the efferent pathway from the frontal eye fields. Large hemispheric lesions that destroy the cortical projection system to the brainstem will abolish the kickback phase of nystagmus. In patients thus afflicted, the slow deviation phase (the vestibular or optokinetic phase) remains. Absence of the cerebral efferent pathway converts the response to merely deviation rather than to an organized nystagmus. Retinal receptors play no part in producing the fast phase of caloric nystagmus. In fact, voluntary fixation tends to inhibit caloric nystagmus. Integrity of the retinal receptors would be necessary for the pursuit phase of optokinetic nystagmus, but the fast—or kickback—phase is related to the integrity of the pathway from the frontal eye fields to the brainstem.

241. The answer is A. (*Adams RD, ed 4. p 970.*) A fused suture prevents skull growth at right angles to the plane of the suture. A compensatory growth occurs in other skull areas not inhibited by the closed suture. When the sagittal suture closes, the head becomes long and thin (scaphocephalic). This type of abnormality can be fixed early in life.

242. The answer is C. (*Adams RD, ed 4. pp 912–913.*) Arsenic can cause a polyneuropathy evolving over days after acute poisoning or over weeks to months with chronic poisoning. The neuropathy is axonal and is associated with anemia, jaundice, hyperkeratosis of the palmar surfaces, brownish cutaneous pigmentation, and Mees' lines (white transverse bands across the nails). Diagnosis can be made definitively with measurement of arsenic in urine or hair.

243. The answer is C. (*Plum, ed 3. p 231.*) Patients with COPD who develop respiratory failure with hypercarbia also develop many brain changes. Increased intracranial pressure from the elevated CO_2 may cause optic disc swelling. Anesthesia may develop along with a dull, diffuse headache, lethargy, or coma. Asterixis and myoclonus are extremely common, whereas seizures are rare.

244. The answer is A. (*Adams RD, ed 4. pp 241–242.*) With end-organ involvement one always observes nystagmus proportional to the severity of the vertiginous symptoms. Labyrinthine dysfunction may be associated with other ear complaints, such as tinnitus and hearing loss, but not always. Central disorders may be accompanied by cerebellar or brainstem signs. The neurologic examination is normal in patients with labyrinthine dysfunction except for gait, which can be ataxic and of the midline cerebellar type, i.e., "drunken." The nystagmus in benign positional vertigo, for example, is usually torsional, is unidirectional, fatigues with repeated Hallpike maneuvers, and is proportional to the symptoms. With central causes the nystagmus varies with gaze direction and the symptoms do not match the signs. Nystagmus does not fatigue with Hallpike maneuvers.

245. The answer is E. (*Adams RD, ed 4. p 970.*) Statistically most enlarged heads in children are due either to hydrocephalus or to a nonpathologic familial hereditary pattern of large heads. However, there are certain conditions in which a large head without significantly enlarged ventricles occurs in the setting of serious neurologic abnormalities. Most degenerative neurologic disorders of children cause small heads. The only three degenerative conditions causing macrocephaly are Tay-Sachs disease, Alexander's disease, and spongy degeneration of infancy. Subdural hematomas in infants should be symptomatic.

246. The answer is B. (*Adams RD, ed 4. pp 1020–1021.*) The EMG finding most indicative of chronic denervation is giant polyphasic motor units. These units are virtually pathognomonic and are absent in normal persons or in patients with dystrophy. They are thought to represent enlargement of the motor units from regenerating nerve sprouts. In many disorders involved in the differential diagnosis of chronic denervation, the EMG will show fibrillations or low-amplitude motor units. Characteristically, patients with chronic denervation show fibrillations and slow positive waves in addition to the giant polyphasic units, but fibrillations also can occur in polymyositis and some dystrophies and lack the pathognomonic significance of the giant polyphasic units. Patients with muscular dystrophy and normal persons show no electrical activity with the muscle at rest.

247. The answer is B. (*Adams RD, ed 4. pp 1021–1022.*) The characteristic EMG pattern of muscular dystrophy is a full interference pattern with low-amplitude potentials. The interference pattern depends on the number of motor units contracting and the number of muscle fibers responding. In dystrophies, the number of motor units remains the same, but the number of muscle fibers available to respond decreases as the disease advances. The reduced number of responding muscle fibers leads to the reduction in amplitude of the interference pattern. The full interference pattern with low-amplitude potentials, in combination with the absence of any of the EMG changes such as fibrillations and giant polyphasic units, lends support to a diagnosis of a primary muscle disease rather than neuronal disease.

248. The answer is E. (*Logigian, N Engl J Med 323:1438–1443, 1990.*) The spectrum of neurologic disorders reported with Lyme disease is large and the clinical course is not yet fully understood. Diagnosis is not always clear cut, as most, but not all patients have a history of ECM and arthritis. The history of a tick bite is more difficult to ascertain because the tick vector is the size of the period at the end of this sentence. Facial and VIIIth nerve lesions occur early, often within a month of the ECM. Polyneuropathy is a common long-term problem, with abnormalities evident on electrophysiologic studies. Improvement in symptoms parallels improvement in electrical studies.

249. The answer is B. (*Mandell, ed 3. pp 1819–1827.*) Facial weakness, often bilateral, is probably the most common cranial neuropathy; however, the neurologic manifestations of Lyme disease include aseptic meningitis, encephalitis, dementia, myelitis, and peripheral nerve problems. The neurologic literature is somewhat hazy because of the frequent difficulty in making the diagnosis if the erythema chronicum migrans or the arthritis was not observed by physicians. No test currently exists to point to active Lyme infection in the CNS other than a finding of pleocytosis, so that the meaning of a positive Lyme titer is not always clear.

250. The answer is A. (*Rowland, ed 8. p 649.*)   Huntington's disease is an autosomal dominant disease that causes the triad of chorea, dementia, and behavioral disorders. It occurs worldwide in all ethnic groups but there have been no cases yet documented of spontaneous mutation. While such a mutation may have occurred, proof would require genetic confirmation of parentage without the disease and either a genetic or pathologic confirmation of the disease. The gene has been localized to the short arm of chromosome 4. Testing is now available to confirm diagnosis if an affected family group is available. Testing will determine carrier status (preclinical disease) in persons planning families.

251. The answer is C. (*Adams RD, ed 4. p 196.*)   The retinal hemorrhage typical of acute increased intracranial pressure occupies the space between the internal limiting membrane of the retina and the hyaloid membrane. Therefore, it is a subhyaloid or preretinal hemorrhage. The blood apparently comes from rupture of the retinal arterioles. The ophthalmoscopic appearance of the various types of hemorrhage depends on the space into which the hemorrhage ruptures or upon the retinal layer into which it ruptures. Common conditions associated with subhyaloid hemorrhages include ruptured intracranial aneurysms and head injuries, often with acute epidural or acute subdural hemorrhage. Occasionally, severe coughing may induce a subhyaloid hemorrhage. The presence of subhyaloid hemorrhages, at least in a comatose patient, requires immediate investigation by CT scan or angiography.

252. The answer is A. (*Adams RD, ed 4. p 210. Patten, pp 62–63.*)   The clinical importance of a vertical gaze palsy lies partly in the localization of mass lesions to the region of the superior colliculus, particularly of the pineal gland, causing Parinaud's syndrome (loss of convergence, light-near pupillary dissociation, retraction nystagmus). The loss of vertical gaze is important in distinguishing progressive supranuclear palsy (PSP) from Parkinson's disease. The superior colliculus is important in initiating saccadic movements only. Clinically, lesions of the superior colliculus affect upgaze, while lesions slightly lower affect only downgaze.

253. The answer is C. (*Glaser, ed 2. p 259.*)   The syndrome of purulent otitis, ipsilateral facial pain, and Vth, VIth, and VIIth nerve palsies is called *Gradenigo's syndrome*. It occurs with extension of the inflammation from the middle ear to the apex of the petrous pyramids over which course the involved nerves. Appropriately placed neoplasms, such as nasopharyngeal carcinoma, can cause a similar syndrome but without the fever.

254. The answer is A. (*Glaser, ed 2. p 172.*)   Bitemporal field cuts are the hallmark of optic chiasm syndromes. Most commonly these do not affect both eyes equally. Pituitary tumors are the most common etiology but other tumors and aneurysms are also in the differential diagnosis. Because the progression is insidious, patients are often unaware of the severity of their deficit.

255. The answer is A. (*Glaser, ed 2. pp 38–39.*)   At maximum abduction, in most normal persons the corneal limbus reaches almost exactly to the apex of the lateral canthus. This is a very precise and reproducible finding. Any departure suggests a disturbance of abduction—either weakness of the lateral rectus muscle action, a lid anomaly, enophthalmos, exophthalmos, or some anomaly of the eyeball itself. The examiner should check for the precision of this relationship every time a patient's range of eye movements is tested.

256. The answer is D. (*Glaser, ed 2. pp 42–43.*)   Excessive action of an intact ocular muscle of one eye that normally is yoked to a paretic muscle of the opposite eye is explained by Hering's law. Hering's law states that the yoke muscles receive equal supranuclear innervation. A patient affected with a weak lateral rectus muscle overinnervates in an effort to activate the paretic muscle. The central connections of the nervous system, in obedience to Hering's law, send an equally strong innervation to the intact medial rectus. The paretic lateral rectus muscle underacts, and the intact medial rectus overacts, causing hyperadduction. The reverse occurs with a medial rectus palsy. When a patient with this deficit attempts to look to the side opposite the medial rectus palsy, the overaction of the intact lateral rectus muscles hyperabducts the eyeball.

257. **The answer is A.** (*Adams RD, ed 4. p 214.*) To test for an intact IVth nerve when the patient has a IIIrd nerve palsy, the examiner asks the patient to look to the side opposite the palsy and down. The examiner then watches for rotation of one of the conjunctival vessels. If the IVth nerve and superior oblique muscle are intact, the examiner will observe intorsion of the eye, although it will fail to adduct. With the eye laterally rotated from the pull of the intact VIth nerve and lateral rectus muscle, the eye is in the position in which the superior oblique muscle has its maximum strength as an intorter. The effort to look medially and down will activate the superior oblique muscle, but it will mainly display its action as an intorter of the eye.

258. **The answer is D.** (*Adams RD, ed 4. pp 1035–1037.*) The patient described in the question has an acutely evolving, flaccid paralysis with areflexia and retention of percussion irritability of muscle. Sensation is only questionably involved, and the patient retains sphincter control. These features argue strongly against myelitis, which would manifest sensory loss and incontinence, even though flaccid paralysis may be present early in the course of the myelitis. Polymyositis usually has a much more indolent onset than occurred in this patient and would not cause acute flaccid paralysis. The electrolyte values are slightly low, but not low enough to cause flaccid paralysis. Familial periodic paralysis of normokalemic type remains a possibility but in terms of probability is much rarer and thus much less likely than the Landry-Guillain-Barré syndrome.

259. **The answer is E.** (*Adams RD, ed 4. pp 1034–1037.*) Normal spinal fluid is compatible with any of the four diagnoses mentioned in the question. Acute myelitis may or may not show a significant change in the CSF; but very mild, acute electrolyte disturbances, polymyositis, and periodic paralysis characteristically would fail to show changes in the components ordinarily measured in a routine CSF examination. In Landry-Guillain-Barré syndrome, the protein level does increase, but occasionally the initial tap may show a normal protein content. The protein level then will increase, usually reaching a peak several weeks after the onset of the illness. Thus, a normal CSF during the acute stage of the illness does not exclude the Landry-Guillain-Barré syndrome.

260. **The answer is E.** (*Rowland, ed 8. p 265.*) A patient with a chronic flaccid paralysis, particularly in the presence of the Landry-Guillain-Barré syndrome, may have increased protein levels for prolonged periods of weeks to months. Such patients may develop papilledema. In the patient discussed in the question, the principle of parsimony in diagnosis calls for a *single* disease to explain the range of clinical manifestations of his illness. To invoke any diagnosis other than the original one of a neuromuscular disease violates this principle. The mechanism of the papilledema and increased pressure with prolonged elevation of CSF protein is probably a result of occlusion of the pacchionian granulations by sludged protein.

261. **The answer is C.** (*Patten, pp 63–64.*) In the medial longitudinal fasciculus (MLF) syndrome, the patient shows nystagmus of the *ab*ducting eye and paresis of the *ad*ducting eye. Both eyes adduct during accommodation. The medial longitudinal fasciculus conveys fibers from the region of the contralateral abducens nucleus to the lower motor neurons of the medial rectus muscle in the IIIrd nerve nucleus. These MLF fibers yoke the medial rectus of one eye with the lateral rectus of the opposite eye to mediate conjugate lateral gaze. Interruption of these MLF fibers causes paresis of adduction of the eye ipsilateral to the MLF lesion. During accommodation, the medial rectus is activated by pathways that run directly into the midbrain without traveling down into the pons and

back through the MLF. The normal medial rectus action during convergence proves that the lower motor neurons of the medial rectus muscle remain intact in the MLF syndrome.

262. The answer is A. (*Rowland, ed 8. p 830.*)   Severe hypothyroidism in adults may cause a large number of neurologic complications. These include cranial neuropathies such as unilateral or bilateral facial weakness, decreased hearing, tinnitus, and vertigo. Delirium, agitation, and psychosis (myxedema madness) may occur as well as acute coma. Myopathy and sensory neuropathy are other rare complications. Laboratory abnormalities in myxedema include low thyroid hormones, elevated TSH, elevated CSF protein, and elevated cholesterol.

263. The answer is A. (*Kelly, Arch Neurol 45:1355–1359, 1988.*)   The laboratory evaluation of peripheral neuropathies should include a protein electrophoresis to look for immune abnormalities. Some of these antibodies have been clearly shown to cross-react with peripheral nerve and are thought to be causal in disease progression and not simply representative of a systemic response to nerve degeneration. The other disorders are also thought to be due to autoimmune dysfunction but have not been linked with benign IgM spikes.

264. The answer is C. (*Rowland, ed 8. p 878.*)   More than 50 percent of infants and children who develop opsoclonus have an associated neuroblastoma, usually in the chest. In adults the most commonly associated malignancy is a small cell cancer of the lung. Opsoclonus may also develop with encephalitis or metabolic and toxic states. In children with a neuroblastoma, opsoclonus is a good prognostic sign. The opsoclonus responds to ACTH.

265. The answer is A. (*Adams RD, ed 4. p 240.*)   The vestibular component of caloric nystagmus is the slow deviation phase and the nonvestibular component is the quick kickback phase. The quick phase depends, in large part, on the cortical efferent system from the frontal eye fields. Interruption of this system will result in loss of the quick phase, but the slow deviation phase in response to caloric irrigation remains. The direction of vestibular or caloric nystagmus unfortunately is named by the direction of the fast component, which is not the primary vestibular action.

266. The answer is D. (*Adams RD, ed 4. p 218.*)   Vertical nystagmus is a brainstem phenomenon. Upbeat nystagmus does not localize well and has been reported in lesions of the pontomedullary or pontomesencephalic junctions and possibly of the anterior vermis as well. Downbeat nystagmus is less common and is seen in lesions of the cervicomedullary junction. These lesions include such abnormalities as Wernicke's encephalopathy and syringomyelia.

267. The answer is B. (*Adams RD, ed 4. p 240.*)   Before performing a caloric irrigation test, an examiner has the patient sit erect, tilting the patient's head 60 degrees backward. The purpose of this maneuver is to place the lateral canal in the exact vertical plane. The lateral canal inclines 30 degrees above the horizontal, and the additional 60 degrees of inclination places it in a vertical position. With the lateral canal in the vertical plane, the effect of gravity plus the temperature effect of the irrigating fluid stimulates circulation of the fluid in the lateral semicircular canal, which in turn stimulates the vestibular receptors.

268. The answer is E (all). (*Rowland, ed 8. p 921.*)   Lead poisoning is more common in children than adults. The latter generally have occupational exposure to lead paint or old car radiators and develop autonomic or motor neuropathies. Children may eat lead paint chips in old houses and develop acute encephalopathies. The signs may include generalized or focal seizures, ataxia, hemiplegia, decerebrate rigidity, lethargy, delirium, or coma.

269. The answer is E (all). (*Musher, Ann Intern Med 113:872–881, 1990.*)   Tertiary syphilis, unlike secondary syphilis, is increased in HIV-positive patients because of the immunodeficiency. The

CSF VDRL test is often negative in HIV-negative as well as HIV-positive patients (30 of 37 HIV-positive patients with neurosyphilis had a negative VDRL test in one study), which makes diagnosis difficult. In the HIV-positive patient, treatment with intravenous penicillin G, 2 to 4 million units every 4 h, is recommended, and on this regimen there are no known failures. The typical delay between primary and tertiary infection appears to be markedly reduced as evidenced by the increasing frequency of young people with tertiary syphilis. Neurosyphilis causes neuroretinitis, deafness, stroke, and acute meningitis. Meningovascular syphilis causes ischemic events and does occur in HIV patients. With syphilitic meningitis, patients present with typical meningitic complaints. Cranial nerve involvement also occurs; the IIrd and VIIIth nerves are most commonly involved.

270. The answer is A (1, 2, 3). (*Adams RD, ed 4. p 212.*) Diagnostic features of nonparalytic (concomitant) heterotropia include the following: (1) the degree of deviation remains the same throughout all directions of movement when both eyes are used; (2) each eye shows a full range of movement when the other is covered; (3) one eye frequently will show an opacity of the media or a severe refractive error; and (4) the patient does not complain of diplopia. In contrast, in paralytic heterotropia from a nerve lesion, the degree of deviation of the eyes increases as the eyes move in the direction of pull of the paretic muscle; the affected eye shows the same restriction of movement when used alone as when both eyes are used together; and the patient *will* complain of diplopia (at least if the nerve lesion occurred after infancy and the patient does not have suppression amblyopia).

271. The answer is B (1, 3). (*Adams RD, ed 4. p 223.*) Adie's syndrome consists of anisocoria, myotonic constriction following response to light accommodation, regular pupillary margin, normal response to mydriatics, and frequent association with hypoactive or absent muscle stretch reflexes. This benign, fairly common syndrome is to be distinguished from other causes of anisocoria, especially the pupillary abnormalities in syphilis in which the Argyll Robertson pupil may be associated with tabes dorsalis and absence of the muscle stretch reflexes. Usually Adie's syndrome is discovered incidentally during an examination for some other complaint. Patients with this syndrome are free of symptoms or complaints despite the pupillary abnormality and hypoactive muscle stretch reflexes.

272. The answer is C (2, 4). (*Glaser, ed 2. p 336.*) Frenzel lenses (strong positive lenses) are placed over a patient's eyes during caloric irrigation in order to occlude visual fixation and to magnify the eye movements for ease of inspection. The strong lenses abolish visual acuity and prevent visual fixation, which inhibits nystagmus. Blocking of fixation by the Frenzel lenses permits faint nystagmus to appear. The strong lenses magnify the eye movements, making it possible to observe faint, low-amplitude nystagmus. The lenses neither produce pupilloconstriction nor abolish the vertigo that may accompany caloric nystagmus.

273. The answer is A (1, 2, 3). (*Rowland, ed 8. pp 727–728.*) Ragged red fibers are found in mitochondrial disorders. The abnormal mitochondria make muscle sections look like ragged red fibers on the Gomori trichrome stain. Mitochondrial disorders cause a wide spectrum of CNS and peripheral abnormalities. The MERRF (myoclonic epilepsy ragged red fibers) syndromes include ataxia. Kearns-Sayre syndrome is a progressive external ophthalmoplegia with cardiac conduction disturbances. Paroxysmal ataxia has no known physiologic, histologic, or biochemical marker.

274. The answer is A (1, 2, 3). (*Rowland, ed 8. pp 831–832.*) Patients with hyperthyroidism may have myasthenic weakness with pathologic fatigability, periodic weakness with low blood levels of potassium, and ophthalmoplegia. Enlarged, firm muscles occur in *hypo*thyroidism. The possibility of thyroid dysfunction should be considered if a patient displays any of these four types of muscle disorders. Enlarged, firm muscles may occur prior to the stage of atrophy in several disorders, including Duchenne's dystrophy, some muscle disorders with myotonia, and glycogen storage disease. The variety of muscle disorders found in association with thyroid disease indicates the importance of testing for thyroid dysfunction in patients who have muscle disorders of obscure origin.

275. **The answer is A (1, 2, 3).** (*Rowland, ed 8. pp 595–597.*)   Progressive external ophthalmoplegia has been the subject of controversy for many years. At one time, it was considered to be an ocular form of progressive motor neuron degeneration, but now it is usually classified as a myopathy. The problem lies in interpreting neurogenic and myopathic changes in eye muscle biopsies. The disease does have an association with retinitis pigmentosa, far more so than do other forms of muscular dystrophy. Patients with progressive external ophthalmoplegia do not characteristically complain of, or present with, diplopia. The eyes may become completely immobile but generally remain in the primary position because all muscles are equally involved. This fact, in conjunction with the extremely gradual evolution of the disease, makes diplopia an uncommon complaint.

276. **The answer is E (all).** (*Adams RD, ed 4. p 12. Mandell, ed 3. p 353.*)   It is well known that the bilirubin pigment from hemoglobin breakdown colors the CSF yellow. This occurs after blood enters the CSF. When protein levels exceed 150 to 200 mg/dL, a yellowish tint appears so that CSF below a spinal canal block from any cause may yield xanthochromic fluid. Less well known but occasionally of clinical importance is the fact that certain pigments in blood cross the blood-brain barrier and color the CSF. Hypercarotenemia (e.g., from ingestion of large amounts of carrots), marked jaundice, and rifampin all cause yellowing of the CSF.

277. **The answer is E (all).** (*Glaser, ed 2. p 127.*)   Optic neuritis is a clinical syndrome characterized by the relatively abrupt impairment of vision progressing over hours to days, usually associated with eye pain. Although it is a common sign heralding the onset of MS, optic neuritis is often idiopathic. Among known associations, presumably etiologic, are various viral and postviral syndromes; granulomatous diseases such as tuberculosis; syphilis; and sarcoid.

278. **The answer is B (1, 3).** (*Adams RD, ed 4. pp 698–700.*)   The severity of the brain lesions caused by closed head injuries varies not only with the force but also with the location of impact and the direction. Linear impacts cause significantly less damage than those with an angular direction. Frontal impacts tend to cause injury mainly at the coup site, whereas posterior impacts tend to cause both coup and contra coup injuries. Regardless of the site or direction of impact, however, most injuries occur in the frontal and temporal regions probably because the inferior surfaces of these regions slide along the irregularities of the skull.

279. **The answer is B (1, 3).** (*DeAngelis, Neurology 41:619–621, 1991.*)   Primary central nervous system lymphomas are increasing in immunocompetent hosts. They are almost always periventricular and frequently involve the basal ganglia. They enhance diffusely with contrast and have little or no edema surrounding them. The tumors may be single or multiple and in 40 percent of cases lyse with steroids, which makes diagnosis impossible. Diagnosis requires a biopsy, which is best performed stereotactically since debulking of lymphomas does not enhance survival, unlike the case with gliomas.

280. **The answer is C (2, 4).** (*Adams RD, ed 4. p 1173.*)   Myotonia usually decreases with increasing use of the involved muscle, is demonstrable by percussion, causes a distinctive EMG pattern, and occurs after a single contraction. These criteria serve to differentiate it from other types of cramps and contractures of the muscle. It is important to have positive criteria by which to identify myotonia because there are many other causes of muscle cramps. In addition, myotonia may be associated with weak muscles (as in myotonia dystrophica) or with strong muscles (as in myotonia congenita).

281. **The answer is A (1, 2, 3).** (*Adams RD, ed 4. p 1045.*)   Diabetes is associated with an increased risk of all neuropathic conditions such as Bell's palsy and carpal tunnel syndromes. In addition to

an axonal, primarily sensory neuropathy, diabetic men are commonly afflicted with impotence on a neurogenic or vascular basis. Diabetic amyotrophy is a particularly disabling problem with back pain, proximal leg weakness leading to atrophy, and a variable degree of sensory deficit. Diabetic third nerve palsies spare the pupils.

282–285. The answers are: 282-C, 283-A, 284-C, 285-E. (*Adams RD, ed 4. pp 785, 976, 1118–1119, 1123–1124.*) Myelomeningocele shows some familial clustering but without a specific mendelian pattern. It has been suggested that clustering is due to environmental agents rather than to a genetic predisposition.

Knowledge of the hereditary nature of a disease is imperative for genetic counseling and for identification of persons at risk for the disorder. A woman who is a carrier for a sex-linked recessive disease can avoid bearing an affected male by choosing to abort all male fetuses. Half of her daughters, however, will be carriers; and the overproduction of carriers throughout several generations can significantly increase the risk of the disease, as occurs in inbred populations.

Myotonic dystrophy exemplifies autosomal dominant disorders, whereas Duchenne's dystrophy and Pelizaeus-Merzbacher disease exemplify sex-linked recessive disorders in which males are afflicted predominantly. In the autosomal dominant disorders, one parent of the affected patient should exhibit clinical evidence of the disease in order to establish the hereditary nature of the patient's disorder.

In the recessive syndromes characterized by inborn errors of metabolism, the parents of affected offspring may show no clinical evidence of the disorder but frequently show biochemical changes. Appropriate biochemical tests can identify the parents as carriers of the disease trait in question and can be used to identify siblings or other relatives at risk as carriers of the disorder.

286–289. The answers are: 286-E, 287-A, 288-B, 289-C. (*Adams RD, ed 4. pp 1104–1106, 1113.*) Myotonic dystrophy is an autosomal dominantly inherited disorder causing progressive weakness and myotonia. Tapping on muscle, particularly the tongue, causes the muscle to painlessly contract. It is often difficult for patients to relax muscles after prolonged contraction. The abnormal gene is located on chromosome 19 and causes widespread systemic abnormalities in the lens, endocrine glands, and skin as well as cardiac rhythm disturbances. The peculiar muscle wasting distribution causes a hatchetlike face due to masseter wasting. Ptosis, frontal baldness, wrinkled forehead, and slender mandible complete the facial changes.

Women develop polymyositis at twice the rate of men. It is a subacute progressive syndrome of weakness that causes pain in only about 15 percent of cases. It generally develops in the age range of 30 to 60 but may occur outside of this. It can sometimes be difficult to distinguish clinically from limb girdle dystrophy when family history is lacking. It is sometimes associated with systemic autoimmune disorders.

Trichinosis is a parasitic disease that, in the acute stage, affects muscles; it shows a predilection for the tongue, masseter, extraocular, and pharyngeal muscles. Involvement is initially painful and affected muscles are swollen. At presentation the face may be swollen as well. In addition the blood often reveals an eosinophilia. Generally the parasites become encysted and calcify and leave the patient asymptomatic.

The enzyme CPT is important in regulating long-chain fatty acids and its absence leads to deposition of lipid vacuoles in muscle fibers. Patients develop recurrent bouts of myoglobinuria starting in the first or second decades, precipitated by cold or a high-fat, low-carbohydrate diet. Between attacks of myoglobinuria the patients are normal, although exercise will cause elevated blood CPK levels.

290–293. The answers are: 290-C, 291-A, 292-E, 293-D. (*Adams RD, ed 4. pp 980, 985.*) Some disorders have well-established chromosomal anomalies and others, although unquestionably hereditary, have no obvious disorders in chromosome number or size. Trisomies and deletions are common disorders of chromosome number or size; of these, trisomies 13 and 21, XXY syndrome, and the

5 deletion syndrome (cri du chat) constitute some of the best known. Neurofibromatosis fails to show a gross disturbance of chromosomal morphology. It has, however, been classified into two forms. In type 1, the defect is on chromosome 17. This is the peripheral form with skin changes and subcutaneous tumors. Type 2, due to a defect on chromosome 22, is the central form and associated with acoustic neuromas. Holoprosencephaly may occur with a normal karyotype, but when a karyotype abnormality exists, it is usually trisomy 13 (although other errors also occur).

By knowing which disorders have gross chromosomal errors, a clinician can offer amniocentesis to mothers at risk for producing infants with that disorder, which allows elective abortion with an identifiable clinical syndrome of malformations. Not only do the affected persons exhibit a clinically recognizable set of external malformations, they often have visceral malformations as well. The majority of patients with gross abnormalities of chromosome number or morphology have some degree of mental deficiency. Thus, a chromosomal deviation may produce a defective brain, but no chromosomal abnormalities are known to be associated with superior intelligence.

Psychiatry Questions for Neurologists

DIRECTIONS: Each question below contains five suggested responses. Select the **one best** response to each question.

294. The sudden onset of a confusional disorder, without language dysfunction and with minimal focal findings, may be seen with infarctions of the

    (A) right occipital lobe
    (B) right parietal lobe
    (C) left parietal lobe
    (D) left occipital lobe
    (E) anterior cerebral artery

295. The production of motor stereotypies by chronic amphetamine use in humans and animals is thought to involve which of the following mechanisms?

    (A) Stimulation of the cholinergic mechanism of the reticular activating system
    (B) Inhibition of the inhibitory outflow from the Purkinje cells to the dentate nuclei
    (C) Direct stimulation of neurons in the motor cortex
    (D) Activation of the substantia nigra neurons
    (E) Activation of the dopaminergic systems

296. All the following are useful in distinguishing psychogenic unresponsiveness from true coma EXCEPT

    (A) roving eye movements
    (B) absent reflexes
    (C) cold caloric induced nystagmus
    (D) eyelid closure after passive eyelid opening
    (E) EEG

297. The most common psychiatric presentation for the AIDS-dementia complex is

    (A) confabulation
    (B) mania
    (C) depression
    (D) delirium
    (E) focal abnormalities such as aphasia, denial, or neglect

298. According to current knowledge, the effect of bifrontal lesions (sparing the motor cortex) on human behavior is best described by which of the following statements?

    (A) Bifrontal lesions are characterized by excessive eating, altered sleep cycles, and hypersexuality
    (B) Bifrontal lesions may cause profound effects on behavior or personality, frequently with little effect on standard IQ tests
    (C) Bifrontal lesions produce behavioral and personality alterations that cannot be produced by lesions elsewhere in the cerebrum
    (D) Bifrontal lesions heighten self-awareness of bodily dysfunction
    (E) A specific frontal lobe syndrome exists that can be recognized by characteristic neurologic signs

299. The most common mental abnormality on presentation with the Wernicke-Korsakoff syndrome is

    (A) a global confusional state
    (B) delirium with hallucinations
    (C) impaired recent memory without confusion
    (D) coma
    (E) stupor

300. The most common hallucinations in schizophrenia are

    (A) visual
    (B) auditory
    (C) tactile
    (D) olfactory
    (E) gustatory

301. Culture-bound psychiatric syndromes are disorders that are found in particular cultures. Which one of the following is an example of a culture-bound disorder in North America?

    (A) Schizophrenia
    (B) Posttraumatic stress disorder
    (C) Autism
    (D) Bulimia
    (E) Conversion reactions

302. Pick's disease is most readily distinguished from other presenile dementias by which of the following histologic findings?

    (A) Granulovacuolar degeneration of the hippocampus
    (B) Neurofibrillary tangles
    (C) Rounded or pear-shaped, pallid cortical neurons
    (D) Absence of gliosis
    (E) Senile plaques

303. Levodopa-induced hallucinations are usually

    (A) auditory
    (B) visual and threatening
    (C) visual and nonthreatening
    (D) auditory and visual
    (E) highly idiosyncratic

304. The transient global amnesia syndrome may be explained on which of the following pathoanatomic bases?

    (A) Infarction of the dentate gyrus
    (B) Destruction of the mamillary bodies
    (C) Lacunar state of the thalamus
    (D) Degeneration of the hippocampal pyramidal cells
    (E) None of the above

305. Fluent aphasic patients lose the ability to

    (A) correct their own speech errors
    (B) speak with prosody
    (C) communicate by gesturing
    (D) understand pantomime or gesture
    (E) understand any spoken or written commands

306. The so-called paradoxical effect of medication in hyperactive children refers to which one of the following responses?

    (A) Calming effect of drugs classed as stimulants
    (B) Calming effect of phenobarbital
    (C) Reduction in hyperactivity from benzodiazepines
    (D) Proven adverse response to salicylates and red dyes
    (E) Minimal response to alcohol as adults

307. The psychosis associated with chronic use of amphetamines resembles naturally occurring schizophrenia. Which of the following, however, is absent in the former?

    (A) Paranoia
    (B) Hallucinations
    (C) Withdrawal and apathy
    (D) Affective flattening and disordered thought associations
    (E) Stereotyped movements, repetitive behaviors, and grimacing

308. Akathisia most resembles

    (A) athetosis
    (B) dystonia
    (C) Gilles de la Tourette's syndrome
    (D) restless legs syndrome
    (E) sleep myoclonia

309. The nature of the hyperkinesias in schizophrenic patients who have not been treated with psychotropic drugs is best described by which of the following statements?

    (A) Prior to the psychotropic drug era, hyperkinesias were commonly described in association with schizophrenia
    (B) The hyperkinesias of schizophrenia closely resemble the standard syndromes of chorea, athetosis, dystonia, and ballismus
    (C) The hyperkinesias are associated with a relatively good prognosis
    (D) The hyperkinetic patients evolve graceful, skilled movement patterns
    (E) The hyperkinesias tend to disappear when the patient walks

310. A man with the recent onset of slightly slurred speech and some questionable difficulty in naming objects failed to protrude his tongue on command but licked his lips a few minutes later. This observation is best explained on the basis of

    (A) negativism
    (B) hysterical overlay
    (C) apraxia
    (D) temporal disorientation
    (E) corticobulbar tract interruption

311. A 50-year-old patient complains of increasing weakness of extremity and trunk muscles of several months' duration, with sparing of the cranial nerve muscles. Examination reveals proximal weakness and possibly atrophy, with preserved muscle stretch reflexes. EMG and muscle biopsy are normal. Screening tests for collagen-vascular disease are negative. Serum enzyme levels are normal. Results of a toxicology screen for heavy metals are negative. These findings warrant which of the following conclusions?

    (A) Organic disease of the neuromuscular system is excluded
    (B) A lumbar puncture should be performed
    (C) A myelogram should be performed
    (D) A psychiatric consultation is required
    (E) Thyroid function tests should be performed

312. Of the five axes in the revised third edition of *Diagnostic and Statistical Manual of Mental Disorders* (*DSM III-R*), the mental disorders are classified by

    (A) I alone
    (B) I and II
    (C) II alone
    (D) I, II, and III
    (E) all five

313. Dissociative states and panic attacks are frequently seen in which of the following psychiatric disorders?

    (A) Depression
    (B) Mania
    (C) Conversion reactions
    (D) Posttraumatic stress disorder
    (E) Gilles de la Tourette syndrome

314. Anosognosia is characteristic of which of the following conditions?

    (A) Diffuse cerebral disease
    (B) Lesions of the frontal lobe
    (C) Lesions of the right posterior parasylvian area
    (D) Lesions of the right lateral occipital gyrus
    (E) None of the above

315. A nondemented patient with a left homonymous hemianopia is unable to orient her
clothes preparatory to dressing. This type
of dressing apraxia suggests a lesion of

(A) the right frontal lobe
(B) the left frontal lobe
(C) the left posterior parasylvian area
(D) the right posterior parasylvian area
(E) both cerebral hemispheres

316. A 25-year-old man who has been treated
with a stable dose of an antipsychotic drug
for a schizophrenia-like illness for 3 years
develops progressive choreiform movements. The presence of which one of the
following would be most helpful in determining whether the patient has tardive dyskinesia (TD) or Huntington's disease (HD)?

(A) Normal brain CT scan
(B) Limb dyskinesias
(C) Rigidity
(D) Dementia
(E) Absence of a family history

317. A 30-year-old woman reports developing
progressive problems writing because her
hand cramps. The results of her neurologic
examination are normal except that when
she attempts to write, her hand cramps. She
can use knives, forks, screwdrivers, and
hairbrushes appropriately and has no difficulty performing delicate tasks. Your leading diagnosis would be

(A) malingering
(B) hysteria
(C) writer's cramp
(D) Hallervorden-Spatz disease
(E) reflex epilepsy

318. A previously normal elderly man is brought
to the emergency room for presumed intoxication. He denies all problems and wants
to go home. Unfortunately he appears to
be blind and bumps into objects and walls
when allowed to walk alone. Otherwise his
examination is normal, including that of his
pupils and eye movements. Your leading
diagnosis would be which one of the following?

(A) Posterior cerebral artery infarction
(B) Right parietal infarction
(C) Conversion reaction
(D) Glutethimide intoxication
(E) Methanol poisoning

319. A patient in a chronic care hospital was normal until middle age, when an acute but unknown illness caused him to become apathetic, hypersexual, aphasic, and amnestic.
In addition he appeared to have difficulty
interpreting how to use various objects, so
that he needed to touch them and sometimes to put them into his mouth. The most
likely cause for this syndrome is

(A) schizophrenia
(B) amphetamine use
(C) MPTP
(D) herpes simplex encephalitis
(E) brain tumor

320. A teen-age boy has a violent temper that
has gotten him arrested on several occasions. In each episode, he has abruptly assaulted his stepfather with seemingly little
provocation. He has never assaulted anyone else. After the episodes he is sometimes amnestic and sometimes contrite.
The most likely explanation is

(A) temple lobe epilepsy
(B) frontal lobe epilepsy
(C) temple lobe damage without seizures
(D) bifrontal disease
(E) none of the above

321. The correct formula for obtaining an IQ score is

   (A) $\dfrac{\text{mental age}}{\text{chronologic age}} \times 100$

   (B) $\dfrac{\text{chronologic age}}{\text{mental age}} \times 100$

   (C) $\dfrac{\text{chronologic age}}{\text{mental age} \times 100}$

   (D) $\dfrac{\text{mental age}}{\text{chronologic age} \times 100}$

   (E) none of the above

322. Oscillopsia is best described as

   (A) a patient's complaint that an object viewed appears to be moving
   (B) an examiner's observation of the eye movements in nystagmus
   (C) a rapid movement of the pupillary margins
   (D) a shimmering scotoma of migraine
   (E) none of the above

323. In Huntington's chorea, the most consistent biochemical abnormality in the basal ganglia is

   (A) an increase in striatal dopamine and tyrosine hydroxylase
   (B) an increase in substantia nigral dopamine and tyrosine hydroxylase
   (C) a decrease in striatal GABA and glutamic acid decarboxylase
   (D) a decrease in nigral serotonin and tryptophan hydroxylase
   (E) none of the above

324. A patient who has a basilar skull fracture complains that sounds seem uncomfortably loud. This symptom most probably represents

   (A) a conversion reaction
   (B) a partial lesion of the VIIIth cranial nerve
   (C) a lesion of the transverse temporal gyri
   (D) interruption of the lateral lemniscus
   (E) stapedius muscle paralysis

325. Hallucinations are defined as

   (A) false beliefs that can be dispelled by reason
   (B) false beliefs that cannot be dispelled by reason
   (C) false sensory perceptions based on natural stimulation of a receptor
   (D) false sensory perceptions not based on natural stimulation of a receptor
   (E) any abnormal sensations from a neurologic lesion

326. A 4-year-old previously normal girl begins to display personality changes. Her parents feel that she does not walk as well as previously. The examination discloses slight clumsiness without overt motor signs. Stretch reflexes are somewhat hypoactive. The history and examination are otherwise noncontributory. The procedure most likely to yield a specific diagnosis is which of the following?

   (A) CT scan with contrast
   (B) Neuropsychological test battery
   (C) Determination of karyotype
   (D) Lysosomal enzyme battery
   (E) Urinary amino acid screen

327. According to *DSM III-R,* which of the following is indispensable to the initial diagnosis of schizophrenia?

   (A) Hallucinations and delusions
   (B) Disorders of perception
   (C) Ideas of reference
   (D) Deterioration of mental function for at least 6 months
   (E) Depersonalization and separation of thought from self

328. Which of the following is a defense process common in obsessive compulsive disorder and in which unacceptable impulses are transformed into their opposites?

   (A) Intellectualization
   (B) Displacement
   (C) Reaction formation
   (D) Sublimation
   (E) Dissociation

DIRECTIONS: Each question below contains four suggested responses of which **one or more** is correct. Select

A	if	**1, 2, and 3**	are correct
B	if	**1 and 3**	are correct
C	if	**2 and 4**	are correct
D	if	**4**	is correct
E	if	**1, 2, 3, and 4**	are correct

329. Patients who are very likely to produce excessive countertransference in male physicians include which of the following?

    (1) Patients with manic-depressive personalities
    (2) Patients with antisocial personality disorders
    (3) Middle-aged, overweight women who are given to complaining
    (4) Attractive young women

330. The neuroleptic malignant syndrome should be treated with which of the following drugs?

    (1) Benztropine
    (2) Bromocriptine
    (3) Valproic acid
    (4) Dantrolene

331. Advantages of benzodiazepines as antianxiety agents include which of the following?

    (1) Wide gap between effective doses and lethal doses
    (2) Relatively low activation of hepatic microsomal enzymes
    (3) Long duration of action
    (4) Relatively low risk of producing physical tolerance

332. Insomnia is frequently associated with

    (1) depression
    (2) periodic movements of sleep
    (3) alcoholism
    (4) Parkinson's disease

333. Characteristic sleep disorders present in depression are

    (1) increased sleep latency
    (2) early morning awakening
    (3) repeated awakening
    (4) excessive sleep

334. Behavioral changes that occur in unmedicated Alzheimer's disease include

    (1) anorexia
    (2) delusions
    (3) insomnia
    (4) hallucinations

335. Correct statements concerning behavior modification therapy include which of the following?

    (1) It regards behavior disorders as maladaptive learning
    (2) It excludes the use of extinction techniques
    (3) It ignores psychodynamic formulations
    (4) It dispenses with desensitization techniques

336. Anticholinergic medications often cause which of the following side effects?

    (1) Dry mouth
    (2) Urinary retention
    (3) Confusion
    (4) Memory dysfunction

337. Brain regions considered part of the limbic system include

    (1) amygdala
    (2) cingulate gyrus
    (3) parahippocampal gyrus
    (4) dorsomedial thalamus

338. Delusions of grandeur are frequently associated with

    (1) mania
    (2) L-dopa psychosis
    (3) general paresis (neurosyphilis)
    (4) lead encephalopathy

339. Rapid eye movement (REM) sleep has which of the following characteristics?

    (1) It occurs cyclically throughout the night
    (2) It exhibits low-voltage fast activity in the EEG
    (3) It is associated with dreaming states
    (4) It is useful in studying causes of impotence

340. Profound memory loss with little involvement of other mental functions is produced by bilateral damage to which of the following structures?

    (1) Dorsomedial nuclei of the thalamus
    (2) Ammon's horn and dentate gyrus
    (3) Parahippocampal gyrus
    (4) Fornix

341. Sleep paralysis is associated with which of the following characteristics?

    (1) It occurs most commonly during transition to or from sleep
    (2) It is initially associated with a strong feeling of fear
    (3) It disappears when a person is called or touched
    (4) It is associated with a shift of potassium into muscle

342. Statements that correctly describe the sexual consequences of neuroanatomic lesions include which of the following?

    (1) Bilateral ventrolateral chordotomy usually causes loss of erection and ejaculation in males
    (2) Destruction of the lumbar sympathetic ganglia causes loss of ejaculation but retention of erectile capacity
    (3) Paraplegic males with complete cord transections may have intercourse and father children
    (4) Destruction of the vulva or amputation of the penis prevents orgasm

343. The ego, as defined by classical psychoanalytic formulations, is described as

    (1) incorporating the reality-testing and cognitive functions
    (2) incorporating the solution-forming, defense-creating aspects of the personality
    (3) bringing about a *modus operandi* for perceiving and relating to other persons
    (4) containing the internalized ideal of what the person should be like

344. The narcolepsy syndrome typically includes which of the following?

    (1) Irresistible sleep under inappropriate circumstances
    (2) Cataplexy
    (3) Hypnagogic hallucinations and sleep paralysis
    (4) Episodic automatic behavior with amnesia

345. Statements that correctly describe the characteristics of the amnesia associated with head trauma and a period of unconsciousness include which of the following?

    (1) The period of retrograde amnesia is usually shorter than the anterograde amnesia
    (2) After recovering consciousness, a patient may seem rational and coherent for days or weeks yet fail to remember the period of unconsciousness
    (3) Frequently, the period of retrograde amnesia shrinks during recovery
    (4) The retrograde and anterograde aspects of amnesia differ greatly in comparing posttraumatic amnesia with amnesia associated with psychomotor seizures

```
SUMMARY OF DIRECTIONS

   A        B       C       D        E
 1, 2, 3   1, 3    2, 4     4     All are
  only     only    only    only   correct
```

346. Clinical features that help to establish a diagnosis of pseudodementia in elderly patients include a tendency on the part of such patients to

    (1) complain greatly about loss of mental faculties
    (2) exhibit low attention span and concentration
    (3) exert little effort to perform on formal tests
    (4) display behavior that is poor relative to mental function

347. Abnormalities required for a diagnosis of psychosis include

    (1) poverty of thought
    (2) hallucinations
    (3) word salad speech
    (4) impaired reality testing

348. Visual hallucinations in an otherwise neurologically intact person can be induced by diseases affecting

    (1) both retinas
    (2) the bilateral vitreous humor
    (3) the optic tract
    (4) the occipital cortex

349. Psychedelic or hallucinogenic drugs are characterized by which of the following features?

    (1) They produce heightened awareness of sensory input
    (2) They have a strong tendency to cause addiction and continued use
    (3) They are generally classified as indoleamines or phenyethylamines
    (4) They are a common cause of auditory hallucinations

350. Correct statements concerning acute alcoholic inebriation include which of the following?

    (1) The odor of the breath serves as a reliable diagnostic aid
    (2) Forcing of oral fluids will reduce the blood alcohol level rapidly
    (3) Hypothermia rules out alcoholic intoxication
    (4) A blood alcohol level of 100 mg/dL constitutes legal drunkenness

351. The major antipsychotic drugs may produce adverse effects such as

    (1) hypotension and hypothermia
    (2) cardiac dysrhythmias
    (3) coma
    (4) seizures

352. Visual field defects that frequently occur in hysterical patients include which of the following?

    (1) Spiral fields on confrontation testing or perimetry
    (2) Paracentral scotomata as demonstrated on tangent screen
    (3) Tubular vision
    (4) Sector defects as demonstrated by tangent screen

353. Electroconvulsive therapy (ECT) is relatively contraindicated in which of the following conditions?

    (1) Brain tumor with edema
    (2) Cardiac arrhythmia
    (3) Evolving stroke
    (4) Epilepsy

354. As classically defined, Gerstmann's syndrome includes

    (1) right-left disorientation
    (2) digital agnosia
    (3) dyscalculia
    (4) dysgraphia

DIRECTIONS: Each group of questions below consists of lettered headings followed by a set of numbered items. For each numbered item select the **one** lettered heading with which it is **most** closely associated. Each lettered heading may be used **once, more than once, or not at all.**

Questions 355–358

For each example of a mental defense mechanism, choose the term with which it is most closely associated.

- (A) Fixation
- (B) Regression
- (C) Identification
- (D) Projection
- (E) Rationalization

355. A shy young man, formerly only moderately interested in athletics, begins to practice throwing a football and frequently organizes touch football games among acquaintances who then become friends. He has his hair cut in the style of Joe Namath and assumes that athlete's mannerisms. When he has a T-shirt imprinted with the great quarterback's number, his new friends nickname him Junior Joe

356. A young woman with a large sexual appetite is married to a man whom she loves and with whom she feels basically compatible. While he is struggling to make a success of a business, she engages in a series of affairs with a variety of men. By most criteria, the husband does not neglect his wife, who nevertheless believes that her husband is more interested in his business than in her. She ascribes her many sexual affairs to traits in her husband rather than in herself

357. A soldier inflicts a wound on himself to escape front-line duty during a war. Later he feels guilty. To ward off the painful resultant anxiety, the soldier blames his physician for neglecting to treat the wound (which is slow to heal) and tries to kill him. The soldier is not consciously aware that, in trying to kill his physician, he is attempting to destroy his own actual deficiencies

358. A 3-year-old child is fully toilet trained until a sibling is born, whereupon he starts to have toileting accidents and wet the bed at night

Questions 359–362

For each definition below, choose the term with which it is most closely associated.

- (A) Palinopsia
- (B) Visual allesthesia
- (C) Micropsia
- (D) Simultagnosia
- (E) Dyschromatopsia

359. Any defect in the perception of color

360. The persistence or recurrence of visual images after the stimulus object has been removed

361. Inability to organize a series of related pictures into the correct sequence or to understand the full meaning of a series of perceived parts

362. The displacement of a visual image from the visual field of perception into the opposite visual field

Questions 363–366

For each clinical description below, choose the term with which it is most closely identified.

- (A) Broca's aphasia
- (B) Conduction aphasia
- (C) Transcortical motor aphasia
- (D) Anomic aphasia
- (E) Transcortical sensory aphasia

363. Nonfluent spontaneous speech; good repetition and comprehension but poor naming

364. Fluent spontaneous speech; good repetition and comprehension but poor naming

365. Nonfluent spontaneous speech; good comprehension but poor repetition and variable naming

366. Fluent spontaneous speech; good comprehension, variable naming, and poor repetition

Questions 367–370

For each clinical description given below, choose the term with which it is most closely associated.

- (A) Negativism
- (B) Catalepsy
- (C) Gegenhalten
- (D) Rigidity
- (E) Catatonia

367. A patient sits quietly, mute and motionless, making no movement of body or face and showing little reaction to environmental events or stimuli, while the eyes remain fixed on a distant point; this behavior alternates with periods of overactivity

368. A patient shows slight resistance to movement but then maintains the body parts in any new position the examiner places them in

369. A patient shows plastic resistance to movement of the body parts in any direction, as if automatically resisting whatever movement the examiner imposes

370. A patient actively resists any effort to be moved or to move in response to command

Questions 371–374

For each clinical feature described below, choose the speech disorder with which it is most closely associated.

- (A) Elective mutism
- (B) Palilalia
- (C) Cluttering
- (D) Aphemia
- (E) Perseveration

371. A patient repeats the last syllable of words or the last phrase

372. A patient runs words together, omitting sounds or entire words

373. A patient talks to selected persons but, under certain circumstances, may fail to speak at all to others

374. A patient suddenly loses the ability to say any words but remains alert and able to understand, read, and write

Questions 375–380

For each stage of sleep or wakefulness listed, choose the EEG pattern with which it most nearly corresponds.

375. Normal waking record

376. Stage 1 sleep

377. Stage 2 sleep

378. Stage 3 sleep

379. Stage 4 sleep

380. REM sleep

Psychiatry Questions for Neurologists

Answers

294. The answer is B. (*Mesulam, J Neurol Neurosurg Psychiatry 39:84–89, 1976. Rowland, ed 8. p 209.*) Right parietal infarctions may present with confusional syndromes and little in the way of focal weakness or obvious signs of neglect and denial. Sometimes testing of these patients is incomplete because of their poor level of cooperation, but even after resolution of the acute state, patients often do not reveal clear signs of laterality on examination. The acute onset of confusional states in the elderly should always raise the possibility of a new infarction.

295. The answer is E. (*Cooper, ed 5. p 293.*) Chronic use of amphetamines in humans or experimental animals results in a motor syndrome characterized by repetitive, stereotyped behaviors. The production of stereotyped behaviors in this situation is believed to result from activation of the dopaminergic systems. These systems arise in either the zona compacta of the substantia nigra where they end in the striatum, or in the interpeduncular region where they play upon the medial basal olfactory and limbic structures. The amphetamine appears to act by increasing the release of dopamine and blocking its reuptake, making more of it available at the postsynaptic ending. L-dopa and methylphenidate produce a similar movement disorder.

296. The answer is B. (*Plum, ed 3. pp 306–308.*) Psychogenic unresponsiveness can be documented using several tests. If the patient is truly awake the EEG should show normal awake activity, although rarely, an EEG may be normal in coma (alpha coma). In awake patients cold water in the ear produces nystagmus with the fast component away from the ear, whereas coma patients either do not react or one or both eyes slowly deviate to the cold water in a smooth fashion. Roving eye movements cannot be simulated by awake persons as voluntary nonpursuit eye movements are saccadic. Eyelid closure in comatose patients occurs in a slow, steady fashion that awake patients cannot mimic. Deep tendon reflexes can be suppressed and can even be absent or asymmetric.

297. The answer is C. (*Dalakos, JAMA 261:2396–2399, 1989.*) It is common early in the development of the AIDS-dementia complex for patients to be depressed. It can be impossible to distinguish a reactive depression due to the presence of the disease itself from an "organic" depression due to HIV infection in the brain. Although the presence of dementia may be a helpful diagnostic clue, this may be very mild and difficult to distinguish from pseudodementia due to the depression. MRI may be helpful in making the diagnosis, whereas spinal fluid analysis may not because the HIV antigen may be present in the CSF of AIDS patients without the AIDS-dementia complex.

298. The answer is B. (*Adams RD, ed 4. pp 356–359.*) While it has long been recognized that bifrontal lesions may profoundly alter behavior and personality, the type and specificity of change remain in question. Similar changes may follow diffuse brain disease or diencephalic lesions. Patients with bifrontal lesions tend to exhibit a syndrome of apathy and indifference that reduces their regard for and concern about bodily dysfunctions. Thus, after a prefrontal lobotomy, chronic cancer patients still report pain but seem to have an attitude of indifference toward it. Yet the results are not always predictable. Some patients with bifrontal lesions become hypomanic or even have a transient state of compulsive walking and may become sexually overactive. In spite of the obvious clinical changes in behavior, patients with bifrontal lesions may score normally on IQ tests; indeed, the failure of routine IQ tests to show the specific effects of frontal lesions and frontal lobotomies was one of the historical reasons for the development of neuropsychology.

299. The answer is A. (*Victor, ed 2. pp 17, 39–52.*) Wernicke-Korsakoff syndrome is a clinical triad consisting of ataxia, oculomotor abnormalities, and mental status impairment, though all three signs may not be present. In 229 patients with the Wernicke-Korsakoff syndrome, 56 percent had a global confusional state at the time of presentation compared with 16 percent with delirium tremens, 5 percent with stupor or coma, and 10 percent without mental abnormality. Although 57 percent had a prominent memory impairment, many of these patients were also confused. Upon resolution of the acute syndrome, some patients return to normal but most evolve into a Korsakoff syndrome, characterized by a retrograde memory loss for months or years prior to onset of the illness and anterograde amnesia.

300. The answer is B. (*Kaplan, Synopsis, ed 6. p 329.*) Although schizophrenics may suffer from any type of hallucination, auditory are the most common. The occurrence of other types should trigger concern that an organic process such as drug intoxication or drug withdrawal is occurring. Visual hallucinations are not rare but other types of hallucinations are. Hallucinations are often perceived as real and patients will commonly talk to and interact with them.

301. The answer is D. (*Kaplan, Synopsis, ed 6. pp 132–133.*) There are multiple psychiatric disorders that appear to be restricted to a single culture or a few related cultures. Eating disorders such as bulimia and anorexia are very much Western-oriented problems related to Western values of body image and striving towards thinness. Other cultures have syndromes virtually unknown in most Western cultures, such as *amok,* a sudden rampage, that occurs in Malaysia or *koro,* an Asian fear that the penis will withdraw into the abdomen and cause death. Some conditions such as *nervios,* seen in Latin America, are also common in North America; this manifests as anxiety and depression.

302. The answer is C. (*Adams RD, ed 4. pp 929–930.*) The histologic feature most typical of Pick's disease is the presence of pear-shaped cortical neurons that stain pallidly with Nissl stains. The substance that appears to distend the neurons may have the appearance of a distinct body, but electron microscopy shows no distinct structure. The material consists of neurofilaments, tubules, and vesiculated endoplasmic reticulum. An intense gliosis accompanies the degenerative process in the cortical neurons. Neurofibrillar tangles and senile plaques, in contrast to their frequency in Alzheimer's disease and senile dementia, are infrequent or absent in Pick's disease. Granulovacuolar degeneration of hippocampal neurons occurs in both Alzheimer's and Pick's diseases.

303. The answer is C. (*Goetz, Am J Psychiatry 139:494–497, 1982.*) Levodopa hallucinations are fairly common but occur mainly in older patients with some degree of cognitive dysfunction, although this is not always the case. The hallucinations may be threatening, but this is extremely uncommon; they are mainly nonthreatening and visual. It is common to hallucinate about children, friendly strangers, or occasionally relatives. The hallucinations may occur in a clear or clouded sensorium and may or may not be recognized as hallucinatory in origin by the patient.

304. The answer is E. (*Adams RD, ed 4. pp 343–344.*)   Transient global amnesia occurs in middle-aged and elderly persons. The patient loses memory for a period of several hours but retains consciousness and many cognitive abilities. Although the differential diagnosis of this condition includes psychomotor seizures, the pathologic substrate remains to be identified. The best surmise is that the syndrome represents a type of transient ischemic attack involving territories irrigated by the posterior cerebral artery, which supplies the inferomedial aspect of the temporal lobes and sends arcades to the hippocampus. The syndrome usually disappears.

305. The answer is A. (*Adams RD, ed 4. pp 383–385.*)   Among other speech deficits experienced by fluent aphasic patients is the inability to correct their own speech errors and, frequently, the failure even to perceive them. Such patients produce an excess of words that are often composed of unrelated syllables—a word salad. The fluent aphasic patient retains the ability to speak with prosody—the normal inflections and rhythms—but loses the faculty to control *content* of speech. Also retained are the ability to understand certain written or spoken commands and a limited ability to communicate by gestures.

306. The answer is A. (*Adams RD, ed 4. p 483.*)   A paradox about hyperactive children (as has been stated in the past) is the observation that drugs classed as stimulants seemed to improve the cardinal symptoms of hyperactivity, impulsiveness, short attention span, and hyperexcitability. Contrarily, drugs that should have sedative action, such as the barbiturates, frequently worsen the target symptoms. One resolution of the paradox lies in the interpretation of the state of arousal. The hyperactivity might be interpreted as a reaction to a *hypo*aroused nervous system. The stimulant drug normalizes the arousal and eliminates the compensating overactive behavior. Barbiturates would further reduce the state of arousal and cause the target symptoms to become correspondingly worse. This formulation might aid in selecting children who could benefit from stimulant medication by subjecting them to tests for hypoarousal.

307. The answer is D. (*Kaplan, Comprehensive Textbook, ed 5. p 719.*)   The chronic abuse of amphetamines may produce a paranoid psychosis that very closely resembles the naturally occurring disease. This psychosis is characterized by paranoid ideation, many stereotypies and mannerisms, hallucinations, and, in the later stages, withdrawal and apathy. Affective flattening and disorders of thought association, which characterize the naturally occurring disease, are absent with the amphetamine-associated psychosis. Amphetamine administration to other primates produces the same motor disturbances seen in humans.

308. The answer is D. (*Kaplan, Comprehensive Textbook, ed 5. pp 1622–1624.*)   Akathisia, often a prominent feature of parkinsonism or drug-induced movement disorders, consists of an irresistible restlessness that compels a patient to shift position or to move around. It is a peculiar state because the patient has an odd mixture of hypokinesia that is broken by compelling movement. Some patients pace incessantly, albeit displaying the parkinsonian gait. The restless legs syndrome, and perhaps to a lesser extent the hyperkinetic child syndrome, together with the manic phase of manic-depressive psychosis all offer parallels to akathisia. Thus, patients with the restless legs syndrome, in which the legs wander aimlessly around at night and prevent sleep, also describe the same irresistible need to move arising in the limbs or muscles that characterizes the parkinsonian patient with akathisia. Akathisia is the most common movement disorder associated with psychotropic medication, including the phenothiazines, butyrophenones, and reserpine.

309. The answer is A. (*Kaplan, Comprehensive Textbook, ed 5. p 766.*)   Even before the advent of psychotropic medications, movement disorders were frequently observed in schizophrenic patients. These usually take the form of stereotypies or mannerisms. These movements appear most frequently in catatonic schizophrenia and suggest a poor prognosis. The movements rarely take the form of skilled or graceful acts—rather they appear ungainly, clumsy, and awkward. The movement pattern of patients may deteriorate over time. The movements not only appear during walking, but often the walking itself involves stereotypies and mannerisms.

310. **The answer is C.** (*Rowland, ed 8. pp 12–13.*) Characteristically, the apraxic patient is unable to execute a movement on command but may do so automatically. Thus, the patient described in the question was unable to protrude his tongue when asked but licked his lips automatically, which indicates that the tongue was not actually paralyzed. Indeed, proof of the ability of a body part to act automatically or inadvertently is necessary to separate apraxia from paralysis. While this patient also could have been negative or hysterical, the dysarthria and possible dysphasia clearly suggest that he may have a lesion of the dominant hemisphere that would predispose to apraxia. Cortico-bulbar tract interruption would cause paralysis rather than apraxia.

311. **The answer is E.** (*Rowland, ed 8. pp 831–832.*) Thyrotoxic myopathy may present with weakness but few other physical or laboratory signs. The affected patient may have none of the classic historical or physical findings of hyperthyroidism. Standard laboratory tests such as EMG and muscle biopsy may fail to show distinct abnormalities. All patients with chronic unexplained weakness should have thyroid function studies. This diagnosable and potentially treatable cause of weakness should not be overlooked. The blood tests for thyroid function are very inexpensive and carry no risk for the patient other than those associated with venipunctures. Since the threat to life arises from involvement of cardiac or respiratory muscles, the affected patient should be carefully followed by clinical examination and laboratory tests for cardiac and pulmonary complications of the disease.

312. **The answer is B.** (*Kaplan, Synopsis, ed 6. pp 223–224.*) *DSM III-R* classifies all known psychiatric disorders based on purely descriptive rather than theoretical terms. It contains five axes. Axis I contains the clinical syndromes while axis II describes the developmental and personality disorders. Axis III lists all physical disorders whether related or not, axis IV rates psychosocial stressors, and axis V is a global assessment of the patient's highest level of function during the preceding year. Thus axes I and II are the only ones that list psychiatric diagnoses.

313. **The answer is D.** (*Kaplan, Synopsis, ed 6. p 410.*) Posttraumatic stress disorder covers a wide range of problems that occur after severe psychological trauma. It was called "shell shock" during World War I but not adequately studied until the Vietnam War. The abnormality extends to all traumatizing events "outside the range of usual human experience, that would be markedly distressing to almost anyone," such as incest, rape, seeing a murder, and so on. The subject often reexperiences the event and undergoes a process of numbing. Dissociative states, in which patients experience fugue states, may occur, as well as panic, guilt, humiliation, illusions, and delusions. Sometimes the dissociative episodes may be described in ways that suggest complex partial seizures.

314. **The answer is C.** (*Rowland, ed 8. p 209.*) Anosognosia is most characteristic in patients with lesions of the right posterior parasylvian area in approximately the same zone that isolated lesions of the opposite hemisphere cause receptive aphasia, or Gerstmann's syndrome. Babinski coined the term to apply to a patient with a left hemiplegia who was unaware of the deficit. Clinicopathologic correlation has repeatedly confirmed the association between posterior right parietal and parasylvian lesions and unawareness of either sensory stimuli or hemiplegia on the left side. This type of anosognosia does not occur with lesions elsewhere in the hemispheres. The term *anosognosia* sometimes is applied to any pathologic unawareness of disease, but in the context of Babinski's original description it implies a specific location of the lesion and a specific neurologic deficit.

315. **The answer is D.** (*Rowland, ed 8. p 209.*) A type of dressing apraxia is characteristic in patients with right posterior parasylvian area lesions. Such patients cannot orient their clothes in preparation

for dressing. For example, they may attempt to put a shirt or blouse on backwards. This type of dressing apraxia aids in localizing the site of the lesion to the right hemisphere and to the posterior parasylvian region of that hemisphere. Other signs of the lesion, such as a left homonymous hemianopia, usually appear. The dressing apraxia may be related to the inability of patients with a right hemisphere lesion to understand spatial concepts that permit them to relate the form and shape of their clothes to the form and shape of their own body. This particular syndrome of dressing apraxia is indicative of a lesion site rather than a lesion type. Any destructive lesion of the right posterior parasylvian area—whether infarct, hemorrhage, abscess, or neoplasm—may produce the same clinical deficit.

316. **The answer is D.** (*Rowland, ed 8. p 650.*) Huntington's disease is a triad of chorea, dementia, and behavioral abnormalities. Aggression, schizophrenic psychoses and depression culminating in suicide all may occur, sometimes preceding the chorea. Although HD is an autosomal dominant genetic disease, family history may be inaccurate. In some cases the gene-carrying parent died before disease onset. In others the affected parent disappeared. Occasionally a biologic parent may be unknown. Rigidity, limb dyskinesias, and normal brain imaging studies all may occur in both HD and TD, as the rigidity is drug-induced. Dementia, however, is not part of the picture in any purely psychiatric disorder. Its presence would indicate HD.

317. **The answer is C.** (*Adams RD, ed 4. p 90.*) Writer's cramp is a form of focal dystonia in which the hand involuntarily cramps when writing. There are two forms of this condition. In simple writer's cramp, the dystonia occurs with writing but with no other maneuvers. In the other form, various activities will induce the dystonia. Similar conditions occur in skilled workers who perform repetitive maneuvers, such as musicians. Of note in writer's cramp is the fact that it transfers sides in a significant percentage of those persons who learn to write using their unaffected hand.

318. **The answer is A.** (*Adams RD, ed 4. p 368.*) This patient clearly suffers from a visual anosognosia. The occurrence of cortical blindness (normal pupils) with denial of the problem is the syndrome of Anton, due to posterior cerebral infarction involving the occipital cortex and the visual association cortex as well. The denial is very similar to that seen with right middle cerebral artery infarcts in which patients deny their weakness and occasionally even deny body parts.

319. **The answer is D.** (*Kaplan, Synopsis, ed 6. p 71.*) The syndrome described is the human analogue to the Klüver-Bucy syndrome in primates. If both medial temporal lobes are resected in a primate, it becomes apathetic and hypersexual and develops agnosias, so that the animal mouths every object. In humans the syndrome is somewhat different and includes aphasia, dementia, and bulimia without the constant mouthing of objects. A bilateral medial temporal lobe deficit in humans is most likely to occur with herpes simplex encephalitis.

320. **The answer is E.** (*Weiger, J Psychiatr Res 22:85–98, 1988.*) Directed rage attacks are not a feature of epilepsy. While rare convulsions involve violence, these are typically undirected attacks. In patients with interictal violent behavior, there tends to be a strong emotional feeling attached—either justification or remorse—whereas this patient was only sometimes remorseful. He always attacked a single person, which suggests an emotion-related problem rather than a nonspecific convulsive attack. After episodic rage attacks patients may have variable degrees of amnesia.

321. **The answer is A.** (*Kaplan, Synopsis, ed 6. p 497.*) The IQ (intelligence quotient) was originally obtained by dividing the mental age by the chronologic age and multiplying by 100. The mental age is a statistical artifact of the test procedure. To develop an IQ test, an examiner gives test items to normal persons of various ages. The average score achieved by the children at each age is then called the *mental age*. A mental age of 5 means that the individual made the same score on the test items as the 5-year-old children who previously took the test. If a patient scores comparably to

other 5 year olds and has a chronologic age of 5 years, the quotient is 5/5 × 100, or 100. If an individual scores comparably to other 5 year olds but is 6 years of age, the IQ becomes 5/6 × 100, or 83. Multiplying by 100 merely converts what could be a decimal to a more convenient number. The person with an impaired brain or less knowledge will score similar to younger persons and thus will have a lower mental age and a lower IQ. The person with a superior brain or more knowledge will score comparably to older persons and thus have a higher IQ. The Wechsler Adult Intelligence Scale (WAIS) now uses the term *IQ* to refer to a statistically derived number.

322. The answer is A. (*Adams RD, ed 4. p 219.*) Oscillopsia refers to a patient's complaint that the object viewed appears to move or to oscillate. It is one of the symptoms of nystagmus acquired after infancy. Patients with early acquired or congenital nystagmus do not complain of oscillopsia, even though they may have extreme and chaotic eye movements. Thus, the absence or presence of oscillopsia gives some evidence as to the time of onset of the nystagmus. Frequently, patients will fail to complain spontaneously of oscillopsia but will acknowledge it upon questioning.

323. The answer is C. (*Rowland, ed 8. pp 647–650.*) The most consistent biochemical abnormality in the basal ganglia in Huntington's chorea is a decrease in the γ-aminobutyric acid (GABA) content of the striatum. Accompanying the decrease in GABA is a decrease in glutamic acid decarboxylase, the enzyme responsible for the synthesis of GABA. Another frequent abnormality in the striatum is a decrease in acetylcholine and its synthetic enzyme, choline acetyl transferase, but this finding is less consistent than the loss of the GABA system. Thus, one would suppose that degeneration of the GABAergic neurons precedes the loss of the cholinergic neurons. These neurons are as yet inconclusively defined but they may consist of small interneurons in the striatum.

324. The answer is E. (*Adams RD, ed 4. pp 695–696, 1082.*) A patient who complains of uncomfortable loudness of sounds (hyperacusis) may have paralysis of the stapedius muscle. This tiny muscle dampens the vibrations of the ossicles and may act as a protective mechanism or modulator of the amplitude of vibrations transmitted to the inner ear. The stapedius muscle receives its innervation from the VIIth nerve. Either the VIIth nerve or its stapedius branch may be damaged by a basilar skull fracture. Trauma may also affect hearing by disarticulating the ossicles; this results in fuzzing or duplication of sound (diplacusis), which may also reflect damage to the inner ear.

325. The answer is D. (*Kaplan, Comprehensive Textbook, ed 5. pp 570–572.*) Hallucinations are false sensory perceptions not based on natural stimulation of a receptor. Hallucinations may, however, be triggered by a structural or biochemical lesion of the relevant areas of the brain. For example, an arteriovenous malformation of an occipital lobe may produce hallucinations of formed or unformed images. In alcoholic persons, the hyperexcitable state of the neurons following the withdrawal of the depressant action of alcohol may trigger hallucinations; auditory hallucinations may persist in such persons. On the other hand, the hallucinations of schizophrenia (such as visions of God, or voices) cannot be explained on the basis of any known structural or biochemical lesion. Hallucinations contrast with illusions, which are false sensory perceptions based on natural stimulation of a receptor. For example, a line may appear longer than another line of equal length because of its relation to a background grid. In this case, the natural receptor functions normally, yet a perceptual error, an illusion, has occurred.

326. The answer is D. (*Adams RD, ed 4. p 795.*) A child with personality changes, gait disturbance, and hypoactive stretch reflexes may be showing signs of a progressive degenerative disease. The combination of a possible central and peripheral nervous system disorder as evidenced by these clinical findings should, first of all, suggest metachromatic leukodystrophy. Because the child described in the question is a girl, Pelizaeus-Merzbacher disease and adrenoleukodystrophy are virtually excluded because both have a sex-linked recessive inheritance pattern. The child's age of 4 years excludes Krabbe's globoid leukodystrophy and her normal somatotype virtually rules out a mucopolysaccharidosis. The normal physical appearance of the child and the absence of malformations, along with the normal period of development, all virtually exclude the possibility of a chromosomal error. The normal retina argues against cerebromacular degeneration. Her previously normal mental state and lack of seizures exclude the usual amino acid disorders. The lysosomal enzyme battery will include tests for deficiency of aryl sulfatase A, which will lead to the specific diagnosis of metachromatic leukodystrophy.

327. The answer is D. (*Kaplan, Synopsis, ed 6. p 333.*)   *DSM III-R* lists deterioration of mental function as the one indispensable criterion for the diagnosis of schizophrenia. Other symptoms include disturbances in thought form and content, perception, affect, sense of self, and relation to the external world. Although schizophrenia almost always involves several of these symptoms, none is necessarily consistently present at the time of the initial diagnosis. Therefore, none is an indispensable criterion for the diagnosis of schizophrenia. *DSM III-R* further states that the deterioration of mental function must have persisted for at least 6 months. The purpose of this stipulation is to exclude the schizophreniform disorders whose symptoms, although similar to schizophrenia, have different external correlates, such as the likelihood of recovery to premorbid levels and lack of a family history. The schizophreniform disorders run the gamut from prodromal through active and residual phases in time periods ranging from 2 weeks to 6 months. Illnesses that begin in older adults also are excluded from schizophrenia and are classified as atypical psychoses.

328. The answer is C. (*Kaplan, Synopsis, ed 6. p 376.*)   Displacement refers to a process in which an emotion related to one idea or object is shifted to another that bears some resemblance to the original. Sublimation is a defense process that allows one to achieve gratification through achievement of more acceptable goals than those actually desired. Dissociation is a major alteration of a person's character to avoid emotional distress, often without memory for the alteration, as with fugue states. Intellectualization is a defense process in which emotions are avoided through a highly rationalized and intellectual interpretation of events.

329. The answer is E (all). (*Kaplan, Comprehensive Textbook, ed 6. pp 1448–1449.*)   Many patients will incite an excessive emotional response—countertransference, as Freud called it—in their physicians. The intensity of the response may then interfere with the physician's objectivity, professional judgment, and ability to treat the patient. Among these patients are those who suffer from manic-depressive psychosis. When manic, they may focus with unremitting zeal on generating antagonisms and difficulties. When depressed, they become mute and withdrawn, manifesting tenacious expressions of pain and anguish, powerless to help themselves or others. For male physicians, the nonpsychotic, overweight, complaining, pain-ridden woman in her forties offers a similar challenge because she is almost invariably depressed. A different problem is presented by the young, physically attractive sociopathic woman who, seemingly cheerful, rational, contrite, and cooperative while hospitalized, may excite the rescue fantasies of the physician who feels he has finally found a responsive patient. Deceived into placing undue trust in his patient, the physician unwisely grants her a weekend pass from the hospital, whereupon she resumes her sociopathic behavior. A similar countertransference may occur on the part of a physician for the attractive young woman who may excite his sexual fantasies, causing the physician to become entrapped in her seductive behavior.

330. The answer is C (2, 4). (*Mueller, Psychosomatics 26:654–662, 1985.*)   The neuroleptic malignant syndrome is a life-threatening complication of dopamine-blocking drugs and also sometimes seen with abrupt withdrawal of L-dopa in Parkinson's disease. It is characterized by high fevers without other explanation, extrapyramidal signs (usually rigidity), autonomic instability, and mental status changes, usually obtundation. The object of treatment is to offset the dopamine deficiency, which is most readily done with a direct dopamine agonist. Dantrolene acts peripherally to loosen the muscles and thereby reduce the fever and the often massive elevations of CPK. Because dantrolene does not act on the brain, where the problem is, it is a second-line drug after bromocriptine or one to be used in concert with bromocriptine.

331. **The answer is E (all).** (*Kaplan, Comprehensive Textbook, ed 5. pp 1580–1583.*) Benzodiazepines have become the most frequently prescribed antianxiety medication. Although overused, they do have specific advantages when they are indicated. These advantages include a wide gap between the effective and lethal doses, low activation of hepatic microsomal enzymes, long duration of action (around 24 h), and relatively low production of physical tolerance. The low activation of hepatic microsomal enzymes means that the benzodiazepines produce little alteration in the metabolism of drugs such as coumarin, antipsychotic agents, tricyclic antidepressants, and certain anticonvulsants, all of which are acted on by these enzymes. The benzodiazepines will, however, add to the pharmacologic effects of other medications, such as increasing the sedation caused by anticonvulsants or alcohol.

332. **The answer is E (all).** (*Rowland, ed 8. pp 810–812.*) Insomnia is a clinically defined problem of initiating or maintaining sleep. It is a common complaint of patients. Although it is often present in patients with depression and mania, only the former complain. It occurs in many neurologic disorders, including periodic movement of sleep, and is a frequent problem for patients with Parkinson's disease. Alcohol and other depressant drugs are a common cause as well.

333. **The answer is A (1, 2, 3).** (*Kaplan, Synopsis, ed 6. p 1109.*) Mood disorders are frequently associated with sleep disorders. The severity of the sleep disorder frequently parallels that of the mood disorder. Depression is associated with normal or increased latency of falling asleep, repeated awakenings during the night, and early morning awakenings. Patients also have shorter-than-normal latencies for developing REM sleep.

334. **The answer is E (all).** (*Kaplan, Synopsis, ed 6. pp 612–613.*) Alzheimer's disease is clinically categorized by the NINCDS and American Association for Retired Persons (AARP) as *definite, probable,* or *possible.* Definite diagnosis requires histopathology. Probable diagnosis requires an abnormal score on a standardized mental status examination, progressive worsening of memory, impaired learning capability, "cortical dysfunction" (language disorder, apraxia), the absence of other explanations, and the absence of the disturbance of consciousness. Associated with the memory and cognitive dysfunction are a host of behavioral changes that include depression, insomnia, loss of social graces, delusions, illusions, hallucinations, weight loss, appetite alterations, and sleep disorders. In addition, nonmental changes may occur, such as mild parkinsonism and myoclonus.

335. **The answer is B (1, 3).** (*Kaplan, Comprehensive Textbook, ed 5. pp 1462–1463.*) Behavior modification is a system of therapy that regards maladaptive behavior as a type of learning disorder. It is assumed that the behavior is perpetuated by environmental contingencies that should be investigated. Behavior therapists attempt neither to formulate the psychodynamics of the behavior nor to rely on insight techniques. They do use extinction techniques (the ignoring by staff and family of unwanted behavior), although there is disagreement about their role. Behavior modification therapists also have tried to treat phobias by desensitization. After a therapist has determined the stimuli that elicit the unwanted behavior, patient and therapist construct a series of scenes that recapitulate the precipitating stimuli. After the patient has been taught deep muscular relaxation, the offending stimulus is conjured by means of mental images. The muscular relaxation is considered to be the means for deconditioning the anxiety initiated by the stimulus.

336. **The answer is E (all).** (*Gilman AG, ed 8. pp 153, 476.*) Acetylcholine receptors are nicotinic (found in skeletal muscle) and muscarinic (central and peripheral). Anticholinergic drugs are antimuscarinic and have a plethora of side effects. They block innervation of the salivary glands and

thus cause dryness of the mouth. They inhibit the brain's cholinergic system, which is important in memory, so that memory impairment is relatively common among the elderly. Antimuscarinic drugs inhibit detrussor muscle contraction, thereby increasing the possibility of urinary retention. The drugs also may produce confusion and hallucinations.

337.   The answer is A (1, 2, 3).   *(Adams RD, ed 4. p 409.)*   The limbic region is not a clearly defined anatomic structure. It is the part of the brain that forms a ring around the corpus callosum and upper brainstem and is involved in emotional control. Because it is not clearly defined anatomically, different authors may include different structures, but all authors include the amygdala; the cingulate, parahippocampal, and dentate gyri; the hippocampal formation; the subcallosal gyrus; and the paraolfactory area. Diseases affecting these areas of the brain will cause emotional and cognitive changes, as in the paraneoplastic syndrome limbic encephalitis.

338.   The answer is B (1, 3).   *(Adams RD, ed 4. pp 576–578, 911.)*   Mania is associated with feelings of unbounded energy and frequently with delusions of omnipotence or omniscience. General paresis of the insane was a common cause of chronic psychiatric hospitalization in the preantibiotic era, and these patients frequently developed, in addition to a slowly progressive dementia, a delusional system in which they were kings or presidents with great powers. L-Dopa produces a wide variety of psychoses, but the most common are paranoid. Lead causes apathy and irritability.

339.   The answer is E (all).   *(Rowland, ed 8. pp 808–810.)*   Rapid eye movement (REM) sleep occurs in cycles of about 90 min throughout the night. The REM state of sleep is characterized by rapid eye movements, a low-voltage fast EEG pattern, irregular breathing and pulse, blood pressure elevation, and diminished muscle tone. Penile erection occurs automatically, a fact that can be used to distinguish functional from organic impotence by demonstrating the integrity of the neural and vascular apparatus for erection. When awakened from REM sleep, a person usually reports dreaming; however, those awakened from non-REM sleep do not. REM sleep occupies a much greater percentage of sleep time in young infants than in adults. From the age of 3 to 5 years to senility, it occupies about 20 percent of sleep time. However, whether or not young infants dream remains a matter of conjecture.

340.   The answer is A (1, 2, 3).   *(Adams RD, ed 4. pp 341–342.)*   Bilateral destruction of several sites in the cerebrum produces a relatively pure loss of memory but leaves cognitive functions relatively intact, including an ability to score in the normal range on IQ tests. Lesion sites that produce an amnestic syndrome include the dorsomedial nuclei of the thalamus, Ammon's horn and dentate gyrus, and the parahippocampal gyrus. Unilateral lesions cause only small or transient memory deficits. Since the fornix is an essential part of the circuitry connecting these structures, it is surprising that transection of the fornices, as has been performed in humans in an attempt to treat epilepsy, does not produce the amnestic syndrome. Although widespread bilateral loss of neurons in the cerebral cortex also causes memory loss, the affected patient will show overt signs of dementia in other areas of mental function. Thus, diffuse cerebral disease does not produce the relatively pure amnestic syndrome equated with lesions in the medial temporal lobes, hippocampal formation, or thalami.

341.   The answer is A (1, 2, 3).   *(Rowland, ed 8. p 815.)*   Sleep paralysis occurs most commonly in the narcolepsy tetrad. It appears during the transition phases of wakefulness-to-sleep and of sleep-to-wakefulness. At the onset it frequently creates fear in the subject, but with repeated episodes patients learn to deal with the phenomenon. It is most frequent when a patient is falling asleep and may be accompanied by dreams, the so-called hypnagogic hallucinations. The striking feature of sleep paralysis is its instantaneous disappearance when the patient is touched or hears a sound. This fact indicates that the disorder is related to a disturbance in the central nervous system rather than to a sudden potassium shift in muscle, which would be too slow to explain so rapid an arousal from sleep paralysis. However, patients with periodic paralysis who have a disturbance in potassium balance also may experience severe fright and anxiety because of a similar feeling of helplessness during their muscular paralysis.

342. The answer is A (1, 2, 3). (*Adams RD, ed 4. pp 441–442.*) In the male, bilateral destruction of the lumbar sympathetic ganglia, particularly the second one, leads to loss of ejaculation but retention of erectile capacity. Erectile capacity requires the integrity of the parasympathetic fibers that travel from the sacral cord to dilate the arterioles of the penis, which allow the penis to fill with blood. In addition, the axons of the pudendal nerve innervate the periurethral muscles, which compress the draining veins of the penis. The fibers that convey sexual sensation and the suprasegmental fibers, which mediate the psychic and brain influences on the genitalia, travel in the ventrolateral quadrant of the spinal cord. Thus, ventrolateral chordotomy causes loss of erection and ejaculation in males and loss of orgasmic capacity in females. Even after vulvectomy or loss of the penis, patients may still experience sexual sensation and even orgasm. A different situation prevails following *complete* cord transection with paraplegia. As part of the exaggeration of certain reflexes after cord transection, erection may be produced by stimulation of the penis and, in fact, priapism may occur as a troublesome complication. Once the paraplegic patient has achieved erection, intercourse and ejaculation can take place.

343. The answer is A (1, 2, 3). (*Kaplan, Comprehensive Textbook, ed 5. pp 372–374.*) Freud, upon whose work much of classical psychoanalytic theory rests, divided the personality into the id, ego, and superego. The id consists of the instinctual drives (which reflect primary biologic needs for food, sexuality, sleep) and the vegetative, homeostatic, and visceral functions. The primitive drives related to these functions produce states of emotion, aggression, fear, pleasure, and satisfaction. The ego is the reality-testing self that deals with the environment through conscious, cognitive processes. It brings about a *modus operandi* for psychosocial adaptation that establishes the manner in which persons both perceive themselves in relation to other persons and relate towards them. The superego, on the other hand, incorporates the ego ideal—the internalized model of what persons think they should be like, as established by childhood perceptions of the kind of person they perceive authority figures wanted them to be.

344. The answer is E (all). (*Kaplan, Comprehensive Textbook, ed 5. pp 1116–1117.*) In addition to the well-known narcolepsy tetrad of symptoms including pathologic sleep, cataplexy, hypnagogic hallucinations, and sleep paralysis, narcoleptic persons often may exhibit episodes of automatic behavior. These episodes might be interpreted as daytime somnambulism. Such persons may remember the beginning of such an attack, then gradually lose awareness of surroundings but continue to perform routine tasks. They may answer simple questions or may burst out with a series of irrelevant words or phrases. These episodes should be distinguished from fugue states, psychomotor seizures, and psychotic intervals. Such attacks of clouding of the sensorium, occurring in more than half of the affected patients, are more common than the better-known episodes of sleep paralysis and hypnagogic hallucinations. Moreover, the classic features of narcolepsy may appear asynchronously over a period of several years, which makes a diagnosis very difficult in patients with only partial expressions of the syndrome. The full expression of the four classic features occurs in only about 10 percent of narcoleptic patients.

345. The answer is A (1, 2, 3). (*Rowland, ed 8. p 375.*) Amnesia following head injuries and amnesia following psychomotor seizures closely resemble each other in a qualitative sense. In either instance, patients show a period of ictal amnesia with retrograde and anterograde components. The retrograde amnesia is shorter than the anterograde and tends to shrink as the patient recovers. During the recovery phase, the patient will display a period of seemingly rational, responsive behavior and consciousness but later may be unable to recall this period of time. For the posttraumatic patient, this period may last days or weeks, but lasts only briefly after the usual psychomotor seizure. The patient who has suffered epileptic status will have a memory deficit quantitatively and qualitatively like that of a posttraumatic patient.

346.   The answer is B (1, 3). (*Kaplan, Comprehensive Textbook, ed 5. p 340.*)   Patients with pseudodementia may manifest many features that suggest an organic brain disorder, although their disorder is actually functional. While no absolute distinction can be made, several features suggest pseudodementia. These include a tendency of such patients to dwell upon their seeming mental incapacity, whereas the organic patient often lacks an appreciation of the degree of disability. The patient with pseudodementia displays little effort or interest in formal testing, preferring to respond with "I don't know," whereas the organic patient usually tries to perform well. In addition, patients with pseudodementia will have normal attention span and ability to concentrate and will retain a high level of successful general behavior in relation to the apparent loss of intellectual function.

347.   The answer is D (4). (*Kaplan, Synopsis, ed 6. p 218.*)   Psychosis is defined as an inability to distinguish fantasy from reality. This is generally associated with several other problems, including the other choices listed in the question. Any particular psychosis, however, might exclude one or more of the listed choices except for impaired reality testing.

348.   The answer is E (all). (*Adams RD, ed 4. p 369.*)   Loss of vision occurs with lesions in any of the listed regions. Visual hallucinations may occur in any patient who is blind. If hallucinations are sudden in onset, one should suspect a brain process, typically in the occipital lobe. These are generally elementary hallucinations such as colors and geometric forms. Hallucinations arising from the visual association cortex are complex; for example, they may involve people and landscapes. With progressive blindness, anywhere in the visual system, one may experience purely visual hallucinations of elementary or complex types. These occur in the blind regions, however, so that a patient with a homonymous hemianopia experiences hallucinations only in the affected field, whereas patients with macular disease see hallucinations in all quadrants.

349.   The answer is B (1, 3). (*Kaplan, Synopsis, ed 6. pp 308–310.*)   Although the psychedelic drugs are difficult to define, they all act to produce a heightened awareness of sensory input; in many instances they cause hallucinations that affect various senses. However, auditory hallucinations are rare in contrast to the state of auditory hallucinosis that follows prolonged use of alcohol. The psychedelic drugs, which, in general, are indoleamines or phenylethylamines, lack strong addictive properties, and recreational users eventually tend to lose interest in them. A high degree of tolerance develops for lysergic acid diethylamide (LSD). Withdrawal symptoms are absent or slight, and fatal intoxication is rare, although severe hallucinations while under the influence of LSD may lead to suicide.

350.   The answer is D (4). (*Rowland, ed 8. p 899.*)   An alcohol blood level of 100 mg/dL constitutes legal drunkenness, while blood levels of 50 to 100 mg/dL together with behavioral evidence of inebriation may still support the diagnosis. Breath odor is an unreliable guide to the degree of acute alcoholic intoxication. Indeed, the offensive "drinker's breath" may result from products in the ingested fluid other than the alcohol. Even in an inebriated patient, the clinical state may result from another problem, like a subdural hematoma. Hypothermia is characteristic of a comatose patient with alcoholic intoxication but also may be associated with other causes of coma. Since the metabolism of alcohol proceeds at a nearly constant rate, fluid ingestion fails to increase the rate of recovery from acute alcohol intoxication.

351.   The answer is E (all). (*Kaplan, Comprehensive Textbook, ed 5. pp 1620–1626.*)   Among the toxic effects common to the major antipsychotic drugs are hypotension and hypothermia, cardiac dysrhythmias, coma, and seizures. The cardiac dysrhythmias may, on rare occasions, result in unexpected death. The other adverse effects can be limited by avoiding an overdose of the drug, by reducing the dose if an adverse effect occurs, or by instituting appropriate remedial therapy. Hypotension is particularly bothersome in the aged patient or in a patient with cerebrovascular disease, because the hypotension may induce transient ischemic attacks or a frank stroke. In epileptic patients who may require antipsychotic medication, the anticonvulsant and antipsychotic medications when combined may produce an addictive sedative effect, but the anticonvulsant medication should be maintained.

352.　The answer is B (1, 3). (*Adams RD, ed 4. pp 201–222.*)　The visual field defects that are typical of hysteria consist of tubular vision and spiral fields. A patient with tubular vision has only a narrow central field of vision, as if looking through a tube. In the periphery of the visual field—which extends medially to 60 degrees from the midpoint and laterally to 80 degrees—the patient is blind. Geometrically, of course, the visual field of the normal person must expand as the visual target moves further away from the eye. In the hysterical patient with spiral fields, the size of the field diminishes as the probing of the periphery continues, which causes a continually reducing spiral of vision. Paracentral scotomata and sector defects, as demonstrated by tangent screens, occur with retinal or optic nerve lesions and provide evidence of an organic type of visual disturbance.

353.　The answer is A (1, 2, 3). (*Kaplan, Synopsis, ed 6. pp 669–672.*)　ECT is an effective therapy for depression and occasionally is used in the treatment of mania and certain forms of schizophrenia. It ameliorates the motor signs of Parkinson's disease for variable periods of time. Contraindications are few. Since seizures increase blood flow and transiently alter the blood-brain barrier, the presence of a tumor or a new stroke is a relative contraindication for fear of worsening a deficit. Cardiac rhythm disturbances may be triggered by the massive sympathetic response to the ECT. Seizure disorders are not contraindications, although the risk of potentially inducing status epilepticus must be kept in mind by the anesthesiologist.

354.　The answer is E (all). (*Adams RD, ed 4. pp 365–366.*)　Gerstmann's syndrome consists of right-left disorientation, digital agnosia, dyscalculia, and dysgraphia. The value of the syndrome is that it combines four elements that superficially seem to bear no necessary relationship to each other into a clinical entity that may indicate a structural lesion in a patient with a mature brain. (The syndrome also can be seen in part as a feature of the developing brain of the young child.) Patients with Gerstmann's syndrome most commonly have a lesion of the left posterior parasylvian area. Because of the location of the lesion, these patients in addition may show some element of dysphasia. If the lesion extends deep into the geniculocalcarine tract, a contralateral homonymous visual field defect may also be present. Gerstmann's syndrome, however, may occur with lesions distant from the posterior parasylvian area. Therefore, the coincidence of the four elements of the syndrome is suggestive, rather than pathognomonic, of a lesion in the posterior parasylvian area.

355–358.　The answers are: 355-C, 356-E, 357-D, 358-B. (*Kaplan, Comprehensive Textbook, ed 5. pp 362–363, 375–376, 1451–1452.*)　In 1896, Freud published his first work on defense mechanisms. Since that time, many other authors, chiefly psychoanalysts, have added to the literature. Kolb has listed 21 basic mental mechanisms and defensive processes. While all can be found in both mentally healthy and mentally ill persons, some mechanisms are more commonly used by mentally ill people, e.g., unrealistic projection, denial, symbolization, and the acting out of conflicts. Also, the mentally ill person uses only a few defenses in a stereotyped nonadaptive way and possesses relatively few appropriately adaptive mechanisms. These include sublimation (the transfer of psychic energy to behavior beneficial to the self or society), altruism, conscious control, and ego-strengthening identification, as exemplified by the Joe Namath admirer described in the question.

　　In contrast, the soldier described in the question, who blamed the physician for his own defection from duty, was using a highly maladaptive, unrealistic projection to save himself from his own painful guilt. Such a projection can lead to murder and other dangerous and self-defeating behavior.

Rationalization is a common mental mechanism used by nearly everyone at some time or another. Frequently, the strongest motives for our behavior are based on greed, gluttony, anger, or other self-centered urges. We like to think, however, that we are rational and fair; therefore, we hide from ourselves the selfish nature of many of our acts and focus on a partial truth (or the semblance of truth) in a situation as the main reason for our behavior. Saving our self-image may cause more trouble than it is worth, for we fail to appreciate where our best interests lie. The young wife described in the question, who rationalized her promiscuity, failed to fully acknowledge a trait she felt guilty about and blamed her husband. This failure, in turn, blocked her search for other solutions that might have strengthened rather than jeopardized her marriage.

Regression is another common defense mechanism of everyday life and frequently occurs during stress. Reverting to a behavior pattern of an earlier developmental period represents an unconscious bid for another person to take care of the sufferer as a young child or infant. The regression, if temporary, can be used to gather strength to fight the battles of the real world on a later occasion. However, continued neglect of developmental problems will, in due course, lead to mental illness.

Mechanisms of defense are subjects for scrutiny in patients undergoing psychoanalysis or dynamic psychotherapy. The rationale behind such exploration is that patients will be able to bring their intelligence to bear on their problems rather than mindlessly engaging in repetitive, destructive behavior whose sole legacy is unhappiness and failure.

359–362. The answers are: 359-E, 360-A, 361-D, 362-B.   (*Adams RD, ed 4. pp 368–369.*)   Dyschromatopsia refers to any disturbance in the perception of color. A defect in color perception will accompany virtually any defect of visual perception due to a cerebral lesion. Thus, color testing is a very sensitive test of visual function. The disorders in color perception may take the form of achromatopsia (lack of color vision), metachromatopsia (change in color perception so that green, for example, may appear as brown), and monochromatopsia (perception of all visual objects as having one color—for example cyanopsia, or blue vision).

Palinopsia refers to the persistence of visual images after removal of the visual stimulus. The object previously seen will persist, often in very vivid form, for minutes or hours. A single object may appear as a chain of many objects (polyopsia). The palinoptic image usually appears in visual fields that are only partially affected rather than completely blind. The causative brain lesions usually are severely destructive, such as infarcts or neoplasms, and will cause other visual and neurologic manifestations as well.

Simultagnosia refers to the inability to organize a series of related pictures into the correct sequence or to understand the meaning of a series of related parts. If given a series of pictures that tells a story, an affected patient is unable to order them into the story-telling sequence but tends to perceive them as a series of independent events. In a series of dots that forms a letter, the patient may see the dots but fail to perceive them as forming a letter. In other words, the patient fails to see the simultaneous relationship of visual sequences.

Visual allesthesia refers to the displacement of a visual image from the visual field of perception into the opposite field. The displacement occurs from the affected to the nonaffected field. Allesthesia also occurs in other sensory modalities, such as in the displacement of tactile stimuli.

363–366. The answers are: 363-C, 364-D, 365-A, 366-B.   (*Adams RD, ed 4. pp 382–388.*)   Aphasias can be characterized in several ways. The current standard format is to categorize language disorders by fluency, auditory comprehension, repetition, naming, reading, and writing. Since many aphasias occur in connection with visual or motor dysfunctions, testing has to take this into account. For example, a patient should attempt to write using the unaffected hand, which will affect penmanship but not spelling or syntax. Broca's aphasia is a paradigmatic, nonfluent aphasia in which comprehension is preserved but patients are unable to speak fluently on command, although they can utter standard phrases fluently when they are frustrated. Because of their inability to speak fluently, they cannot repeat and may have problems naming. Generally they can select the correct name for an object when given choices.

Conduction aphasia is a type in which the arcuate fasciculus is interrupted, which causes a disruption in the pathway connecting Wernicke's and Broca's areas. Speech is fluent but subject to paraphasias. Comprehension for spoken and written words is good but naming is variably affected.

The transcortical aphasias are characterized by the preservation of repetition. There are three types of transcortical aphasias: motor, sensory, and mixed. Anomic aphasia, which is not of the transcortical type, also has preserved repetition. The transcortical motor is a Broca's type of aphasia but with preserved repetition; that is, it is nonfluent with good comprehension for spoken and written words. Transcortical sensory is a Wernicke's type with preserved repetition—the patient is fluent but with impaired comprehension. Anomic aphasia is a fluent aphasia with preserved repetition, auditory comprehension, and impaired naming.

367–370.   The answers are: 367-E, 368-B, 369-C, 370-A.   (*Adams RD, ed 4. p 62. Kaplan, Synopsis, ed 6. p 217.*)   Many terms are available to describe states of immobility or resistance to movement. The patient with catatonia remains mute and statuesque, showing little reaction to the usual environmental stimuli. Catatonia was described by Kahlbaum in 1874 as a component of the disorder newly termed *dementia praecox*, later to be supplanted by Bleuler's term *schizophrenia*. He noted that it was frequently associated with flexibilitas cerea, or catalepsy.

Catalepsy refers to the condition in which patients maintain their body or limbs in whatever position, however uncomfortable, the examiner places them. While this feature is classically associated with schizophrenia, it also occurs in dementia and in the twilight states of disturbed consciousness of any origin, including seizures. Catatonia as such seems today to be a much less frequent finding in schizophrenia than formerly, judging by the older literature on the subject.

In gegenhalten (paratonia or motor negativism), patients show plastic resistance to any movement the examiner seeks to impose. The resistance, while relatively slight, remains nearly constant throughout the course of movement and will remain so regardless of where the movement starts or stops. The resistance will increase if the examiner tries to move the part too quickly, or will nearly disappear if the examiner moves the part very slowly. It may be unilateral. Gegenhalten occurs in the intact limbs of stroke victims while these patients have obtundation of consciousness, and under a variety of other conditions associated with altered consciousness.

Negativism is a general term for resistance by patients to any effort to move body parts, either passively by the examiner or in response to the examiner's command. This feature, often seen in the disturbed or retarded child, may totally defeat the parent when it pervades the whole behavior of the child. It may have partial expression in mutism and refusal to eat or dress or to go to school. The active opposition to the parental goal and the preservation of consciousness readily distinguish negativism from other resistances.

371–374.   The answers are: 371-B, 372-C, 373-A, 374-D.   (*Adams RD, ed 4. p 387. Kaplan, Synopsis, ed 6. pp 218–220, 756.*)   Disorders of verbal expression take many forms. One method of classifying them is to recognize the differences between disorders of speech, of language, and of thought. Among the disorders of speech are stuttering, cluttering, palilalia, and several varieties of mutism. Disorders of language include the aphasias, echolalia, and perseveration.

Among the speech disorders, palilalia consists of the repetition of the final word or phrase. There is an increased speed of repetition but loss in volume of voice until the sound and lip movements fade away, with a patient then making only lip movements (aphonic palilalia). Sometimes, in exasperation at the repetitions, the patient may interrupt them by an expletive. Palilalia stands in contrast to stuttering, which involves the first sound of the word.

Cluttering consists of very rapid speech with the omission of entire sounds or words, resulting in incomprehensible speech in severe cases. Patients will say something like, "torow go toping" for "Tomorrow I want to go shopping." Asked to repeat the phrase, the patient says the same incomprehensible thing but, if cautioned to slow down, can produce the words individually. Nevertheless, the patient will revert to the cluttering upon making the next statement.

Among the many forms of mutism is elective mutism. In this disorder, a patient—usually a young child—consistently fails to speak to some persons or under certain conditions but can talk normally or almost normally under other conditions. The child may fail to speak when introduced to anyone new or strange or may not speak in the presence of a particular family member or other familiar person. Particular forms of mutism include akinetic mutism, due to a lesion of the brainstem or septal region, and aphemia.

Aphemia, or pure word mutism, is a particular type of aphasia. The patient suddenly loses all speech because of a lesion in the posterior inferior frontal region (Broca's area) but remains alert and able to write, read, and behave normally. Other terms for aphemia are *pure word dumbness,* *cortical anarthria,* and *subcortical motor aphasia.*

375–380. The answers are: 375-C, 376-A, 377-E, 378-D, 379-B, 380-F. (*Adams RD, ed 4. pp 304–305.*)   The stages of normal sleep, while continuous, exhibit fairly characteristic EEG patterns that must be recognized and distinguished from patterns of abnormal sleep. It is particularly important not to interpret early drowsiness as pathologic slowing, or vertex sharp waves as spikes. The EEG of the normal, awake person shows an occipitally dominant alpha rhythm of 8 to 12 cps and low-voltage, mixed-frequency activity. As drowsiness evolves, the EEG shows some activity in the theta range, and in stage 1, the lightest stage of sleep, it shows low-voltage desynchronized activity and low-to-moderate amplitude waves in the theta range (4 to 6 cps). Such a person displays slow, roving eye movements during stage 1 sleep. The EEG pattern is similar during rapid eye movement (REM) sleep.

Stage 2 sleep features 12 to 15 cps sleep spindles and K-complexes. K-complexes consist of high-amplitude, mixed sharp-slow waves, usually with a central or frontal dominance and often followed by sleep spindles. K-complexes will appear during attempts to arouse a sleeping person, as well as spontaneously. The spindles and K-complexes appear against a background of low-voltage, mixed-frequency waves.

Stage 3 sleep displays moderate amounts of high-amplitude, slow-wave activity. Some waves in the delta range (0.5 to 3 cps) appear. In stage 4 sleep, delta waves dominate the record.

The various stages of sleep alternate in cycles during the night, and although transitions occur between stages, the records can be scored as to how much of the night is spent in each stage. In young adults, stage 1 occupies 3 to 5 percent of the night; stage 2, 50 to 60 percent; stages 3 and 4, 10 to 20 percent; and REM, about 20 to 25 percent. The amount of time spent in the various stages of sleep varies with age. REM sleep occupies about 50 percent of the cycle in young infants. The elderly have very little stage 3 and 4 sleep.

The delta stage, stage 4, is generally interpreted as the deepest stage of sleep, in the sense that the person is least arousable during this stage. All the first four stages taken together occupy the first 70 to 120 min of the night's sleep. Then, the first cycle of REM sleep occurs. The EEG resembles that of stage 1 sleep, but the person now undergoes a phase of dreaming. Although the REM stage is often thought of as a lighter stage of sleep, the person is not necessarily easier to arouse. It is also called *paradoxical sleep* because of the dreaming in conjunction with profound loss of muscle tone. It is not readily categorized as light or deep sleep, rather as a different *kind* of sleep. Repeat REM cycles occur at intervals of 90 to 100 min throughout the night. REM stages of sleep appear in all mammals and even in birds and thus have some profound biologic significance. Daytime napping is associated with REM sleep that appears earlier and is of greater duration than in nocturnal sleep.

PSYCHIATRY

Biologic Dimensions of Psychiatry

DIRECTIONS: Each question below contains five suggested responses. Select the **one best** response to each question.

381. Currently accepted statements about the heritability of psychiatric disorders include all the following EXCEPT

    (A) there is an increased incidence of mood disorders among the families of patients suffering from anorexia nervosa
    (B) the first-degree relatives of patients with schizoaffective disorder are more likely to suffer from mood disorders than from schizophrenia
    (C) the child of two schizophrenic patients has a 5 percent chance of developing schizophrenia
    (D) unipolar affective disorder is the most frequent psychiatric disorder among the families of patients with bipolar affective disorder
    (E) there is an increased incidence of mood disorders among the parents of depressed teenagers

382. Which of the following is a true statement about Tourette's disorder?

    (A) The disease usually presents initially during adulthood
    (B) Abnormalities in serotonin metabolism appear to be the primary mechanism in the pathogenesis of the condition
    (C) The patient's tics are usually aggravated by periods of emotional stress
    (D) The concordance rate for the disorder among monozygotic twins is extremely low
    (E) There is a higher rate of sociopathy among patients with the disorder than in the general population

383. Identified risk factors in schizophrenia include all the following EXCEPT

    (A) having a dizygotic twin with schizophrenia
    (B) male sex
    (C) a history of perinatal birth injury
    (D) being born in winter
    (E) having a first-degree relative who suffers from schizophrenia

384. The neuropathologic changes found in Huntington's chorea

    (A) primarily involve limbic structures
    (B) seldom influence cognitive functioning
    (C) are localized to the caudate nucleus and globus pallidus
    (D) are determined by an autosomal recessive gene
    (E) are linked to the presence of the Huntington gene located on the short arm of chromosome 4

385. Closed head injury is most likely to result in traumatic lesions of

    (A) the reticular activating system and its projections
    (B) deep subcortical structures
    (C) the orbitomedial frontal and anterior temporal lobe areas
    (D) areas CA1 and CA2 of the hippocampus
    (E) the cerebellar vermis

386. Risk factors for the development of Alzheimer's disease include all the following EXCEPT

    (A) head trauma
    (B) smoking
    (C) increasing age
    (D) a sibling with Alzheimer's disease
    (E) Down's syndrome

387. An amnestic disorder may follow which of the following?

    (A) A lesion of the caudate nuclei
    (B) A lesion of the amygdaloid complex
    (C) Bilateral hippocampal lesions
    (D) A lesion of the corpus callosum
    (E) A lesion of the globus pallidus

388. True statements about the limbic system include all the following EXCEPT

    (A) the term refers to those neural structures primarily involved in the pursuit of innate biologic drives
    (B) the medial temporal cortex forms a significant portion of the limbic system
    (C) the limbic system has clearly defined neuroanatomic boundaries
    (D) the hypothalamus represents an integral part of the system
    (E) the fornix forms the largest outflow tract from the hippocampus

389. A craniopharyngioma may involve all the following structures EXCEPT

    (A) the pituitary gland
    (B) the optic chiasm
    (C) the third ventricle
    (D) the hypothalamus
    (E) the anterior cerebral artery

390. A destructive lesion involving both anterior temporal lobes would produce which of the following clinical syndromes?

    (A) Bizarre repetitive automatisms with repeated lip smacking
    (B) An inability to distinguish left from right, finger agnosia, and acalculia
    (C) Hyposexuality, perseveration, distractibility, and poor impulse control
    (D) Hyperorality, hypersexuality, placidity, visual agnosia, and amnesia
    (E) Alexia without agraphia

391. Computed tomography (CT) is a more sensitive investigation than magnetic resonance imaging (MRI) for which of the following?

    (A) A posterior fossa tumor
    (B) A calcified parasagittal meningioma
    (C) Multiple sclerosis
    (D) Medial temporal sclerosis
    (E) Binswanger's disease

392. All the following statements about evoked potentials are correct EXCEPT

    (A) they may be used to determine the prognosis in coma
    (B) the procedure may be useful in the evaluation of multiple sclerosis
    (C) evoked potentials are not specific to any particular sensory modality
    (D) evoked potentials may be helpful in diagnosing conversion disorders
    (E) the technique is helpful in diagnosing deafness in newborns

393. A young man presents with a complaint of recurrent olfactory and gustatory hallucinations and associated feelings of déjà vu and dysphoria. A routine EEG with standard leads performed while the patient was awake was reported as normal. The next appropriate study could be any of the following EXCEPT

    (A) mapping of brain electrical activity
    (B) repeat EEG with anterior temporal leads
    (C) repeat EEG with nasopharyngeal leads
    (D) sleep-deprived EEG recording
    (E) repeat standard EEG leads with patient asleep

394. The normal resting EEG in a healthy young adult is characterized by

    (A) an evoked response in the frontal lobes with stroboscopic stimulation
    (B) increasing frequency of the background rhythm during stages 1 through 4 sleep
    (C) a background of 4 to 7 Hz alpha rhythm
    (D) alpha rhythms predominantly over the frontal lobes when the eyes are closed
    (E) attenuation of the background alpha rhythm and the appearance of beta waves in the frontal regions symmetrically when the eyes are opened

DIRECTIONS: Each question below contains four suggested responses of which **one or more** is correct. Select

A	if	**1, 2, and 3**	are correct
B	if	**1 and 3**	are correct
C	if	**2 and 4**	are correct
D	if	**4**	is correct
E	if	**1, 2, 3, and 4**	are correct

395. The activation of adenylate cyclase

    (1) may result in either an inhibitory or stimulatory response
    (2) may be triggered by more than one neurotransmitter
    (3) is an example of a second messenger system
    (4) facilitates the opening of chloride channels

396. The activation of a dopamine autoreceptor

    (1) increases the release of dopamine at the synapse
    (2) produces an inhibitory feedback loop
    (3) occurs at the postsynaptic membrane
    (4) results in decreased dopamine synthesis

397. The catabolism of dopamine involves which of the following enzymes?

    (1) Monoamine oxidase
    (2) Tyrosine hydroxylase
    (3) Catechol-*O*-methyltransferase
    (4) Dopa decarboxylase

398. Inhibitory neurotransmitters include which of the following?

    (1) Glutamate
    (2) Glycine
    (3) Aspartate
    (4) γ-Aminobutyric acid (GABA)

399. Prolactin secretion is correctly characterized by which of the following statements?

    (1) It is stimulated by dopamine secretion in the hypothalamus
    (2) It is increased by a generalized tonic clonic convulsion
    (3) It is diminished by the administration of neuroleptics
    (4) It occurs in the anterior pituitary

400. Which of the following statements regarding *N*-methyl-D-aspartate is true?

    (1) It is an excitatory amino acid
    (2) It may cause convulsions if injected intracerebrally
    (3) It may cause neuronal damage
    (4) It produces depolarization at the synapse

401. Serotoninergic 5-HT2 receptors are the probable site of action of

    (1) buspirone
    (2) fluoxetine
    (3) haloperidol
    (4) hallucinogens

402. Increased serum levels of endogenous opioids have been reported in

    (1) exercise
    (2) starvation
    (3) stress
    (4) pain

403. True statements about neurotransmitters include

    (1) they are released into the synaptic cleft when repolarization occurs at the presynaptic terminal
    (2) they influence the electrical and biochemical properties of the postsynaptic membrane
    (3) they are resistant to catabolism
    (4) they are found in highest concentration in the presynaptic terminal

404. The production of melatonin

    (1) requires tryptophan as a precursor
    (2) takes place in the pineal gland
    (3) is decreased by light stimulation
    (4) is increased by noradrenaline (norepinephrine)

405. Monoamine oxidase A is correctly described by which of the following?

    (1) It selectively deaminates serotonin and noradrenaline (norepinephrine)
    (2) It is reversibly inhibited by phenelzine
    (3) It is selectively inhibited by clorgiline
    (4) It increases intracellular levels of noradrenaline (norepinephrine)

406. Second messengers include

    (1) calcium
    (2) acetylcholine
    (3) protein kinases
    (4) dopamine

407. Dopamine D1 receptors are

    (1) situated on the presynaptic membrane
    (2) autoreceptors
    (3) selectively blocked by haloperidol
    (4) located primarily in the parathyroid gland

408. Recognized treatments for sleep apnea include

    (1) protriptyline
    (2) uvulopalatopharyngoplasty
    (3) tracheostomy
    (4) clonazepam

409. The sleep pattern in patients with the recurrence of a major depressive episode is characterized by

    (1) decreased rapid eye movement (REM) latency
    (2) decreased stages 3 and 4 sleep
    (3) prolonged first REM period
    (4) early morning awakening

410. Normal changes in sleep architecture that occur with aging include

    (1) increased slow-wave sleep
    (2) increased REM sleep
    (3) decreased awakenings
    (4) decreased total sleep time

411. Chronic alcohol abuse produces which of the following changes in sleep architecture?

    (1) Decreased stages 3 and 4 sleep
    (2) Increased REM sleep
    (3) Decreased total sleep time
    (4) Decreased awakenings

412. Clinical features of narcolepsy include

    (1) sleep paralysis
    (2) increased REM latency
    (3) cataplexy
    (4) myoclonic jerks

413. An 8-year-old boy occasionally awakens screaming and terrified in the middle of the night, at which time he is sweating, anxious, and confused. Correct statements about this event include

    (1) the child is likely to have significant psychopathology
    (2) the event probably occurred during REM sleep
    (3) the child should receive psychotherapy
    (4) sleep terror is the most likely diagnosis

414. A middle-aged man presents with the complaint of daytime drowsiness. Possible etiologies include

    (1) a major depressive disorder
    (2) alcoholic dependency
    (3) sleep apnea
    (4) restless legs syndrome

DIRECTIONS: Each group of questions below consists of lettered headings followed by a set of numbered items. For each numbered item select the **one** lettered heading with which it is most closely associated. Each lettered heading may be used **once, more than once, or not at all.**

Questions 415–418

Select the EEG recording that would be most likely in each of the following clinical vignettes.

    (A) EEG A
    (B) EEG B
    (C) EEG C
    (D) EEG D
    (E) EEG E

415.   A young woman is brought to the emergency room in a semicomatose state. She says that she ingested a large number of "sleeping pills" 1 h prior to her arrival at the hospital

416.   A 60-year-old man is accompanied by his wife to the emergency room. She states that her husband is unable to speak and has developed shaking of his right arm and leg

417.   A 40-year-old alcoholic is brought to the emergency room confused and belligerent

418.   A normal young male falls asleep while having a routine EEG as part of a research protocol

A

B

C

D

E

Questions 419–423

The axial MRI scan below is of a 9-month-old infant at the level of the third ventricle and basal ganglia. Match the numbered structures with the appropriate letters on the scan.

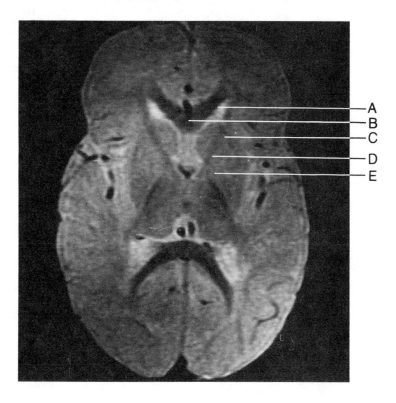

Adapted from Fischer and Ketonen, Fig. 2-71, with permission.

419. Genu of corpus callosum

420. Head of caudate nucleus

421. Anterior limb of internal capsule

422. Frontal horn of lateral ventricle

423. Globus pallidus

Questions 424–427

Match the following.

   (A) Raphe nuclei
   (B) Nucleus basalis
   (C) Locus coeruleus
   (D) Red nucleus
   (E) Ventral tegmental area

424. Origin of long-tract dopaminergic projections

425. Origin of cholinergic pathways

426. Primary serotonin cell bodies

427. Numerous noradrenergic projections

Biologic Dimensions of Psychiatry

Answers

381. The answer is C. (*Kaplan, ed 5. pp 879–881.*)   Although the genetic transmission of psychiatric disorders remains largely unknown, certain patterns of heritability have emerged. There is a 35 to 45 percent chance that the child of two schizophrenic parents will develop schizophrenia. Families of schizoaffective patients have a higher incidence of mood disorders and there is a much greater concordance for schizoaffective disorder among monozygotic twins. The increased incidence of mood disorders among the first-degree relatives of patients with anorexia nervosa has been replicated several times. The prevalence of unipolar mood disorders among relatives with bipolar and unipolar mood disorders is 14.9 and 16.6 percent, respectively. The prevalence of bipolar mood disorder among relatives with bipolar and unipolar disorders is 8 and 2.9 percent, respectively.

382. The answer is C. (*Kaplan, ed 5. pp 1865–1878.*)   The precise prevalence of Tourettes's disorder and the other tic disorders is unknown. The condition has a male:female ratio of 3:1 and usually presents in childhood—virtually every case has begun by age 15. The genetic mode of transmission is unknown, but there is a higher prevalence of tic spectrum disorders among first-degree family members (5 percent). The concordance rate among monozygotic twins is between 77 and 87 percent and is 25 percent in same-sex dizygotic twins. The pathogenesis of the condition remains unknown but is postulated to involve striatal dopamine receptor supersensitivity; the efficacy of high-potency neuroleptics in alleviating motor symptoms has been taken as support for this model. The suggested association between Tourette's disorder and attention-deficit hyperactivity disorder or obsessive-compulsive disorder remains unproven. There is no evidence for any typical personality traits among these patients. High-potency neuroleptics are effective in markedly reducing the frequency of tics in 80 percent of patients; unfortunately patients with Tourette's disorder usually gain a considerable amount of weight on these medications.

383. The answer is B. (*Kaplan, ed 5. pp 702–705.*)   Studies that take gender differences in age of onset into consideration have demonstrated no difference in the prevalence of schizophrenia between males and females. Females tend to experience the onset of the disease between 25 and 34 years, whereas males tend to present earlier between 15 and 24 years. Males tend to display more profound negative symptoms with a more chronic debilitating course. Schizophrenics are more likely than the general population to have been born during the winter months. This correspondence has been used to support a viral etiology of the illness. Replicated retrospective studies have found a high incidence of perinatal birth injuries among schizophrenics and suggest that this is associated with more negative symptomatology and a poorer prognosis. The concordance rate for schizophrenia among monozygotic twins is 33 to 78 percent and in dizygotic twins is 8 to 28 percent.

384. The answer is E. (*Adams, ed 4. pp 932–935.*)   Huntington's disease is transmitted by a monohybrid autosomal dominant gene with complete penetrance located at chromosome 4. The disease is more common in males and usually presents in the fourth or fifth decades although it may often present earlier. Neuropathologic changes are limited to the caudate and putamen and produce profound wasting of these structures, which may be seen on CT and MRI scans. Clinical features include personality change, mood disorders, cognitive change, and the characteristic choreiform motor disorder. Treatment is symptomatic and haloperidol (Haldol) has proved most effective in suppressing motor abnormalities. Patients usually die within 2 decades of the onset of the illness.

385. The answer is C. (*Kaplan, ed 5. pp 635–637.*)   The anterior temporal and orbitomedial frontal areas are most frequently damaged in closed head injuries because of their site in the anterior fossa positioned between the sphenoidal wings and frontal ridge. Since these cortical structures make up part of the paralimbic system, closed head injuries often lead to alterations in personality. These changes usually include poor impulse control, diminished insight and planning, and emotional lability.

386. The answer is B. (*Kaplan, ed 5. p 614.*)   Although the etiology of Alzheimer's disease remains unknown, it is clear that there is a genetically determined predisposition to the condition. This is most apparent in families that exhibit early-onset Alzheimer's disease but is also evident in late-onset dementias. The high incidence of early-onset Alzheimer's disease in patients with Down's syndrome suggests a causative locus at chromosome 21.

387. The answer is C. (*Strub, pp 287–290.*)   The amnestic syndrome may be defined as an inability to learn new material (anterograde amnesia) in the presence of normal attention. The degree of retrograde amnesia (i.e., memory of previously known material) will vary in each case. The study of amnestic disorders provides a template for understanding the anatomy of memory. In simple terms, a bilateral lesion of limbic structures is required for the development of an amnestic disorder. The best known clinical example of an amnestic disorder is the Wernicke-Korsakoff syndrome in which necrotic lesions in the mamillary bodies and dorsomedial nuclei of the thalamus are found. Bilateral lesions of the hippocampus also cause memory loss and are typically seen in severe head trauma, anoxia, carbon monoxide poisoning, and limbic encephalitis. Unilateral limbic lesions may produce modality-specific memory deficits, e.g., in language or visuospatial functions.

388. The answer is C. (*Strub, pp 18–31.*)   The limbic system derives its name from the Greek word *limbus* meaning *rim*. The system has a vital role in determining the emotional valency of and appropriate behavioral response to an environmental stimuli. Despite its pervasive and critical role in behavior, the neuroanatomic boundaries of the system are poorly defined. The system contains the hypothalamus, thalamic nuclei, limbic components of the cortex (i.e., orbitofrontal and mediotemporal structures), and the limbic striatum (i.e., nucleus accumbens, olfactory tubercle, and ventral tegmentum). The circuit of Papez forms an integral pathway linking the components of the limbic system and includes the hippocampus, fornix, anterior thalamus, hypothalamus, and cingulate gyrus.

389. The answer is E. (*Adams, ed 4. p 537.*)   The craniopharyngioma is a germ cell tumor arising from Rathke's pouch, which is situated at the junction between the infundibular stem and the pituitary gland. The anatomic relationships of the tumor therefore parallel those of the sella turcica. These structures include the pituitary gland, hypothalamus, optic chiasm, and third ventricle. Patients with the condition may therefore typically present with decreased vision, declining libido, general lethargy, headache, confusion, or amenorrhea. With neurosurgical intervention and the careful monitoring of the patient's endocrine status, mortality is 5 to 8 percent.

390. The answer is D. (*Strub, p 291.*) Bilateral destruction of the anterior temporal lobes produces a distinct neurobehavioral disorder—the Klüver-Bucy syndrome. This disorder was first described in monkeys who had undergone surgical ablation of both anterior temporal lobes but is now well recognized in humans. The most common causes are limbic encephalitis, head trauma, Alzheimer's disease, and anoxia. Clinical features consist of placidity, hypersexuality with indiscriminate sexual interest in both animate and inanimate objects, amnesia, hyperorality, and visual agnosia.

391. The answer is B. (*Adams, ed 4. p 17.*) Although MRI represents the most sensitive neuroimaging tool available, it is essentially "blind" to calcified structures. The technology offers particular advantages for the visualization of lesions of matter, brainstem, posterior fossa, and the anterior temporal region. The ability of MRI to produce multiplanar images provides more potential information than standard CT procedures. The adjunctive use of paramagnetic contrast materials further improves resolution and increases the sensitivity of the procedure.

392. The answer is C. (*Kaplan, ed 5. pp 80–83.*) In simple terms, evoked potentials are the electrical response produced by specific sensory stimuli and represent the neural conduction of modality-specific (e.g., vision, hearing) information. They have been recorded from cortical areas, brainstem, spinal cord, and peripheral nerves. The primary clinical use of evoked potentials is to determine the integrity of the visual, auditory, and somatosensory systems. The presence of normal evoked response patterns is helpful in confirming the diagnosis of conversion disorder. Although the use of evoked potentials in psychiatric disorders remains unclear, several studies have suggested that a reduced P300 amplitude is found in schizophrenia. The P300 late evoked potential is becoming of increasing interest to psychiatrists and may represent the motivational valence attributed by the subject to a particular environmental stimulus.

393. The answer is A. (*Kaplan, ed 5. p 79.*) The patient described most likely suffers from complex partial seizures with a temporolimbic focus. Standard electroencephalographic electrode placements are relatively insensitive to abnormal discharges from the anterior temporal area. The use of nasopharyngeal, sphenoidal, and anterior temporal leads will improve sensitivity because of their closer proximity to anterior temporal structures. Although the computerized mapping of data (BEAM) does provide interesting data, the technique does not offer any increased sensitivity to temporolimbic spike and wave activity. Sleep-deprived recordings, by increasing the likelihood that the patient will fall asleep during the EEG, increase the likelihood that abnormalities will be manifested even on a routine EEG montage.

394. The answer is E. (*Adams, ed 4. pp 20–30.*) When the subject is at rest with the eyes closed, the normal EEG pattern consists of a background alpha frequency within the range of 8 to 13 Hz. This pattern is replaced by a faster, lower-voltage beta activity when the subject is anxious, concentrating, or using minor tranquilizers. Stroboscopic visual stimulation will produce an evoked response (photic driving) in the occipital lobes if the subject can perceive light. Normal sleep produces a decrease in the background frequency through stages 1 through 4 with the appearance of 1 to 3 Hz activity during the deep sleep of stages 3 and 4. Rapid eye movement (REM) sleep is associated with asynchronous, low-voltage fast activity.

395. The answer is A (1, 2, 3). (*Kaplan, ed 5. pp 46–47.*) The activation of adenylate cyclase is mediated via guanosine triphosphates (GTP), which act as coupling proteins. The presence of different mediating (G) proteins, which may be either facilitory or inhibitory, allows several different neurotransmitters to activate the adenylate cyclase cascade. Adenylate cyclase can therefore be activated by dopamine, norepinephrine, serotonin, and histamine. This type of second messenger transmission is slower than simple "lock and key" allosteric transmission. The second messenger system is also capable of amplifying the initial signal because of the initiation of a cascade response.

The opening of a chloride channel is produced by the binding of γ-aminobutyric acid (GABA) at its particular receptor site and is an example of allosteric binding.

396. The answer is C (2, 4). (*Kaplan, ed 5. p 1611.*)   Autoreceptors are situated on the presynaptic membrane and respond to increased levels of a particular neurotransmitter (e.g., dopamine) by activating an inhibitory feedback on the synthesis and release of that neurotransmitter. Blocking the dopamine postsynaptic receptor will therefore result in increased dopamine synthesis and release. Some degree of tolerance, however, eventually develops. Autoreceptors are therefore responsible for autoregulation at the synapse.

397. The answer is B (1, 3). (*Kaplan, ed 5. pp 48–49.*)   Catecholamines are inactivated at the synapse either by active reuptake at the nerve terminal or by enzymatic catabolism. The two enzymes involved in this breakdown are monoamine oxidase and catechol-*O*-methyltransferase (COMT). Monoamine oxidase is situated on the external mitochondrial membrane and is available to catabolize free catecholamines within the cell cytosol. COMT is situated on the outer membrane cell membrane and involved with the degradation of catecholamines in the synaptic cleft. These catabolic enzymes are found not only in the central nervous system but also in the intestine and liver. Tyrosine hydroxylase and dopamine decarboxylase are involved in the synthesis of the catecholamines. Tyrosine hydroxylase is the rate-limiting enzyme in this pathway.

398. The answer is C (2, 4). (*Kaplan, ed 5. pp 50–51.*)   GABA and glycine are both inhibitory neurotransmitters. Both of these neurotransmitters act rapidly via allosteric (i.e., "lock and key") binding at their receptor sites and induce a rapid hyperpolarization by increasing the chloride permeability of the neuronal cell membrane. GABA receptor activity is gaining increasing interest and importance in psychopharmacology. In particular, benzodiazepines have been found to bind at GABA receptors and act as agonists by increasing the affinity of these receptors for GABA. The development of a benzodiazepine antagonist offers the potential for the rapid, controlled reversal of benzodiazepine activity. This may offer important clinical uses in anesthesia and benzodiazepine overdose. GABA agonists are also under development and may have therapeutic uses in seizure disorders and behavioral disorders. Glycine is an inhibitory neurotransmitter confined to the brainstem and spinal cord. Both aspartate and glutamate are excitatory amino acids.

399. The answer is C (2, 4). (*Kaplan, ed 5. pp 108–109.*)   Prolactin is secreted in the anterior pituitary. Its secretion is directly inhibited by dopamine released into the tuberoinfundibular system. Secretion is further modulated by negative feedback. Thyrotropin-releasing hormone (TRH), endogenous opiates, and L-tryptophan stimulate prolactin secretion. Somatostatin inhibits response. Patients with hyperprolactinemia report dysphoria, reduced tolerance to stress, oligomenorrhea, and galactorrhea. There is a sharp rise in plasma prolactin following generalized seizure activity.

400. The answer is E (all). (*Kaplan, ed 5. p 51.*)   *N*-methyl-D-aspartate (NMDA) is one of several agonists for the excitatory receptors. Through its actions at ion channels it produces depolarization and therefore excitation. Intracerebral injection of NMDA results in tonic clonic convulsions and neuronal degeneration at the site of injection. This phenomenon has been now termed "excitotoxicity." Antagonists to these excitatory neurotransmitters offer promise as anticonvulsants and as a means of reducing neuronal injury following seizures, anoxia, hypoglycemia, or cerebrovascular accidents. Other potentially neurotoxic excitatory amino acids include quisqualate and kainate. Each excitatory amino acid appears to have a distinct receptor distribution in the brain.

401. The answer is C (2, 4). (*Kaplan, ed 5. p 50.*)   The 5-HT2 serotonin receptors are found primarily in the cortex. They are the primary site of action of fluoxetine as well as LSD and other hallucinogens and have therefore been implicated in the production of psychotic states. Buspirone is thought to act as a 5-HT1a receptor agonist. An increasing number of heterogeneous serotonin receptors with diverse activities are being discovered.

402. The answer is E (all). (*Kaplan, ed 5. p 106.*) Raised serum levels of the endorphins have been found in each of the situations described. The pattern of endorphins in psychiatric disorders is less clear. The endorphins increase appetite and have been shown to rise significantly with exercise. Endorphins are a heterogeneous group of peptides derived from one of three precursor proteins: proenkephalin, prodynorphin, and proopiomalanocortin (POMC). Unlike monoamines, which are metabolized in the nerve terminal from dietary sources, neuropeptides are synthesized in the ribosomes and require mRNA. Neuropeptides appear to exert a neuromodulating effect upon monoaminergic neurotransmission. Other neuropeptides include substance P, cholecystokinin, vasoactive intestinal polypeptide, somatostatin, bombesin, and neurotensin.

403. The answer is C (2, 4). (*Davis, p 73.*) Neurotransmitters are released into the synaptic cleft from the presynaptic terminal when depolarization occurs. A number of criteria for neurotransmitters have been outlined. These include the following: (1) they should be present in highest concentration in the presynaptic terminal; (2) they should be released with depolarization; (3) they should produce a similar response to electrical stimulation at the receptor; (4) there must be a method of rapid inactivation; (5) they should bind to the receptor in a selective manner; and (6) presynaptic electrical stimulation and neurotransmitter application should be similarly altered by drug actions.

404. The answer is E (all). (*Kaplan, ed 5. p 110.*) Melatonin is an indoleamine produced in the pineal gland. The synthesis of melatonin requires tryptophan as a precursor. The uptake of tryptophan into the pineal is increased by noradrenaline. The production of melatonin is highest at nighttime with a peak at about 0300 hours and is suppressed by light stimulation. Melatonin synthesis follows a circadian 24-h cycle, which is entrained via environmental light and the suprachiasmatic nucleus. Its production appears to be unaffected by other circadian components such as the sleep/wake cycle or temperature. Melatonin is under increasing scrutiny as a potential marker for several psychiatric disorders.

405. The answer is B (1, 3). (*Kaplan, ed 5. p 1651.*) There are two types of monoamine oxidase (MAO): MAO-A and MAO-B. MAO-A selectively inhibits serotonin and noradrenaline, whereas MAO-B deaminates phenylethylamine, tyramine, tryptamine, and phenylethanolamine. MAO-A is selectively inhibited by clorgiline, whereas pargyline selectively inhibits MAO-B activity. Currently used MAO inhibitors such as phenelzine, tranylcypromine, and isocarboxazid are nonselective and influence both enzymes. Most MAO inhibitors irreversibly inhibit the activity of the enzyme, and although they have a short half-life will result in a depletion of enzyme activity that lasts several weeks after discontinuation of the drug.

406. The answer is B (1, 3). (*Kaplan, ed 5. pp 61–63.*) Second messengers are intracellular mediators for other neurotransmitters. Most monoamine neurotransmitters operate via a second messenger. These second messengers may amplify an initial response and therefore serve a modulatory function. Three broad groups of second messengers are currently recognized: cyclic nucleotides (cAMP, cGMP), calcium ions, and phospholipid metabolites (ITP, arachidonic acid). A single neurotransmitter can activate several second-messenger systems.

407. The answer is D (4). (*Kaplan, ed 5. pp 718–719.*) There are at least two different subtypes of dopamine postsynaptic receptors: D1 and D2 receptors. The D1 receptor has been identified in the parathyroid gland (and influences parathormone secretion) and in the retina. The D2 receptor is more widely distributed in the dopaminergic system and is found in mesostriatal, mesolimbic, mesocortical, and tuberoinfundibular distributions. Most currently available neuroleptics are nonselective and produce blockade at both receptor subtypes. Flupenthixol appears to have the highest affinity for D2 receptors, while domperidone and sulpiride exhibit a high affinity for D2 receptors.

408. The answer is A (1, 2, 3). *(Kaplan, ed 5. p 1111.)* Sleep apnea is a condition in which there are repeated episodes of sleep-associated cessation of breathing. Two broad categories of sleep apnea have been identified: obstructive and central sleep apnea. Many persons, however, will exhibit a mixed pattern. Clinical features of sleep apnea include excessive daytime somnolence, fatigue, sleep attacks, headaches, hypertension, episodic confusion after awakening, and probably mood disorders. There is a high incidence of cardiac arrhythmias and sudden death among these patients. Recognized treatments include tracheostomy, uvulopalatopharyngoplasty, weight loss, and administration of protriptyline and medroxyprogesterone.

409. The answer is E (all). *(Kaplan, ed 5. p 1114.)* Characteristic changes are found in major depressive disorder. These changes include decreased REM latency, prolonged first REM period, decreased slow-wave sleep, more frequent awakenings, and early morning awakening. These changes mean that sleep is likely to be less refreshing, and excessive daytime drowsiness is often reported.

410. The answer is D (4). *(Kaplan, ed 5. pp 86–92.)* There are significant alterations in sleep architecture with aging. Total sleep, slow-wave sleep, and REM sleep all attain peak duration during childhood, stabilize after puberty, and then go into a steady decline with advancing age. These are normal physiologic changes and are not indicative of pathology. Although there may be variation among different persons, the sleep pattern of an individual is relatively stable. As a result of these changes, elderly people may complain of sleeping problems and therefore receive more sedatives. Older patients may also take more daytime naps to compensate for these changes.

411. The answer is B (1, 3). *(Kaplan, ed 5. p 1111.)* Chronic alcohol abuse leads to a significant disruption of sleep architecture. Changes include fragmented and decreased REM duration, decreased sleep time, and increased awakenings. Alcohol withdrawal produces decreased slow-wave sleep, difficulty initiating sleep, and usually REM rebound. In severe alcoholics REM may remain depressed.

412. The answer is B (1, 3). *(Kaplan, ed 5. pp 1116–1117.)* Narcolepsy is characterized by the classic tetrad of sleep attacks, cataplexy, sleep paralysis, and hypnopompic/hypnogogic hallucinations. In reality all four of these symptoms are seldom present and the sleep attacks usually precede the other symptoms. The disease usually has its onset in the second decade. There is a strong familial trend with equal frequency in both sexes. An association of HLA-B7 and HLA-DR2 with narcolepsy has been postulated. Diagnosis is made by demonstrating a shortened REM latency on polysomnography. Psychostimulants are the treatment of choice.

413. The answer is D (4). *(Kaplan, ed 5. p 1122.)* Sleep terrors are one of the parasomnias and occur in 1 to 4 percent of the population with an onset usually between ages 4 and 12. The disorder is usually benign and does not indicate any psychopathology or predisposition to mental illness later in life. The disorder may have its onset later in life and is then associated with an increased incidence of anxiety disorders. The episodes usually occur during the first part of the night during a period of slow-wave sleep. There is usually clinical evidence for sympathetic outflow and occasionally the subject may exhibit automatisms. There is no vivid dream recall. The child and his family should be gently reassured about the condition and its implications.

414. The answer is E (all). *(Kaplan, ed 5. pp 1115–1117.)* The disorders of excessive somnolence (DOES) have been classified by the Association of Sleep Disorders Centers (ASDC) under a number of different subheadings: (1) psychophysiologic (causes under this heading include acute or chronic stress situations); (2) associated with psychiatric disorders (e.g., mood disorders); (3) associated with drug use; (4) sleep apnea; (5) narcolepsy; (6) "restless legs" syndromes; (7) environmental; and (8) Kleine-Levin syndrome. The appropriate treatment will of course depend on the etiology.

415–418. The answers are: 415-B, 416-D, 417-A, 418-C. (*Adams, ed 4. pp 20, 24, 26. Kaplan, ed 5. p 86.*) EEG tracing B demonstrates the expected findings in a subject who is using minor tranquilizers. These findings are typically low-voltage, symmetric, fast-frequency wave forms found particularly over the frontal areas. The encephalopathy produced by lithium is characterized by diffuse slowing of the background rhythm. The EEG may provide valuable clues when investigating any alteration in attention, particularly when a drug overdose is suspected.

Tracing D demonstrates spike discharges localized to the left hemisphere. These changes are consistent with partial focal epilepsy of the right hemisphere. Although this is a classic ictal pattern, it is important to remember that 40 percent of patients with generalized epilepsy will have a normal EEG on single random recording. A single normal EEG tracing does not rule out epilepsy and the procedure should be repeated if necessary. All electrophysiologic data should only be interpreted in the context of the clinical findings.

Tracing A demonstrates the typical features of a hepatic encephalopathy. These changes include background slowing and bilateral synchronous "triphasic waves." The EEG abnormality closely correlates with the clinical stage of coma and may be helpful in following the patient's clinical course.

Tracing C demonstrates the "sleep spindles," K complexes, and background theta waves normally found in stage 2 sleep. Stage 1 sleep consists of an increasing percentage of theta-wave activity (4 to 7 Hz) with low-voltage, fast-background activity and vertex sharp waves. Stages 3 and 4 sleep are characterized by delta-wave predominance (1.5 to 3 Hz). The EEG of REM sleep closely approximates the waking state with the occurrence of hypotonia and REMs.

419–423. The answers are: 419-B, 420-C, 421-D, 422-A, 423-E. (*Fischer, p 125.*) The structures shown on the axial MRI scan in the question are identified in the figure below.

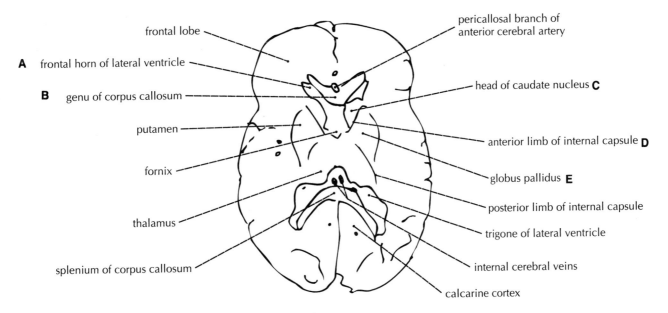

Adapted from Fischer and Ketonen. Fig. 2-71. with permission.

424–427. The answers are: 424-E, 425-B, 426-A, 427-C. (*Davis, pp 74–81.*) There is a clear neuroanatomic distribution of the major biogenic amines and their projections. Five distinct dopaminergic tracts exist: (1) nigrostriatal, (2) mesolimbic, (3) mesocortical, (4) tuberoinfundibular, and (5) retinal. Long tracts arise from areas A9 (substantia nigra) and A10 (ventral tegmental area), while medium tracts arise from the hypothalamus. The nigrostriatal tract regulates motor activity and innervates the striatum. The mesocortical tracts and mesolimbic tracts are involved in the motor expression and the subjective experience of emotional states. The tuberoinfundibular system influences the activity of the anterior pituitary gland.

The cell bodies of the noradrenergic system lie in the hindbrain; the major collection is found in the locus coeruleus. The diffuse projections from these sites to virtually all areas of the neuraxis suggest primarily a neuromodulatory function.

The raphe nuclei are the major sites for serotoninergic projections to diffuse areas of the brain including the cortex, limbic structures, spinal cord, and lateral geniculate nucleus. The system appears to have inhibitory effects on behavioral response to environmental cues, including the suppression of aggression, sexual interest, and arousal. This neuromodulating activity is supported by the tonic firing of the raphe nuclei, which appears to act as a behavioral "pacemaker."

Cholinergic projections arise from cell bodies situated around the medial septal area: the nucleus basalis, preoptic nucleus, and diagonal band of Broca. Destruction of the nucleus basalis, which has dense projections to the hippocampus, has been postulated to be partly responsible for the memory disturbances found in Alzheimer's disease. Diffuse cholinergic projections are to (1) ventral horn cells to all muscles, (2) striatal interneurons, (3) cortex, and (4) hippocampus.

Psychosocial Issues and Phenomenology

DIRECTIONS: Each question below contains five suggested responses. Select the **one best** response to each question.

428. Each of the following is considered a mature ego defense mechanism EXCEPT

    (A) sublimation
    (B) humor
    (C) repression
    (D) suppression
    (E) altruism

429. According to classical psychoanalytic theory, the functions of the ego include each of the following EXCEPT

    (A) the control of instinctual drives
    (B) development of moral codes of behavior
    (C) maintenance of an appropriate relationship to reality
    (D) reality testing
    (E) development of satisfying object relationships

430. According to Margaret Mahler's object relations theory, the period of consolidation and object constancy is characterized by each of the following EXCEPT

    (A) the child becomes comfortable during periods of mother's absence
    (B) the child internalizes an image of the mother as stable and reliable
    (C) the child is able to accept substitutes for the mother
    (D) the child develops a social smile
    (E) this stage of development is usually reached by age 3

431. The ego defense mechanism of splitting

    (A) is a neurotic level defense mechanism
    (B) transforms one unacceptable impulse into its opposite
    (C) results in the suppression of conflict-ridden impulses
    (D) produces oscillating interpersonal relationships
    (E) isolates ego dystonic affect

432. Each of the following statements about Erik Erikson's theory of personality development is true EXCEPT

    (A) integrity versus despair represents the final stage of personality development
    (B) personality development follows a predictable sequence of critical stages
    (C) trust versus mistrust represents the first developmental stage
    (D) a person must accomplish each developmental task before progressing to the next stage
    (E) personality development is completed by early adulthood

433. True statements regarding the pleasure principle include

    (A) it is a learned function
    (B) it is modulated by the reality principle
    (C) it is directed toward increasing tension
    (D) it attempts to create disequilibrium within the organism
    (E) it persists only until late adolesence

434. Formal operational thinking is characterized by which of the following?

    (A) It is usually achieved by the end of the latency period
    (B) It is necessary for the development of social skills
    (C) It is necessary for abstraction
    (D) It heralds the acquisition of speech
    (E) It is achieved by the majority of adults

435. The ego defense mechanism of projective identification

    (A) is the product of a rigid superego
    (B) is the prominent defense of the compulsive personality
    (C) is a manifestation of the ego-ideal
    (D) often makes the therapist uncomfortable
    (E) produces a sudden change in the subject's character

436. All the following circumstances are exceptions to the psychiatrist's obligation to maintain confidentiality EXCEPT

    (A) the patient is involuntarily committed
    (B) the patient is involved in child abuse
    (C) a medical emergency exists
    (D) the patient has a venereal disease and is sexually active
    (E) the patient's lawyer requests information

437. The competency of a patient is correctly described by which of the following?

    (A) It is task-specific
    (B) It is determined by the psychiatrist
    (C) It is necessary for involuntary commitment
    (D) It is necessary for confidentiality
    (E) It is necessary if informed consent is to be obtained

438. The principle of *respondeat superior*

    (A) determines the patient's moral sanity
    (B) describes the patient's right to dictate treatment decisions
    (C) demands the confidentiality of medical records
    (D) involves the vicarious responsibility an attending physician has for the treatment decisions of his resident
    (E) dictates the moral imperative

439. The elements of medical malpractice include each of the following EXCEPT

    (A) the presence of a doctor-patient relationship
    (B) the dereliction of duty by the physician
    (C) a direct causation between the physician's behavior and the damage experienced by the patient
    (D) injury as a direct result of the physician's negligence
    (E) the competency of the patient

440. The American Law Institute rule

    (A) provides the basis of the insanity law
    (B) dictates the requirements for any malpractice suit
    (C) states the requirements for the right to refuse treatment
    (D) outlines the requirements of seclusion and restraint
    (E) provides guidelines for involuntary commitment

441. Which of the following statements regarding the Tarasoff II decision is true?

    (A) It determines the requirements for involuntary hospitalization
    (B) It does not influence confidentiality
    (C) It dictates the clinicians' responsibility to inform any person who might be harmed by their patient
    (D) It is binding on all psychiatrists in the U.S.
    (E) It does not apply to patients who are psychotic

442. The patient's right to bar information shared within the professional relationship from judicial hearings is referred to as

    (A) confidentiality
    (B) privilege
    (C) *parens patriae*
    (D) *respondeat superior*
    (E) obstruction

443. The structural model of family therapy considers family dysfunction to be a result of

    (A) communication deficits
    (B) deficient reward systems within the family
    (C) poor problem-solving within the family
    (D) malfunctioning boundaries within the family
    (E) triangulation within the family

444. "Collusive defense" in couple's therapy refers to

    (A) the unconscious alliance that may develop between the therapist and one member of the couple
    (B) the couple's shared distortions
    (C) an attempt by one partner to sabotage treatment
    (D) an unconscious strategy by both members to devalue the therapist
    (E) transgenerational patterns exhibited in the couple

445. Each of the following is a true statement about incest EXCEPT

    (A) the majority of cases involve father-daughter relationships
    (B) mothers are very rarely aware of the incest
    (C) alcoholism in the family is a risk factor
    (D) the mother in the family is often physically abused
    (E) the victim is usually a prepubertal child

446. The number of cases of an illness at a particular time is known as the

    (A) incidence
    (B) point prevalence
    (C) frequency
    (D) risk factor
    (E) cohort

447. The results of an experimental drug trial demonstrate that a drug definitely known to be effective is ineffective. This is an example of a

    (A) negative skew
    (B) standard error
    (C) between-sample variance
    (D) type I error
    (E) type II error

448. The term *pseudologia fantastica* describes

(A) bizarre neologisms
(B) word salad
(C) reduplicative paramnesia
(D) repeated incredible lying
(E) fixed delusions

449. According to classical psychoanalytic theory, conversion disorder

(A) represents fixation at the oral phase of ego development
(B) is the consequence of a rigid superego
(C) indicates an unresolved oedipal conflict
(D) is an extension of female penis envy
(E) suggests inappropriate toilet training

450. Which of the following clinical features would mitigate against a diagnosis of conversion disorder?

(A) A dermatome distribution of sensory loss
(B) Convulsive movements
(C) Astasia-abasia
(D) Coordination disturbance
(E) Rhythmic tremors

451. Each of the following is a true statement about the prognosis of conversion disorder EXCEPT

(A) the majority of conversion symptoms rapidly resolve
(B) at least 25 percent of patients will develop another conversion disorder
(C) recurrent conversion symptoms are not always the same
(D) the presence of another psychiatric disorder is a poor prognostic indicator
(E) the presence of a severe psychosocial precipitant is a poor prognostic indicator

452. Monosymptomatic delusional hypochondriasis is correctly characterized by which statement?

(A) It is most effectively treated with a high-potency neuroleptic
(B) It frequently remits with hypnosis
(C) It is more common in males
(D) It usually has its onset in adolescence
(E) It seldom interrupts the affected person's life-style

453. Following a cerebrovascular accident, an elderly man claims that he can no longer recognize friends or relatives. This is most likely to be

(A) a conversion disorder
(B) Balint's syndrome
(C) prosopagnosia
(D) confabulation
(E) Capgras syndrome

454. Catatonia is characterized by each of the following features EXCEPT

(A) negativism
(B) echopraxia
(C) stereotypies
(D) mutism
(E) perseveration

455. Acute confusional states are characterized by each of the following EXCEPT

(A) complex motor tics
(B) perseveration
(C) lack of persistence
(D) distractibility
(E) fluctuating consciousness

456. The ego defenses of isolation of affect, reaction formation, and undoing are employed by which of the following personalities?

(A) Histrionic
(B) Sociopathic
(C) Compulsive
(D) Borderline
(E) Self-defeating

457. The primary ego defense mechanism employed in the development of a specific phobia is

    (A) acting out
    (B) isolation of affect
    (C) somatization
    (D) displacement
    (E) suppression

458. A young woman meets a man only once. Following this encounter, she "falls madly in love" with him and writes about their love affair in her secret diary each day for the next year. This is best described as

    (A) acting out
    (B) an erotic transference
    (C) anticipation
    (D) a schizophreniform psychosis
    (E) schizoid fantasy

459. At the end of the oedipal stage a boy becomes allied with his father. This is the classic example of

    (A) acting out
    (B) identification with the aggressor
    (C) sublimation
    (D) idealization
    (E) reaction formation

460. A patient with borderline personality disorder would be expected to employ each of the following ego defenses EXCEPT

    (A) reaction formation
    (B) projective identification
    (C) regression
    (D) splitting
    (E) somatization

DIRECTIONS: Each question below contains four suggested responses of which **one or more** is correct. Select

A	if	**1, 2, and 3**	are correct
B	if	**1 and 3**	are correct
C	if	**2 and 4**	are correct
D	if	**4**	is correct
E	if	**1, 2, 3, and 4**	are correct

461. Alexithymia is characterized by

(1) an inability to appreciate the feelings of others
(2) an association with chronic pain syndromes
(3) prolonged periods of depression
(4) a subjective unawareness of one's emotions

462. Secondary process thinking may be described as

(1) a consequence of thought derailing
(2) a phenomenon found in schizophreniform psychosis
(3) a manifestation of a core delusional experience
(4) a logical process

463. The positive symptoms of schizophrenia

(1) tend to be resistant to neuroleptic medication
(2) imply a poor prognosis
(3) are more common in male schizophrenics
(4) include paranoid delusions

464. Schneiderian first-rank symptoms include

(1) thought withdrawal
(2) auditory hallucinations
(3) thought broadcasting
(4) thought hearing

465. The classic interictal personality disorder is characterized by

(1) hypergraphia
(2) hyperviscosity
(3) hypermoralism
(4) hyposexuality

466. Characteristics of hypnopompic hallucinations include that they

(1) occur at sleep onset
(2) are associated with narcolepsy
(3) usually indicate psychosis
(4) often occur in normal persons

467. Typical features of a fugue state include

(1) the assumption of a new identity
(2) repetitive stereotypic movements
(3) amnesia for previous life experiences
(4) bizarre somatosensory experiences

468. An uncomplicated grief reaction may include which of the following?

(1) Somatic symptoms such as insomnia, weight loss, and loss of appetite
(2) Social withdrawal
(3) Emotional numbing
(4) Marked functional impairment and psychomotor retardation

469. The speech of a schizophrenic patient may be characterized by

(1) neologisms
(2) mutism
(3) verbigeration
(4) dysprosody

470. Obsessive ruminations may be found as a manifestation of

(1) major depressive disorder
(2) schizophrenia
(3) Tourette's disorder
(4) conversion disorder

471. Trichotillomania may be characterized as

    (1) a mood-congruent psychotic disorder
    (2) a disorder usually associated with advanced dementia
    (3) an example of a factitious disorder
    (4) an irresistible urge to pull out one's hair

472. Symptoms typical of posttraumatic stress disorder include

    (1) emotional numbing
    (2) increased distractibility
    (3) amnesia for the traumatic event
    (4) social avoidance

473. Alcoholic hallucinosis may be described by which of the following?

    (1) It is associated with an acute confusional state
    (2) It may persist for several weeks
    (3) It only involves visual hallucinations
    (4) It usually occurs within 48 h of cessation of alcohol use

DIRECTIONS: Each group of questions below consists of lettered headings followed by a set of numbered items. For each numbered item select the **one** lettered heading with which it is **most** closely associated. Each lettered heading may be used **once, more than once, or not at all.**

Questions 474–477

For each definition appearing below, choose the statistical term that is most appropriate.

    (A)   Mean
    (B)   Median
    (C)   Standard deviation
    (D)   *t*-Distribution
    (E)   Normal distribution

474. A bell-shaped frequency distribution curve such as would be generated by plotting the height of a large number of people

475. The arithmetic sum of the observations divided by the number of observations

476. A bell-shaped curve with the tails containing more area than a *z*-distribution

477. The square root of the variance

Questions 478–481

For each definition appearing below, choose the type of validity that it most accurately describes.

    (A)   Construct validity
    (B)   Predictive validity
    (C)   Correlative validity
    (D)   Concurrent validity
    (E)   Content validity

478. Extent to which the items in a rating scale sample the universe of behaviors to the observer, e.g., in a rating scale for depression, how well the items of the rating scale reflect the behaviors actually found in depression

479. Relation between test results and another criterion evaluated at about the same time, e.g., a comparison of self-rating depression scale results with ratings made on the basis of clinical judgment

480. Ability of a measuring instrument to forecast another measurement by a different criterion at a different time, e.g., comparison of results of a self-rating depression scale

481. Demonstration that certain explanatory constructs—e.g., depression or anxiety—account for some portion of variability of the ratings

Questions 482–485

For each set of primary goals of psychotherapy listed below, select the originator with whom it is most closely identified.

- (A) Alfred Adler
- (B) Harry Stack Sullivan
- (C) Karen Horney
- (D) Jules Masserman
- (E) Eric Berne

482. To relieve immediate distress and guide the patient by any ethical means to more satisfying ways of living and a new life philosophy

483. To increase the patient's social interest so that the patient can feel an equal among peers and abandon unrealistic views of life

484. To free the patient from compulsions and resistance to change so that creative forces can be expressed

485. To develop and maintain a patient's self-esteem and interpersonal security

Questions 486–490

Match the following.

- (A) *Mens rea*
- (B) *Lex talionis*
- (C) *Non compos mentis*
- (D) *Habeas corpus*
- (E) *Parens patriae*

486. The right to challenge the lawfulness of detention

487. Lack of capacity to exercise sound judgment

488. The guilty mind

489. Retributive justice

490. The right of the state to hold a dangerous person in custody

Questions 491–496

For each clinical vignette, choose the defense mechanism of which it is illustrative.

- (A) Fixation
- (B) Resistance
- (C) Dissociation
- (D) Displacement
- (E) Restitution

491. An epileptic adult, with no cognitive deficits, continually forgets to buy his medication, loses it when he buys it, and forgets to take it when his wife brings it home for him

492. A juvenile male enters therapy because of an inordinate feeling of anger toward and hatred of policemen. He fears that he will attack or assault a policeman because he becomes enraged by the sight of any male wearing a uniform. The patient comes from a broken home with a harsh, punitive father whom he, nevertheless, claims to love

493. An adult in psychoanalytic therapy is making satisfactory progress but then begins to arrive late at therapy sessions and seems disgruntled with the therapist

494. A 20-year-old woman who had recently become engaged experienced three episodes in which she wandered aimlessly on the streets; she did not harm herself or others during these episodes. She describes complete amnesia for these episodes. Neurologic examination and EEG results were normal

495. An 18-year-old woman enters therapy after having a child out of wedlock. The conception occurred several months after her younger sister died from rheumatic heart disease. The patient expresses strong feelings of guilt and responsibility for her sibling's death and the grief it has caused in her parents

496. A 9-year-old boy is presented for therapy because of his mother's complaints of his excessive mouthing of objects, excessive appetite, and thumb sucking. These have been lifelong behaviors. The child is dressed like—and acts like—a much younger child

Questions 497–501

For each clinical sketch below, choose the type of resistance to which it most closely corresponds.

    (A)   Secondary gain resistance
    (B)   Superego resistance
    (C)   Id resistance
    (D)   Transference resistance
    (E)   Conscious resistance

497. During a session of free association, a patient thinks about describing having masturbated the night before but does not tell the analyst because of feelings of shame and embarrassment

498. During a therapy hour, a patient begins by freely discussing his feelings about his father, using veiled criticism with no display of affect. The therapist listens quietly. The patient becomes silent for a period, then somewhat angrily says, "Why don't you say something? You are just sitting there"

499. In discussing her repetitious hand-washing, a patient is unable to connect the act with the early desire she had to handle her brother's genitals. On many occasions, the therapist had, by gentle interpretation, suggested to the patient the possibility of a connection when the hand-washing and early fantasy had been repeatedly linked by the patient while free associating

500. A patient struggling with an offer of a job far better than any held by his siblings or father is unable to make a decision to accept it. The analysis discloses strong feelings that the patient wants to be the most loved and successful member of the family, and this is attended by much guilt

501. With many years of indulgence on the part of her husband for her headaches and infirmities, a patient has improved in her ability to work and complete household chores like grocery shopping. She cannot induce herself to learn to drive, however, and insists that her husband drive her wherever she goes

Psychosocial Issues and Phenomenology

Answers

428. The answer is C. (*Kaplan, ed 5. p 375.*) Repression is considered a neurotic ego defense. It describes the process of expelling a thought or feeling from consciousness without being aware that one is doing it. The ego defense of suppression describes the process whereby one consciously and deliberately avoids paying attention to a thought or feeling. A hierarchy of ego defense mechanisms has been described by Dr. George Vaillant: psychotic (narcissistic), immature, neurotic, and mature ego defenses. Other mature ego defenses are anticipation and asceticism.

429. The answer is B. (*Kaplan, ed 5. pp 372–374.*) The ego essentially functions as a mediator between a person's instinctual libidinous drives and instincts and the reality of the outside world. Each of its functions is therefore directed toward this goal. According to classical psychoanalytic theory, the ego is responsible for the following functions: (1) control and regulation of instinctual drives; (2) development of an appropriate relationship to reality; (3) the capacity to develop and sustain appropriate object relationships; and (4) primary autonomous functions such as speaking, thinking, learning, intelligence, perception, and intuition. The ability to "self-evaluate" one's behavior is a function of the superego, which emerges with resolution of the Oedipus complex. It represents the incorporation and integration of parental standards and the development of an "ego-ideal."

430. The answer is D. (*Kaplan, ed 5. pp 399–401.*) Margaret Mahler described three developmental phases based on the theory of object relations. In the normal autistic phase (birth to 4 weeks), the major task is to achieve homeostatic equilibrium with the environment. In the normal symbiotic phase (4 weeks to 4 months), the child behaves as if he or she and the caretaker were undifferentiated. The child also develops a social smile at this age. The third phase is separation/individuation (5 to 36 months). This phase is further divided into four subphases: differentiation, practicing, rapprochement, and consolidation and object constancy. During the subphase of differentiation (5 to 10 months), the child is emerging from his or her cocoon and exploring the outside world. The sensorium therefore develops and the child exhibits stranger anxiety. Practicing (10 to 16 months) is typified by further exploration and walking. The child will also develop separation anxiety during this period. During the rapprochement subphase (16 to 24 months), the child is ambivalent about separation from the mother and may both seek and reject nurturance by her. The final subphase of separation-individuation (24 to 36 months), which is consolidation and object constancy, is characterized by the child's development of a stable internal image of the mother. The child is able to tolerate periods of separation and accept brief maternal substitutes and also develops a better sense of time and improved verbal skills during this period.

431. The answer is D. (*Kaplan, ed 5. p 375.*)   Splitting is a narcissistic (or psychotic) level ego defense mechanism in which all objects are experienced by a person as either "good" or "bad." These subjective categorizations are unstable and may oscillate rapidly between the two extremes. This process, by necessity, dictates that objects (including the self) must either be idealized or devalued. This defense mechanism therefore results in unstable relationships and extremes in the subject's mood. Splitting is considered to be the primary defense used by the borderline personality structure.

432. The answer is E. (*Kaplan, ed 5. pp 404–408.*)   Erik Erikson postulated eight stages of personality development extending from infancy into old age. Each stage of development is critical and each developmental task must be accomplished before progressing to the next stage. Erikson described a tripartite model for understanding personality development. This model includes the somatic, ego, and cultural-historical aspects of the person's experience, and the resolution of each developmental "crisis" is influenced by each of these factors. Erikson's eight stages of personality development are trust vs. mistrust, autonomy vs. shame and doubt, initiative vs. guilt, industry vs. inferiority, identity vs. role confusion, intimacy vs. isolation, generativity vs. stagnation, and finally integrity vs. despair.

433. The answer is B. (*Kaplan, ed 5. p 362.*)   The pleasure principle was conceptualized by Sigmund Freud. It refers to the inborn tendency of the organism to seek equilibrium by the discharge of tension. This is achieved by seeking pleasure rather than pain. The pleasure principle is modulated by the reality principle, which develops with maturation of the ego. The delay of immediate gratification by the reality principle was postulated to result eventually in greater pleasure. Freud postulated that a disequilibrium between these two systems results in psychopathology.

434. The answer is C. (*Kaplan, ed 5. pp 256–260.*)   Formal operational thinking is the final stage of Piagetan cognitive development and begins in early adolescence. The acquisition of this degree of cognitive sophistication is not universal, however, and it is estimated that approximately 25 percent of adults are capable of formal operational thinking. It is characterized by the ability to abstract and manipulate theoretical concepts. Entry into this stage invites an increasing interest in politics, religion, and philosophy. The four stages of Piagetan cognitive development are sensorimotor (birth to 2 years), preoperational thought (2 to 7 years), concrete operations (7 to 11 years), and formal operational thinking (11 years to adulthood).

435. The answer is D. (*Kaplan, ed 5. p 375.*)   Projective identification is a narcissistic level ego defense mechanism. Through this mechanism subjects deposit uncomfortable aspects of themselves on the observer and thereby distance themselves from these experiences. These experiences are modified by the recipient. This defense is commonly employed by persons with borderline personality disorder and often makes the therapist uncomfortable.

436. The answer is E. (*Kaplan, ed 5. pp 2118–2119.*)   Confidentiality is defined as the responsibility of the physician not to disclose to any third party information shared by the patient. Breach of confidentiality is grounds for, and is a common cause of, litigation by patients against their physicians. The exceptions to the confidentiality rule are (1) emergency situations (since there is no clear definition of what constitutes an emergency, the physician must use sound clinical judgment as to what constitutes an emergency); (2) patient incompetence—in this situation the patient's guardian or the court should be asked permission to release information; (3) information necessary to commit a patient; (4) reportable conditions—the abuse of minors or the presence of communicable diseases requires reporting to the appropriate agency; (5) the legal right of third-party payers to some aspects of the patient's record.

437. The answer is A. (*Kaplan, ed 5. pp 2112–2113.*)   *Competence* is a task-specific term that refers to a person's ability to perform certain tasks through a capacity to use information and make a decision based on the person's own value system. The concept of global competency is therefore invalid and each determination of competency should be made with only the particular task in mind; for example, a patient may be competent to make decisions regarding treatment choices but incompetent to handle finances. Informed consent is obtained through the patient's guardian. Although the psychiatrist may be asked to make a professional assessment of a person's competence, the court ultimately makes the ruling. A patient's competency does not influence confidentiality.

438. The answer is D. (*Simon, pp 386–388.*) The term *respondeat superior* (literal translation from the Latin: "Let the master respond") refers to the vicarious responsibility that attending physicians have for the negligence of those they directly supervise (e.g., resident staff or paramedical therapists). This legal concept has important implications for physicians working in multidisciplinary settings such as community mental health centers. In any situation where the physician is responsible for signing insurance forms to enable nonmedical therapists to receive payment, that physician is considered ethically, morally, and medically responsible for the treatment that those personnel provide.

439. The answer is E. (*Kaplan, ed 5. pp 2108–2109.*) The elements of malpractice incorporate four factors often referred to as the "4 D's": (1) *dereliction* or negligence by the physician, (2) a breach of the physician's *duty* to his patient, (3) *damages* (injury) experienced by the patient, and (4) a *direct* causation between the physician's negligence and the damage. All these factors must be present for a claim of medical malpractice to be successful.

440. The answer is A. (*Kaplan, ed 5. p 2121.*) The American Law Institute rule has become an integral part of American insanity law. It states that a person is not responsible for an alleged crime if that person (1) lacks the ability to appreciate that the alleged act was wrong or (2) is incapable of behaving in accordance with the law. This law provides the judge and jury with considerable flexibility in reaching their determination about a particular defendant's sanity.

441. The answer is C. (*Kaplan, ed 5. pp 2119–2120.*) The Tarasoff II decision held that therapists have a duty to take all reasonable steps to protect a third party from physical assault by their clients. This represents an extension of the Tarasoff I decision, which stated that the therapist simply had a responsibility to warn any potential victim. According to this ruling, the therapist therefore has a responsibility to both the patient and third parties. It determines that the therapist should predict the likelihood of potential violence and overrides the confidentiality of the patient-doctor relationship. The specific Tarasoff II ruling applies only to therapists in California; each state has its own precedents.

442. The answer is B. (*Kaplan, ed 5. pp 2118–2119.*) Privilege is the right of the patient to bar from the court (or any judicial hearing) any information disclosed within the doctor-patient relationship. Exceptions to the rule of privilege are (1) patient litigation, (2) the patient's making his or her mental state part of the legal argument, (3) child custody, and (4) duty to protect third parties. Confidentiality is the obligation of the therapist not to disclose any information about the patient without the patient's permission.

443. The answer is D. (*Kaplan, ed 5. p 1540.*) The structural model of family therapy is based on the concept that families require clearly defined boundaries with a strong parental hierarchy. The system must, however, be adaptive to environmental change and allow for the growth of individual family members. Family malfunction stems from deficits in the establishment of defined but malleable boundaries. The goal of therapy is therefore to disrupt the family's current dysfunctional system and establish these clear boundaries and parental hierarchy.

444. The answer is B. (*Kaplan, ed 5. pp 1551–1552.*) ''Collusive defense'' refers to the tendency of a couple to share distortions and projective identifications designed to fulfill the unconscious needs of each partner. This suggests that both partners are responsible for maintaining the couple's pattern of behavior. This concept has significant ramifications for therapy of both couples and individuals and predicts that change by either partner will disrupt this shared defense and threaten the integrity of the system. It is also important to appreciate that not every collusive defense is necessarily pathologic; it may indeed provide the basis for a stable and healthy relationship.

445. The answer is B. (*Kaplan, ed 5. pp 1101–1103.*) Although it is difficult to estimate the true incidence of incest, most recent statistics suggest that approximately 15 percent of women and 6 percent of men have been sexually abused and that about half of these cases involve incest. Father-daughter incest accounts for 75 percent of incest and often involves more than one daughter. Most cases involve the eldest daughter around the age of 10. Risk factors include fathers with a history of alcoholism, poor impulse control, psychosis, depression, or chronic illness. A higher incidence of incest has been reported in lower socioeconomic groups and in families where a parent has been married before. Several characteristic patterns of family dynamics have been described. One typical pattern is a father characterized by alcohol abuse and a mother who is habitually physically assaulted and sanctions the incest.

446. The answer is B. (*Kaplan, ed 5. pp 313–315.*) *Point prevalence* refers to the number of cases of a disorder at a specific point in time. *Period prevalence* is the number of cases present within a certain period. The *incidence* is the number of new cases of a disorder that have their onset within a specific time period. A *cohort* is a sample of a well-specified population. The *relative risk* is the incidence in the group with the risk factor divided by the incidence in the group without the risk factor.

447. The answer is E. (*Kaplan, ed 5. p 345.*) The null hypothesis states that differences between samples are secondary to chance alone, i.e., that the effect being investigated does not exist. A type I error occurs when the null hypothesis is rejected when it should have been retained. A type II error occurs when the null hypothesis is retained when it should have been rejected.

448. The answer is D. (*Kaplan, ed 5. pp 1136–1138.*) *Pseudologia fantastica* describes the incredible, usually self-aggrandizing stories that patients with a factitious disorder such as Münchausen's syndrome may construct. These patients will fabricate elaborate, extensive life histories to gain acceptance (e.g., medical symptoms and histories in Münchausen's syndrome in an attempt to receive medical treatment). Patients appear to have an inadequate sense of self and attempt to develop relationships based on their imaginary identities. Developmental histories are characterized by an unstable family of origin often with neglect or abandonment.

449. The answer is C. (*Kaplan, ed 5. p 1013.*) Conversion disorder describes the subjective alteration of a particular bodily function in the absence of any identifiable physical pathology. The incidence of the condition appears to be decreasing and is more common among females, lower socioeconomic groups, and rural and poorly educated persons. The presence of other psychiatric disease also predisposes to the condition. It usually occurs in persons with histrionic, passive-aggressive, and dependent personalities. Conversion disorders were the breeding ground for early psychodynamic theory and inspired Freud's attempts to outline psychoanalytic principles. These earliest psychodynamic constructs considered conversion disorders to be a failure to resolve incestuous oedipal conflicts. They have been expanded to include the presence of any unconscious intrapsychic conflict and the presence of any primary or secondary gain. Neurobehavioral theory suggests that the conversion disorder is secondary to alterations in cortical arousal served primarily by the right hemisphere. This theory would explain why the majority of conversion symptoms are left-sided.

450. The answer is A.   (*Kaplan, ed 5. pp 1015–1016.*)   Conversion disorders may present with motor or sensory symptoms or both. The most common are hemianesthesia, gait disturbance (astasia-abasia), glove-and-stocking anesthesia, tunnel blindness, pseudoseizures, and tremors. Symptoms that correlate with neuroanatomic boundaries (e.g., dermatome sensory loss) suggest physical pathology. *La belle indifference* describes the patient's apparent lack of concern for his or her predicament, and although this symptom was once considered pathognomonic of conversion, it is now considered an unreliable sign.

451. The answer is E.   (*Kaplan, ed 5. p 1016.*)   Although the initial conversion symptom remits rapidly in 90 percent of patients, at least 25 percent have a recurrence within 6 years. It has been estimated that as many as 60 percent of patients initially diagnosed as suffering from a conversion disorder will eventually be found to have an organic etiology for their symptoms. After excluding any physical basis for the symptom, treatment focuses on reassuring the patient and identifying psychosocial precipitants. Hypnosis and amobarbital (Amytal) may be helpful in identifying occult factors. Once these precipitants have been identified, individual, family, and behavioral therapy may all be effective in developing more productive coping skills in the patient and family.

452. The answer is A.   (*Kaplan, ed 5. pp 1025–1027.*)   Monosymptomatic delusional hypochondriasis refers to the delusion that one is suffering from a single, specific physical affliction. The most common example is delusional parasitosis (i.e., the belief that one is infested by a parasite). The disorder is more common in females with an average age of onset of 55. The disease may profoundly negatively influence the life-style of the person and may occasionally result in suicide. High-potency neuroleptics (pimozide has been most extensively studied) are effective in alleviating the delusion.

453. The answer is C.   (*Strub, pp 277–278.*)   The term *agnosia* describes a deficit in cognition. In particular, *prosopagnosia* describes an inability to recognize familiar faces. A person with prosopagnosia may be able to recognize the voices of family members without recognizing their facial features. The condition is caused by bilateral lesions in the visual association cortices. Many other modality-specific agnosias have been described; these include tactile, auditory, and visual agnosias.

454. The answer is E.   (*Kaplan, ed 5. pp 770–773.*)   Catatonia is currently divided into two broad subtypes: stuporous and excited catatonia. Stuporous catatonia is characterized by stereotypy, bizarre postures, mutism, waxy flexibility, negativism, echolalia, and echopraxia. *Excited catatonia* appears to be a misnomer and is now seldom used. The excited catatonic is described as agitated, talkative, and driven by delusions. It is most likely that these patients are in fact suffering from manic psychosis. Perseveration describes a person's inability to change set and is normally associated with prefrontal lesions.

455. The answer is A.   (*Strub, pp 112–117.*)   The acute confusional state (delirium) is a rapidly developing alteration in the level of arousal and attention. The disorder is a nonspecific symptom of an encephalopathy of any etiology. The clinical features of an acute confusional state include perseveration, distractibility, lack of persistence, alteration in consciousness, and hallucinations. Since attention is the "bedrock" of cognitive functioning, it is misleading to interpret higher cognitive functioning in the context of an acute confusional state. The presence of an encephalopathy is confirmed by diffuse background slowing on electroencephalography.

456. The answer is C.   (*Kaplan, ed 5. pp 1382–1384.*)   The obsessive-compulsive personality uses the ego defenses of isolation of affect and reaction formation as a means of controlling uncomfortable, ego-dystonic affect. This need for control results in perfectionism and undoing, which paralyzes the person's attempts at decision-making. A genetic predisposition to obsessive-compulsive personality has been documented. Freud conceptualized these persons as fixated at the anal stage of psychosexual development and bound in a conflict between libidinous drives and parental expectations. Erikson postulated that this arrest at the anal stage leads to a dilemma between the choices of autonomy and shame.

457. The answer is D. (*Kaplan, ed 5. pp 974–976.*)   Phobias provided Freud with material for much of his early work in psychoanalysis. In particular, his study of little Hans who suffered from a phobia of horses provided the template for the development of his theory that displacement is the mechanism necessary for the development of phobias. By this mechanism, affect can be directed from the initial object toward one less threatening and can be thus avoided. In the case of Hans, Freud postulated that the boy's repressed and hostile feelings (oedipal conflict) toward his father could be redirected toward horses. Since Hans was able to avoid horses, his anxiety could be subjectively avoided.

458. The answer is E. (*Kaplan, ed 5. p 375.*)   Schizoid fantasy is an immature level ego defense mechanism. Through this mechanism the person retreats into an autistic environment in which conflicts can be resolved and gratification obtained without the perceived threat of intimacy. The person does not believe the content of the fantasy and does not act it out. Other immature ego defenses include acting out, blocking, hypochondriasis, introjection (e.g., identification with the aggressor), passive-aggressive behavior, projection, regression, and somatization.

459. The answer is B. (*Kaplan, ed 5. p 375.*)   Identification with the aggressor is an example of introjection—an immature ego defense mechanism. Although the internalization of objects is a necessary part of development, the introjection of the punitive traits of the aggressor will result in self-punitive symptoms. By introjecting a feared object, one feels more control of the anxiety-provoking affect.

460. The answer is A. (*Kaplan, ed 5. p 384.*)   The borderline personality uses narcissistic level ego defenses. In particular, splitting and projective identification are considered to be the primary defensive strategies of the borderline personality. In splitting, external objects are viewed as either "all good" or "all bad" and the subject's perception of the object may change rapidly. This instability will result in unstable and volatile dyadic relationships.

461. The answer is C (2, 4). (*Kaplan, ed 5. p 470.*)   Alexithymia describes the inability to experience emotions at a subjective level. The alexithymic person can be expected to respond to situations of emotional conflict and dysphoria with somatic complaints. These persons therefore have a higher incidence of chronic pain syndromes and somatization disorders. The genesis of alexithymia is unknown but it does appear to be a disorder of temperament.

462. The answer is D (4). (*Kaplan, ed 5. p 560.*)   The concept of primary and secondary process thinking was introduced by Freud. Primary process thinking uses symbols, metaphors, and images to produce an illogical cognitive style. Freud considered that this form of thinking was involved in dreaming and creative thinking. Secondary process (primarily language-based) thinking relies on sequential, rational processes in the production of a predictable, logical cognitive style. Secondary process thinking is therefore helpful in abstract thinking, planning, and problem-solving.

463. The answer is D (4). (*Kaplan, ed 5. pp 774–775.*)   There has been a resurgence in interest in attempting to define the positive and negative subtypes of schizophrenia. Positive symptoms include hallucinations, delusions, and agitation. Negative symptoms include apathy, social withdrawal, poverty of affect of speech, and cognitive deficits associated with schizophrenia. Positive symptoms are associated with an acute episode or acute exacerbation of illness and tend to respond to neuroleptics. Negative symptoms tend to be insidious and associated with poor social functioning. Females tend to exhibit more positive symptoms.

464. **The answer is E (all).** (*Kaplan, ed 5. p 458.*) Schneider attempted to delineate symptoms that could distinguish the psychosis of schizophrenia from other secondary psychoses (i.e., those secondary to an "organic" process). Although experience has demonstrated that the Schneiderian first-rank symptoms are not pathognomonic for process schizophrenia, they are still frequently referred to and have been incorporated into current nosology such as that found in the *DSM III-R.* First-rank symptoms include audible thoughts, thought hearing, broadcasting and withdrawal, auditory hallucinations, experiences of influence, and alienation. Schneider also described the nonspecific second-rank symptoms of emotional impoverishment, depressed or elevated mood, and other perceptual disturbances.

465. **The answer is E (all).** (*Strub, pp 410–411.*) The features of the classic interictal personality of temporo-limbic epilepsy include (1) hyperviscosity (not being able to change the subject of conversation); (2) hypergraphia (excessive writing); (3) hypermoralism; (4) a sense of personal destiny; (5) hyposexuality; (6) circumstantiality; (7) dependence and passivity; (8) lack of humor; (9) elation or euphoria; (10) compulsive behavior; (11) hostility and aggressive behavior; (12) paranoia; (13) increased emotionality; and (14) depression. These represent stable characteristics in the temperament of some patients with temporo-limbic epilepsy and are probably not influenced by anticonvulsants.

466. **The answer is C (2, 4).** (*Kaplan, ed 5. p 571.*) Hypnopompic and hypnagogic hallucinations are predominantly visual and occur at the time of waking and falling asleep, respectively. They are frequently experienced by normal persons and are not suggestive of any underlying psychotic disorder. The hallucinations have a "dreamlike" quality and may elicit extreme anxiety in those who first experience them. They are found in as many as 50 percent of patients with narcolepsy and they have also been reported with increased frequency in patients with temporo-limbic epilepsy.

467. **The answer is B (1, 3).** (*Kaplan, ed 5. pp 1032–1033.*) Fugue states are characterized by the sudden onset of periods of altered identity often associated with travel away from the person's usual place of routine. These persons are unaware that they are in an altered state of perception and, while in the fugue, have amnesia for past life experience. Their actions appear purposeful and seldom appear unusual to those unfamiliar with the person. Once they have returned to their usual mental status, they have no recollection of their behaviors during the period of fugue.

468. **The answer is A (1, 2, 3).** (*Kaplan, ed 5. pp 1346–1347.*) As described by *DSM III-R,* an uncomplicated grief reaction may last several months and include feelings of depression associated with somatic symptoms such as insomnia and loss of energy, appetite, and weight. The development of functional impairment and psychomotor slowing suggests the emergence of a complicated grief reaction. Survivors may hoard and "enshrine" the possessions of the deceased and may imagine that they see that person during the first few months after death. Complicated grief may be characterized by prolonged denial, clinical major depressive disorder, or a failure to resolve the affective distress associated with the initial stages of an uncomplicated grief.

469. **The answer is E (all).** (*Kaplan, ed 5. p 765.*) The speech of the schizophrenic may exhibit each of the features listed. Verbigeration describes the repetitive use of meaningless words or phrases. The schizophrenic may invent new words (neologisms) or simply refuse (or be unable) to communicate. Apart from the semantic and lexical errors described, the schizophrenic may also exhibit abnormalities in the nonverbal aspects of communication, which results in the production of inappropriate emotional coloring to a conversation (dysprosody). The automatic repetition of what the schizophrenic hears (echolalia) and word salad have also been described.

470. **The answer is A (1, 2, 3).** (*Kaplan, ed 5. pp 996–997.*) Obsessive ruminations do not constitute an encapsulated psychiatric syndrome but a symptom with a differential diagnosis. Approximately

30 percent of patients with a major depressive disorder exhibit obsessive ruminations, which will be considerably diminished once the patient is euthymic. Transient obsessive ruminations may be found in process schizophrenia, but their incidence is probably much less than previously thought. Approximately 3 to 12 percent of patients with obsessive-compulsive disorder (OCD) will develop a schizophreniform psychosis. There is an increased incidence of OCD among patients with Tourette's disorder.

471. The answer is D (4). (*Kaplan, ed 5. pp 1149–1151.*) Trichotillomania describes the irresistible urge to pull one's hair. Delaying the act causes increasing tension and the pulling of hair produces immediate reduction in anxiety—in this respect the disorder resembles obsessive-compulsive disorder. The incidence of the condition is unknown but is estimated at 1 to 3 percent of the population. A higher incidence is found among the mentally retarded. Behavior modification has been the major therapeutic modality although several recent studies have demonstrated the efficacy of tricyclic antidepressants.

472. The answer is E (all). (*Kaplan, ed 5. pp 1000–1008.*) The symptoms of posttraumatic stress disorder may occur at any time after the initial stressor. In simple terms, these symptoms may be divided into two broad categories: intrusive and avoidant. These symptoms essentially represent the person's attempts to cope with the initial stressor and avoid further incidents. Intrusive symptoms include distractibility, decreased sleep, nightmares, increased startle response, irritability, and difficulty concentrating. The person may reexperience the traumatic event with recurrent flashbacks or subjective reenactments. Avoidant symptoms include social withdrawal, emotional numbing, attempts to avoid reminders of the event, diminished interest in activities, and psychogenic amnesia for the event.

473. The answer is C (2, 4). (*Kaplan, ed 5. p 635.*) Alcoholic hallucinosis describes the development of auditory and visual hallucinations that normally occur within 24 to 48 h of alcohol withdrawal in an alcohol-dependent person. The hallucinations occur in the presence of a clear sensorium and last several weeks after cessation of alcohol use. Neuroleptics are effective in reducing the hallucinosis.

474–477. The answers are: 474-E, 475-A, 476-D, 477-C. (*Kaplan, ed 5. pp 340–345.*) No physician can read the clinical or experimental literature critically without at least a minimum knowledge of experimental design and statistics. Many statistical analyses compare the mean of some variable in an experimental group with the mean of a control group. The mean, or arithmetic average, is defined as the total value of the observations added together, divided by the number of observations. The mean is usually the most useful measure of the central tendency of the data.

   Other measures of central tendency are the median and the mode. The median is the midpoint between the highest and lowest point. The mode is the most frequently occurring value.

   To describe the numerical characteristics of a population requires knowledge of the variation of the data. The values used for this purpose are the range, variance, and standard deviation. The range is the difference between the highest and lowest values in the data. The variance is the average squared deviation of the individual values of the mean.

   A *t*-distribution resembles a bell-shaped normal distribution but has more area in the two tails of the curve. The *t*-distribution reflects the fact that for small samples (less than 30), the standard deviation will, on average, be larger than in an infinite population. Therefore, in order to achieve statistical significance with small numbers of subjects, the difference between the control groups has to be greater than is the case with large numbers of subjects.

478–481. The answers are: 478-E, 479-D, 480-B, 481-A. (*Kaplan, ed 5. pp 313–314.*) Behavior rating instruments are usually examined for several kinds of validity. Before the validity of any scale can be determined, its reliability must be examined. Reliability, defined as the consistency of the instrument in differentiating one subject from the other, is most efficiently determined by applying correlational measures to ratings established by different judges.

While all forms of validity are interrelated, there are differences. A rating scale may have one form of validity and not another. Before researchers decide to employ a certain scale, they must determine whether the scale has content validity, i.e., whether it measures the behavior it is meant to.

A second important type of validity, concurrent validity, is determined by comparing test results with some other independent criterion of measurement. For example, the scores of a self-rated depression scale could be compared with the clinical judgment of a psychiatrist following an interview.

In predictive validity, a determination is made as to how well a measurement can predict another measure by another means at a later time. The difference between concurrent and predictive validity involves differences in time periods when the criterion measures are obtained; i.e., concurrent validity measures are performed at the same time and predictive measures at different times.

Construct validity refers to the extent to which an instrument measures an explanatory construct. A researcher must make predictions that certain types of scores will be obtained if the test adequately measures the researcher's construct.

482–485. The answers are: 482-D, 483-A, 484-C, 485-B. (*Kaplan, ed 5. pp 411–431.*) Six people are commonly thought of as belonging to the cultural and interpersonal school of psychoanalytic thought, and all are widely acclaimed as effective and innovative therapists. Alfred Adler (1870–1937) was a member of Freud's circle from 1902 to 1911. When Adler disputed Freud's theory of innate aggressive drive, he became disassociated from Freud. Best known for his theory of the "inferiority complex" and striving for superiority as motivating human behavior, Adler also introduced a number of other widely held theories regarding the basic social nature of humans and the necessity for taking responsibility for one's own behavior. In his therapeutic practice, he finally came to stress that patients must increase their social interest in order to increase their self-esteem.

Karen Horney (1885–1952) was trained in psychoanalysis by Karl Abraham and his school in Berlin and came to the United States, where her creativity was encouraged. In her famous book *The Neurotic Personality of Our Time,* she presented evidence to demonstrate that culture and environmental events are potent etiological factors in the production of neurosis. Horney based her therapy primarily on the reduction of "blockages," or resistances, in order to free patients from a "compulsive," stereotyped approach to life.

The name Harry Stack Sullivan (1892–1949) is practically synonymous with the "interpersonal" approach to psychiatry and human behavior. Trained in the United States, he underwent classical analysis but early in his career rejected classical psychoanalysis on both theoretical and pragmatic grounds. Sullivan's guiding principle in therapy was to preserve and increase a patient's self-esteem. He also regarded each psychiatric interview, no matter how short, as an opportunity for therapy.

Sandor Rado (1890–1971) materially tried to change the field of psychoanalysis, but never broke from it. He endeavored to increase the scientific underpinning of psychoanalysis and keep it within the fold of medicine. Rado defined an emotionally healthy person as self-reliant and capable of experiencing affection, pride, friendliness, optimism, and joy. Accordingly, his therapy was aimed at enhancing these characteristics in his patients in addition to developing their independence.

Jules Masserman was trained in psychoanalysis by Franz Alexander and in psychobiology by Adolf Meyer. His research and clinical career have been devoted to an amalgamation of biologic and psychological concepts. He has used laboratory methods to investigate methods of psychotherapy and has evolved an eclectic approach that invokes all ethical procedures in helping patients find a better life-style and life-view.

Transactional analysis was developed by Eric Berne in the fifties after he decided traditional psychoanalysis took too long to effect change in patients. He was originally influenced by Paul

Federn and the Vienna Psychoanalytic Society, but parted ways in a friendly spirit from classical analysis. Berne developed not only script analysis but also a total theory of personality in which he took ideas from California group therapists. Frederick Perls' gestalt techniques were particularly useful to Berne in delineating ego states and interpersonal games. In his therapy, Berne tried to demystify the complexities of human behavior by reducing problem behavior to its simplest form, thereby helping patients to see destructive forms of human interaction ("games"). The final phase of therapy was to help patients interrupt their games.

The above six pioneers, through their writings and speeches, have influenced not only several generations of psychiatric trainees but the general public as well. Adlerian groups exist throughout the world, and Berne fostered a creativity in his followers that has enabled transactional analysis to grow in the decade since his death.

486–490. The answers are: 486-D, 487-C, 488-A, 489-B, 490-E. (*Kaplan, ed 5. pp 2107–2123.*) The traditional approach to crime and punishment holds that persons are endowed with free will and therefore are responsible for their behavior, and that the threat of punishment deters antisocial behavior. According to these concepts, a person who by free will chooses to commit antisocial acts should receive punishment as a deterrence against such acts in the future, as well as a deterrence to persons who might otherwise be tempted to commit similar acts. When an antisocial act has been judged the result of free will, the doctrine of *lex talionis* applies. This doctrine, enunciated in the code of Hammurabi, justifies the taking of "an eye for an eye or a tooth for a tooth." Offenders are punished in kind for their misdeeds. Traditional doctrine holds that the degree of punishment depends on the state of mind of the person, which supposedly can be determined by the court's evaluation of legal and psychiatric evidence. It is, of course, possible to challenge every one of these assumptions. Nevertheless, some legal machinery is required to protect society.

The doctrine of *parens patriae* holds that the state may intervene and hold in custody persons deemed dangerous to themselves or others. This doctrine leads to commitment procedures for those persons judged incompetent, insane, or dangerous to self or others.

All societies recognize that mental illness and dementia may ameliorate the doctrine of responsibility. The doctrine of *non compos mentis* recognizes that patients thus affected may lack the capacity to exercise free will and therefore are less responsible for their behavior.

The concept of *mens rea,* the guilty mind, applies to a person accused of an antisocial act who is capable of having committed the act with deliberation and malice aforethought. If the accused person is judged not to have the guilty mind, the punishment is correspondingly ameliorated. The psychiatrist's role has been to advise the court of the mental state of the accused person. The court then decides on the weight to be accorded this information in setting the sentence, either for a prison term or detention in a mental institution.

Habeas corpus refers to the right of any detained person to have a hearing to determine the legality of the detainment. At a hearing, a judge will decide on the legality of the procedures involved in confining the person. This right applies to prisoners as well as to patients in mental institutions.

491–496. The answers are: 491-B, 492-D, 493-B, 494-C, 495-E, 496-A. (*Kaplan, ed 5. pp 375–376.*) Ego defense mechanisms attempt to counter the anxiety generated by unresolved drives. Although these defenses diminish anxiety, if they become rigid and inflexible they may produce psychopathology.

Fixation describes the persistence of an immature mode of coping. It is postulated to occur as a result of stress during critical periods of ego development. The described patient's mouthing, sucking, and oral manipulation represent fixation at the oral stage.

Resistance describes opposition to the therapeutic process. In its simplest form, it describes a patient who "forgets" or refuses to comply with the terms of the therapeutic relationship. To the described patient, his medication symbolized his illness and he therefore believed that by not taking his medication he could deny the existence of his illness. This represents a prelogical or magical form of thinking. Resistance in the psychotherapeutic relationship provides productive material for the therapist to work with.

In displacement, the person transfers affect from one object to another more acceptable object. Through this mechanism the person may be able to tolerate the expression of an uncomfortable affect toward a less anxiety-provoking object. In the patient described, the link between his father and other authority figures is not difficult to extrapolate; the connection to the displacement object, however, is not always so clear.

In restitution, the subject relieves guilt by committing an act or adopting a life-style that is intended to atone for a perceived transgression. This should not be confused with reaction formation in which subjects do the opposite of their ego-dystonic drives.

497–501. The answers are: 497-E, 498-D, 499-C, 500-B, 501-A. (*Kaplan, ed 5. p 1448.*) A keystone of psychoanalysis is the recognition and management of resistances. Resistances arise when some distressing material in a person's unconscious threatens to become conscious.

Conscious resistance takes the form of deliberate censorship of material during free association, material that patients feel will cause the analyst to think poorly of them, or that will engender within themselves feelings of shame, guilt, or embarrassment.

The ego may expend much energy in repression resistances, which keep instinctual impulses from reaching conscious recognition. Repression resistance describes the efforts of the ego to prevent disclosures during the analytic process. If analysts can help their patients overcome the repression resistances, the ego will finally accept or reject the repressed instinctual material, thereby disposing of a permanent threat and the need to expend energy previously required to maintain the repression.

Patients with transference resistance transfer to the therapist significant feelings generated by some previously encountered person for whom the therapist acts as a symbol. Transference resistance has the particular quality of both reflecting and expressing the patient's struggle with early experience and feeling. Although the transference can be positive, it frequently takes a negative form that may be evidenced by silence, sarcasm, or by a veiled or overtly hostile question or remark. Therapists must recognize these kinds of responses as clinical transference phenomena and not respond in kind. The patient described in the question may have been struggling to cope with feelings about his father, but he was unable to connect his veiled criticisms of his father with their instinctual origins—an example of repression resistance. He then transferred the resistance to recognizing his feelings about his father to the analyst, whom he criticized for being silent. Such resistances appearing as transference can be dealt with very effectively by the analyst. A transference resistance can become a transference attachment. Alternatively, the negative aspects of the transference resistance may dominate and seriously impede the therapeutic relationship.

Id resistance refers to the inability to change some ingrained behavioral pattern, often in the form of a compulsion, which derives from a particular instinctual drive that is very powerful. The washing of hands as a manifestation of unacceptable sexual impulses is an example. The resistance is to unlearning the ingrained, maladaptive pattern of behavior that serves to mask, as it were, unacceptable impulses from which the behavior originates.

In superego resistance, patients on the verge of achieving some seemingly cherished goal find themselves too guilt-ridden about the achievement to accept it. Such promptings of the conscience prevent these patients from making their desired changes.

Patients with secondary gain resistance cling to the advantages that stem from their sick role, such as attention, comfort, and avoidance of responsibility. This is often seen in cases where financial compensation is involved.

Anxiety Disorders

DIRECTIONS: Each question below contains five suggested responses. Select the **one best** response to each question.

502. Panic disorder may be characterized as

    (A) usually having its onset in middle age
    (B) being a self-limiting disorder
    (C) occurring in approximately 10 percent of the population
    (D) having equal sex distribution
    (E) tending to run in families

503. A 65-year-old man with severe chronic obstructive airways disease complains of severe generalized anxiety. The most appropriate psychotropic would be

    (A) alprazolam
    (B) carbamazepine
    (C) fluvoxamine
    (D) buspirone
    (E) clonazepam

504. According to classical psychoanalytic theory, anxiety represents

    (A) unresolved separation from the mother
    (B) an undifferentiated id
    (C) the cause of repression
    (D) fixation at the oral stage of ego development
    (E) anger directed against the self

505. Each of the following is a true statement about posttraumatic stress disorder (PTSD) EXCEPT

    (A) the majority of a population experiencing a natural disaster will exhibit PTSD
    (B) the onset of the disorder may be delayed weeks or years after the stressor
    (C) PTSD is more common in children than in adults following a stressor
    (D) symptoms usually resolve within 1 week
    (E) PTSD is a frequent consequence of rape

506. The symptoms of generalized anxiety disorder

    (A) tend to worsen with age
    (B) are precipitated by intravenous lactate infusion
    (C) demonstrate diurnal variation
    (D) include difficulty initiating and maintaining sleep
    (E) have a 1-year prevalence of 1 percent in the general population

507. Each of the following is considered a long-acting benzodiazepine EXCEPT

   (A) clorazepate
   (B) diazepam
   (C) oxazepam
   (D) chlordiazepoxide
   (E) clonazepam

508. The compulsions found in a patient with obsessive-compulsive disorder

   (A) are usually ego-syntonic
   (B) are usually an attempt to modify or control a primary obsession or compulsion
   (C) are nonpurposeful
   (D) are usually considered reasonable by the patient
   (E) are usually a direct acting out of the patient's obsessive thoughts

509. Flooding therapy for agoraphobia

   (A) is effective in reducing symptoms in at least 60 percent of patients
   (B) causes the majority of patients to drop out of therapy
   (C) requires several weeks treatment
   (D) is less effective than cognitive therapy
   (E) has limited efficacy because of the emergence of extinction

510. The differential diagnosis of a patient exhibiting obsessive-compulsive behavior includes each of the following EXCEPT

   (A) schizophrenia
   (B) panic disorder
   (C) phobic disorder
   (D) Tourette's disorder
   (E) major depression

DIRECTIONS: Each question below contains four suggested responses of which **one or more** is correct. Select

A	if	**1, 2, and 3**	are correct
B	if	**1 and 3**	are correct
C	if	**2 and 4**	are correct
D	if	**4**	is correct
E	if	**1, 2, 3, and 4**	are correct

511. Which of the following medical conditions may mimic panic disorder?

  (1) Pheochromocytoma
  (2) Complex partial seizures
  (3) Caffeine intoxication
  (4) Hypoglycemia

512. True statements regarding buspirone include that it

  (1) is a potent GABA agonist
  (2) has significant potential for abuse
  (3) decreases psychomotor performance
  (4) acts at the 5-HT1 receptor

513. Agents that have demonstrated efficacy in panic disorder include

  (1) clonazepam
  (2) propranolol
  (3) desipramine
  (4) buspirone

514. Symptoms of withdrawal from diazepam

  (1) usually subside within 10 days of discontinuing the drug
  (2) may include generalized convulsions
  (3) are unlikely if the drug was used at therapeutic dosage
  (4) may include paranoid delusions

515. Sleep terrors in children

  (1) occur during REM sleep
  (2) are heralded by a scream
  (3) are usually indicative of psychopathology
  (4) normally occur during the first half of the night

516. Which of the following medications should alleviate the symptoms of alprazolam withdrawal?

  (1) Carbamazepine
  (2) Clonazepam
  (3) Propranolol
  (4) Buspirone

517. Patients with somatoform pain disorder are often

  (1) alexithymic
  (2) workaholics
  (3) suffering from a major depressive disorder
  (4) counterdependent

518. A 30-year-old woman is referred to a psychiatrist by her family doctor. Despite the fact that she is extremely attractive, she ruminates constantly over her perception that her nose is huge, bulbous, and deformed. Her distress

  (1) is likely to resolve spontaneously
  (2) will be alleviated by plastic surgery
  (3) should resolve with cognitive psychotherapy
  (4) may necessitate neuroleptic medication

519. The symptoms of posttraumatic stress disorder

  (1) may be aggravated by unrelated life stressors
  (2) include cognitive difficulties
  (3) may include psychogenic amnesia
  (4) usually disappear with time

520. Premature ejaculation is accurately described by which of the following statements?

    (1) It is more common among college-educated males
    (2) It is frequently associated with an anxiety disorder
    (3) It may be caused by urethritis
    (4) It occurs in approximately 30 percent of males

521. Appropriate initial treatment interventions for premature ejaculation include

    (1) hypnosis
    (2) anxiolytics
    (3) topical lidocaine jelly
    (4) the "squeeze technique"

522. True statements regarding sexual aversion disorder include that it

    (1) is almost completely confined to females
    (2) usually necessitates psychopharmacologic intervention
    (3) carries a poor prognosis despite treatment
    (4) is often found in association with panic disorder

523. The person who engages in "cross-dressing"

    (1) is almost always male
    (2) is usually homosexual
    (3) has frequently been engaged in other paraphiliac behavior
    (4) has a female sexual identity

524. When prescribing a benzodiazepine to an 80-year-old woman, the physician should expect

    (1) an increased half-life of the drug
    (2) increased absorption
    (3) decreased hepatic metabolism
    (4) decreased CNS sensitivity to the drug

Anxiety Disorders

Answers

502. **The answer is E.** (*Kaplan, ed 5. pp 958–960.*) Panic disorder is a common condition with an estimated 6-month prevalence of 0.6 to 1.0 percent. The prevalence of agoraphobia may be as high as 6 percent. Anxiety disorders are more common among females and usually have their onset in adolescence or young adulthood. Although genetic factors have been demonstrated in both generalized anxiety and panic disorders, the evidence suggests that there is a stronger genetic loading in panic disorder. The long-term course of panic disorder remains uncertain; it is clear, however, that most patients continue to experience recurrent episodes. The prognosis of generalized anxiety tends to be more favorable than that of panic disorder.

503. **The answer is D.** (*Hollister, ed 3. pp 22–24.*) The treatment of anxiety disorders in patients with compromised respiratory function often presents a therapeutic dilemma. Conventional anxiolytics (i.e., sedative hypnotics) may depress respiratory drive and further aggravate the patient's condition. Since it produces no such respiratory depression, the novel anxiolytic buspirone offers significant advantages in treating this group of patients. Buspirone produces no more sedation than a placebo. Indeed, several studies have suggested that the drug may improve psychomotor performance.

504. **The answer is C.** (*Kaplan, ed 5. p 961.*) Freud's earliest theory postulated that anxiety was the result of a failure to discharge libidinous energy. Later, he developed a more complex theoretical framework that included the concept of repression. According to this scheme, conscious ideas, emotions, and impulses that are unacceptable to the ego are forced into the unconscious by repression. Freud postulated that anxiety is secondary to that repression. Finally, as part of his structural model of the psyche, Freud postulated that anxiety is an expression of the ego's response to instinctual forces arising from the id. According to this theory, anxiety is considered to arise from the ego and is a primary psychological force.

505. **The answer is D.** (*Kaplan, ed 5. pp 1000–1008.*) As many as 80 percent of people who experience a catastrophic stressor will develop posttraumatic stress disorder (PTSD). Although symptoms may occur almost immediately following the stressor, they are more usually delayed weeks or years. PTSD may occur in any age group but is most common in children. Rather than resolve, the symptoms of PTSD may grow worse. A 20-year follow-up study of World War II veterans demonstrated an increase in symptoms with time. Although longitudinal studies are limited, it appears that PTSD is a cyclical disorder with periods of exacerbation precipitated by life stressors.

506. **The answer is D.** (*Kaplan, ed 5. pp 954–955.*) Generalized anxiety disorder usually has its onset in late adolescence or young adulthood and is more common in women. The onset of the disorder

after age 40 should raise the suspicion of an underlying medical precipitant. Physical symptoms reflect autonomic arousal. Although the condition tends to be chronic, the symptoms do subside with age. The 1-year prevalence in the general population is estimated at 6.4 percent.

507. The answer is C. (*Kaplan, ed 5. p 2040.*) Oxazepam has an elimination half-life of 8 h and is therefore classified as a short half-life benzodiazepine. The benzodiazepines may be divided into two groups based on their biotransformation characteristics. One group has inactive metabolites (e.g., lorazepam, oxazepam, and temazepam), while the other is metabolized to active compounds (e.g., chlordiazepoxide, diazepam, and clonazepam). The elimination half-life should not be confused with the drug's effective duration of action, since this is ultimately determined by the drug's lipid solubility (as a determinant of penetration of the blood-brain barrier), absorption, and receptor binding. Although oxazepam has a shorter elimination half-life than diazepam, its duration of action is longer because of its slow absorption and low lipid solubility.

508. The answer is B. (*Kaplan, ed 5. pp 994–995.*) The compulsive act is normally an attempt to control a primary obsession or compulsion. The compulsive ritual is seldom a direct acting out of the primary impulse and is therefore unlikely to dissipate the anxiety provoked by the primary obsession. The compulsions are usually ego-dystonic and are recognized by the subject as being irrational.

509. The answer is A. (*Kaplan, ed 5. p 1465.*) The behavioral technique of flooding is an effective treatment for agoraphobia and has proved superior to all other treatment modalities. This technique exposes the patient to the feared stimulus for brief but intense periods. Flooding is rapidly effective in reducing symptoms, but for the most sustained results the exposure should be spaced and regularly repeated. The goal of flooding is extinction—the elimination of the dysfunctional response to the feared stimulus. Ideally this technique should be used in conjunction with psychopharmacologic interventions.

510. The answer is B. (*Kaplan, ed 5. pp 997–998.*) Attempting to separate the syndrome of obsessive-compulsive disorder (OCD) from other psychiatric disorders may be difficult. Patients with a number of psychiatric conditions may exhibit obsessive-compulsive behavior as part of their condition. Differentiating the obsessive-compulsive syndrome from other conditions is important if appropriate treatment modalities are to be selected. Approximately 30 percent of patients with depressive disorder exhibit obsessive-compulsive symptoms and a similar fraction of patients with obsessive-compulsive disorder will develop a major depressive disorder. Patients with process schizophrenia often exhibit obsessive-compulsive behavior. It may also be difficult at times to distinguish the bizarre magical thinking of obsessive-compulsive disorder from schizophreniform delusions.

511. The answer is E (all). (*Kaplan, ed 5. pp 968–969.*) It behooves the physician to consider and exclude medical conditions that mimic panic disorder prior to commencing treatment. A number of conditions may produce symptoms similar to panic disorder. These symptoms essentially represent marked autonomic sympathetic overflow and may be caused by acute myocardial infarction, pheochromocytoma, hypoglycemia, caffeine intoxication, cocaine, and complex partial seizures. The relationship between mitral valve prolapse and panic disorder remains unclear, and although the two conditions may be found together, no direct causal relationship has been established. An electroencephalogram with anterior temporal or nasopharyngeal leads should be performed in all patients to explore the possibility of a complex partial seizure disorder.

512. The answer is D (4). (*Kaplan, ed 5. p 1665.*) Buspirone is a novel anxiolytic with demonstrated efficacy and a benign side effect profile. The drug is thought to act at the 5-HT1a autoreceptor with additional dopaminergic activity at higher doses. The drug produces no sedation and has been shown to improve psychomotor testing in the laboratory. Apart from mild dizziness, no significant side effects have been reported and the drug is safe far in excess of the therapeutic dosage.

513. The answer is B (1, 3). (*Kaplan, ed 5. pp 970–971.*)   A number of psychotropic drugs have proven efficacy in panic disorder. Tricyclic antidepressants take several weeks to produce maximum benefit and should be used in doses equivalent to those required for antidepressant effect. Monoamine oxidase inhibitors are effective in as many as 90 percent of patients but have a limited clinical role because of their potentially hazardous side effects. High-potency benzodiazepines (e.g., clonazepam, alprazolam) are rapidly effective and are useful adjuncts to antidepressants, particularly during the initial phase of treatment. Although beta blockers are probably effective in generalized anxiety disorder, they are not effective in panic disorder.

514. The answer is C (2, 4). (*APA Task Force Report, pp 15–21.*)   Physical dependence on benzodiazepines may occur at therapeutic dosage after just a few weeks' use. The temporal pattern of symptoms of discontinuance is largely dependent on the pharmacokinetic characteristics of the particular benzodiazepine. There may be an initial rebound of anxiety symptoms within a few days of stopping the drug. With a benzodiazepine of long half-life, such as diazepam or clonazepam, this period is followed in the first 10 days by a confusional state with tachycardia, hallucinations, and autonomic overflow. Paranoid delusions or frank psychosis may persist for as long as several months. Withdrawal seizures normally occur within a few days and are more common with high-potency benzodiazepines.

515. The answer is C (2, 4). (*Kaplan, ed 5. p 1122.*)   Sleep terrors usually have their onset before age 12 but may occasionally occur as late as the third decade. Their occurrence does not usually indicate underlying psychopathology in young children, but adults with the condition have a high incidence of anxiety disorders. Each episode is usually heralded by a scream and occurs during the first half of the evening during stages 3 and 4 (i.e., NREM) sleep. Subjects are unable to remember the content of their "terror," and this distinguishes the disorder from nightmares.

516. The answer is A (1, 2, 3). (*APA Task Force Report, pp 35–38.*)   Patients are more likely to experience symptoms following the withdrawal of short half-life, high-potency benzodiazepines (e.g., alprazolam, triazolam). The recent increase in the therapeutic use of these agents has increased the frequency of withdrawal symptoms. Tapering doses of long half-life benzodiazepines (e.g., clonazepam) usually provides an effective means of reducing withdrawal. Early data suggest that carbamazepine is effective in preventing withdrawal symptoms, although the drug's mode of action in this situation remains a matter of debate. Beta blockers and clonidine are helpful in reducing the autonomic overflow usually associated with withdrawal from benzodiazepines. Finally, phenobarbital substitution and tapering has also demonstrated efficacy in this situation.

517. The answer is E (all). (*Kaplan, ed 5. p 1021.*)   Somatoform pain disorder is a common and disabling condition in which the patient experiences severe disabling pain with no identifiable etiology. The symptoms must be present for at least 6 months to meet criteria for a diagnosis of this condition. It has been estimated that as many as half of these patients are suffering from a major depressive disorder and the remainder usually meet criteria for a dysthymic disorder. Several personality styles have been associated with the condition. These include the "pain-prone" patient who is pessimistic and self-punitive, the alexithymic patient who is unable to generate affective experience at a conscious level, and the counterdependent workaholic who finds nurturance unacceptable and therefore develops somatic complaints to validate dependent needs.

518. The answer is D (4). (*Kaplan, ed 5. pp 1025–1027.*)   Body dysmorphic disorder (which is also referred to as *monosymptomatic delusional hypochondriasis*) describes an irrational preoccupation with a symptom or perceived body deformity. Common examples include delusional parasitosis and a preoccupation with one's body odor or physical imperfections. The disorder may occur in isolation or in association with other psychiatric disorders such as major depression or schizophrenia or following neurologic injury. The illness tends to run a chronic, relapsing course. Treatment is primarily pharmacologic. The high-potency neuroleptic pimozide has documented efficacy. In addition, there have been isolated reports of a positive response to other neuroleptics, tricyclics, and monoamine oxidase inhibitors.

519. The answer is A (1, 2, 3). (*Kaplan, ed 5. pp 1005–1006.*) Symptoms of posttraumatic stress disorder may occur immediately following the stressor or more typically may be delayed months or years. Symptoms may be divided into three broad categories—those of intrusion, hyperarousal, and avoidance. Patients frequently exhibit deficits in attention with subsequent difficulties in short memory. The majority of patients experience chronic symptoms with periods of acute exacerbation.

520. The answer is E (all). (*Kaplan, ed 5. pp 1054–1055.*) There is no single definition of premature ejaculation. Masters and Johnson define it as an inability of the male to satisfy his female partner 50 percent of the time. This definition of course implies that the female partner is capable of achieving orgasm normally. Premature ejaculation implies ejaculation within ten thrusts or within 2 min of penetration. The condition occurs in 30 percent of males and is often associated with sexual naivete, anxiety disorders, and the male's preoccupation with satisfying his partner. The condition may be caused by abdominal and pelvic surgery, lower spinal cord lesions, prostatitis, and urethritis. The higher incidence of premature ejaculation among men with college education probably reflects their increased concern for their partner's satisfaction.

521. The answer is D (4). (*Kaplan, ed 5. pp 1054–1055.*) Treatment of premature ejaculation consists primarily of the squeeze technique in which the female partner squeezes the coronal ridge of the penis just prior to ejaculation. In most circumstances this will eventually result in more sustained periods of penile erection and decreased performance anxiety on the part of the male. Although patients are frequently anxious, psychotropic medications are seldom indicated. Psychodynamic psychotherapy may be helpful in some cases in which the patient appears to harbor deep hostility toward women.

522. The answer is C (2, 4). (*Kaplan, ed 5. p 1050.*) Sexual aversion disorder describes a persistent avoidance of almost all sexual contact. Patients will describe their repulsion of the sexual act. The disorder often has its genesis in previous episodes of abuse or assault or in dyspareunia. Patients usually require multimodal treatment and assessment.

523. The answer is B (1, 3). (*Kaplan, ed 5. pp 1075–1076.*) Transvestite fetishism usually occurs in males and has its onset in adolescence. The transvestite is usually heterosexual and has a male sexual identity. These persons have frequently been involved in other paraphilias, such as exhibitionism, frottage, or voyeurism.

524. The answer is B (1, 3). (*Jenike, pp 254–256.*) Significant alterations in drug metabolism occur with aging. Decreased splanchnic blood flow and an increased gastric pH result in decreased absorption from the gut. The higher percentage of body fat in the elderly prolongs the half-life of lipid-soluble drugs, while the decreased relative water content increases the effective concentration of water-soluble drugs. Decreased serum albumin increases the percentage of unbound, i.e. "active," drug. Decreased cytochrome P-450 activity and renal clearance prolong excretion. The elderly brain tends to be more sensitive to the effects of psychotropics.

Childhood Disorders

DIRECTIONS: Each question below contains five suggested responses. Select the **one best** response to each question.

525. Each of the following is a characteristic of the fragile X syndrome EXCEPT

    (A) macro-orchidism
    (B) large ears
    (C) occurrence limited to males
    (D) mental retardation
    (E) short stature

526. The mother of a 4-year-old girl complains that the child wets her bed three times a week. She should be told that

    (A) bed-wetting is the result of premature toilet training
    (B) the family should come in for evaluation
    (C) the child requires imipramine
    (D) the child requires a physical examination and urinalysis
    (E) the child should receive psychotherapy

527. A child suffering from reactive attachment disorder

    (A) usually has delayed developmental milestones
    (B) is frequently mentally retarded
    (C) seldom responds to treatment
    (D) often has motor abnormalities
    (E) is usually male

528. A child with an IQ of 60

    (A) is usually diagnosed before attending school
    (B) usually requires institutional care
    (C) may be able to live independently as an adult
    (D) seldom learns vocational skills
    (E) is unlikely to develop stable relationships

529. Compared with the pervasive developmental disorders, schizophrenia with childhood onset

(A) usually has a later age of onset
(B) has a higher incidence of perinatal complications
(C) has a worse prognosis
(D) is more likely to be found in association with mental retardation
(E) is seldom associated with a family history of schizophrenia

530. A 14 year old who commits suicide

(A) is unlikely to have suffered from a major depressive disorder
(B) is unlikely to have exhibited prior signs of psychopathology
(C) is more likely to be female
(D) is more likely to be black
(E) often has a family member who had attempted or completed suicide

531. All the following neuroendocrine findings are associated with anorexia nervosa EXCEPT

(A) increased 24-h plasma cortisol levels
(B) dexamethasone nonsuppression
(C) normal thyroid-stimulating hormone
(D) increased follicle-stimulating hormone
(E) blunted adrenocorticotropic response to corticotropin-releasing hormone

532. A person with trisomy 21 has a higher incidence of

(A) hyperthyroidism
(B) hyperparathyroidism
(C) hypertonia
(D) hearing impairment
(E) diabetes mellitus

Questions 533–534

A 10-year-old boy is referred to you for evaluation of his behavior. His parents describe 2 years of rudeness, disobedience, and cheekiness. The boy refuses to participate in family activities and "throws a tantrum" when he is confronted about his behavior. The child has broken furniture, smashed ornaments, and kicked his mother. His schoolteacher has made no derogatory comments about his behavior and his grades have been satisfactory.

533. The most appropriate initial diagnostic step would be

(A) electroencephalography
(B) projective psychological testing
(C) formal school reports
(D) family interview
(E) methylphenidate treatment trial

534. The child's most likely diagnosis is

(A) conduct disorder—aggressive type
(B) attention-deficit hyperactivity disorder
(C) oppositional defiant disorder
(D) identity disorder of childhood
(E) inhalant substance abuse

DIRECTIONS: Each question below contains four suggested responses of which **one or more** is correct. Select

A	if	**1, 2, and 3**	are correct
B	if	**1 and 3**	are correct
C	if	**2 and 4**	are correct
D	if	**4**	is correct
E	if	**1, 2, 3, and 4**	are correct

535. Developmental reading disability is characterized by which of the following statements?

    (1) It is associated with a high incidence of juvenile delinquency
    (2) It has a familial pattern
    (3) It is more common in boys
    (4) It is usually found in people of lower intellect

536. The core symptom complexes of infantile autism include

    (1) deficits in reciprocal social interaction
    (2) restricted repertoire of activities
    (3) impaired verbal communication
    (4) absence of imaginative behavior

537. True statements regarding normal adolescence include

    (1) gender identity disturbances are usual
    (2) emotional turmoil is an expected part of this developmental period
    (3) acting out is an appropriate ego defense during this stage of development
    (4) rebellious behavior is normal

538. Medications with proven efficacy in attention-deficit hyperactivity disorder include

    (1) pemoline
    (2) clorgyline
    (3) desipramine
    (4) tranylcypromine

539. A 30-year-old man has a history of attention-deficit hyperactivity disorder. He is more likely than the general population to suffer from

    (1) Briquet's syndrome
    (2) obsessive-compulsive disorder
    (3) dysthymia
    (4) schizotypal personality disorder

540. A 4-year-old child who has been abused may exhibit

    (1) assaultive behavior toward parents
    (2) developmental delays
    (3) passivity
    (4) hypervigilance

541. You examine a child in the emergency room who you believe has been the victim of child abuse. As the treating physician

    (1) you must report the case to the police immediately
    (2) you should consult a social worker immediately
    (3) you must obtain a sworn statement from the child's parents
    (4) you should perform all necessary diagnostic procedures even without the parent's consent

542. A child receiving psychotropic medications

    (1) will exhibit greater tolerance to the drug than will an adult
    (2) will require higher dosages compared with an adult
    (3) requires therapeutic plasma levels similar to those of an adult
    (4) will frequently exhibit a paradoxical response

543. Medical complications of bulimia nervosa include

    (1) metabolic alkalosis
    (2) hypercarotenemia
    (3) parotid enlargement
    (4) thrombocytopenia

544. Characteristics of complex motor tics include that they

    (1) are stable over time
    (2) are purposeless
    (3) cannot be suppressed by the patient
    (4) are nonrhythmic

545. In the first week of life, the behavior of a normal neonate includes

    (1) orienting the head toward a human voice
    (2) a long latency between a painful stimulus and crying
    (3) a tendency to fix the eyes on a human face
    (4) absence of a grasp reflex

546. Statements that follow from the tabula rasa (clean slate) theory of personality development, as espoused by Watson's behaviorist school, include which of the following?

    (1) Innate drives and genetic predeterminants have little to do with personality development
    (2) If given sufficient control over environmental factors, the behaviorist could produce a child with any specified personality
    (3) Mental illness is the consequence of faulty parenting or environment
    (4) Their theory of archetypes attempts to explain most of the aspects of personality structure

DIRECTIONS: Each group of questions below consists of lettered headings followed by a set of numbered items. For each numbered item select the **one** lettered heading with which it is **most** closely associated. Each lettered heading may be used **once, more than once, or not at all.**

Questions 547–550

Match the descriptions below with the appropriate test.

(A) Peabody
(B) Rorschach
(C) Halstead-Reitan
(D) Bender
(E) Wechsler

547. A test originally designed to disclose the structure, dynamics, and boundaries of personality and which may also produce inferences about intelligence

548. A test originally designed to test visuomotor abilities in children but which may also serve as a memory and projective test

549. A test battery originally designed to disclose the effects of brain lesions on mental, motor, and sensory performance

550. A test battery originally designed to evaluate cognitive, verbal, and performance abilities; it can also disclose patterns of organic deficit and be used projectively

Questions 551–554

For each of the following sets of essential clinical information, select the *DSM III-R* diagnosis with which it is most closely associated.

(A) Oppositional disorder
(B) Avoidant disorder
(C) Overanxious disorder
(D) Separation anxiety disorder
(E) Generalized anxiety disorder

551. Great distress when either parent or child leaves the home; persistent fears of danger to self or close relatives; phobias about monsters, death, or being kidnapped; sleep disturbances and nightmares

552. A failure to involve self with unfamiliar peers, embarrassment, timidity, and lack of social contact even though it is desired; lack of motor activity and initiative; poor articulation despite good language skills

553. Excessive worry and fear unrelated to stress or specifics of the environment; excessive worry about possible injury, school tests, or friendships; excessive self-doubt; sleep difficulties and psychophysiologic symptoms

554. Resistance to authority and to demands; unresponsiveness to persuasion; provocativeness, stubbornness, and procrastination

Childhood Disorders

Answers

525. The answer is C. (*Kaplan, ed 5. pp 1741–1742.*) The fragile X syndrome is the second most common cause of mental retardation (behind Down's syndrome). Females are the carriers of the gene. Although it was thought that the clinical syndrome was limited to males, it is now recognized that it may also be expressed in females. In fact, only one-third of female carriers are normal; the remainder are either learning disabled or mentally retarded. Phenotypically normal males with the fragile X have also been reported. Physical characteristics are short stature, long face, large ears, pectus excavatum, and macro-orchidism. Cognitive deficits typically involve functions of the right hemisphere.

526. The answer is D. (*Kaplan, ed 5. pp 1879–1882.*) Over 80 percent of 2 year olds, 50 percent of 3 year olds, 25 percent of 4 year olds, and 7 percent of 5 year olds are enuretic. There is often a family history of enuresis. The condition is more common in lower socioeconomic groups and broken homes and in neglected and abused children. It is crucial to evaluate children for a medical cause of their enuresis (e.g., infection, posterior urethral valves, meatal stenosis, spina bifida occulta, or diabetes). A physical etiology will be found in 5 percent of enuretics. Psychotropics should be reserved for children who have failed to respond to more conservative treatment (i.e., behavioral methods).

527. The answer is A. (*Kaplan, ed 5. p 1781.*) The reactive attachment disorder of infancy or early childhood is a result of social deprivation. Although the child may exhibit delays in developmental milestones, these are a result of an impoverished psychosocial experience rather than indicative of neurodevelopmental deficits. The child usually has the capacity for normal social interaction and development. The majority of children have the capacity to benefit considerably from treatment interventions provided the period of deprivation has not been too prolonged. It is important, therefore, to evaluate a child's psychosocial experience before concluding that he or she is mentally retarded.

528. The answer is C. (*Kaplan, ed 5. pp 1729–1730.*) The IQ range of 50 to 70 is defined as mild retardation and accounts for 85 percent of all retarded persons. Most persons with mild retardation are capable of learning prevocational skills and eventually living independently. They are also capable of developing long-term, stable interpersonal relationships. These children are seldom recognized prior to attending school and even then the diagnosis may be significantly delayed. It is important to realize that the IQ score is not necessarily an accurate indication of the person's functional capacity.

529. The answer is A. (*Kaplan, ed 5. pp 1977–1980.*)   The onset of schizophrenia before age 12 is rare, particularly in girls. The genetic basis for the childhood onset form of the illness appears to be similar to that for the adult onset form of schizophrenia. A high incidence of abnormalities on electroencephalography has been demonstrated; however, the incidence of perinatal complications is lower than that found in patients with pervasive developmental disability. The majority of children with childhood onset schizophrenia have IQ scores within the normal range, while 75 percent of autistic children are retarded. The long-term prognosis for childhood-onset schizophrenia is unknown.

530. The answer is E. (*Kaplan, ed 5. pp 1991–1992.*)   Adolescent suicide is a common and increasing problem with no predilection for any particular social class or racial group. Although the incidence of suicide attempts is higher in adolescent females than in adolescent males, the incidence of completed suicide is higher in males. The majority of adolescents who attempt suicide are suffering from a major depressive disorder or substance abuse or have been the victims of abuse. The majority will also have communicated their suicidal ideation prior to their suicidal act.

531. The answer is D. (*Kaplan, ed 5. p 1858.*)   The neuroendocrine changes found in anorexia nervosa are a reflection of both weight loss and the mood disorder that accompanies the disorder. The amenorrhea that accompanies the profound weight loss is reflected in decreased FSH and LH levels. Approximately 90 percent of patients will have nonsuppression on dexamethasone challenge and will have consistently raised plasma cortisol levels. Thyroid function is usually normal or marginally diminished. Bulimia nervosa is not normally associated with dexamethasone non-suppression or alterations in gonadotropic hormones.

532. The answer is D. (*Kaplan, ed 5. pp 1739–1740.*)   Down's syndrome is the most common cause of mental retardation in the developed world. The condition is associated with a high incidence of a number of physical abnormalities including duodenal atresia, hypotonia, seizures, endocardial cushion defects, hypothyroidism, and hearing loss. Neuropathologic changes similar to those of Alzheimer's disease are commonly seen in Down's syndrome. These persons do not often demonstrate the typical dementia associated with the neurofibrillary plaques and tangles.

533–534. The answers are: 533-D, 534-C. (*Kaplan, ed 5. pp 1842–1844.*)   Children with oppositional defiant disorder are often simply described as "difficult kids." The majority of their behavioral problems occur in the context of their relationship with parents or other emotionally concerned adults. The clinical features essentially reflect the normal behavioral problems seen in the "terrible 2's." These children are described as rude, resentful, touchy, hostile, impertinent, and often precocious. They typically confront their parents' authority, although their behavior with teachers and other authority figures is usually less troublesome. Their behavior does not include the antisocial problems demonstrated by children with conduct disorders. Family dysfunction is often a precipitant for this behavior and the children may be performing their roles as scapegoats within this family system. Family therapy with particular emphasis on behavioral control by the parents is the mainstay of treatment. The concurrence of an attention-deficit disorder should be evaluated by a thorough examination of the child and his or her social system.

535. The answer is A (1, 2, 3). (*Kaplan, ed 5. p 1791.*)   Developmental reading disorder is a common condition occurring in 5 to 10 percent of schoolchildren. The disorder is four times more common in males. There is a strong familial pattern and the concordance for the disorder between monozygotic twins is 87 percent. The incidence of sociopathy is estimated at 15 to 20 percent. By definition, the reading disability is not part of more global deficits.

536. The answer is E (all). (*Kaplan, ed 5. p 1779.*)   Numerous items are listed in the criteria of infantile autism. They may be divided into three broad groups: (1) Impairment in reciprocal social interaction. This includes behaviors such as an indifference to other people's feelings, an inability to make friends, impaired imitation, and lack of social play. (2) Qualitative impairment in verbal and nonverbal (prosodic) communication and imagination. This includes absent or abnormal communication such as grunting or echolalia and an inability to maintain gaze or use body language appropriately. (3) Restricted repertoire of motor behaviors. This describes stereotypic movements, compulsive rituals, and a preoccupation with maintaining routine.

537. **The answer is D (4).** (*Kaplan, ed 5. pp 1712–1713.*)   Contrary to public opinion, emotional turmoil is not an expected part of adolescent development. Although teen-agers may experience transient periods of dysphoria and anxiety, these reach significant proportions in only approximately 7 percent of subjects. Rebelliousness toward authority figures represents a normal part of the emancipation process. Despite this rebellion, the majority of teen-agers continue to share their parents belief and value systems. When adolescents do suffer from significant psychological difficulties, there is no reason to believe that they will necessarily outgrow these difficulties. The limited repertoire of symptoms exhibited by these teen-agers often makes it difficult to precisely categorize their psychiatric disorder.

538. **The answer is E (all).** (*Kaplan, ed 5. p 1835.*)   There is no doubt that methylphenidate is an effective treatment for attention-deficit hyperactivity disorder (ADHD). But the drug's short half-life and side effect profile (insomnia, growth retardation, motor tics, and appetite suppression) and the development of tolerance to the drug have prompted alternative treatment strategies. Both the monoamine oxidase inhibitors and tricyclic antidepressants have proven efficacy in reducing the child's hyperactivity and improving attention.

539. **The answer is B (1, 3).** (*Kaplan, ed 5. p 1834.*)   Approximately one-third of adults with a history of ADHD in childhood will eventually develop a psychiatric disorder in adulthood. The most common disorders in this group are antisocial personality disorder, alcoholism, ADHD (residual type), and Briquet's syndrome (somatization disorder). Many will also complain of chronic dysphoria, low self-esteem, and poor career achievements. The dysphoric symptoms usually respond to psychotropic treatment of the ADHD.

540. **The answer is E (all).** (*Kaplan, ed 5. p 1964.*)   The response of the preschool child to abuse may include withdrawn despondency or aggressive behavior directed toward caretakers and peers. Many of the small child's responses suggest a syndrome similar to posttraumatic stress disorder in the adult. Children will often exhibit a diminished attachment to their mothers and diminished separation anxiety. Delays in motor, cognitive, and emotional development are also typical.

541. **The answer is C (2, 4).** (*Kaplan, ed 5. p 2130.*)   It is the responsibility of the physician to report suspected child abuse to the appropriate agency immediately. All states have an identified agency responsible for the investigation of all such cases. This agency is required to make a determination about the most suitable placement for the child. Many hospitals have an identified department or person who can facilitate these referrals. The physician's duty to protect the child against further injury overrides any consideration of confidentiality. The physician may pursue any investigations or treatment considerd necessary for the child's care.

542. **The answer is A (1, 2, 3).** (*Kaplan, ed 5. p 1577.*)   The increased metabolism and renal clearance of medications in children necessitates the use of higher oral dosages. It is important to monitor serum levels in children rather than rely on oral dosage. Children usually tolerate psychotropics well and should not exhibit paradoxical responses.

543. **The answer is E (all).** (*Kaplan, ed 5. p 1860.*)   The medical complications of the eating disorders may be life-threatening. Recognized sequelae to anorexia nervosa include osteoporosis, hypothermia, bradycardia, arrhythmias, hypotension, edema, reduced renal clearance, renal calculi, and

pancytopenia. The repeated vomiting of bulimia nervosa results in a metabolic alkalosis, parotid enlargement, dental caries, and traumatic injury to the upper gastrointestinal tract. The chronic abuse of ipecac by bulimic patients is reported to produce a myopathy that may include a cardiomyopathy.

544. The answer is C (2, 4). (*Kaplan, ed 5. p 1866.*)　Tics may be motor, vocal, or sensory. They are rapid, brief, nonrhythmic, and purposeless. Although they are involuntary, they can usually be suppressed by the sufferer for short periods. Tics have a variable response to stress and may be aggravated, unchanged, or improved. The nature and pattern of the tic may change over time and may include other modalities. Motor tics are the most common type and account for three-quarters of initial presentations with the facial muscles the area most frequently involved.

545. The answer is B (1, 3). (*Kaplan, ed 5. p 155.*)　Neonates exhibit a number of innate responses that appear to promote infant-maternal interaction. A neonate will orient its head to a human voice and learn to respond preferentially to its own mother's voice. It will fix its eyes on the human face. The grasp reflex allows the infant to grasp its mother, just as an arboreal primate would. The normal infant cries immediately following a painful stimulus.

546. The answer is A (1, 2, 3). (*Kaplan, ed 5. pp 434–440.*)　The Watson school of behavioral psychology places little emphasis on genetic or prenatal influences on behavior, believing that parenting and the environment are prepotent in shaping it. Their theory is that a person is born with a "clean slate," which then receives indelible impressions from the environment. Therefore, if the personality is aberrant, environmental factors must have been at fault.

547–550. The answers are: 547-B, 548-D, 549-C, 550-E. (*Strub, pp 76–89.*)　Among the widely used psychological tests with clinical application are those devised by Rorschach, Wechsler, Bender, and Halstead and Reitan. As originally designed, each test was meant to serve some specific purpose, such as intelligence testing, assessment of personality structure, or evaluation of sensory perception. Some of the tests also assess motor function. Although designed to serve a specific goal, each test allows the interpreter to draw certain conclusions about a patient's mental capacity, psychodynamics, and the organic integrity of the patient's brain. Clinicians must have knowledge of the validity and sensitivity of the tests for each of these various aspects of brain function.

　　Wechsler tests are available in two forms, one for adults and another for children. Results of these tests are widely used by clinicians to derive IQ scores and to make inferences about the organic integrity of the brain, although in this regard the tests' limitations need fuller appreciation. While some examiners use the Wechsler test results projectively to assess personality structure, either the Rorschach or Bender tests or the Minnesota Multiphasic Personality Index is much more commonly used for this purpose. The IQ score is derived as a full-scale score, a verbal score, and a performance score. Certain brain lesions will be reflected in the test scores, but a normal Wechsler score does not exclude organic disorders of the brain. In general, patients with lesions of the right hemisphere score poorly on the performance scales, and those with lesions of the left hemisphere score poorly on the verbal scales. As arbitrarily incorporated in the scaling, the verbal and performance IQs in normal subjects should be about the same. Any large discrepancy suggests an organic disorder, but Wechsler test results alone can neither establish nor exclude an organic lesion. The results have to be integrated with the information from a patient's history, physical examination, neuroradiologic studies, EEG, or autopsy findings before a diagnosis can be made.

　　Lauretta Bender adopted the Gestalt figures of Wertheimer to test the visuomotor skills of children as a function of their maturation and to study the effects of brain lesions and retardation. The patient copies nine designs, which are then scored for accuracy, rotation, relation to each other, excesses or deletions, size, and pressure of lines. Generally, children younger than age 3 cannot perform the test, whereas most normal 12-year-old children can. Because the examiner gives few instructions, patients are compelled to call upon their own resources. While some overlap exists between subjects who are normal and those who have brain damage, brain-damaged subjects in general perform less well than normal subjects. Usually, patients with lesions of the right parietal lobe perform most poorly, whereas patients with lesions in other locations may produce essentially normal results. By asking a subject to produce the designs without looking at the originals, the examiner can test the patient's memory. By interpreting the distortions in the patient's drawings, the examiner may make inferences about the personality dynamics of the patient.

The Rorschach test requires the subject to respond to ten cards with inkblot figures, some of which are multicolored. What patients perceive in the relatively formless figures expresses their personality. A major criticism of the test is that the personality of the interpreter cannot always be separated from that of the patient. The examiner scores a patient's responses according to location, determinants, and content. The location refers to the areas of the figure to which the patient responds, as well as to whether the response involves the figure partially or as a whole. A large number of responses to the figure as a whole is associated with high intelligence and organizational ability. The content score indicates the breadth and range of the patient's interests and includes whether the patient responds in human, animal, sexual, or natural terms. The determinants of each response indicate the factors that made the patient produce the particular response, such as the form, shading, color, and sense of apparent movement. For example, an overemphasis on form would suggest an inhibited, rigid personality; a lack of perception of form might suggest inadequate control, inability to comply, or poor organizational ability. (The Murray Thematic Apperception Test has applications similar to the Rorschach. The Sentence Completion Test also has similar projective uses, but is thought to tap data at a more conscious level than the other projective tests like the Rorschach and the Murray.)

The Halstead-Reitan battery was devised because the psychological instruments available in the 1940s—such as the Wechsler, Rorschach, and Bender tests—too often failed to disclose abnormalities in patients with confirmed brain lesions. Halstead at the University of Chicago and Reitan at Indiana University School of Medicine worked with patients from neurologic and neurosurgical services who had confirmed brain lesions. They devised new tests and new interpretations of old tests based on empirical correlations of test results with clinical, neuroradiologic, and postmortem findings. The resultant battery includes the new versions of the Wechsler, the Halstead category tests, and a variety of motor and sensory tests. Originally designed to evaluate adults, a battery is now available for children as young as 5 years. The battery requires several hours to administer but includes the widest variety of tests and yields the most complete assessment of brain function of any neuropsychological instrument now available. The work has put to final rest a holy grail of psychologists, which was to develop a single test for evaluating brain damage. The complexity and range of brain functions cannot be tested on one dimension. Clinical conclusions based on converging lines of evidence from many sources are far more secure than conclusions relying on a single pathognomonic finding, which, when present, relieves the clinician of having to struggle with the diagnosis. The Halstead-Reitan battery, with its many cognitive, performance, and sensory tasks—some taken from the standard neurologic examination—recognizes this principle.

551–554. The answers are: 551-D, 552-B, 553-C, 554-A. (*Kaplan, ed 5. pp 1846–1852.*) Anxiety disorders make up a considerable part of the practice of child psychiatry. Anxiety-ridden children struggle with the burden of terror-filled ideas that disaster awaits them or those they love. When the child is unable to displace anxiety onto a symbolic object or situation, the anxiety becomes free-floating rather than phobic. This free-floating anxiety may manifest as separation anxiety, avoidant disorder, or overanxious disorder. These conditions are manifestations of the child's fear of separation, contact, or both. Although a certain amount of oppositional behavior is normal to the development of a clear ego identity, when it becomes prolonged and intense and interferes with social functioning, it is regarded as an oppositional disorder. This disorder is more common in males, while anxiety disorders are more common in females. In separation disorder the family tends to be enmeshed. Avoidant children usually have at least one parent who is avoidant. The parents of a child with oppositional disorder are often preoccupied with issues of control.

Mood Disorders

DIRECTIONS: Each question below contains five suggested responses. Select the **one best** response to each question.

555. The term *double depression* describes

    (A) a particularly severe episode
    (B) melancholic depression
    (C) coincident mood disorder and substance abuse
    (D) iatrogenic exacerbation of depressed mood
    (E) major depression coincident with a dysthymic disorder

556. Patients with bipolar II disorder exhibit

    (A) only episodes of hypomania
    (B) prolonged periods of mania and depression
    (C) mania induced only by antidepressants
    (D) brief periods of hypomania followed by a major depressive disorder
    (E) consecutive manic episodes

557. The period between cycles of depression

    (A) remains stable
    (B) rarely exceeds 5 years
    (C) decreases with age
    (D) exhibits no clear pattern
    (E) averages 1 year in bipolar mood disorder

558. Adjustment disorders are accurately described by the statement that they

    (A) are most common in adult males
    (B) are most commonly associated with an anxious mood
    (C) are usually present for more than 6 months
    (D) seldom interfere with occupational functioning
    (E) carry a worse prognosis in adolescents than in adults

559. Which of the following psychotropics has an identified "therapeutic window"?

    (A) Haloperidol
    (B) Fluoxetine
    (C) Nortriptyline
    (D) Buspirone
    (E) Bupropion

560. A 26-year-old single woman presents with the symptoms of chronic depression, social avoidance, panic episodes, rejection sensitivity, carbohydrate craving, and weight gain. These symptoms have been intensified since the termination of a romance. The psychotropic most likely to be effective is

(A) trazodone
(B) thioridazine
(C) phenelzine
(D) lithium
(E) nortriptyline

561. Following a serious suicide attempt, a 72-year-old man presents with the clinical features of a major depressive disorder with mood-congruent psychotic features. On examination, the patient exhibits moderate Parkinsonism and mild congestive heart failure. An electrocardiogram demonstrates a left bundle branch block and frequent ventricular extrasystoles. The most appropriate treatment at this time would be

(A) supportive psychotherapy
(B) electroconvulsive therapy (ECT)
(C) nortriptyline and haloperidol
(D) deprenyl
(E) thioridazine

562. Each of the following is a true statement about suicide EXCEPT

(A) females complete suicide more frequently than males
(B) most suicide victims have identifiable axis 1 disorders
(C) suicide ranks among the top 10 causes of death in the United States
(D) suicide tends to run in families
(E) the majority of suicide victims have communicated their intent prior to the act

563. The natural course of unipolar depression is characterized by which of the following statements?

(A) The first episode is by age 20 in the majority of patients
(B) The untreated episode lasts an average of 3 months
(C) The mean is six episodes per lifetime
(D) Twenty percent of patients will have more than one episode
(E) Sixty percent of patients will become chronically disabled

564. Major depressive disorder in childhood

(A) carries a good long-term prognosis
(B) is estimated to occur in 15 percent of 10 year olds
(C) fails to respond to antidepressants
(D) seldom has somatic symptoms
(E) is frequently associated with mood-congruent psychotic features

565. Each of the following statements about the postpartum blues is true EXCEPT

(A) it normally occurs shortly after delivery
(B) it is self-limiting
(C) there is a significant risk of suicide
(D) it occurs in up to 50 percent of women
(E) it lasts less than 30 days

566. Which of the following statements about lithium maintenance therapy is true?

(A) It is effective prophylaxis in 50 percent of patients with bipolar illness
(B) It is indicated in all patients with bipolar illness
(C) It may cause sustained leukopenia
(D) It invariably impairs thyroid function
(E) It should maintain blood levels between 0.8 and 1.2 meq/L

567. The presence of melancholia with a major depressive disorder is associated with each of the following EXCEPT

   (A) diurnal variation in symptoms
   (B) anorexia
   (C) good response to ECT
   (D) anhedonia
   (E) premorbid personality disorder

568. According to Sigmund Freud, melancholia develops as a consequence of

   (A) a self-defeating cognitive stance
   (B) anal-sadistic impulses
   (C) the internalization of a "bad object" during infancy
   (D) harsh criticism by the superego
   (E) a diminished sense of self

569. Each of the following is a true statement about late luteal phase dysphoric disorder EXCEPT

   (A) the onset of the disorder tends to be after age 30
   (B) oral contraceptives are effective in reducing symptoms
   (C) symptoms worsen with age
   (D) symptoms remit a few days after onset of the follicular phase
   (E) the disorder causes disruption in work and social activity

570. Diagnostic criteria for anorexia nervosa include each of the following EXCEPT

   (A) in females, the absence of at least three consecutive menstrual cycles
   (B) an intense fear of gaining weight
   (C) weight loss of at least 15 percent
   (D) distorted body image
   (E) delusions about food

571. All the following antihypertensives have been demonstrated to cause depression EXCEPT

   (A) propranolol
   (B) reserpine
   (C) captopril
   (D) nifedipine
   (E) methyldopa

572. Which of the following is an absolute contraindication to ECT?

   (A) Intracranial tumor
   (B) Hypertension
   (C) Myocardial infarction within 6 weeks
   (D) Seizure disorder
   (E) None of the above

DIRECTIONS: Each question below contains four suggested responses of which **one or more** is correct. Select

A	if	**1, 2, and 3**	are correct
B	if	**1 and 3**	are correct
C	if	**2 and 4**	are correct
D	if	**4**	is correct
E	if	**1, 2, 3, and 4**	are correct

573. Which of the following psychotropics should be avoided in a breast-feeding patient?

   (1) Diazepam
   (2) Lithium
   (3) Phenothiazines
   (4) Barbiturates

574. For augmenting tricyclic antidepressants in a treatment-resistant major depressive disorder, agents with demonstrated efficacy include

   (1) cyproheptadine
   (2) triiodothyronine (T_3)
   (3) nifedipine
   (4) lithium

575. Rapid-cycling bipolar mood disorder

   (1) describes four or more episodes of mood disorder per year
   (2) occurs in 25 percent of bipolar patients
   (3) is more common in females
   (4) may indicate occult hyperthyroidism

576. The patient with chronic intractable pain

   (1) most often has a family history of mood disorder
   (2) is most likely a blue-collar worker
   (3) is often alexithymic
   (4) is most often male

577. According to Beck's cognitive theory, elements essential to the development of depression include

   (1) logical errors
   (2) the cognitive triad
   (3) silent assumptions
   (4) parataxic distortion

578. Dysthymic disorder is correctly characterized by which of the following statements?

   (1) It seldom improves with antidepressants
   (2) It is often accompanied by mood-congruent psychotic features
   (3) It usually responds to long-term psychotherapy
   (4) It is often complicated by a superimposed major depressive disorder

579. Suicide in the elderly

   (1) is more common than in other age groups
   (2) is highest in men age 80 to 89
   (3) is usually associated with a major depressive disorder
   (4) is increasing

580. True statements regarding fluoxetine include that

   (1) it is primarily metabolized by the liver
   (2) it is extensively bound to serum proteins
   (3) it takes more than 1 month to achieve steady state
   (4) its absorption is not influenced by food intake

581. Dexamethasone nonsuppression is accurately described by which of the following?

   (1) It persists well beyond treatment response
   (2) It is found most commonly among patients with a major depression with psychotic features
   (3) It predicts a rapid response to antidepressants
   (4) It is found in anorexia nervosa

582. In the treatment of a major depressive disorder,

   (1) cognitive psychotherapy has been shown to be effective
   (2) antidepressants are most effective in alleviating vegetative symptoms
   (3) combined psychotherapy and pharmacotherapy is most effective
   (4) placebo is as effective as psychotherapy

583. Characteristics of phototherapy include that it

   (1) may be used to augment antidepressants
   (2) may cause hypomania
   (3) is more effective if administered in the morning
   (4) is most effective at 400 lux

584. An appropriate candidate for short-term dynamic psychotherapy must

   (1) be motivated
   (2) not be suffering from a mood disorder
   (3) possess at least average intelligence
   (4) be capable of tolerating interpersonal conflict

585. According to Bowlby's theory of separation, the infant demonstrates which of the following stages?

   (1) Denial
   (2) Protest
   (3) Distortion
   (4) Detachment

586. The serum lithium level will be raised by which of the following?

   (1) Furosemide (Lasix)
   (2) Naproxen
   (3) Aspirin
   (4) Low-salt diet

587. Which of the following investigations would be necessary prior to starting lithium therapy in a healthy 25-year-old man?

   (1) CBC
   (2) BUN and creatinine
   (3) T_4 and TSH
   (4) Creatinine clearance test

588. Risk factors for completed suicide in a patient with a major depressive disorder include

   (1) female sex
   (2) low social class
   (3) age of less than 30 years
   (4) psychotic features

589. According to Elisabeth Kübler-Ross, the stages of dying

   (1) are successfully negotiated by most people
   (2) follow a predictable sequence
   (3) are shaped by cultural attitudes and beliefs
   (4) usually include a period of panic

590. ECT that uses a brief-pulse waveform current pattern as opposed to a sine-wave current pattern

   (1) produces a longer seizure
   (2) produces less confusion in the subject
   (3) is less effective in treating depression
   (4) requires less energy

591. Depression following a left frontal cerebrovascular accident

   (1) is usually resistant to antidepressants
   (2) is seldom incapacitating
   (3) is a manifestation of pseudobulbar affect
   (4) is more likely with opercular lesions

592. Carbamazepine can accurately be described by which of the following statements?

    (1) It is as effective as lithium in preventing relapse in bipolar affective disorder
    (2) It is effective in preventing only the depressive phase of bipolar illness
    (3) It is an effective antimanic agent
    (4) It is ineffective in patients with rapid-cycling bipolar mood disorder

593. Acute severe lithium toxicity

    (1) is usually secondary to deliberate overdose
    (2) may require emergency hemodialysis
    (3) is likely to produce a fulminant hepatitis
    (4) may produce cardiac arrhythmias

594. Mood disorders in the mentally retarded are

    (1) not usually accompanied by somatic symptoms
    (2) usually resistant to psychotropics
    (3) usually short-lived
    (4) often accompanied by aggressive behavior

595. Side effects of monoamine oxidase inhibitors include

    (1) significant weight gain
    (2) suppression of rapid eye movement (REM) sleep
    (3) peripheral neuropathy
    (4) generalized edema

596. Cardiovascular effects of tricyclic antidepressants include

    (1) quinidine-like actions
    (2) decreased sensitivity to circulating catecholamines
    (3) prolonged QT interval
    (4) prominent P waves

597. Which of the following are considered valid animal models of depression in humans?

    (1) Maternal separation
    (2) Learned helplessness
    (3) Reserpine administration
    (4) Chronic stress

Mood Disorders

Answers

555. The answer is E. (*Kaplan, ed 5. pp 902–903.*) *Double depression* describes patients who develop a major depression in addition to a concurrent dysthymic disorder. These patients are at higher risk for recurrence of their major depression and are less responsive to medication.

556. The answer is D. (*Goodwin, p 21.*) Bipolar II disorder is characterized by brief periods of hypomania followed by a major depressive disorder. According to *DSM III-R* this would be classified as "bipolar disorder not otherwise specified." Although the characteristics of patients with this type of mood disorder have not been fully elaborated, certain features have been reported. These patients appear to have a higher incidence of other psychopathology, including alcoholism, drug abuse, obsessive-compulsive disorder, and antisocial personality. They also appear to have an earlier age of onset and higher risk of suicide than patients with bipolar I or unipolar depression.

557. The answer is C. (*Kaplan, ed 5. pp 893–894.*) The duration of the period between successive episodes of mood disorder in unipolar and bipolar patients decreases with increasing age. This decrease with each successive cycle is approximately 20 percent in unipolars and 10 percent in bipolars. Nearly all cycles in unipolar will be between 4 months and 52 years and between 4 months and 30 years in bipolar mood disorder. The average cycle length in bipolar mood disorder is 33 months and in unipolar mood disorder 45 months.

558. The answer is E. (*Kaplan, ed 5. pp 1143–1146.*) An adjustment disorder is a reaction, within 3 months, to an identifiable psychosocial stressor. The maladaptive reaction includes occupational impairment or symptoms that are in excess of the expected norm or both. The adjustment disorder does not, by definition, persist beyond 6 months. Adjustment disorders carry a poor prognosis in adolescents and 56 percent will have evidence of a psychiatric disorder 5 years after the initial adjustment disorder. There are nine subtypes of adjustment disorder; depression is by far the most common.

559. The answer is C. (*Lader, pp 146–147.*) The issue of defined "therapeutic windows" for psychotropic medications remains controversial. Nortriptyline is the only one with a defined plasma level "therapeutic window" of approximately 50 to 170 ng/mL. Routine monitoring of nortriptyline plasma concentrations is not justified unless the patient has proved to be nonresponsive to standard dosages of the medication. There are no data to support an upper limit of plasma level for other tricyclic antidepressants; it is clear, however, that the incidence and severity of side effects rises steadily above a plasma level of 350 ng/mL. Most data suggest that a standard dose of fluoxetine, 20 mg, is adequate for the treatment of major depressive disorders.

560. The answer is C. (*Lader, pp 158–159.*)   The patient described exhibits the symptoms of an "atypical depressive disorder." Although this category of depressive disorders has not yet been incorporated into *DSM III-R* nosology, several studies have demonstrated that this disorder has a differential responsivity to the monoamine oxidase inhibitors. Also occasionally referred to as "hysteroid dysphoria," the clinical features of atypical depression include social avoidance, panic attacks, rejection sensitivity, hypochondriasis, chronic suicidal ideation, hypersomnia, weight gain, carbohydrate craving, substance abuse, mood lability, and dysphoria. These patients often experience a dysphoric response to tricyclic antidepressants and poor response to ECT. Their illicit drug of choice is usually amphetamines.

561. The answer is B. (*Lader, p 340.*)   The main indications for ECT in patients with a major depressive disorder are (1) failure to respond to psychotropics, (2) mood-congruent delusions or hallucinations, (3) high suicide risk, (4) life-threatening psychomotor retardation, (5) previous response to ECT, and (6) medical contraindications to the use of standard psychotropics. The patient described clearly meets these criteria. ECT provides a safe, rapid, and effective treatment of major depression in the elderly.

562. The answer is A. (*Kaplan, ed 5. pp 1414–1416.*)   Suicide is the fifth most common cause of death in the Western world. It has been estimated that approximately 90 percent of patients who commit suicide are suffering from a psychiatric illness. There is a strong familial and genetic determinant to suicide. The vast majority of persons who attempt or complete suicide will have informed someone of their intention prior to the act. Although the incidence of suicide attempts is higher among females, males complete suicide more frequently. Males tend to employ more violent means of self-destruction (e.g., guns, hanging).

563. The answer is C. (*Kaplan, ed 5. pp 892–893.*)   The majority of patients with unipolar depression will have their first episode by age 40. As many as 50 to 85 percent of patients will have at least two episodes. The mean number of episodes per lifetime is six. The average duration of an untreated unipolar depression is 6 to 13 months, while treated depressions last approximately 3 months. An attempt to withdraw antidepressants in less than 3 months will almost always result in immediate recurrence of symptoms. Approximately 20 percent of patients with unipolar mood disorder will exhibit a significant chronic impairment in functioning. Men carry a poorer long-term prognosis.

564. The answer is E. (*Kaplan, ed 5. pp 902–903.*)   It is estimated that the incidence of major depressive disorders in 10 year olds is 1.7 percent. The illness is more likely to be found in the children of parents with mood disorders; the incidence is doubled with one afflicted parent and quadrupled with both parents afflicted. Children may frequently develop somatic complaints, agitation, and mood-congruent psychotic features. The onset of a major depressive disorder suggests a poor long-term prognosis. Children will respond to antidepressants in a similar fashion to adults. There is a much higher incidence of oppositional behavior, learning problems, and substance abuse among children with major depression.

565. The answer is C. (*Kaplan, ed 5. pp 902–903.*)   The postpartum blues is considered to fall under the category of an adjustment disorder with depressed mood. Postpartum dysphoria, headaches, tearfulness, and irritability occur in 50 percent of women. This disorder is most common in primiparae and symptoms usually peak within 10 days and resolve within 30 days of delivery. No formal psychiatric intervention is normally required, although a small percentage of these patients may go on to develop a major depressive disorder. The etiology is unknown but presumed to be secondary to rapid alterations in estrogen, progesterone, and prolactin.

566. The answer is D. (*Kaplan, ed 5. p 926.*)   Lithium maintenance therapy is effective in preventing relapse in 70 to 80 percent of patients with bipolar illness. There are no well-defined criteria for implementing long-term lithium therapy. Most clinicians would agree that two or three episodes within a few years or devastating episodes are an indication for maintenance therapy. Ultimately the decision should be made only after discussion with the patient. Long-term side effects include a uniform suppression of thyroid function, tremor, weight gain, and diarrhea. High peak levels have been associated with encephalopathy and nephrotoxicity. In order to minimize these possible side effects, the recommended maintenance blood level is 0.5 to 0.8 meq/L. Lithium may produce a leukocytosis rather than leukopenia.

567.   The answer is E.   *(APA, DSM III-R, p 224.)*   According to *DSM III-R*, a major depressive disorder with melancholia is associated with at least five of the following: (1) loss of interest or pleasure in all, or almost all, activities, (2) lack of reactivity to usually pleasurable stimuli, (3) depression worse in the morning, (4) early morning awakening, (5) psychomotor retardation or agitation, (6) anorexia or weight loss, (7) no significant premorbid personality disorder, (8) one or more previous major depressive episodes followed by recovery, (9) previous good response to somatic therapies.

568.   The answer is D.   *(Kaplan, ed 5. pp 392–393.)*   Freud outlined his early theory about melancholy in the 1915 treatise "Mourning and Melancholia." He postulated that in mourning the psychic pain is the consequence of the loss of an external object, whereas in melancholia this pain may be precipitated by an actual or perceived loss. The self-reproach and self-punitive attitude of the melancholic is the consequence of a harsh superego activated by the aggressive impulses generated by the ego's sense of abandonment. The melancholic directs this hostility inward rather than against the lost object.

569.   The answer is B.   *(Kaplan, ed 5. pp 1333–1334.)*   Late luteal phase dysphoric disorder has been included in the appendix of the *DSM III-R* but remains a controversial diagnostic entity since 90 percent of women experience some symptoms during the premenstrual period. The varied symptoms of the disorder have their onset during the late luteal phase (i.e., the week before menses) and remit a few days after the onset of the follicular phase (i.e., a few days after the menses). The disorder usually starts after age 30 and the symptoms often increase with age. Typical symptoms include affective lability, irritability, decreased interest, difficulty concentrating, hypersomnia/insomnia, and numerous physical symptoms. Oral contraceptives are ineffective in reducing symptoms. Recent studies suggest that fluoxetine may be helpful in reducing affective symptoms and bromocriptine is effective in reducing breast swelling.

570.   The answer is E.   *(Kaplan, ed 5. p 1854.)*   The presence of delusional thought content is not necessary to make a diagnosis of anorexia nervosa, though patients do exhibit a distorted body image that is not malleable to outside suggestion. The illness may, however, coexist with schizophrenia, obsessive-compulsive disorder, or anxiety disorders.

571.   The answer is C.   *(Kaplan, ed 5. p 1188.)*   Cardiovascular medications have been associated with many behavioral changes. Captopril has not been implicated in causing depression and may actually possess antidepressant properties. Apart from inducing dysphoria, beta blockers may produce physical and mental lethargy and nightmares. Confusion and hallucinations have been reported with digoxin, procainamide, and disopyramide. Guanethidine, beta blockers, and methyldopa commonly cause impotence.

572.   The answer is E.   *(APA, Treatments, pp 1805–1806.)*   According to the recent report of the APA Task Force, there are no absolute contraindications to performing electroconvulsive therapy; however, a number of medical conditions place the patient at higher risk. The most important physiologic stress is increased cardiac output and also possibly an immediate 5- to 10-s period of bradycardia or asystole immediately following the electrical stimulus. Patients with a history of hypertension, recent myocardial infarction, or compromised cardiac function are at increased risk for complications. Digoxin therapy may in particular predispose to prolonged bradycardia. Modern cardiac pacemakers are electrically shielded and therefore relatively immune to any interference. The degree of raised intracranial pressure that occurs during the ECT-induced seizure does not represent an absolute contraindication to ECT in patients with intracranial tumors and arteriovenous malformations. ECT may be safely administered at any stage of pregnancy.

573. **The answer is E (all).** (*Kaplan, ed 5. p 1578.*) As a rule of thumb, all psychotropics should be avoided if a mother is breast feeding. Benzodiazepines and barbiturates in the mother's milk will produce drowsiness in the child. Lithium concentrations in breast milk may approach those of maternal serum and present a potent potential hazard to the child (e.g., encephalopathy). Although the concentrations of tricyclic antidepressants and fluoxetine are generally lower in breast milk than in the maternal circulation, their use in the lactating woman should be undertaken with caution.

574. **The answer is C (2, 4).** (*APA, Treatments, pp 1792–1802.*) There is no universal definition of the treatment-resistant major depressive disorder. However, it is generally agreed that a failure to respond to an adequate dose (i.e., >150 mg daily) of imipramine after 4 to 6 weeks of treatment is resistance to treatment. The most common causes of treatment resistance are inadequate dosage or duration of treatment and noncompliance. The possibility of drug interactions or occult medical illness may also hamper treatment response. Recognized pharmacologic treatment augmenters for treatment-resistant cases include lithium, T_3, stimulants, neuroleptics, and L-tryptophan. The combination of antidepressants may also prove effective and recent research suggests that the combination of a tricyclic with fluoxetine may produce rapid response. Nonpharmacologic interventions include sleep deprivation, sleep phase advancement, and high-intensity light. Finally, ECT is often effective in those cases that fail to respond to the above interventions.

575. **The answer is B (1, 3).** (*APA, Treatments, pp 1934–1936.*) Rapid-cycling bipolar affective disorder may be defined as four or more episodes of mood disorder per year. The condition is postulated to occur in as many as 10 percent of patients with bipolar disorder. It is more common among females and in patients who have received tricyclic antidepressants for prolonged periods. A significant percentage of patients will be found to have subclinical hypothyroidism in association with long-term lithium use. Although there are no rigorous guidelines for the treatment of "rapid cyclers," a number of agents have demonstrated efficacy in this group. These include carbamazepine, valproic acid, clonazepam, propranolol, and verapamil. An attempt should be made to avoid tricyclic antidepressants.

576. **The answer is A (1, 2, 3).** (*APA, Treatments, pp 1901–1904.*) The *DSM III-R* diagnosis of somatoform pain disorder describes severe, prolonged pain in the absence of plausible physical pathology. The condition is most common in females and blue-collar workers. Their family history is often positive for alcohol abuse and major depressive disorder. A significant percentage of patients will have psychophysiologic markers for depression (i.e., DST nonsuppression and shortened REM latency). Patients benefit from antidepressants and psychosocial and educational intervention. Since these patients express their affective discomfort through physical symptoms, it is not surprising that there is an increased incidence of alexithymia.

577. **The answer is A (1, 2, 3).** (*APA, Treatments, pp 1834–1835.*) The cognitive theory of depression suggests that automatic, negatively biased thinking is responsible for precipitating and perpetuating depressive episodes. The cognitive triad describes the negative view that depressives hold about themselves, their world, and their future. Silent assumptions are psychological constructs that make the person vulnerable to a helpless and hopeless depressive position. Logical errors produce a distortion that also predisposes to a depressed position. Cognitive therapy attempts to identify these self-defeating cognitive patterns and replace them with more productive patterns.

578. The answer is D (4). (*Kaplan, ed 5. pp 903–904.*)   Dysthymic disorder describes a syndrome of chronic dysphoria persisting for more than 2 years (1 year in children and adolescents). There are none of the somatic symptoms usually associated with a major affective disorder. The condition may occur concurrently with other psychopathology, most commonly a major affective disorder (producing the so-called double depression). Recent research suggests that a significant percentage of dysthymic patients (50 percent) will benefit from tricyclic antidepressants. A family history of affective disorder suggests a good response to antidepressants. No psychotherapeutic techniques have demonstrated efficacy for this group of patients.

579. The answer is E (all). (*Jenike, pp 43–46.*)   The elderly are at highest risk for suicide with a 50 percent higher rate than young adults. The incidence of suicide among the elderly is increasing with men between 80 and 89 and women between 50 and 65 years of age at highest risk. Compared with young people, the elderly are less likely to communicate their suicidal ideation or make ''manipulative'' gestures and tend to employ more lethal methods. Approximately 75 percent of these elderly suicide attempters will be found to have a major depressive disorder. The presence of mood-congruent psychotic features increases the possibility of suicide.

580. The answer is E (all). (*PDR—1991, p 902.*)   Fluoxetine absorption is not influenced by food. The drug is metabolized by the liver to an active metabolite, norfluoxetine. The half-life of fluoxetine is 2 to 3 days and that of its metabolite is 7 to 9 days. This means that more than 30 days are required to reach steady state levels. Serum protein binds 94.5 percent of serum fluoxetine. Other protein-bound drugs, such as digoxin or warfarin, may be displaced and therefore become more bioavailable. The serum concentration of tricyclic antidepressants may be increased several fold by the concomitant use of fluoxetine.

581. The answer is C (2, 4). (*Kaplan, ed 5. p 873.*)   The dexamethasone suppression test is a nonspecific test for psychiatric disorders. Although a number of contradictory studies have been published, some clear patterns have emerged. The highest incidence of nonsuppression is found in patients with a psychotic depression. Patients with a family history are more likely to be nonsuppressors. The return of suppression indicates treatment response, and patients tend to ''run true'' with each episode of mood disorder. Any significant medical illness or weight loss can cause nonsuppression. Dementia may also produce nonsuppression.

582. The answer is A (1, 2, 3). (*APA, Treatments, pp 1817–1823.*)   The major studies have all been consistent in demonstrating that combined psychotherapy and pharmacotherapy is most effective for treating a major depressive disorder. Psychotherapy has demonstrated the most efficacy in the areas of problem-solving and psychosocial dysfunction. Pharmacotherapy is most effective for treating vegetative symptoms and preventing relapse. Patients with an identified psychosocial precipitant responded best to psychotherapy. Combined treatment appears to produce better long-term outcome.

583. The answer is A (1, 2, 3). (*Kaplan, ed 5. pp 1685–1686.*)   The intensity of the light source used for phototherapy should be above 2500 lux. Phototherapy is most effective if administered in the early morning for at least 30 min; it appears that 2 h is necessary for adequate clinical response, and a typical dose response curve has been demonstrated. Several cases of hypomania following light treatment have been reported.

584. The answer is E (all). (*APA, Treatments, p 1876.*)   Appropriate patient selection is probably the most important factor in achieving a positive outcome from short-term dynamic psychotherapy. Despite the well-defined selection criteria for suitable patients, a broad range of patients will benefit from the technique. Selection criteria include (1) motivation for change, (2) ego strength, (3) psychological mindedness, (4) the ability to tolerate ''focal'' interpersonal conflict, and (5) the ability to develop affective involvement. Patients with narcissistic and immature level ego defense structures are unlikely to benefit from short-term psychotherapy.

585. The answer is C (2, 4). (*APA, Treatments, p 1952.*)   Bowlby described three stages of infant response to separation from the mother. These stages are protest, despair, and detachment. Bowlby considers the mother-infant attachment bond to be a paradigm for depression. According to this theory, if the infant is separated from the mother for prolonged periods of time, a hopeless depression may persist throughout life.

586. The answer is C (2, 4). (*Kaplan, ed 5. pp 1661–1662.*)   The excretion of lithium is almost entirely renal. Any drug that reduces the renal clearance of lithium will therefore raise serum levels. Increased levels occur with thiazide diuretics, nonsteroidal anti-inflammatory drugs, low sodium intake, and dehydration. Loop diuretics (furosemide, ethacrynic acid) increase renal clearance and may therefore reduce serum levels. Although the combination of lithium and haloperidol has been implicated in causing an encephalopathy, this association has not been confirmed. Verapamil may lower serum lithium levels. A prolonged response to neuromuscular blocking agents has been reported when they are used in conjunction with lithium.

587. The answer is A (1, 2, 3). (*APA, Treatments, pp 1926–1927.*)   The appropriate use and efficacy of lithium therapy is dependent on a thorough evaluation, appropriate dosage, and close monitoring. Initial evaluation is necessary to ensure appropriate patient selection and objective parameters for follow-up. In addition to a thorough history and physical examination, a young (<40 years), healthy subject requires the following: weight measurement, CBC, T_4/TSH, fasting blood sugar and electrolytes, urinalysis, and BUN and creatinine. Older patients require additional evaluation, including ECG, EEG, thyrotropin-releasing hormone test, 24-h urine volume, and creatinine clearance and concentration test. In patients on a maintenance schedule, with no clinical evidence for side effects, follow-up requires annual thyroid function tests and quarterly serum creatinine and lithium levels.

588. The answer is C (2, 4). (*Kaplan, ed 5. pp 1423–1427.*)   Although females have a higher rate of suicide attempts, males are more likely to complete a suicide. Risk factors for suicide include (1) male sex, (2) divorce or widowhood and living alone, (3) age over 45, (4) unemployment, (5) chaotic family background, (6) alcohol or drug abuse, (7) psychosis, (8) chronic illness, and (9) poor insight. Recent work suggests that there are subgroups of high-risk subjects in different age groups, each with its own demographic features; for example, the group over age 55 tends to contain less alcoholism and fewer personality disorders but more widowhood and chronic illness than the group under age 35. The demographic profile of the geriatric population at risk has yet to be established.

589. The answer is B (1, 3). (*Kaplan, ed 5. p 1341.*)   Despite the intensity of emotional distress that the dying process involves, most people are able to cope with this period effectively. The ability to navigate this traumatic period is determined by a number of factors, including past experiences and familiarity with death, sociocultural norms, religious beliefs, cognitive development, and personality structure. Kübler-Ross has defined a number of stages in the dying process. Although they have become embedded in current medical and social thinking, these stages do not always follow a predictable sequence. The five stages are (1) shock and denial, (2) anger, (3) bargaining, (4) depression, and (5) acceptance.

590. The answer is C (2, 4). (*Kaplan, ed 5. p 1673.*)   The goal of modern ECT equipment is to induce seizure activity with the fewest possible side effects. This is accomplished by delivering the minimum amount of current for the shortest possible duration. Traditional equipment has used the sine-wave type of electrical current available through domestic circuits. The development of brief-pulse waveforms allows the administration of the current only during a small peak period of the cycle. This produces an equivalent clinical response for only one-third of the energy expenditure and therefore reduces cognitive side effects such as postictal confusion and memory loss. The brief-pulse waveform has demonstrated efficacy equal to that of the sine-wave method.

591. **The answer is D (4).** (*Kaplan, ed 5. p 632.*)   Affective disorders are common following cerebrovascular accidents. The likelihood of a major depressive disorder appears to be directly proportional to the proximity of the lesion to the left frontal pole. Mania appears to be more likely with right frontopolar lesions. The development of a mood disorder during the period of rehabilitation can profoundly impede progress and diminish the possibility of functional recovery. It is therefore extremely important that the mood disorders are recognized early and treated aggressively. Nortriptyline has proved effective for the treatment of "poststroke depression."

592. **The answer is B (1, 3).** (*Hollister, ed 3. pp 148–150.*)   Carbamazepine has proven efficacy as prophylaxis in bipolar affective disorder and as an antimanic agent. Although the drug should theoretically possess antidepressant properties, this has yet to be confirmed clinically. The drug has been proved equivalent to lithium in preventing relapse of both the manic and depressive phases of the illness. The serum level necessary to obtain the acute and chronic effects has not been fully elaborated, but it would appear that it correlates with anticonvulsant levels. One major study suggested the following predictors of a good antimanic response to carbamazepine: (1) greater severity of symptoms, (2) anxiety and dysphoria, (3) rapid cycling, and (4) negative family history of mood disorder.

593. **The answer is C (2, 4).** (*Hollister, pp 145–146.*)   The majority of lithium intoxications occur accidentally during treatment, i.e., through the presence of dehydration or salt depletion or the addition of drugs that raise serum lithium levels (thiazides, nonsteroidal anti-inflammatory drugs). The severity of clinical symptoms does not always follow the serum lithium level. During the early stages the serum level may be highest and antecede the development of florid clinical signs. Early signs of intoxication include diarrhea, vomiting, tremor, and lethargy. These will be followed by evidence of encephalopathy, including myoclonus, increased muscle tone, extensor plantar responses, seizures, and decreasing consciousness. Cardiac arrhythmias and respiratory arrest may be terminal events. Treatment of lithium intoxication includes saline alkaline diuresis with adjunctive theophylline or loop diuretics, hemodialysis, and cardiorespiratory support. Bronchial toilet is particularly important since viscous bronchial secretions are likely to develop. With the onset of coma, the mortality of lithium toxicity approaches 50 percent.

594. **The answer is D (4).** (*Kaplan, ed 5. p 1756.*)   Mood disorders are common among the mentally retarded and are frequently unrecognized. They may exhibit both unipolar and bipolar disease. The mentally retarded will use primitive ego defenses in coping with their illness and are more likely to become aggressive or show somatization. The usual somatic symptoms found in a mood disorder will be present but sometimes difficult to recognize. These patients will respond to conventional psychotropics, but they may be more sensitive to side effects.

595. **The answer is E (all).** (*Jenike, pp 71–78.*)   The primary advantage of monoamine oxidase inhibitors in the elderly is their relative lack of anticholinergic side effects. The side effects that are most common are hypotension and insomnia. The development of orthostatic hypotension is particularly hazardous in the elderly. A peripheral neuropathy can be prevented by the adjunctive use of vitamin B$_6$ (pyridoxine). Generalized edema, if it occurs, usually resolves within a week of commencing treatment. Weight gain with carbohydrate craving may be marked. A reversible lupuslike reaction and hyperprolactinemia have been reported. Reference to a standard text should always be made prior to starting any medication concomitant with a monoamine oxidase inhibitor.

596. **The answer is B (1, 3).** (*Lader, p 149.*)   The tricyclic antidepressants exhibit quinidine-like effects on the cardiovascular system. Possible dose-related cardiac side effects include prolonged QT

interval; flattened or inverted T waves; prominent Q waves; prolonged AV conduction; bradycardia or tachycardia; atrial and ventricular arrhythmias; and diminished cardiac output. Accordingly, patients with compromised cardiac functioning or conduction abnormalities should not receive tricyclic antidepressants if they can be avoided.

597. The answer is E (all). (*Kaplan, ed 5. pp 330–331.*)   The learned helplessness model is produced by exposing the animal to an inescapable stress such as an electric shock. Although animals will initially protest and become agitated, they will soon assume a helpless and submissive position. This state has been correlated with decreased central noradrenergic drive, which can be restored with antidepressants or by allowing the animal to regain some control over the noxious stimulus. Maternal separation results in a predictable sequence of protest, despair, and denial in the infant. The physiologic changes associated with this state are reversed by tricyclic antidepressants. The antihypertensive provided the first physiologic model of depression and produces alterations in central biogenic amines in a manner similar to that of a major depressive disorder. Chronic stress (e.g., changing cage mates or housing conditions) produces physiologic changes similar to those of depression; these changes are reversed by tricyclics and monoamine oxidase inhibitors. Chronic stress models use repeated unpredictable stressors (e.g., tail pinching) that produce a decrease in exploratory behavior. This change is reversed by antidepressants and ECT.

Personality Disorders

DIRECTIONS: Each question below contains five suggested responses. Select the **one best** response to each question.

598. According to Otto Kernberg's theory, the basis of the borderline personality is

    (A) an inability to mobilize productive ego defenses
    (B) the presence of an atypical mood disorder
    (C) an inability to integrate both positive and negative self and object representations
    (D) an inability to differentiate the self from the maternal and paternal objects
    (E) an inability to differentiate between fantasy and reality

599. The person with a schizoid personality disorder

    (A) feels abandoned and alone
    (B) uses fantasy as a major ego defense
    (C) frequently distorts reality
    (D) is seldom capable of abstract thinking
    (E) is not an appropriate candidate for group therapy

600. Features of hysteroid dysphoria include each of the following EXCEPT

    (A) hypersomnia
    (B) rejection sensitivity
    (C) carbohydrate craving
    (D) mood lability
    (E) low-level paranoia

601. Each of the following disorders has an increased incidence among the family of origin of a person with antisocial personality disorder EXCEPT

    (A) substance abuse
    (B) histrionic personality disorder
    (C) schizophrenia
    (D) somatization disorder
    (E) antisocial personality disorder

602. When attempting psychotherapy with a patient suffering from a paranoid personality disorder, the therapist

    (A) should avoid zealous interpretations
    (B) must assume a passive position
    (C) must be unusually warm and ingratiating toward the patient
    (D) should assume a stance of technical neutrality
    (E) almost always requires the use of adjunctive neuroleptic medication

DIRECTIONS: Each question below contains four suggested responses of which **one or more** is correct. Select

A	if	**1, 2, and 3**	are correct
B	if	**1 and 3**	are correct
C	if	**2 and 4**	are correct
D	if	**4**	is correct
E	if	**1, 2, 3, and 4**	are correct

603. According to the *DSM III-R*, diagnostic criteria for borderline personality disorder include

    (1) chronic feelings of loneliness and emptiness
    (2) affective instability
    (3) recurrent suicidal threats or gestures
    (4) episodes of micropsychosis

604. Characteristics of all persons with a personality disorder include

    (1) interpersonal conflict
    (2) suppression
    (3) inflexible responses to stress
    (4) mood lability

605. The person with a passive-aggressive personality disorder

    (1) is difficult to engage in psychotherapy
    (2) usually had punitive, insensitive parents
    (3) has learned to retroflex aggressive feelings
    (4) often exhibits ideas of reference

606. In the psychotherapy of a person with obsessive-compulsive personality disorder,

    (1) overt dependency needs frequently inhibit the patient's autonomy
    (2) humor provides ready access to covert fears
    (3) cognitive therapy is the most effective modality
    (4) the therapist should be nondirective and unassertive

607. Client-centered psychotherapy recognizes which of the following principles?

    (1) Clients are admonished to suppress feelings about the therapist
    (2) Therapists cultivate a caring, unconditional regard for the client
    (3) Clients are encouraged to change their life-style
    (4) Therapists express their own affective responses generated by their relationship with the patient

DIRECTIONS: The group of questions below consists of lettered headings followed by a set of numbered items. For each numbered item select the **one** lettered heading with which it is **most** closely associated. Each lettered heading may be used **once, more than once, or not at all.**

Questions 608–611

For each of the case histories below, choose the disorder (according to *DSM III-R* criteria) with which it most closely corresponds.

(A)   Schizotypal personality disorder
(B)   Schizoid personality disorder
(C)   Self-defeating personality disorder
(D)   Paranoid personality disorder
(E)   Avoidant personality disorder

608.   A 39-year-old man reluctantly submits to a psychiatric examination at the urging of his siblings, whom he accuses of treachery in the family business and plotting against him. Unable to relax, he is guarded and totally humorless. He does not love his female companion but is jealous of anyone who makes amorous advances toward her. He attends the psychiatric interview only to appease his family, and he is concerned that they are attempting to institutionalize him

609.   A 24-year-old college graduate submits to a psychiatric examination more in deference to her parents than from self-concern. The patient has a degree in education but is content with a job filing books in the library. She has no friends and spends her time collecting recipes and cooking for herself. She seems indifferent to criticism and has never had a romantic relationship

610.   A 46-year-old woman is referred to a psychiatrist by her 25-year-old daughter, who complains that her mother is hostile toward everyone. The daughter describes her mother as always being eccentric and superstitious. Her mother has joined a cult that believes in communicating with the dead and household pets. She believes she has telekinesis and clairvoyance and is the reincarnation of an Egyptian queen

611.   A 29-year-old man comes to a psychiatrist complaining that he cannot find friends who will accept him "for who he is." In the interview, the patient appears tense and anxious. The psychiatrist encourages the patient to meet persons of both sexes, but the patient ruminates constantly over his sense of inadequacy, fear of rejection, and anxiety in social situations

Personality Disorders

Answers

598. The answer is C. (*Tasman, p 51.*) The concept of splitting forms the cornerstone of Kernberg's theory of the borderline personality structure. This primitive level defense is indicative of the dilemma that borderline personalities face in their inability to internalize both positive and negative self and object relations. The borderline personality is therefore incapable of developing a mature relationship, which will, by necessity, involve ambivalent feelings. Intolerable affects generated within a relationship are therefore split off and attached to another object (i.e., person). The genesis of the borderline personality's inability to integrate mixed affect is considered to be secondary to either excessive ego-dystonic aggression or an environment that has not allowed the child to integrate the polarized feelings.

599. The answer is B. (*Kaplan, ed 5. p 1366.*) The person with a schizoid personality disorder is incapable of generating and nurturing social relationships and leads a quiet, retiring life with virtually no intimacy with others. Rather than feeling alone and abandoned, this person uses schizoid fantasy as the major ego defense mechanism. Complex and satisfying desires are fulfilled through these fantasies, thereby, limiting the need for interpersonal contact and heightening the person's social isolation. The schizoid personality is often intelligent and involved in creative, but solitary professional pursuits. Provided the therapist is patient, the schizoid person can benefit greatly from individual and group therapy.

600. The answer is E. (*Tasman, p 27.*) The concept of the hysteroid dysphoric was first proposed by Klein, who has suggested that it represents a subgroup of borderline patients characterized by affective instability. Clinical features include rejection sensitivity, mood lability, xenophobia, hypersomnia, hyperphagia, and carbohydrate craving. These patients appear to have a differential response to monoamine oxidase inhibitors and fluoxetine.

601. The answer is C. (*Kaplan, ed 5. pp 1373–1376.*) The transmission of antisocial personality appears to have both genetic and environmental components. Antisocial personality disorder is three times more common among males. Female siblings have a much higher incidence of histrionic personality disorder. Conversion disorder and substance abuse also cluster in these family cohorts.

602. The answer is A. (*Kaplan, ed 5. p 1366.*) Psychotherapy can be particularly challenging with paranoid personalities. Since these patients, by definition, have difficulty with intimacy and trust, it is difficult to establish a productive therapeutic alliance. Interpretations should be used sparingly, and it is preferable for the therapist to allow the patient to volunteer areas for discussion. The therapist should maintain a polite and professional manner and explain clearly any deviation from routine. The patient should not be made to feel humiliated at any time. The paranoid person will be frightened if the therapist is perceived as weak or disorganized. The efficacy of neuroleptics in this disorder is currently unproven.

603. The answer is A (1, 2, 3). (*Kaplan, ed 5. p 1388.*)   The diagnostic criteria for borderline personality disorder have always been an area of controversy. The most recent criteria outlined in the *DSM III-R* have excluded the presence of micropsychosis. These criteria remain descriptive and have not attempted to define or identify any core pathologic process. They include intense and unstable interpersonal relationships, repetitive self-destructive behavior, chronic fear of abandonment, chronic dysphoric affect, cognitive distortions, impulsivity, and poor social adaptation.

604. The answer is B (1, 3). (*Kaplan, ed 5. pp 1352–1353.*)   The basic deficit in the personality disorders is the persistent use of lower level ego defenses and an inability to be flexible in response to stress. The discomfort of the personality disordered person is played out in the context of interpersonal relationships, i.e., externalized. This defensive style makes it difficult for these persons to develop stable relationships and leaves them feeling helpless, dysphoric, and overwhelmed. It also results in a tendency to alienate and aggravate others. This maladaptive coping style therefore results in a cycle of unproductive and painful relationships that further compound the person's distress.

605. The answer is A (1, 2, 3). (*Kaplan, ed 5. pp 1384–1385.*)   Persons with a passive-aggressive personality disorder have usually had punitive and insensitive parents. As children they have had to learn to retroflex aggressive impulses for fear of angering their parents and thereby place their relationships in jeopardy. This results in the indirect communication of negative affect, i.e., passive-aggressive behavior. They procrastinate any confrontation and become sullen and withdrawn when criticized. The passive-aggressive person is likely to experience a conflictual transference in psychotherapy and sabotage attempts to work through painful issues. This makes it difficult to sustain a productive therapeutic relationship.

606. The answer is C (2, 4). (*Kaplan, ed 5. pp 1384–1385.*)   Professionals often find it extremely difficult to develop a therapeutic alliance with a person with an obsessive-compulsive personality disorder. This is because many professionals themselves possess compulsive traits that make it difficult for them to relinquish overt control, which their patient requires (at least initially) to feel comfortable within the therapeutic relationship. The therapist should assume a nondirective, unassertive position and encourage the patient to explore his or her affective, rather than cognitive, experience of the world. Attempts at cognitive therapy may simply compound the patient's intellectualization and diffuse the affective intensity generated by the therapeutic relationship. Isolation, displacement, and undoing are the primary ego defenses employed by the obsessive-compulsive personality.

607. The answer is C (2, 4). (*Kaplan, ed 5. pp 1482–1494.*)   The client-centered therapy developed by Carl Rogers demands that the therapist is genuine in response to the patient, has an unconditional regard for the patient, and is sensitive to the patient's subjective experience of the world. The method does not insist that the therapist reveal every passing thought but does require the therapist to divulge any persistent responses to the patient's behavior.

608–611. The answers are: 608-D, 609-B, 610-A, 611-E. (*Kaplan, ed 5. pp 1352–1405.*)   The symptoms of personality disorders usually become apparent by adolescence, are prominent features of the person's life-style, and interfere with work and relationships. The paranoid personality is characterized by extreme, unrealistic distrust and suspiciousness; exaggerated social hypersensitivity; and cold, restricted, humorless affect. The schizoid personality displays an absence of tender feelings and an indifference to the opinions or feelings of others. This person displays coldness, aloofness, and social isolation. The avoidant personality seeks intimacy but is overwhelmed by the anxiety that social contact elicits. Heightened rejection sensitivity and low self-esteem further compound the difficulty in forming relationships. The schizotypal personality exhibits odd or eccentric behavior, magical thinking, social anxiety, and few friends. Although a florid thought disorder is absent, the schizotypal personality may display ideas of reference or paranoid ideation.

Substance Abuse

DIRECTIONS: Each question below contains five suggested responses. Select the **one best** response to each question.

612. Withdrawal symptoms from heroin

    (A) occur within 4 h of the last dose
    (B) reach their peak at 24 h
    (C) may induce generalized convulsions
    (D) may last several weeks
    (E) can be alleviated by naloxone

613. The lifetime prevalence of alcoholism in the United States is approximately

    (A) 2 percent
    (B) 7 percent
    (C) 13 percent
    (D) 21 percent
    (E) 32 percent

614. Type 2 alcoholics are characterized by

    (A) equal sex distribution
    (B) onset of illness after age 25
    (C) antisocial personality traits
    (D) a high incidence of depressive disorder
    (E) low novelty seeking and high harm avoidance

615. The probability that the son of an alcoholic father will himself develop alcoholism is

    (A) 5 percent
    (B) 10 percent
    (C) 20 percent
    (D) 30 percent
    (E) 50 percent

616. Alcoholics Anonymous is characterized by each of the following statements EXCEPT

    (A) members cannot receive psychoactive drugs
    (B) the twelve-step program is an essential component of recovery
    (C) anonymity of members is preserved
    (D) spirituality is a central theme in recovery
    (E) many members are from the middle and upper social classes

DIRECTIONS: Each question below contains four suggested responses of which **one or more** is correct. Select

A	if	**1, 2, and 3**	are correct
B	if	**1 and 3**	are correct
C	if	**2 and 4**	are correct
D	if	**4**	is correct
E	if	**1, 2, 3, and 4**	are correct

617. Disorders associated with an increased incidence of alcoholism include

(1) panic disorder
(2) major depressive disorder
(3) phobic disorders
(4) schizophrenia

618. True statements regarding disulfiram include that it

(1) binds irreversibly to aldehyde dehydrogenase
(2) may precipitate psychosis
(3) may be fatal in combination with alcohol
(4) may enhance the intoxication produced by alcohol

619. After prescribing disulfiram to an alcoholic man, you advise him

(1) the drug will take 2 days before it is effective
(2) reactions with alcohol may occur as long as 2 weeks after stopping the drug
(3) he may safely use rubbing alcohol
(4) reactions usually last a few hours

620. Clinical signs of cocaine toxicity include

(1) myocarditis
(2) formication
(3) respiratory depression
(4) visual hallucinations

621. The cocaine withdrawal syndrome is characterized by

(1) hypersexuality
(2) anorexia
(3) motor tics
(4) hypersomnia

622. Chronic cannabis abuse may result in

(1) decreased fertility in females
(2) panic attacks
(3) glaucoma
(4) bronchial carcinoma

623. Clinical features of phencyclidine intoxication include

(1) seizures
(2) stereotypic movements
(3) muscle rigidity
(4) myoclonic jerks

624. A patient is brought to the emergency room after ingesting a large overdose of phencyclidine (PCP) 30 min earlier. Appropriate treatment interventions at this time include

(1) diazepam
(2) gastric suction
(3) isolation
(4) haloperidol

625. Contraindications to nicotine gum include

(1) seizure disorder
(2) recent myocardial infarction
(3) peptic ulceration
(4) lactation

626. Amphetamines and cocaine may be characterized as

(1) producing similar euphoric effects
(2) acting as local anesthetics
(3) tending to produce paranoid ideation
(4) having a similar duration of action

SUMMARY OF DIRECTIONS

A	B	C	D	E
1, 2, 3 only	1, 3 only	2, 4 only	4 only	All are correct

627. Physiologic effects of nicotine include which of the following?

(1) EEG alerting pattern with low-amplitude fast activity
(2) Decreased muscle tone and stretch reflexes
(3) Peripheral vasoconstriction
(4) Antiemetic effect

628. True statements regarding elderly alcoholics include

(1) they often begin drinking heavily late in life
(2) they are often not recognized
(3) they are frequently suffering from a major depressive disorder
(4) they are more likely to have a family history of alcoholism than are younger alcoholics

Substance Abuse

Answers

612. The answer is D. (*Kaplan, ed 5. pp 649–650.*) The acute phase of withdrawal from short-acting opiates usually begins 8 to 12 h after cessation of the drug and consists of craving, dysphoria, lacrimation, yawning, diaphoresis, rhinorrhea, piloerection, muscle aches, hot and cold flushes, and palpitations. This period is followed in severe cases of withdrawal by vomiting, diarrhea, low-grade fever, hypertension, and tachypnea. This initial phase of withdrawal usually lasts 7 to 10 days and is followed by a protracted period of withdrawal including insomnia, dysphoria, and generalized malaise. This final stage of withdrawal may last several weeks and contribute to relapse. The longer-acting opiates such as methadone may produce an even more prolonged period of withdrawal symptoms.

613. The answer is C. (*Tasman, p 295.*) The Epidemiological Catchment Area study found the lifetime prevalence of alcoholism to be approximately 13 percent. The prevalence is higher in males but is rapidly increasing in females. The age of onset appears to be decreasing. The incidence is highest among 25 to 44 year olds and lowest among persons over 65.

614. The answer is C. (*Tasman, pp 294–295.*) Two distinct categories of alcoholics have been identified based on their genetic and behavioral characteristics. Type 1 alcoholics ("milieu-limited") usually have their disease onset after age 25, prolonged and repeated binges, pervasive guilt, high harm avoidance (i.e., shy and pessimistic), and low novelty seeking. These persons are reinforced by the reduction in anxiety elicited by alcohol and rapidly develop tolerance and dependency. Both parents often exhibited similar patterns of behavior. Type 2 alcoholics are characterized by antisocial personality traits, impulsiveness, novelty seeking, criminality, and low harm avoidance. Their disease usually has its onset before age 25. These patients usually experience euphoria with alcohol. This type of alcoholism is more common in males, and the fathers (but not the mothers) of these patients tend to have exhibited similar behavior patterns.

615. The answer is D. (*Tasman, pp 298–299.*) The prevalence of alcoholism among the sons of alcoholic fathers is approximately 35 percent; the prevalence among grandsons of an alcoholic 12 percent. The genetic loading for alcoholism is highest in type 2 alcoholics. The concordance between monozygotic twins is estimated at 70 percent; between dizygotic twins 33 percent. The risk of recurrent alcohol abuse is 7 percent in the general population and appears to be rising.

616. The answer is A. (*APA, Treatments, pp 1151–1162.*) The membership of Alcoholics Anonymous is heterogeneous. Many members are middle class, employed, and married. The percentage of female members has increased to approximately 34 percent in recent years. The majority of initial contacts with AA are made during a period of crisis; these "newcomers" are allocated a more experienced member, or "sponsor," who is available to support the person's sobriety and provide advice. Although this "one to one" approach is important, the major philosophy of the AA program is a self-help process outlined by the "twelve steps." Spirituality is a cornerstone of this twelve-step recovery process, which is designed to provide the way to a "spiritual awakening."

617. The answer is A (1, 2, 3). (*Tasman, pp 330–331.*)   Anxiety disorders, panic disorders, and phobias in particular are associated with alcoholism. While the lifetime prevalences of panic disorder and phobic disorders are 1 to 2 percent and 8 to 23 percent in the general population, respectively, their lifetime prevalences are more than doubled in alcoholics. Unipolar affective disorder, but not bipolar affective disorder, is also more common among alcoholics. The influence of comorbidity upon treatment outcome and sobriety has not yet been fully evaluated. The incidence of antisocial personality has been estimated as high as 79 percent in alcoholics as opposed to approximately 1 percent in the community.

618. The answer is E (all). (*Tasman, pp 366–368.*)   Most studies have demonstrated the efficacy of disulfiram in reducing alcoholic relapse. This data is difficult to evaluate since studies have obviously been limited by their ability to select only those patients who would agree to take the drug. Disulfiram binds irreversibly to aldehyde dehydrogenase and may inhibit the activity of this enzyme for as long as 2 weeks. The drug also inhibits dopamine β-dehydroxylase and may therefore precipitate a psychotic reaction in susceptible persons. Other side effects include autoimmune hepatitis, peripheral neuropathy, and cardiac conduction abnormalities. Disulfiram may enhance the intoxicating effects of small quantities of alcohol.

619. The answer is C (2, 4). (*Tasman, pp 366–368.*)   The adverse reaction after alcohol ingestion is caused by a five- to tenfold increase in serum acetaldehyde. This produces facial flushing, headache, nausea, vomiting, palpitations, syncope, and blurred vision. Life-threatening reactions include respiratory depression, seizures, cardiac arrhythmias, and congestive heart failure. Reactions may occur as long as 2 weeks after discontinuing disulfiram and may occur following the topical application of alcohol.

620. The answer is C (2, 4). (*Kaplan, ed 5. p 1436.*)   Cocaine blocks the presynaptic uptake of dopamine and norepinephrine. These changes result in euphoria and the sympathetic surge that cocaine users experience. Intoxication may produce a psychosis, cardiac arrhythmias, hypertension, hyperthermia, coronary artery spasm, seizures, and cerebrovascular accidents. Treatment of these symptoms is supportive.

621. The answer is C (2, 4). (*Kaplan, ed 5. pp 671–672.*)   The cocaine withdrawal syndrome can be divided into three stages. Stage 1 (0 to 4 days) consists initially of agitation, depression, anorexia, and high cocaine craving. This initial period is followed by fatigue, hypersomnia or normal sleep, hyperphagia, and decreased craving. Stage 2 is initially characterized by normalized sleep, energy, and appetite but is usually followed by periods of anergy, dysphoria, and increased craving precipitated by cues associated with cocaine use. Stage 3 is a period of extended vulnerability to relapse.

622. The answer is C (2, 4). (*Kaplan, ed 5. pp 673–675.*)   The most widely recognized consequences of cannabis abuse are euphoria, hyperphagia, altered perceptions, and apathy. In susceptible persons the drug may precipitate a panic attack, organic delusional attack, or exacerbation of comorbid schizophrenia. Chronic use in males results in smaller testicles and azoospermia. The suppression of prolactin in females actually increases fertility, although use of the drug during pregnancy inhibits fetal growth and maturation. Cannabis has powerful antiemetic effects and reduces intraoccular pressure. An increased incidence of chronic obstructive airway disease and bronchial carcinoma has been reported in chronic abusers. The drug has actions on the immune system resulting in decreased humoral and cell immunity.

623. The answer is B (1, 3). (*Kaplan, ed 5. p 676.*) Phencyclidine produces alterations in neurotransmitters at multiple sites, including the hippocampus, cortex, striatum, and amygdala. Acute intoxication may present in a number of ways: catatonia, acute psychosis, or delirium. Patients will exhibit hypertension, nystagmus, seizures, diminished pain response, ataxia, and muscle rigidity. Treatment is symptomatic; benzodiazepines may reduce agitation.

624. The answer is A (1, 2, 3). (*Kaplan, ed 5. pp 675–677.*) Phencyclidine (PCP or "angel dust") has been used by as many as 8 million Americans. In low doses the drug produces an intoxication similar to that of alcohol. However, in larger doses the drug has a number of potentially hazardous effects, some of which may be fatal. Clinical features include ataxia, hyperreflexia, seizures, hypertensive crisis, muscular rigidity, nystagmus, coma, and eventually death. Treatment is essentially supportive. Stimulation should be reduced as much as possible. Since the drug is extensively bound to acidic gastric contents, a gastric lavage will considerably reduce eventual absorption. Acidification of urine plus diuretics will increase urinary excretion. Diazepam is useful in reducing agitation and muscular rigidity and decreasing the chance of seizures.

625. The answer is C (2, 4). (*APA, Treatments, p 1275.*) Nicotine gum has proved to be a useful aid to smoking cessation. However, patients should have instruction in the correct method of using and chewing the gum if they are to be successful. The gum should not be used while the patient is still smoking. Contraindications to nicotine gum include recent myocardial infarction, unstable angina, severe arrhythmias, pregnancy, and lactation.

626. The answer is B (1, 3). (*Kaplan, ed 5. pp 669–670.*) Amphetamines and cocaine have similar central nervous system effects—anorexia and euphoria. They may both produce a toxic psychosis with paranoid features. Amphetamines have a considerably longer duration of action than cocaine. Cocaine may be used as a local anesthetic.

627. The answer is A (1, 2, 3). (*Kaplan, ed 5. p 680.*) Nicotine reduces muscle tone and stretch reflexes, perhaps by stimulating the Renshaw cells, which inhibit the ventral motor neurons. The stimulant effect of nicotine may be mediated through nicotinic and dopaminergic neurons. It triggers the emesis center of the medulla oblongata and therefore stimulates emesis rather than inhibits it. Nicotine produces low-amplitude fast activity on EEG.

628. The answer is A (1, 2, 3). (*Jenike, pp 319–327.*) Substance abuse is a common but often unrecognized problem in the elderly. As many as 60 percent of elderly patients admitted to some general hospitals may have evidence of alcoholism. Compared with younger alcoholics, older alcoholics are less likely to have a family history of alcoholism. As many as 25 percent of elderly alcoholics have a major depressive disorder and many begin drinking later in life after a significant personal loss.

Thought Disorders

DIRECTIONS: Each question below contains five suggested responses. Select the **one best** response to each question.

629. Which of the following tests would one expect to be abnormal in a patient with chronic undifferentiated schizophrenia in remission?

    (A) Digit span
    (B) Block design
    (C) Wisconsin card sort
    (D) Boston aphasia examination
    (E) Rey-Osterrieth figure

630. All the following medications have been implicated in causing neuroleptic malignant syndrome EXCEPT

    (A) clozapine
    (B) amantadine
    (C) L-dopa
    (D) haloperidol
    (E) buspirone

631. All the following factors indicate poor prognosis in schizophrenia EXCEPT

    (A) poor premorbid work record
    (B) low IQ
    (C) early age of onset of psychosis
    (D) paranoid type
    (E) single marital status

632. An elderly man with no previous psychiatric history suddenly begins to ruminate continuously about his love for a woman he has never actually met. Which of the following syndromes does this describe?

    (A) Capgras
    (B) de Clerambeault
    (C) Ganser
    (D) Othello
    (E) Balint

633. Risk factors for tardive dyskinesia include each of the following EXCEPT

    (A) the presence of a mood disorder
    (B) increasing age
    (C) female sex
    (D) "negative symptom" schizophrenia
    (E) neuroleptic treatment of several years' duration

634. Clozapine-induced agranulocytosis is accurately described by the statement that it

    (A) seldom occurs within 4 weeks of starting treatment
    (B) occurs in approximately 5 percent of patients
    (C) is seldom life-threatening
    (D) is not an indication for discontinuing the drug
    (E) is usually self-limiting

635. The interictal psychoses can be described as

    (A) being usually self-limiting
    (B) responding to anticonvulsant medications
    (C) primarily consisting of positive symptoms
    (D) carrying a good prognosis
    (E) being paroxysmal

636. Alcoholic hallucinosis is correctly described by which of the following statements?

    (A) It occurs during alcoholic binges
    (B) It may persist for several weeks
    (C) It only involves visual hallucinations
    (D) It occurs in the context of an attentional deficit
    (E) It is more common in patients with a family history of schizophrenia

637. Which of the following statements regarding suicide in schizophrenia is true?

    (A) It occurs in 10 percent of patients
    (B) It is more common in females
    (C) It is usually in response to command auditory hallucinations
    (D) It seldom occurs in the period following discharge from the hospital
    (E) It usually occurs after decades of illness

DIRECTIONS: Each question below contains four suggested responses of which **one or more** is correct. Select

A	if	**1, 2, and 3**	are correct
B	if	**1 and 3**	are correct
C	if	**2 and 4**	are correct
D	if	**4**	is correct
E	if	**1, 2, 3, and 4**	are correct

638. Prodromal symptoms of schizophrenia include

    (1) decreased personal hygiene
    (2) magical thinking
    (3) inappropriate affect
    (4) somatic delusions

639. Which of the following drugs may precipitate an acute psychosis?

    (1) Amantadine
    (2) Nifedipine
    (3) Bromocriptine
    (4) Captopril

640. A patient with catatonia may exhibit

    (1) echopraxia
    (2) waxy flexibility
    (3) unprovoked outbursts
    (4) improvement with lorazepam

641. Acute dystonic reactions are characterized by which of the following statements?

    (1) They usually occur soon after starting a neuroleptic
    (2) They predict the development of tardive dyskinesia
    (3) They most often affect facial muscles in the elderly
    (4) They rapidly respond to benzodiazepines

642. Compared with low-dose treatment with neuroleptics, the technique of rapid neuroleptization

    (1) is more effective in controlling delusional thought content
    (2) reduces the possibility of relapse
    (3) requires high-potency neuroleptics
    (4) causes more dystonic reactions

643. Correct statements about the use of electroconvulsive therapy (ECT) in schizophrenia include

    (1) it is more likely to be effective in patients with catatonia
    (2) 5 to 10 percent of chronic schizophrenics will respond to ECT
    (3) it is most likely to be effective when there is evidence of a mood disorder
    (4) it is more effective if the patient has a chronic relapsing course

644. True statements regarding Meige's syndrome include that it

    (1) is more common in males
    (2) responds to anticholinergics
    (3) usually involves truncal musculature
    (4) may be induced by neuroleptics

645. First-rank Schneiderian symptoms of schizophrenia include

    (1) thought insertion
    (2) abulia
    (3) auditory hallucinations
    (4) ambivalence

646. The person with schizotypal personality

    (1) is often paranoid
    (2) more often develops schizophrenia than does the general public
    (3) often uses metaphorical language
    (4) usually requires maintenance neuroleptic medication

647. Ego defenses employed by the patient with an acute schizophreniform psychosis include

    (1) isolation of affect
    (2) denial
    (3) suppression
    (4) schizoid fantasy

648. The ophthalmic side effects of neuroleptics

    (1) are most common with high-potency agents

    (2) are promoted by exposure to sunlight

    (3) include retinal degeneration

    (4) are related to the total lifetime dose received

649. Compared with a male, a female suffering from schizophrenia has

    (1) a later age of onset

    (2) more negative symptoms

    (3) more affective symptoms

    (4) a poorer response to neuroleptics

650. True statements regarding delusional disorder include that it

    (1) is more common in females

    (2) usually has its onset in middle age

    (3) is more common in lower social classes

    (4) is more common among immigrants

651. A 70 year old complains of the recent onset of formed visual hallucinations. This suggests

    (1) the development of paraphrenia

    (2) an occipital lobe cerebrovascular accident

    (3) a complex partial seizure disorder

    (4) probable deficits in vision

Thought Disorders

Answers

629. The answer is C. *(Kaplan, ed 5. p 767.)* There are no diagnostic neuropsychological tests for schizophrenia. However, patients with chronic undifferentiated schizophrenia consistently demonstrate deficits in those tests designed to assess the function of the dorsolateral convexities of the prefrontal lobes. The Wisconsin card sorting test is a good measure of the functions of this area.

630. The answer is E. *(Kaplan, ed 5. pp 1624–1625.)* Neuroleptic malignant syndrome (NMS) has been reported with agents other than the neuroleptics. In particular, agents with dopaminergic activity (e.g., L-dopa, bromocriptine, and amantadine) have been implicated as etiologic agents. The relatively selective D2 blocker clozapine has been associated with several cases of NMS. Characteristic features of NMS include rigidity, fever, autonomic instability, elevated creatinine phosphokinase, leukocytosis, and rhabdomyolysis.

631. The answer is D. *(Kaplan, ed 5. p 768.)* Approximately 40 to 60 percent of patients with schizophrenia are chronically impaired by their illness. Good prognostic indicators include late age of onset, obvious precipitating factors, positive symptoms, affective symptoms, and acute onset. The absence of an appropriate social support system and the presence of predominantly negative symptoms (e.g., poverty of affect or poor motivation and organizational skills) are negative prognostic factors.

632. The answer is B. *(Kaplan, ed 5. p 824.)* The case describes erotomania (*psychose passionelle*, or de Clerambeault syndrome), a disorder in which the person has a delusional belief that he or she is having a love affair with someone. This may occur in the context of a delusional, mood, or organic disorder. The Othello syndrome describes a conjugal paranoia in which the subject falsely believes his or her spouse to be guilty of infidelity. Capgras syndrome (reduplicative paramnesia) describes the delusion that familiar figures are actually impostors who have assumed the identity of people known to the subject. Balint's syndrome describes a defect in visual scanning secondary to an occipital or parieto-occipital lesion.

633. The answer is D. *(Kaplan, ed 5. p 1623.)* Tardive dyskinesia usually develops after several years of neuroleptic treatment; however, some patients may develop the disorder in a considerably shorter period. The incidence of tardive dyskinesia is approximately 4 to 5 percent per year for the first 5 years, but this is higher in older patients. The presence of a mood disorder clearly increases the risk of developing tardive dyskinesia, and patients with schizoaffective disorders are therefore at particular risk. The symptoms of tardive dyskinesia often first appear following a reduction in neuroleptic dosage, but as many as 30 percent of patients will eventually remit off neuroleptics.

634. The answer is A. (*Kaplan, ed 5. pp 1621–1622.*) The incidence of clozapine-induced psychosis is approximately 1 percent. The side effect seldom occurs during the first 4 weeks of treatment, and this allows a relatively safe window in which to determine the efficacy of the drug in a particular patient. The agranulocytosis is not self-limiting and carries a mortality of 40 percent if a superadded infection supervenes. Once clozapine is discontinued, the granulocyte count should return to normal levels in 2 to 4 weeks.

635. The answer is C. (*Strub, pp 406–408.*) The interictal psychoses usually occur in patients with partial complex seizures of temporolimbic origin. Several studies have suggested that the condition is more common in patients with left-sided foci. The condition tends to have a later age of onset than process schizophrenia and presents with positive symptomatology. Patients with this disorder tend to exhibit better interpersonal skills and more affective symptomatology than "process schizophrenics." Anticonvulsants are ineffective in alleviating the thought disorder (indeed, they may precipitate symptoms), and neuroleptics are necessary to control the delusional thought content and hallucinations.

636. The answer is B. (*Kaplan, ed 5. p 635.*) Alcoholic hallucinosis occurs in alcohol-dependent persons within 48 h of abstinence. The hallucinations may involve any sensory modality and, unlike delirium tremens, occur in the context of a clear sensorium. The hallucinations usually remit within a few days but may persist for several months after abstinence. The patient is seldom delusional and does not meet criteria for a schizophreniform psychosis. Neuroleptics are often necessary to control symptoms.

637. The answer is A. (*Kaplan, ed 5. pp 1419–1420.*) Suicide in the person with schizophrenia usually occurs in the context of depressive symptoms rather than as a response to command auditory hallucinations. In half the cases, the patient has been discharged from the hospital within the last few weeks and has been ill for a few years. Single males are at highest risk.

638. The answer is A (1, 2, 3). (*Kaplan, ed 5. p 769.*) Recognized prodromal symptoms of schizophrenia include social withdrawal; impairment in social performance; blunted or inappropriate affect; vague and overelaborate speech; odd beliefs and magical thinking; unusual perceptual experiences; lack of initiative; and peculiar behavior.

639. The answer is B (1, 3). (*Kaplan, ed 5. p 835.*) Psychosis may be precipitated by any dopamine agonist. Anti-parkinsonism medications are therefore the most common cause. Approximately 15 to 30 percent of patients receiving L-dopa will develop a psychosis. The agitated delirium associated with anticholinergic toxicity may also resemble an acute psychosis. Via their inhibitory action on dopamine β-hydroxylase, corticosteroids may precipitate an acute psychosis.

640. The answer is E (all). (*Kaplan, ed 5. pp 770–773.*) The neurophysiologic and phenomenological underpinnings of catatonia remain unclear. Catatonia has classically been divided into three subgroups: stuporous, excited, and periodic. The validity of and rational for this classification are controversial and provide no clear guidelines for etiology or treatment. Stuporous catatonia is characterized by mutism, social withdrawal, and markedly diminished motor activity. Patients demonstrate echopraxia, echolalia, and stereotypies and seldom initiate any original spontaneous motor behavior. Agitated catatonia is described as a state of extreme psychomotor agitation with increased verbal output. Whether this represents a true schizophreniform psychosis or simply mania remains unclear. Lorazepam has demonstrated efficacy in stuporous catatonia.

641. The answer is A (1, 2, 3). (*Kaplan, ed 5. pp 761–762.*) Acute dystonic reactions usually occur within a few hours of receiving the neuroleptic—50 percent of cases occur within 48 h. Episodes may last anywhere from a few minutes to several hours. Reactions usually involve the facial and neck muscles, although the extremities may occasionally be involved. Blepharospasm and an oculogyric crisis may occur. The incidence of acute dystonic reactions is uncertain and estimates range from 2 to 25 percent. Anticholinergics are the most effective treatment for acute dystonic reactions. Benzodiazepines are often helpful in akathisia.

642. The answer is D (4). *(Kaplan, ed 5. p 1601.)* There is no evidence that the use of large doses of neuroleptics during the period of acute psychosis is more effective than lower doses in reducing delusional thought content. Patients on higher doses will exhibit more acute extrapyramidal symptoms and sedation. The concomitant use of neuroleptics and benzodiazepines is finding increasing support owing to the lower incidence of side effects.

643. The answer is A (1, 2, 3). *(Kaplan, ed 5. p 1277.)* Electroconvulsive therapy is most efficacious in patients with positive or affective symptoms. Only 5 to 10 percent of patients with chronic process schizophrenia can be expected to improve with a course of ECT. ECT remains the most effective and rapid treatment for a major depressive disorder with psychotic features.

644. The answer is D (4). *(Adams RD, ed 4. p 89.)* Meige's syndrome describes an orofacial dyskinesia. Patients exhibit blepharospasm, protrusion of the tongue, retraction of the platysma, and forceful opening or closure of the mouth. Patients receiving neuroleptics may develop a Meige's syndrome or a similar orofacial dyskinesia characterized by chewing movements, lip smacking, and licking movements.

645. The answer is B (1, 3). *(Kaplan, ed 5. p 588.)* Schneider attempted to identify some symptoms that, in the absence of organic mental disease, he considered to be diagnostic of a process schizophrenia. His "first-rank" symptoms were auditory hallucinations, experiences of influence, experiences of alienation (this will include the experience that "foreign thoughts" are being inserted into one's head), and thought broadcasting. These symptoms are now recognized in association with affective disorders and are therefore no longer considered diagnostic of schizophrenia.

646. The answer is A (1, 2, 3). *(Kaplan, ed 5. p 1369.)* As many as 10 percent of patients with a diagnosis of schizotypal personality disorder will eventually develop schizophrenia. Overall, the long-term prognosis for the person with a schizotypal personality disorder is better than that of a schizophrenic. Brief periods of paranoid ideation are not unusual, and these personalities often employ magical thinking and consider themselves to have special powers.

647. The answer is C (2, 4). *(Kaplan, ed 5. p 375.)* The person with a schizophreniform psychosis uses psychotic level defenses that, in simple terms, attempt to distort the external world to comply with that person's experience. Examples of these narcissistic level defenses include denial, distortion, projection, schizoid fantasy, projective identification, and splitting.

648. The answer is C (2, 4). *(Kaplan, ed 5. p 1625.)* Several ophthalmologic side effects have been reported with neuroleptics. Retinitis pigmentosa is associated with high maintenance doses of thioridazine and may result in blindness. Whitish-brown granular deposits have been found in the anterior chamber and lens of patients on long-term maintenance chlorpromazine; however, these do not present a hazard to eyesight. These "benign" ocular changes appear to correlate with the development of a bluish-gray skin discoloration and are accelerated by exposure to sunlight.

649. The answer is B (1, 3). *(Kaplan, ed 5. pp 717–718.)* Although the incidence of schizophrenia is similar in both sexes, there are significant differences in symptoms. Females tend to have a later age of onset with more positive symptoms and a somewhat better response to neuroleptics. The concordance rate for schizophrenia is higher between monozygotic females.

650. The answer is E (all).   (*Kaplan, ed 5. pp 819–826.*)   The delusional disorders are a heterogeneous group of disorders with varying content. The mean age of onset is 40 years and although the majority of sufferers will be employed and married, there is a higher incidence among the lower social classes. Immigrants who are unable to speak the local language are at particular risk for developing a paranoid delusional system. There appears to be some familial clustering but the precise genetic basis for the condition remains unclear. Long-term follow-up reveals that the disorder remains stable over time and does not develop into a schizophreniform psychosis or mood disorder.

651. The answer is D (4).   (*Jenike, pp 213–215.*)   The most usual cause of formed visual hallucinations in the elderly is declining vision. This was first described in the eighteenth century by Charles Bonnet and the syndrome bears his name. Neuroleptics have not proved effective and patients usually respond to reassurance and correction of visual deficits, if possible.

Neurology Questions for Psychiatrists

DIRECTIONS: Each question below contains five suggested responses. Select the **one best** response to each question.

652. All the following would be considered part of normal aging in an 80-year-old man EXCEPT

    (A) loss of vibration sense in the legs
    (B) short, uncertain steps
    (C) decreased stage 4 sleep
    (D) decreased vocabulary
    (E) loss of large cortical neurons

653. A 55-year-old man presents for evaluation of his behavioral change. His family describe his recently increasing belligerence, inappropriate social behavior, sexual promiscuity, and foul language. Examination reveals an intact memory and visuospatial functions, word-finding difficulties, and frontal lobe deficits. The most likely diagnosis is

    (A) Alzheimer's disease
    (B) neurosyphilis
    (C) Pick's disease
    (D) AIDS dementia complex
    (E) multi-infarct dementia

654. Each of the following is a true statement of AIDS dementia complex (ADC) EXCEPT

    (A) the syndrome usually has a slow onset
    (B) deficits in attention are usually significant
    (C) behavioral changes are often prominent
    (D) amnesia is usually the earliest clinical sign
    (E) psychomotor slowing is usually pronounced

655. A young woman with a history of borderline personality disorder complains of a gradual loss of sensation extending from her shoulders to her hands. Examination reveals loss of pain sensation and position sense but intact touch perception in both hands. Reflexes are absent in both arms and the muscles of her hands are atrophied. The most likely diagnosis is

    (A) tabes dorsalis
    (B) vitamin B_{12} deficiency
    (C) syringomyelia
    (D) amyotrophic lateral sclerosis
    (E) alcoholic neuropathy

656. Following a cerebrovascular accident an elderly woman states that she recognizes the voices but not the faces of family members. The probable site of the lesion is

(A) bilateral occipitotemporal
(B) right hippocampal
(C) left hippocampal
(D) biparietal
(E) mediodorsal nucleus of the thalamus

657. Persons with transient global amnesia

(A) are usually young and female
(B) know who they are
(C) usually have a psychiatric history
(D) are likely to have several episodes
(E) should have a sodium amytal interview

658. One month following a cerebrovascular accident, a 50-year-old man is asked to complete the letter cancellation test. His performance is shown below. The probable site of the cerebrovascular accident is the

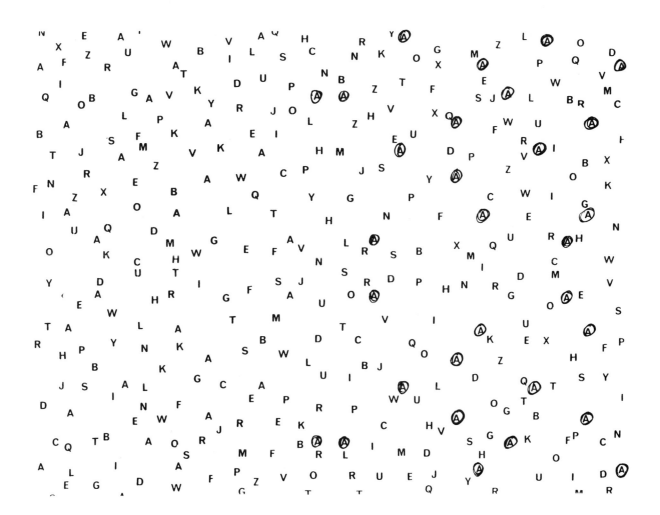

(A) frontal lobes
(B) left temporal lobe
(C) right parietal lobe
(D) right occipital lobe
(E) left occipitotemporal area

659. An elderly man was asked to reproduce the sample drawing. His performance suggests

SAMPLE DRAWING

PATIENT'S REPRODUCTION

(A) Parkinson's disease
(B) a right parietal lobe lesion
(C) a right temporal lobe lesion
(D) occipital lobe lesions
(E) frontal lobe lesions

660. Following the resection of an anterior communicating artery aneurysm, a patient may exhibit each of the following EXCEPT

(A) amnesia
(B) personality change
(C) akinetic mutism
(D) expressive aphasia
(E) urinary incontinence

661. Upon routine admission screening, a 70-year-old demented man is found to have a positive VDRL (Venereal Disease Research Laboratory) test. The most appropriate next step would be to

(A) treat the patient for neurosyphilis
(B) isolate the patient
(C) inform his wife that she, too, probably has syphilis and should be tested
(D) obtain CSF for another VDRL test
(E) obtain a fluorescent treponemal antibody absorption (FTA-ABS) test

662. A 35-year-old male executive presents with a complaint of irregular incapacitating headaches, which may last several weeks. He describes them as a steady pressure extending from his neck to the top of his head and says they are often associated with lightheadedness. The pain, which is relieved by alcohol, is present in the morning and worsens as the day progresses. The most likely diagnosis is

(A) cluster headache
(B) tension headache
(C) classic migraine
(D) raised intracranial pressure
(E) temporal arteritis

663. Complete interruption of the right optic tract produces

(A) bitemporal hemianopia
(B) right homonymous hemianopia
(C) left homonymous hemianopia
(D) right quadrantanopia
(E) left quadrantanopia

664. The site at which a small lesion will produce complete loss of consciousness with minimal effect on other functions is the

(A) medullary tegmentum
(B) caudal pontine tegmentum
(C) midbrain tegmentum
(D) diencephalon
(E) cerebral cortex

665. The combination of acalculia, right-left disorientation, finger agnosia, and agraphia without alexia suggests a lesion of the

    (A) right posterior parasylvian region
    (B) left medial temporal area
    (C) left angular gyrus
    (D) left calcarine cortex
    (E) left prefrontal cortex

666. If an examiner shines a light in one eye of a normal person, which of the following pupillary responses occurs?

    (A) Both pupils constrict equally
    (B) The ipsilateral pupil constricts more than the contralateral one
    (C) The contralateral pupil constricts more than the ipsilateral one
    (D) Only the ipsilateral pupil constricts
    (E) Only the contralateral pupil constricts

667. To reinforce the stretch reflex of a hypoactive quadriceps femoris muscle, an examiner requests the patient to

    (A) think about an emotionally stimulating event
    (B) count slowly to 10
    (C) close the eyes
    (D) grasp one hand with the other and pull
    (E) walk briskly around the room

668. A young man presents to your office complaining of rapidly increasing weakness, which began in his feet and is now affecting his legs and arms. He also complains of pain in the back, legs, and arms. Physical examination reveals diminished motor power and arreflexia in the legs more than the arms, autonomic instability, and intact sensation. The most likely diagnosis is

    (A) motor neuron disease
    (B) polio
    (C) conversion disorder
    (D) Guillain-Barré syndrome
    (E) multiple sclerosis

669. A 17-year-old girl presents to the emergency room in an acute confusional state. She complains of double vision, difficulty swallowing, weakness of her legs, and abdominal pain. She had been treated with a sulfonamide for a urinary tract infection 3 days prior to admission but complained that her urine still appeared foul. On examination she was apyrexial with evidence for a motor peripheral neuropathy. CSF examination revealed only a mild elevation of protein. The most likely diagnosis is

    (A) herpes encephalitis
    (B) acute intermittent porphyria
    (C) gonococcal meningitis
    (D) multiple sclerosis
    (E) mercury poisoning

670. A 70-year-old man is unable to follow simple multistep directions such as to fold a letter, place it in an envelope, and affix a postage stamp. He is, however, capable of performing each of these tasks individually. This is an example of

    (A) motor apraxia
    (B) an amnestic disorder
    (C) ideational apraxia
    (D) autopagnosia
    (E) simultagnosia

671. A 32-year-old farm worker is brought to the emergency room by the police, who describe him as violent and irrational. On examination he is found to be in a confusional state. Physical examination reveals excessive salivation, fever, miosis, muscle weakness and fasciculations, and piloerection. The most likely diagnosis is

    (A) Wernicke's encephalopathy
    (B) rabies
    (C) benzene intoxication
    (D) intoxication with peyote
    (E) acute organophosphate poisoning

672. If a patient displays complete paralysis of some muscles of an extremity with normal power in adjacent muscles of that extremity, it is most likely that the patient has a

(A) lower motor neuron lesion
(B) upper motor neuron lesion
(C) combined upper and lower motor neuron lesion
(D) motor cortex lesion
(E) myopathy

673. To elicit clonus, an examiner does which of the following?

(A) Quickly jerks a part of the body that is at rest
(B) Slowly pulls a part of the body that is at rest
(C) Quickly jerks a part of the body that is under voluntary tension
(D) Slowly pulls part of the body that is under voluntary tension
(E) Forces the body part back and forward

674. Aphasic patients characteristically lose which of the following types of speech?

(A) Automatic, expletive, or emotional speech
(B) Propositional speech
(C) Lingual sounds of speech
(D) Vowel sounds of speech
(E) All forms of speech in equal degree

675. A patient with normal pressure hydrocephalus

(A) benefits from diuretic treatment
(B) exhibits gait apraxia early in the course of the illness
(C) should not have a lumbar puncture performed
(D) frequently develops papilledema
(E) exhibits significant cortical atrophy on MRI scanning

676. When asked to describe his problem after his stroke, a patient said, "I cannot sum gook sib fib trans anymore." The lesion is likely to be situated in

(A) the left temporoparietal area or arcuate fasciculus
(B) the left anterior temporal lobe
(C) the left prefrontal lobe
(D) the left parahippocampal gyrus
(E) the globus pallidus

677. The most consistent and reliable sign of cerebellar dysfunction is

(A) unsteadiness of gait
(B) excessive swaying with the eyes closed
(C) nystagmus
(D) weakness
(E) tremor

678. The cognitive changes associated with Parkinson's disease

(A) primarily involve memory
(B) primarily involve cortical functions
(C) are late manifestations of the disease
(D) usually include deficits in visuospatial functioning
(E) are frequently associated with depression

679. The single most important part of the motor examination is

(A) elicitation of the plantar reflexes
(B) inspection for fasciculations
(C) strength testing
(D) palpation
(E) observation of gait

680. Occlusion of the posterior inferior cerebellar artery will cause

(A) ipsilateral paralysis and loss of pain and temperature sensation
(B) contralateral paralysis and ipsilateral cerebellar ataxia
(C) ipsilateral facial nerve palsy and cerebellar ataxia
(D) contralateral loss of pain and temperature sensation and ipsilateral ataxia
(E) pseudobulbar palsy

681. Causes of parkinsonism include each of the following EXCEPT

    (A) carbon monoxide poisoning
    (B) AIDS
    (C) dementia pugilistica
    (D) chronic alcoholism
    (E) Wilson's disease

682. A 40-year-old man is seen in the emergency room. He is unable to provide a clear history. On examination he is found to be in a confusional state with ataxia, nystagmus, and ophthalmoplegia. He is afebrile, his pupils are normal and reactive, funduscopy is normal, and he has a large hematoma on his forehead. As the treating physician your first order should be

    (A) an immediate spinal tap and CSF evaluation for xanthochromia
    (B) thiamine intravenously and intramuscularly
    (C) intravenous line with a 10% dextrose infusion
    (D) emergency head CT scan without contrast media
    (E) emergency head CT scan with contrast media

683. In persons with normal hearing, tests for efficiency of air and bone conduction of sound (Rinne test) demonstrate that

    (A) air conduction is better than bone conduction for all frequencies
    (B) bone conduction is better than air conduction for all frequencies
    (C) bone and air conduction are equal for high-frequency sounds
    (D) air conduction is superior for high-frequency sounds
    (E) air conduction is better in children and bone conduction is better in adults

684. A supranuclear palsy is characterized by each of the following EXCEPT

    (A) clonus
    (B) marked atrophy
    (C) spasticity
    (D) hyperreflexia
    (E) normal electromyographic tracing

685. A lesion of the cerebellum may be associated with each of the following EXCEPT

    (A) ataxia
    (B) dysmetria
    (C) hypertonia
    (D) titubation
    (E) scanning speech

686. A 65-year-old woman, who has been referred for evaluation of dementia, walks into your office. You observe that her trunk is bent forward, her steps are short and shuffling, and her feet hardly clear the ground. Her legs are stiff and bent at the knees and she does not swing her arms. The probable diagnosis is

    (A) peripheral neuropathy
    (B) spastic diplegia
    (C) parkinsonism
    (D) astasia-abasia
    (E) normal pressure hydrocephalus

687. A benign essential tremor

    (A) is limited to the upper limbs
    (B) occurs at rest
    (C) may have an autosomal dominant inheritance
    (D) is aggravated by alcohol
    (E) has a frequency of 8 to 12 Hz

688. The most effective method of visualizing the demyelinating plaques of multiple sclerosis is

    (A) contrast-enhanced MRI with a long T2 weighted image
    (B) contrast-enhanced MRI with a short T1 weighted image
    (C) contrast-enhanced MRI with a long T1 weighted image
    (D) single proton emission computed tomography
    (E) CT with contrast media

689. Lumbar puncture and cerebrospinal fluid examination reveal a normal opening pressure, mild turbidity, 50 lymphocytes per millimeter, protein of 100 mg/mL, and glucose of 50 mg/mL. The most likely diagnosis is

   (A) fungal infection
   (B) tuberculosis
   (C) meningococcal meningitis
   (D) viral meningitis
   (E) Guillain-Barré syndrome

690. Huntington's disease is correctly described by which of the following statements?

   (A) It frequently presents with personality change
   (B) It is associated with degeneration of the red nucleus
   (C) It is linked to a gene located on the short arm of chromosome 8
   (D) It usually manifests in the second decade
   (E) It produces cortical atrophy visible on MRI

691. A 40-year-old man is able to stand upright with his feet close together. When asked to close his eyes, however, he begins to sway. Appropriate laboratory investigations include each of the following EXCEPT

   (A) complete blood count
   (B) VDRL test
   (C) serum lead levels
   (D) serum vitamin B_{12} level
   (E) serum folate level

DIRECTIONS: Each question below contains four suggested responses of which **one or more** is correct. Select

A	if	**1, 2, and 3**	are correct
B	if	**1 and 3**	are correct
C	if	**2 and 4**	are correct
D	if	**4**	is correct
E	if	**1, 2, 3, and 4**	are correct

692. Features of Broca's (expressive) aphasia include

(1) sparse, telegraphic speech
(2) absence of prepositions, articles, and conjunctions of speech
(3) dysprosody
(4) associated alexia and visual field defects

693. The Brown-Séquard syndrome is characterized by

(1) enduring loss of sphincter control
(2) contralateral loss of pain and temperature sensation
(3) ipsilateral cerebellar ataxia
(4) ipsilateral loss of position sense

694. Loss of position sense may be caused by lesions of the

(1) peripheral nerves
(2) dorsal roots or columns
(3) medial lemniscus
(4) parietal cortex

695. A tumor confined to the internal auditory canal would be very likely to cause

(1) facial palsy
(2) tinnitus
(3) vestibular dysfunction
(4) diplopia

696. Correct statements about the tremor of Parkinson's disease include which of the following?

(1) It does affect the tongue
(2) It is present during sleep
(3) It is present at rest
(4) It has a frequency of 6 to 8 Hz

697. Correct statements about the optic disc include which of the following?

(1) The palest sector is lateral
(2) The optic disc appears pink
(3) The pigment ring is more conspicuous laterally
(4) The large vessels pierce the disc peripheral to the optic cup

698. Peripheral nerve and dermatomal distributions coincide in the

(1) head
(2) neck
(3) arm
(4) thorax

699. The AIDS dementia complex (ADC)

(1) is secondary to opportunistic central nervous system infection
(2) is characterized by psychomotor slowing
(3) occurs in approximately 10 percent of patients with HIV infection
(4) usually has an insidious onset

700. The Klüver-Bucy syndrome is characterized by

(1) hypometamorphosis
(2) amnesia
(3) compulsive rituals
(4) hypersexuality

701. A person with progressive supranuclear palsy

(1) usually has a flexed neck
(2) has difficulty reading
(3) often exhibits dyskinetic movements
(4) often appears anxious

SUMMARY OF DIRECTIONS				
A	B	C	D	E
1, 2, 3 only	1, 3 only	2, 4 only	4 only	All are correct

702. A person with herpes simplex encephalitis

    (1) usually has an abnormal electroencephalogram
    (2) has often had symptoms for several months prior to initial presentation
    (3) often exhibits personality change
    (4) seldom survives with or without treatment

703. Seizures after head injury

    (1) have an incidence of 50 percent after compound skull fractures
    (2) usually occur in people with a family history of seizures
    (3) are less likely to recur in patients who have their first seizure at the time of trauma rather than months later
    (4) seldom generalize

704. A young woman is diagnosed as suffering from multiple sclerosis (MS). True statements about her illness include

    (1) approximately one-third of patients with MS have no functional disability after 10 years
    (2) cognition is almost always spared in MS
    (3) the risk of recurrence is increased by stress
    (4) optic neuritis almost always develops into disseminated MS

705. Central nervous system manifestations of Lyme disease include

    (1) facial nerve palsy
    (2) quadriparesis
    (3) cerebellar ataxia
    (4) behavioral change

706. Anoxic encephalopathy may result in

    (1) an amnestic state
    (2) a major depressive disorder
    (3) a progressive dementing illness
    (4) an acute psychotic episode

707. The neuropathologic changes of Alzheimer's disease

    (1) are most commonly localized to the paralimbic areas
    (2) do not usually include significant cortical neuronal cell loss
    (3) are characterized by the presence of Lewy bodies
    (4) usually involve the locus ceruleus

708. Which of the following would normally be found in a patient with a large meningioma of the olfactory groove?

    (1) Amotivation
    (2) Poor impulse control
    (3) Unilateral optic atrophy
    (4) Papilledema

709. Occlusion of the superior branch of the right middle cerebral artery may produce

    (1) deviation of the eyes to the right
    (2) left-sided motor weakness
    (3) left-sided sensory deficit
    (4) a left homonymous hemianopia

710. A left oculomotor nerve palsy produces

    (1) diplopia on straight-ahead gaze
    (2) a dilated unreactive left pupil
    (3) lateral deviation of the left eye
    (4) ptosis of the left eye

711. Features that are helpful in distinguishing multi-infarct dementia from Alzheimer's disease include

    (1) age of onset
    (2) abnormal reflexes
    (3) CSF pleocytosis
    (4) stepwise progression

712. Causes of tunnel vision include

    (1) glaucoma
    (2) migraine
    (3) papilledema
    (4) hysteria

713. Which of the following may cause absent knee and ankle jerks with an extensor plantar response?

    (1) Transection of the cord at the level of T12
    (2) Tabes dorsalis
    (3) Lead intoxication
    (4) Diabetes mellitus

714. Papilledema may be caused by

    (1) lead poisoning
    (2) hypertensive encephalopathy
    (3) optic neuritis
    (4) normal pressure hydrocephalus

715. The serum level of phenytoin is raised by the concomitant use of

    (1) carbamazepine
    (2) fluoxetine
    (3) clonazepam
    (4) sulfonamides

716. True statements regarding chronic subdural hematomas include

    (1) they are normally associated with a normal electroencephalogram
    (2) they very seldom cause focal neurologic signs
    (3) they seldom cause significant symptoms
    (4) they may resorb spontaneously

717. Infection of the nervous system with HIV may result in

    (1) an acute onset paraplegia
    (2) acute meningoencephalitis within a few days of exposure
    (3) a peripheral neuropathy
    (4) urinary incontinence

718. Features of the Ramsay Hunt syndrome include

    (1) orofacial dyskinesia
    (2) "crocodile tears"
    (3) dysphagia
    (4) pain in the region of the ear and mastoid

719. A 60-year-old man develops wasting of the small muscles of his hand. Before considering a diagnosis of amyotrophic lateral sclerosis, which of the following conditions should be considered as part of the differential diagnosis?

    (1) Cervical spondylosis
    (2) Multiple sclerosis
    (3) Syphilis
    (4) Myasthenia gravis

720. Which of the following would be expected to produce episodic "dyscontrol" or violence?

    (1) Left prefrontal cerebrovascular accident
    (2) Herpes encephalitis
    (3) Raised intracranial pressure
    (4) Meningioma of the olfactory groove

721. A patient has recently been diagnosed as suffering from tardive dyskinesia. Correct statements about the condition include

    (1) approximately 40 percent of cases resolve over the first 12 months after discontinuing neuroleptics
    (2) symptoms may be improved by increasing the dose of neuroleptic
    (3) reserpine may reduce the intensity of symptoms
    (4) symptoms will increase with sodium valproate

722. The afferent tracts and relays for transmitting pain sensation to the cortex include

    (1) the posteromedial funiculus
    (2) the lateral neospinothalamic tract
    (3) the dorsomedial nucleus of the thalamus
    (4) the spinoreticulothalamic tract

	SUMMARY OF DIRECTIONS			
A	B	C	D	E
1, 2, 3 only	1, 3 only	2, 4 only	4 only	All are correct

723. Features of the Argyll Robertson pupil include

    (1) small, equal pupils
    (2) response to mydriatic drugs
    (3) failure to constrict on accommodation
    (4) failure to react to light

724. A person with vertebrobasilar migraine may present with

    (1) temporary blindness
    (2) staggering
    (3) stupor
    (4) quadriplegia

725. Clinical features that suggest a subcortical rather than a cortical dementia include

    (1) early onset of apraxia
    (2) bradyphrenia
    (3) language disturbance
    (4) movement disorder

726. Nonmetastatic neurologic complications of bronchial carcinoma include

    (1) personality change
    (2) dementia
    (3) psychosis
    (4) parkinsonism

727. True statements regarding trigeminal neuralgia include which of the following?

    (1) It usually has its onset in early adulthood
    (2) It may be a manifestation of motor neuron disease
    (3) It is associated with an area of sensory loss appropriate to the branch of the trigeminal nerve involved
    (4) It is more common in females

728. A patient with the Dejerine-Roussy syndrome

    (1) has a sensory loss
    (2) has a thalamic lesion
    (3) has unusual pain in the affected area
    (4) usually recovers

729. Inappropriate and jocular affect is likely to be produced by a lesion in which of the following sites?

    (1) Left prefrontal cortex
    (2) Right posterior parietal cortex
    (3) Left periventricular area
    (4) Right prefrontal cortex

730. Typical features of cluster headaches include

    (1) pain that wakes the patient at night
    (2) focal neurologic deficits
    (3) lacrimation and nasal congestion
    (4) relief of the pain with alcohol

731. A 60-year-old man has just suffered a transient ischemic attack. He could accurately be told

    (1) he has a 20 percent chance of eventually having a major cerebrovascular accident within 5 years
    (2) he has a 20 percent chance of having a myocardial infarction within 5 years
    (3) he will have no neurologic deficit from the episode
    (4) he should have a carotid endarterectomy as soon as possible

732. Causes of a mononeuritis multiplex include

    (1) HIV infection
    (2) chronic alcoholism
    (3) diabetes mellitus
    (4) lead poisoning

DIRECTIONS: Each group of questions below consists of lettered headings followed by a set of numbered items. For each numbered item select the **one** lettered heading with which it is **most** closely associated. Each lettered heading may be used **once, more than once, or not at all.**

Questions 733–737

For each of the neuropathologic findings listed below, choose the movement disorder with which it is most closely associated.

    (A)   Hemiballismus
    (B)   Chorea
    (C)   Parkinson's disease
    (D)   Wide-based gait
    (E)   Akinetic mutism

733.   Bilateral hemorrhage into the cingulate gyri

734.   Lewy bodies

735.   Degeneration of the caudate nuclei

736.   Infarction of the subthalamic nucleus

737.   Evidence of previous meningitis

Questions 738–740

For each of the following clinical syndromes, select the artery that is occluded.

    (A)   Anterior cerebral artery
    (B)   Middle cerebral artery
    (C)   Posterior cerebral artery
    (D)   Carotid artery
    (E)   Vertebrobasilar artery

738.   Contralateral sensory loss, contralateral homonymous hemianopia, and alexia without agraphia

739.   Urinary incontinence, paratonia, transcortical aphasia, and abulia

740.   Contralateral hemiparesis, hemisensory loss, homonymous hemianopia, and aphasia syndromes

Questions 741–745

Match each clinical presentation of a seizure disorder with the likely cause.

    (A)   Hippocampal sclerosis
    (B)   Orbitofrontal lesion
    (C)   Left temporal glioma in Heschl's gyrus
    (D)   Occipital lobe infarct
    (E)   Lesion in the right supplementary motor area

741.   A 40-year-old woman turns her eyes to the right. Initially the fingers of her left hand start to twitch, followed by her face, leg, and then her whole body. She then loses consciousness and is incontinent of urine

742.   A 25-year-old man complains of a foul odor, epigastric discomfort, and dysphoria. He then exhibits a motionless stare for 1 min. He later denies any knowledge of this event

743.   A 50-year-old man complains of brief periods of "flashing lights and strange colors"

744.   A 17-year-old girl complains of episodes of flushing, excessive sweating, palpitations, and dry mouth

745.   A 20-year-old man complains of brief periods during which he believes he is hearing Beethoven's Ninth Symphony

Questions 746–750

Match the clinical syndrome with the site of pathology.

(A)   Right temporoparietal area
(B)   Left prefrontal lobe
(C)   Orbitomedial frontal lobes
(D)   Right anteromedial temporal lobe
(E)   Right inferoparietal lobe
(F)   Left peristriate area
(G)   Hypothalamus

746.   A 35-year-old man is referred by his internist. The family has recently noticed a change in his demeanor. They describe him as apathetic, slovenly, and lazy. He lies around the house all day and watches television or sleeps. However, he has also embarrassed his family by making sexual advances toward old family friends and upset the parish priest by telling dirty jokes outside church

747.   A 25-year-old man is referred to the student counselor by his college professor. The professor states that he is "exhausted" by the young man's enthusiasm for his class. Each day, the student has voluntarily been handing in 30-page assignments on biblical texts and ruminates constantly over his subjective sense of personal destiny and his moral outrage over the decadence in the world. According to the professor, the student "never stops talking" and claims to have become celibate

748.   A 16-year-old girl presents to the emergency department accompanied by the police. She apparently "ran amok" in the classroom and attacked several students without provocation. The episode lasted a few minutes and the girl denies any recollection of the incident

749.   A 60-year-old man is found wandering the streets. He is confused and disoriented to time and place. There is no evidence for any substance or alcohol use. No abnormalities are found on metabolic screening

750.   A 40-year-old computer expert is referred by his psychiatrist for a second opinion. Despite prolonged psychotherapy and appropriate psychotropic medication, the patient remains profoundly depressed

652. The answer is D. (*Adams RD, ed 4. pp 489–491.*) Neurologic changes that are expected to occur with the process of aging include each of those mentioned plus presbycusis, decreased smell, decreased motor movement, small pupils, diminished pupillary reflexes, decreased upward gaze, impaired fine coordination and agility, and decreased muscle power. Although it was originally believed there is a linear decrease in cognitive abilities with age, this has not proved to be true. A decline in abstraction and the ability to process and store new material appear to be the changes associated with aging. Along with other pathologic changes, the population of large cortical neurons decreases with age.

653. The answer is C. (*Adams RD, ed 4. pp 929–930.*) Pick's disease is a rapidly progressive degenerative disorder primarily affecting the frontal and temporal lobes. Histopathology reveals marked loss of neurons in the first three cortical layers and argentophilic bodies (Pick bodies) within the remaining neurons. Clinical features essentially reflect the lobar distribution of these pathologic changes. Patients display apathy, amotivation, and shallowness alternating with periods of inappropriate stimulus-bound behavior. A gradual deterioration in language from an initial fluent aphasia into palilalia and finally mutism is typical. The cause of the disorder is unknown, but a genetic basis appears likely. The disease runs a rapid downhill course with death usually occurring in 2 to 5 years.

654. The answer is D. (*Tasman, p 600.*) Approximately 60 percent of patients will exhibit clinical evidence of central nervous system involvement in AIDS. At postmortem almost 90 percent of patients will be found to have neuropathologic changes associated with the disease. The dementing illness associated with HIV infection essentially reflects the subcortical neuropathologic changes found in the illness. Patients usually display the gradual onset of a "dilapidated" cognition characterized by marked psychomotor slowing, impersistence, and confusion. It is important to remember that these patients may develop many of the other secondary complications of the illness (e.g., infection, lymphomas) and therefore present with virtually any possible constellation of signs and symptoms.

655. The answer is C. (*Adams RD, ed 4. pp 748–751.*) Syringomyelia is a progressive degenerative condition of the spinal cord caused by a congenital abnormality—a syrinx (tube), which occupies the central gray matter of the cervical spinal cord. Gradual enlargement of the syrinx causes compression of surrounding structures and a neurologic deficit. The syrinx initially extends into the anterior and posterior horns and later into the lateral and posterior funiculi. The onset of symptoms is usually insidious and characterized by a dissociative loss of pain and temperature sensation, but not touch, over a capelike distribution of the neck, shoulders, and arms. Other clinical signs include muscle weakness and atrophy, loss of reflexes, and ataxia. Eventually a spastic paraparesis may result from involvement of the corticospinal tracts. There are frequently other congenital abnormalities associated with syringomyelia, such as fused cervical vertebrae, platybasia, and the Arnold-Chiari malformation. The condition is easily identified by MRI.

656. The answer is A.   *(Adams RD, ed 4. p 370.)*   The inability to recognize a previously familiar face is known as prosopagnosia. This is an example of a visual agnosia, i.e., the inability to identify or categorize an object or stimulus despite an intact visual system. Other examples of visual agnosias include color agnosia, topographic agnosia (an inability to recognize geographic landmarks), and simultagnosia (an inability to synthesize all the components of a visual field).

657. The answer is B.   *(Adams RD, ed 4. pp 344–345.)*   Transient global amnesia usually occurs in middle-aged or elderly people. The period of amnesia lasts a few hours and does not involve personal identity. The person is capable of normal language and intellectual functioning. Attention is normal throughout the period of amnesia. The etiology of transient global amnesia is unknown but is postulated to be a transient ischemic attack in the posterior cerebral circulation. The disorder usually lasts a few hours and seldom recurs. No emergency treatment is indicated.

658. The answer is C.   *(Adams RD, ed 4. p 364.)*   The letter cancellation test demonstrates a typical example of left hemineglect. This syndrome is typically caused by a lesion in the right parietal lobe and is characterized by an inattention to somatosensory experiences located in the person's left hemifield. The person with hemineglect will be oblivious to activity or stimuli in the left half of the visual field and will also be unaware of the left side of the body. Since lesions of the left superior parietal lobe do not cause neglect, it is postulated that the right hemisphere is dominant for directing attention.

659. The answer is E.   *(Adams RD, ed 4. pp 356–359.)*   The patient's drawing demonstrates perseveration and an inability to change set. This is suggestive of frontal lobe deficits. Other abnormalities that might be found in this patient are amotivation, apathy, poor impulse control, lack of insight, and emotional lability. Since the prefrontal lobes are primarily involved in the integration and execution of sophisticated motor and cognitive behavioral functions, it is difficult to evaluate their functioning within the confines of the structured neuropsychological laboratory. When considering the possibility of frontal lobe deficits, the examiner is well advised to observe the patient's behavior within the context of an ambiguous social environment.

660. The answer is D.   *(Adams RD, ed 4. p 629.)*   The anterior cerebral artery supplies the medial, medial-orbital, and lateral surface of the frontal lobes. In addition the artery supplies most of the corpus callosum. Deep proximal branches also supply the head of the caudate, anterior limb of the internal capsule, and the anterior part of the globus pallidus. A bilateral lesion of this artery, such as the resection of an aneurysm, will produce profound deficits in the prefrontal lobe, such as personality change; urinary incontinence; gait apraxia; amnesia; paraplegia; sensory loss over foot, toes, and leg; and paratonia.

661. The answer is E.   *(Kaufman, ed 3. p 126.)*   The VDRL test, which has a sensitivity of 85 percent, is currently the test used most frequently as a screen for neurosyphilis. False positives on the VDRL test may be found with old age, autoimmune disease, and addictive disorders. False negative results may occur many years after initial exposure or after previous treatment (even if inadequate). More specific, but more expensive, tests such as the fluorescent treponemal antibody absorption (FTA-ABS) or treponema micro-hemagglutination (MHA-TP) tests should be used if the VDRL test is positive or a false negative result is suspected. CSF testing should be performed when asymptomatic or symptomatic persons test positive on the FTA-ABS or MHA-TP or when a patient with HIV infection exhibits mental status change. CSF VDRL testing is highly specific and diagnostic for neurosyphilis but does have a high rate of false negatives.

662. **The answer is B.** (*Kaufman, ed 3. pp 171–172.*)   A thorough history and full physical examination are essential when evaluating the symptoms of headache. The pain of a tension headache is thought to be secondary to muscle contraction precipitated by fatigue, emotional stress, bright lights, or noise. The pain typically worsens as the day progresses and is often relieved by alcohol or exercise. The condition is more frequent in women and tends to run in families. Treatment is essentially empiric and includes simple analgesics, relaxation techniques, or low-dose tricyclic antidepressants.

663. **The answer is C.** (*Adams RD, ed 4. pp 201–204.*)   Interruption of the right optic tract causes a left homonymous hemianopia. One optic tract contains the nondecussated axons from the lateral half of the ipsilateral retina and decussated axons from the medial half of the contralateral retina. Thus, the axons in one tract unite homonymous visual fields, and their interruption results in a contralateral homonymous field defect. A complete lesion of the visual pathway between the origin of one optic tract and the calcarine cortex will cause a complete contralateral homonymous hemianopia. Therefore, the localization of the lesion depends on the associated neurologic findings rather than on the visual field defect per se.

664. **The answer is C.** (*Adams RD, ed 4. pp 277–285.*)   A small lesion in the midbrain tegmentum located a few millimeters ventral to the aqueduct will completely interrupt consciousness with little effect on other functions. A lesion at this site interrupts the reticular ascending system, which is responsible for maintaining arousal. Lesions of the medullary or caudal pontine tegmentum do not selectively abolish consciousness. Lesions at the diencephalon or the cortex must be extensive to abolish consciousness and will alter other bodily functions.

665. **The answer is C.** (*Adams RD, ed 4. pp 365–366.*)   The tetrad of (1) agraphia without alexia, (2) finger agnosia, (3) loss of right-left discrimination, and (4) acalculia characterizes Gerstmann's syndrome. This results from a lesion in the left anterior parietal area (i.e., the left angular gyrus). The syndrome appears to represent a defect in cross-modal matching. For example, patient's with Gerstmann's syndrome can maintain appropriate conversation and can read but cannot understand a sentence if it contains complex statements about relationship (e.g., the man who came after the second woman). Similar processing difficulties explain the problems with calculation, finger agnosia, and left-right orientation.

666. **The answer is A.** (*Adams RD, ed 4. pp 220–221.*)   In normal persons, both pupils constrict equally when light is flashed in one eye. The contralateral connections of the afferent retinal fibers disperse the pupillary reflex equally over both IIIrd cranial nerves. Any difference in the response of the two pupils is evidence of a lesion somewhere in the reflex arc, i.e., between the retinal receptor and pupilloconstrictor muscle of the iris. When the pupils react differently to light, the examiner must inspect the retina, the visual fields, the oculomotor nerve, and the sympathetic innervation of the iris and investigate for possible midbrain lesions.

667. **The answer is D.** (*Adams RD, ed 4. pp 6–7.*)   To reinforce a quadriceps femoris muscle stretch, the examiner may try the maneuver of Jendrassik in which the patient grasps his or her own hands and pulls hard, while the examiner attempts to elicit the stretch reflex. The voluntary innervation of the part not being tested "overflows" to augment the innervation of the lower motor neurons of the quadriceps. Some persons normally have such a high threshold for the muscle stretch reflex that reinforcement is necessary to demonstrate that the reflex arc is intact and that no pathology exists.

668. The answer is D. (*Adams, ed 4. pp 1035–1040.*) Guillain-Barré is an acute demyelinating polyradiculoneuropathy that manifests as a rapid ascending paralysis with autonomic neuropathy and minimal sensory loss. The onset is rapid and paralysis may ascend to involve the cranial nerves within days or weeks. Patients may require respiratory support secondary to phrenic nerve palsy. The condition is presumed to be an autoimmune response to host myelin, which has been linked to a number of infectious diseases such as hepatitis, Lyme disease, and infectious mononucleosis. The disease has also been associated with lymphomas, insect bites, sarcoidosis, and connective tissue diseases. Plasmapheresis is currently the only therapeutic intervention but is of doubtful efficacy. Patients may require several months to regain their muscle power.

669. The answer is B. (*Adams RD, ed 4. p 1040.*) Acute intermittent porphyria (Swedish-type porphyria) is an autosomal dominant metabolic disorder of hemoglobin synthesis resulting in excessive production and urinary excretion of porphobilinogen and δ-aminolevulinic acid. Clinical symptoms include abdominal discomfort, dark urine, encephalopathy occasionally with seizures, polyneuropathy, cranial nerve palsies (e.g., dysphagia, facial palsy), and autonomic arousal. Attacks are precipitated by estrogens, sulfonamides, barbiturates, phenytoin, and succinimides. Treatment is supportive and intravenous glucose is administered to inhibit hemoglobin production. Pyridoxine supplements may also be beneficial.

670. The answer is C. (*Adams RD, ed 4. pp 46–48.*) Apraxia is the inability to carry out previously learned motor sequences despite intact motor ability. This group of disorders may be considered the motor equivalent of the aphasias. The apraxias are examples of disconnection syndromes in which different modalities are separated from one another (e.g., speech from motor functions). In *ideational apraxia* the subject cannot perform sequential motor tasks but can perform each component step; this is caused by dementia or other pathologic processes. In *ideomotor apraxia* the subject is unable to perform simple motor sequences (e.g., buttoning a shirt). This form is caused by dominant posterior frontal or anterior parietal lesions. And in *constructional apraxia* the subject is unable to put together the parts of the whole—a disorder caused by a right parietal lesion.

671. The answer is E. (*Adams RD, ed 4. p 914.*) The organophosphates are powerful acetylcholinesterase inhibitors. The most common cause of intoxication is chronic exposure of the skin to insecticides that may impregnate the clothing of farm workers. Clinical signs of organophosphate poisoning include muscarinic effects such as salivation, sweating, bradycardia, hypotension, and involuntary urination. Nicotinic effects include muscle weakness and fasciculations, respiratory depression, and copious bronchial secretions. High doses cause a confusional state, which may progress into coma and seizures. The diagnosis may be confirmed by low red blood cell and plasma acetylcholinesterase levels. Treatment consists of atropine titration, pralidoxime as a binding agent, and supportive measures.

672. The answer is A. (*Adams RD, ed 4. pp 39–46.*) Complete paralysis of a set of muscles with preservation of adjacent muscles is evidence of a lower motor neuron lesion. Upper motor neuron lesions, in principle, do not cause paralysis of individual muscles. Instead, following the dictum of Hughlings Jackson, upper motor neurons paralyze movements. This statement holds true whether the lesion affects the motor cortex, hemispheric white matter, internal capsule, brainstem, or spinal cord. Although the myopathies may have a predilection for certain muscle groups, they tend to involve all muscles to some degree.

673. The answer is A. (*Adams RD, ed 4. pp 83–84.*) To elicit clonus the examiner quickly jerks a part of the body that is at rest. The quick jerk is necessary to stretch the muscle spindles to set off the repetitive series of stretch reflexes that constitute the clonus. The examiner should ensure that the part of the patient's body is at rest and placed in a position that allows control of the amount of tension and movement to be imparted.

674. The answer is B. (*Adams RD, ed 4. pp 382–385.*)   Aphasic patients, as Hughlings Jackson pointed out, characteristically lose propositional speech but retain emotional or automatic speech (particularly expletives). Aphasic patients lose the ability to speak in terms of proposals (i.e., a subject removed from the present) but are able to express the nature of their current state of mind. Thus, after struggling and failing to produce the propositional sentence "I think it will rain tomorrow," the patient will say with clarity "Damn, I can't do it!"

675. The answer is B. (*Adams RD, ed 4. pp 507–508.*)   Normal pressure hydrocephalus usually presents with the classic triad of gait apraxia, urinary incontinence, and dementia. The gait is typically "magnetic" (i.e., patients have difficulty shifting their weight forward) and wide-based and the patient often walks on tiptoes. Aberration in gait is typically the first sign of the disease and its severity is proportional to the stage of the disease. The urinary incontinence is typically urgency and frequency, but patients may become completely incontinent. Although there is significant ventricular dilatation, the amount of cerebral atrophy is usually minimal. Lumbar puncture and CSF withdrawal may help the patient significantly. Surgical shunting is presently the only effective treatment.

676. The answer is A. (*Adams RD, ed 4. pp 382–389.*)   The described patient exhibits the typical features of a fluent aphasia, that is, paraphasic errors, neologisms, clang associations, and circumlocution. The patient will be able to convey his emotional state by the use of nonverbal cues (i.e., prosodic behavior). Patients with fluent aphasias may be misdiagnosed as psychotic because of the similarities of their speech to schizophrenic speech. These patients may also experience paranoia. Fluent aphasia is caused by discrete lesions in the dominant temporoparietal area or arcuate fasciculus.

677. The answer is A. (*Adams RD, ed 4. pp 73–75.*)   An unsteady gait is the most consistent sign of cerebellar dysfunction. The Romberg sign is a test of posterior column function. The interpretation of nystagmus is complex and often nonspecific. Lesions of the cerebellar vermis secondary to alcohol, in particular, will cause gait abnormality. Cerebellar lesions may also cause an intention tremor, an inability to perform rapid alternating movements (dysdiadochokinesia), past pointing (dysmetria), scanning speech, and truncal ataxia. Common causes of cerebellar dysfunction include chronic phenytoin (Dilantin) therapy and alcohol abuse.

678. The answer is E. (*Adams RD, ed 4. p 930.*)   Parkinson's disease results in a subcortical dementia. The subcortical dementias are characterized by "dilapidated" cognition. Although neocortical systems are intact, the affected person appears to lack the motivation to engage in cognitive tasks. Patients will classically respond to questions with statements such as "I don't know. I just can't do it." Enthusiastic encouragement by the examiner will normally significantly improve the subject's performance. A significant percentage of patients with Parkinson's disease develop a major depressive disorder sometimes referred to as bradyphrenia. These clinical syndromes parallel the motor symptoms, which are normally the major focus of treatment.

679. The answer is E. (*Adams RD, ed 4. pp 94–99.*)   The most important part of the motor examination is watching a patient walk. Unfortunately many examiners fail to do so. Since pathology of the central nervous system, peripheral nerves, muscles, or joints will manifest in the patient's gait, most motor system abnormalities can be diagnosed from simply observing the patient walk.

680. The answer is D. (*Adams RD, ed 4. p 639.*)   Occlusion of the posterior inferior cerebellar artery produces damage in the lateral medulla and is therefore referred to as the *lateral medullary syndrome* (*Wallenberg's syndrome*). Damage is incurred by the cerebellar peduncle, trigeminal nerve nucleus, spinothalamic tract, nucleus ambiguus, and sympathetic fibers. Damage to these structures causes a complex clinical picture consisting of ipsilateral pain and numbness over the face; limb ataxia; vertigo, nausea, and vomiting; Horner's syndrome; dysphagia, hoarseness, vocal cord paralysis, and decreased gag reflex; hiccup; and numbness of arm, trunk, or leg. Contralateral signs are decreased pain and temperature sensation over half the body.

681. The answer is D. (*Adams RD, ed 4. pp 937–941.*) Apart from the idiopathic disease, the symptoms of parkinsonism have numerous possible etiologies. "Post encephalitic Parkinson's disease" was common following the encephalitis lethargica epidemic of 1914. There are many other causes of the syndrome, however. These include carbon monoxide poisoning, anoxia, dementia pugilistica, Wilson's disease, AIDS, manganese poisoning, and dopamine blocking drugs. Recently, the "designer" street drug MPTP (methylphenyl pyridine) has caused several cases of fulminant parkinsonism and provided a possible research model for the disorder.

682. The answer is B. (*Adams RD, ed 4. pp 821–827.*) The patient presents with the classic symptoms of Wernicke's encephalopathy. This is a medical emergency and demands immediate parenteral thiamine supplementation. Since thiamine is a safe therapeutic agent, it can be prescribed before other possible differential diagnoses have been excluded. Despite the prompt use of thiamine, approximately one-fourth of patients with Wernicke's encephalopathy will develop an amnestic disorder. The use of intravenous glucose prior to thiamine may precipitate or aggravate a Wernicke's encephalopathy and should be avoided in confused or comatose patients until thiamine administration. A definitive diagnosis of thiamine deficiency is confirmed by a low erythrocyte transketolase level.

683. The answer is A. (*Adams RD, ed 4. p 230.*) Air conduction is better than bone conduction in normal persons of all ages. Thus, the usual channel for sound perception through the ear is better than the artificial channel of bone stimulation. If bone conduction is better than air conduction, there must be a problem in the external canal, eardrum, or ossicles. The Weber test consists of placing the tuning fork in the midline of the forehead. A normal person will hear the sound equally in both ears. In neural deafness the sound will be localized in the normal ear; in conductive deafness the sound is localized to the affected side.

684. The answer is B. (*Adams RD, ed 4. p 46.*) An upper motor neuron or supranuclear palsy is characterized by (1) more than one muscle affected, (2) slight atrophy secondary to disuse, (3) spasticity with hyperreflexia, (4) normal nerve conduction studies, and (5) an extensor plantar response. Lower motor neuron palsy is characterized by (1) marked wasting, (2) fasciculations, (3) flaccidity and hyporeflexia, (4) the possibility of individual muscles' being affected, and (5) an abnormal EMG study.

685. The answer is C. (*Adams RD, ed 4. pp 73–75.*) Cerebellar dysfunction may give rise to hypotonia, ataxia (incoordination affecting voluntary movement), and disorders of equilibrium and gait. Hypotonia is usually due to extensive lesions of the cerebellar hemispheres or peduncles and is more pronounced with acute lesions. For example, "pendular reflexes" are caused by decreased tone in the quadriceps and hamstrings. Examples of ataxia include dysmetria, dyssynergia, and dysdiadochokinesis. The cerebellar gait is typified by a wide base, lateral veering, irregular steps, and unsteadiness. Titubation describes the anteroposterior head nodding that these patients may exhibit. Disorders of equilibrium and gait are usually secondary to cerebellar vermis lesions.

686. The answer is C. (*Adams RD, ed 4. pp 94–99.*) The patient exhibits the festinating gait that is typical of parkinsonism. These patients also have difficulty initiating their gait and exhibit retro- and anteropulsion. The gait of normal pressure hydrocephalus is characterized by a short step and wide base. Patients with a sensory ataxia have to watch the floor to determine the position of their feet, which are raised high and often stamped down. The spastic diplegic has a classic "scissor gait" with no flexion at the hip, knee, or ankle and therefore limited movement and short steps.

687. The answer is C. (*Adams RD, ed 4. pp 78–82.*)   An essential tremor may be familial and transmitted as an autosomal dominant trait, occur with old age (senile tremor), or occur on a sporadic basis in young people (essential tremor). It is an action tremor with a frequency of 4 to 8 Hz that usually affects the upper limbs but may also involve the axial and cervical musculature causing a typical head nodding tremor. The tremor is relieved by alcohol. Beta blockers and primidone have both demonstrated efficacy in reducing the tremor, although the condition seldom requires treatment.

688. The answer is A. (*Kaplan, ed 3. pp 440–448.*)   Tissue exposure to a powerful electromagnetic field causes its excitation. The energy of the electromagnetic pulse is absorbed by the tissue and subsequently released until the tissue once again relaxes completely. This period of relaxation (i.e., energy release) produces two relaxation constants that are tissue-specific—the T1 and T2 constants. The scan may be set to produce an image of either of these signals and also a balanced T1/T2 image. The long T1 weighted image demonstrates fluid with a low density and provides a better definition of brain tissue and anatomy. Since T2 weighted images ascribe a high density to fluid, they are useful in documenting tumors, inflammation, and infarction where edema is suspected. The paramagnetic contrast media such as gadolinium provide higher definition images and aid in the delineation of even small areas of inflammation.

689. The answer is D. (*Kaufman, ed 3. pp 429–430.*)   CSF examination provides reliable evidence for the type of intracranial infection. Viral meningitis causes a low-grade pleocytosis, moderately elevated protein, and possibly a mild decrease in glucose. The appearance of the CSF is normal or mildly turbid and Gram stain is negative. Bacterial infections cause a marked polymorphonuclear leukocytosis, decreased glucose, and elevated protein; Gram stain frequently demonstrates the pathogen. TB and fungal infections produce a greater lymphocytosis and protein elevation than does a viral infection; special stains and antigen studies (e.g., cryptococcal) may be diagnostic. Guillain-Barré syndrome may produce mild elevation in serum protein with a very low pleocytosis.

690. The answer is A. (*Adams RD, ed 4. pp 932–935.*)   Although the motor components are the most visible clinical aspect of the disorder, it is important to consider all the aspects of Huntington's disease (HD). Degeneration of the caudate nucleus produces deficits in cognition, behavior, and movement. The personality changes are usually the first to appear and are characterized by shallowness, lability, poor planning, and poor impulse control. Patients with HD may develop mood disorders and thought disorders. Because of the extensive reciprocal connections between the head of the caudate and the prefrontal lobes, the dementia is primarily subcortical with features suggestive of prefrontal deficits. HD is an autosomal dominant disorder with occasional sporadic cases. The responsible gene has been identified on the short arm of chromosome 4.

691. The answer is C. (*Adams RD, ed 4. pp 833–835.*)   The patient demonstrates a positive Romberg's sign. This is indicative of a loss of proprioception and therefore of dorsal column pathology. The most common cause of this syndrome is subacute combined degeneration of the cord (SACD) secondary to vitamin B_{12} deficiency. This produces a demyelination peripheral neuropathy and involvement of the lateral and dorsal columns of the spinal cord. Clinical signs are therefore a classic "glove and stocking" sensory loss, loss of position sense, muscle weakness, spastic gait, and absent ankle jerks. Late in the illness, optic atrophy may occur as well as other symptoms secondary to demyelination of the central nervous system. Chronic lead intoxication produces a peripheral neuropathy with no loss of proprioception. Tabes dorsalis can produce a clinical picture similar to SACD.

692. The answer is A (1, 2, 3). (*Adams RD, ed 4. pp 382–383.*)   Features of a Broca's aphasia are sparse, telegraphic speech; absence of prepositions and conjunctions in speech; and dysprosody. Alexia and visual field defects are associated with lesions in the parieto-occipito-temporal region (posterior parasylvian region) and therefore are more likely to occur in association with a Wernicke's aphasia. Patients with a nonfluent aphasia are aware of their inability to communicate and this may aggravate or precipitate a major depressive disorder. Most patients also exhibit dysgraphia with letters misspelled or poorly formed.

693. The answer is C (2, 4). (*Adams RD, ed 4. pp 129–130.*)   The Brown-Séquard syndrome describes a hemisection of the spinal cord. This results in ipsilateral loss of dorsal column function with loss of position sense and in contralateral loss of pain and temperature. Interruption of the ipsilateral corticospinal tract causes hemiplegia and therefore precludes testing cerebellar function. Tactile sensation is not affected since the fibers from one side of the body are distributed via the posterior columns and anterior spinothalamic tract to both sides of the body.

694. The answer is E (all). (*Adams RD, ed 4. p 126.*)   Loss of position sense may occur following lesions to the peripheral nerves, dorsal roots or columns, medial lemniscus, thalamus, internal capsule, and parietal cortex. The clinician should therefore consider this pathway when determining the etiology in a particular case. Abnormalities of position sense are determined in a number of ways: with arms outstretched and eyes closed the affected arm will stray from its position; outspread fingers will change posture ("piano playing" movements); and a positive Romberg's sign will be present.

695. The answer is A (1, 2, 3). (*Adams RD, ed 4. pp 838–839.*)   A tumor confined to the internal auditory canal would affect only the VIIth and VIIIth cranial nerves, producing a facial palsy and disturbances of both the vestibular and auditory components of the VIIIth nerve. An acoustic neuroma would cause diplopia only if extended out of the canal into the adjacent cerebellopontine angle, thereby compressing the VIth nerve and eventually the Vth, IXth, Xth nerves; brainstem; and cerebellum. The earliest symptom is usually hearing loss, but by the time of the first neurologic examination the clinical picture is quite complex.

696. The answer is B (1, 3). (*Adams RD, ed 4. pp 78–79.*)   The tremor of Parkinson's disease is a resting tremor that is aggravated by emotional stress. It is absent during sleep. Tremors occurring with action (i.e., intention tremors) are usually secondary to a lesion in the cerebellum or its pathways. The parkinsonian tremor is coarse with a frequency of 3 to 5 Hz and is often referred to as a "pill rolling tremor" because of the characteristic movements of the thumb and fingers. The tongue, eyelids, and jaw are all subject to the tremor, which has a constant frequency.

697. The answer is B (1, 3). (*Adams RD, ed 4. pp 192–195.*)   The normal optic disc is palest laterally and has the most conspicuous pigment deposition along the lateral boundary. The large vessels of the retina pierce the disc within the optic cup. The cup itself appears white. The clinician must be familiar with these normal anatomic features of the disc in order to identify lesions or congenital abnormalities of that area. Other significant features of the disc that should be noted during the ophthalmoscopic examination include the size of the disc, the color of the nerve fiber layer and its degree of capillarity, the size of the vessels, and the distinctness of the disc margins.

698. The answer is D (4). (*Adams RD, ed 4. p 122.*)   Peripheral nerve and somite distributions coincide only in the thoracic region. Rearrangement of the somites by development of the head and limbs produces a situation in which the peripheral nerves carry either more or fewer fibers than those from one somite. In the thorax, the somites retain their simple segmental arrangement, which coincides with the peripheral nerve. The muscles and bones derived from each somite display a similar pattern. In the limbs, many of the muscles and bones are formed from more than one somite and therefore receive innervation from more than one source.

699. The answer is C (2, 4). (*Adams RD, ed 4. pp 612–613.*)   Approximately 50 percent of patients with HIV infection will eventually develop clinical evidence of an HIV encephalitis. This is currently referred to as the AIDS dementia complex (ADC) and is not considered to be a manifestation of an opportunistic infection. The disease normally has an insidious onset and has the features suggestive of a subcortical dementing process. It is therefore characterized by apathy, psychomotor slowing, and impersistence as well as motor abnormalities and ataxia. Neuropathologic features are a diffuse multifocal rarefaction of the cerebral white matter with perivascular infiltrates of lymphocytes and multinucleated cells.

700. The answer is C (2, 4). (*Kaufman, ed 3. p 331.*) The Klüver-Bucy syndrome describes the behavioral changes following bilateral anterior temporal damage. The most common causes of the syndrome are herpes encephalitis, trauma, bilateral lobectomies, infarction, and end-stage Alzheimer's disease and Pick's disease. Clinical features include indiscriminate hypersexuality for both animate and inanimate objects, aggression, amnesia, hyperorality, and hypermetamorphosis (excessive exploration of the environment).

701. The answer is C (2, 4). (*Adams RD, ed 4. p 944.*) Progressive supranuclear palsy usually occurs in people over age 60. Pathologic changes are the loss of neurons and gliosis in the periaqueductal gray matter, superior colliculus, subthalamic nucleus, red nucleus, pallidum, dentate, pretectal and vestibular nuclei, and occulomotor nucleus. Clinical features include difficulty in downward gaze and later in horizontal gaze; axial dystonia; dysarthria and dysphagia; gait ataxia; and extension of the neck. The patient often exhibits personality changes characterized by anxiety, dependency, and dysphoria. The occular changes and cervical extension give the patient an "apprehensive" appearance.

702. The answer is B (1, 3). (*Adams RD, ed 4. pp 602–604.*) Herpes simplex encephalitis may occur at any age. Although the disease is probably due to the dissemination of a reactivated cold sore virus, the presence of these sores is not helpful in making a diagnosis. Patients may present with a wide range of nonspecific symptoms and signs including fever, personality change, delerium, seizures, ataxia, cranial nerve palsies, and hemiparesis. About one-third demonstrate the amnesia classically associated with the condition. The disease is usually rapidly progressive over 1 to 2 weeks. A brain biopsy is required to confirm or dispute the diagnosis, which may have been incorrect in as many as half the clinically suspected cases. Acyclovir has reduced the mortality of the disease from 70 to approximately 20 percent. As many as 45 percent of patients have made a successful recovery by 6 months.

703. The answer is A (1, 2, 3). (*Adams RD, ed 4. pp 709–710.*) The incidences of seizures after closed and open head injuries are approximately 5 and 50 percent, respectively. Patients who experience their first seizure at the time of injury are less likely to experience recurrence than those who have a delayed onset of seizures. The frequency of seizures tends to decrease with time and as many as 30 percent will remit completely.

704. The answer is B (1, 3). (*Adams RD, ed 4. pp 764–765.*) Approximately 20 to 40 percent of patients with solitary optic neuritis will eventually go on to develop the clinical features of multiple sclerosis. The initial manifestations of the disease range from mild to severe. About 10 percent of patients will develop a steadily progressive downhill course; however, approximately one-third of patients will not be functionally disabled after 10 years. The majority of patients with progressive disease will develop cognitive deficits. The chance of relapse is markedly increased by emotional or physical stress.

705. The answer is E (all). (*Adams RD, ed 4. pp 580–581.*) Lyme disease is caused by the spirochete *Borrelia burgdorferi,* whose usual vector is the deer tick. The peak incidence of the disease is between June and September. Patients usually present with the insidious onset of malaise, low-grade fever, and arthralgias. The classic skin rash associated with the illness is erythema chronicum migrans, which consists of a central red spot surrounded by a ring of erythema. Like another spirochete, *Treponema pallidum, Borrelia burgdorferi* is a great imitator and may present with diverse multisystem pathology. Neurologic involvement may produce peripheral and cranial nerve palsies, meningoencephalitis, seizures, and headache. The peripheral neuropathy may resemble a Guillain-Barré syndrome and rapidly progress to a quadriparesis. The lethargy, malaise, and dysphoria may sometimes be misinterpreted as a major depressive disorder. Dementia and psychosis have both been attributed to Lyme disease.

706. The answer is B (1, 3). (*Adams RD, ed 4. pp 846–850.*) Anoxia results in the catabolism of neurons and the accumulation of catabolic products that cause further cellular destruction. The areas of initial and major destruction are the watershed zones. The permanent neurologic sequelae of anoxic encephalopathy are persistent coma, dementia, amnesia, extrapyramidal and choreoathetoid syndromes, myoclonus, and cerebellar ataxia. A progressive postanoxic encephalopathy may produce delayed and progressive neurologic deficits. Although patients may develop a chronic confusional state, they will not exhibit psychosis.

707. The answer is D (4). (*Adams RD, ed 4. pp 926–927.*) The pathology of Alzheimer's disease is characterized by the following: cortical atrophy and neuronal loss usually involving the frontal, temporal, and parietal lobes; neuritic plaques; neurofibrillary tangles; and granulovacuolar degeneration of neurons. These cellular changes are normally most pronounced in the temporoparietal association areas and in the hippocampus and subicular and presubicular regions. Lewy bodies are normally found in Parkinson's disease. Despite the apparent clarity and specificity of the above pathologic changes, individual variations are not unusual.

708. The answer is E (all). (*Adams RD, ed 4. p 543.*) Meningiomas of the olfactory groove often reach massive proportions before coming to the attention of the physician. They initially grow into the inferior orbitofrontal lobes, where they produce the personality changes of amotivation, jocularity, poor impulse control, and low insight. Compression of the ipsilateral optic nerve will produce optic atrophy, while the raised intracranial pressure will produce contralateral papilledema (the Kennedy syndrome). Patients may therefore develop unilateral or total blindness. Despite their size, these tumors can usually be successfully excised.

709. The answer is A (1, 2, 3). (*Adams RD, ed 4. p 628.*) Most occlusions of the middle cerebral artery are embolic and usually involve one of the branches of the artery, i.e., the superior or inferior divisions and their branches. The superior branch supplies the rolandic and prerolandic areas, while the inferior branch supplies the inferior parietal and lateral temporal areas. Occlusion of the superior division causes a dense contralateral sensorimotor deficit and deviation of the head and eyes to the side of the occlusion. Left-sided lesions produce a motor aphasia with deficits in the comprehension of written and spoken words. Occlusion of the inferior branch produces a Wernicke's aphasia and a homonymous hemianopia.

710. The answer is E (all). (*Kaufman, ed 3. pp 34–35.*) Disruption of the oculomotor nerve produces ipsilateral ptosis; a dilated, unreactive pupil; and diplopia. The ipsilateral eye is deviated downward and outward because of paresis of the medial rectus, inferior oblique, inferior rectus, and superior rectus. Diplopia is aggravated by attempting to adduct the affected eye. The third nerve nucleus is situated in the midbrain and passes through the red nucleus and corticospinal tract.

711. The answer is C (2, 4). (*Strub, p 219.*) It is sometimes difficult to distinguish completely between an Alzheimer's dementia and multi-infarct dementia. Many patients have evidence for both pathologies. Features that may help to distinguish the two conditions include a history of hypertension or transient ischemic attacks; stepwise progression of the illness; the presence of neurologic signs such as abnormal reflexes or motor and sensory abnormalities; and pseudobulbar signs. The amnesia of the multi-infarct dementia is seldom as dominant a part of the clinical picture as that of Alzheimer's disease. The presence of multiple white matter lesions on MRI will support a diagnosis of multi-infarct dementia.

712. The answer is E (all). *(Adams RD, ed 4. p 201.)* Tunnel vision describes a concentric diminishment of the visual field. Apart from hysteria, there are several causes of tunnel vision. These include glaucoma, retinal disease (retinitis pigmentosa and choroidoretinitis), papilledema, bilateral lesions of the anterior calcarine cortex, acute ischemia (e.g., migraine), and chronic syphilitic optic neuritis. A useful clue to distinguishing hysterical from true tunnel vision is to remember that, even with tunnel vision, the area of the visual field will increase with distance from the object.

713. The answer is C (2, 4). *(Adams RD, ed 4. pp 1028–1034.)* The combination of absent ankle and knee jerks and an extensor plantar response suggests a mixed upper and lower motor neuron pathology. Conditions that may produce this clinical picture are subacute combined degeneration of the cord, syphilitic taboparesis, Friedreich's ataxia, motor neuron disease, diabetes mellitus, or a lesion at the level of the conus medullaris.

714. The answer is B (1, 3). *(Adams RD, ed 4. pp 198–201.)* The pathogenesis of papilledema is not fully understood but is currently thought to be caused by swelling of the optic nerve fibers due to stasis of anterograde axoplasmic flow. The later vascular changes (i.e., hyperemia of the disc, capillary dilatation, and hemorrhages) are secondary to edema of the disc. Anything that induces axoplasmic stasis of the optic nerve can therefore cause papilledema. Recognized causes include raised intracranial pressure, arterial hypertension, optic neuritis, obstructed retinal venous drainage (e.g., from a tumor or cavernous sinus thrombosis), hypercapnia, hypoparathyroidism, vitamin A poisoning, lead poisoning, and exophthalmos.

715. The answer is C (2, 4). *(Adams RD, ed 4. p 268.)* Phenytoin is metabolized by the liver. The plasma half-life is about 17 h. Anything that inhibits the microsomal metabolism of phenytoin will effectively raise its blood level and increase the risk of side effects. Among those agents demonstrated to increase levels are disulfiram, chloramphenicol, and fluoxetine.

716. The answer is D (4). *(Adams RD, ed 4. pp 705–706.)* The incidence of chronic subdural hematoma is highest in the elderly and often follows an apparently trivial head injury. In the weeks that follow, headache, dizziness, confusion, and occasionally seizures are the principal symptoms. Patients may develop a gradual onset of hemiparesis and aphasia. As the condition progresses the patient will display a fluctuating level of consciousness. EEG may demonstrate slow high-voltage waves. Lumbar puncture will demonstrate an elevated pressure with normal protein and xanthochromia. CT will normally demonstrate the fluid collection, but this may sometimes be isodense and therefore not discernible. MRI provides a clear but more expensive alternative.

717. The answer is E (all). *(Adams RD, ed 4. pp 612–613.)* HIV has become "the great impersonator" and may produce virtually any constellation of acute or chronic neurologic signs and symptoms. These may result from the virus itself or the presence of an opportunistic infection or other complication of infection with the HIV. Currently documented syndromes include an acute meningoencephalitis shortly after exposure to the virus, a dementia (ADC), peripheral neuropathy, mononeuritis multiplex, myelopathy, polymyositis, and aseptic meningitis.

718. The answer is D (4). *(Adams RD, ed 4. p 597.)* The Ramsay Hunt syndrome consists of the constellation of symptoms that may occur when the reactivation of a latent varicella-zoster virus (shingles) involves the geniculate ganglion. Vesicles are normally seen in the external auditory canal. Other clinical features are facial nerve paresis, ipsilateral loss of pain in the anterior two-thirds of the tongue, deafness, dizziness, pain in the ear and mastoid, and hyperacusis.

719. The answer is B (1, 3).   (*Adams RD, ed 4. pp 953–954.*)   It is important to rule out treatable causes of muscle wasting before accepting a diagnosis of amyotrophic lateral sclerosis. The most common cause is cervical spondylosis, and myelography or MRI is indicated to evaluate this possibility. Other conditions that should be excluded are cervical cord tumor or compression, syringomyelia, meningovascular syphilis, Klumpke's paralysis, cervical ribs, and ulnar or median nerve palsies. Disuse secondary to local injury or arthritis will also produce wasting.

720. The answer is C (2, 4).   (*Strub, pp 456–459.*)   No clear definition of *episodic dyscontrol* exists. In simple terms one may state that the more primitive or the more inappropriate the violence is, the more likely it is that a neuropathologic substrate for the behavioral change will be found. Nonpurposeful rage attacks are often associated with lesions in the area of the hypothalamus. Orbitofrontal deficits will result in lack of impulse control and a "short fuse" and violence that is typically triggered by a perceived threat or insult. These patients are often remorseful after they have calmed down. Patients with chronic confusional states are often involved in aggressive behavior that is nonpurposeful and short-lived. The relationship between epilepsy and violence remains controversial. Patients may be violent as a consequence of their ictal/periictal confusion. It is most unlikely that a seizure can manifest as a nonstereotypic violent act. Interictal personality change may result in a hypermoral personality that feels justified in pursuing violence as a means to an end.

721. The answer is A (1, 2, 3).   (*Kaufman, ed 3. pp 394–395.*)   Tardive dyskinesia usually occurs after at least 1 year of neuroleptic treatment. The symptoms remit in 40 percent of patients after discontinuing the neuroleptic. Numerous drugs have been used to treat the condition; reserpine is usually considered the most effective. Other agents used include clonazepam; acetylcholine precursors such as deanol, lecithin, and choline; sodium valproate; baclofen; and diltiazem.

722. The answer is C (2, 4).   (*Adams RD, ed 4. pp 106–107.*)   Axons from the secondary nociceptive neurons decussate in the anterior spinal commisure and ascend in the anterolateral funiculus. There are two major ascending spinal pathways: the lateral spinothalamic tract, which acts as a fast relay system, and a slower spinoreticulothalamic pathway. The fast system, the (neo)spinothalamic system, projects to discrete areas of the sensory cortex and is responsible for discriminative functions. The slower (paleo)reticulothalamic tract projects via the laminar and intralaminar nuclei to diffuse limbic and frontal projections and is involved in determining the affective or motivational relevance of a nociceptive stimulus.

723. The answer is D (4).   (*Adams RD, ed 4. p 223.*)   The Argyll Robertson pupil is characterized by small, unequal pupils; failure to react to light or mydriatic drugs; constriction on accommodation; and occasional atrophy of the iris. Similar signs are occasionally seen with diabetes, Lyme disease, multiple sclerosis, and pinealomas.

724. The answer is E (all).   (*Adams RD, ed 4. p 139.*)   Vertebrobasilar migraine most commonly occurs in young women. Symptoms include transient blindness, vertigo, ataxia and perioral tingling. Occasionally, patients may develop an atypical psychosis, alteration in consciousness, or even quadriplegia. These symptoms usually precede the headache and last about 30 min.

725. The answer is C (2, 4).   (*Strub, p 228.*)   In simple terms, patients with cortical dementia have lost the cortical "hardware" to perform complex cognitive tasks while patients with subcortical dementia have lost the "drive" necessary to perform. Patients with a subcortical dementia will therefore present with a "dilapidated" cognition characterized by apathy and dysphoria, and their performance will be influenced by the emotional valence of the situation (or the enthusiasm of the examiner). Cortical dementias will present early with deficits in cortical function: apraxia, agnosia, language deficits, and memory deficits. Subcortical dementias will be accompanied by other evidence of the primary disease process, e.g., movement disorder.

726. The answer is A (1, 2, 3). (*Adams RD, ed 4. pp 549–550.*) Apart from intracranial seeding of metastases, bronchial carcinoma may produce a number of varied nonmetastatic syndromes (paraneoplastic disorders). These include limbic encephalitis, which may produce changes in mood, comportment, thought processes, and cognition; peripheral neuropathy; cerebellar degeneration; myopathy; and myasthenia gravis.

727. The answer is D (4). (*Adams RD, ed 4. p 150.*) Trigeminal neuralgia usually has its onset in middle or late adult life and is three times more common in females. Patients experience 10- to 30-s paroxysms of stabbing or burning pain in an area supplied by a branch of the trigeminal nerve. These paroxysms may persist for several weeks and there may be a chronic low-grade hypersensitivity or dull ache in the area between attacks. There is no associated motor or sensory loss.

728. The answer is A (1, 2, 3). (*Adams RD, ed 4. pp 114–115.*) The Djerine-Roussy syndrome is caused by a lesion in the posterolateral thalamus. The immediate consequence is a contralateral sensory loss. After a delay of several weeks or months, with or without the return of sensory function, the patient experiences unusual pain in the area of original sensory loss. This dysesthesia is aggravated by factors such as change of temperature or touch. There is no simple or effective treatment and the condition is usually chronic.

729. The answer is D (4). (*Adams RD, ed 4. p 364.*) Inappropriate and jocular affect (so-called pseudo-hypomania) is found in patients with right-side lesions. In particular, patients with right frontal lesions may exhibit an inappropriate response to their illness and appear almost impervious to the consequences of any resultant disability. This is referred to as *anosognosia* and may be mistaken for a mild hypomania. Right subcortical and periventricular lesions have also been found in association with hypomanic states. Patients with a left prefrontal lesion usually develop dysphoria that may meet criteria for a major depressive disorder.

730. The answer is B (1, 3). (*Adams RD, ed 4. pp 144–145.*) Cluster headaches usually occur in men aged 20 to 40. They consist of episodes of pain involving, and localized to, the eye on one side and are often associated with lacrimation and nasal congestion. Occasionally the patient exhibits a partial Horner's syndrome. The pain characteristically lasts 20 to 30 min and awakens the patient several hours into sleep. The pain is usually aggravated by alcohol. Each "cluster period" lasts about 6 weeks and tends to recur at the same time each year. Possible treatments are steroids, propranolol, methysergide, or lithium.

731. The answer is A (1, 2, 3). (*Adams RD, ed 4. pp 651–655.*) Transient ischemic attacks (TIAs) are almost always associated with atherosclerotic thrombosis. By definition, they produce no neurologic deficit beyond 24 h. TIAs indicate significant atherosclerotic disease and therefore predict a higher incidence of myocardial infarction and cerebrovascular accidents. The patient may experience only a single TIA or many hundred and a major occlusive event may occur at any time. The use of surgical resection remains controversial and should probably be limited to those patients who have severe extracranial stenosis or ulcerating plaques.

732. The answer is B (1, 3). (*Kaufman, ed 3. pp 64–65.*) Mononeuritis multiplex describes a lesion in two or more nerves. Conditions that may produce this pattern are diabetes, HIV infection, leprosy, sarcoidosis, rheumatoid arthritis, polyarteritis nodosa, and carcinoma.

733–737. The answers are: 733-E, 734-C, 735-B, 736-A, 737-D. (*Adams RD, ed 4. pp 63, 66, 276, 507, 941.*) Lewy bodies are eosinophilic cytoplasmic inclusions found in the cell bodies of the substantia nigra in patients with Parkinson's disease. Close scrutiny will often detect similar bodies in cortical neurons and the sympathetic ganglia.

Obliteration of the subarachnoid state by previous or low-grade meningitis may result in normal pressure hydrocephalus (NPH). The classic triad of NPH is a wide-based gait, urinary incontinence, and dementia. Other etiologies of NPH include previous subarachnoid hemorrhage, achondroplasia, and Paget's disease.

Chorea describes an involuntary, jerky, arrhythmic movement. Grimacing and peculiar respiratory sounds may also be associated with the condition. Muscle tone tends to be reduced in all limbs and the reflexes are pendular. Chorea is caused by damage to the caudate nuclei. Possible etiologies include Huntington's disease, pregnancy, Sydenham's chorea, and use of neuroleptics.

Hemiballismus is characterized by wild flinging movements of the arm or leg. It is caused by a lesion of the subthalamic nucleus.

Akinetic mutism describes a state in which the patient is awake and vigilant but makes no attempt to communicate or interact with the outside world. The state has also been called a "coma vigil." This clinical picture may be caused by lesions of the basis pontis or bilateral cingulate cortex.

738–740. The answers are: 738-C, 739-A, 740-B. (*Adams RD, ed 4. pp 624–642.*) Because each of the major cerebral arteries supplies a specific territory, it is possible to delineate the site of a cerebrovascular accident. The anterior cerebral artery supplies the frontal pole, anterolateral frontal lobe, anterior limb of the internal capsule, the head of the caudate nucleus, and the putamen. Obstruction of this system produces contralateral motor and sensory loss and behavioral changes associated with frontal lobe lesions.

The middle cerebral artery splits into superior and inferior divisions and supplies the insula; posterior limb of the internal capsule; external capsule; caudate, frontal, and temporal lobes; and part of the parietal and occipital lobes.

The posterior cerebral artery supplies the midbrain, thalamus, and inferomedial portions of the temporal and occipital lobes.

The vertebral arteries supply the spinal cord and give rise to the basilar artery, which in turn supplies the pons, midbrain, and cerebellum.

741–745. The answers are: 741-E, 742-A, 743-D, 744-B, 745-C. (*Adams RD, ed 4. pp 252–258.*) A thorough history will often provide reliable information about the site of a seizure focus. Describing what he witnessed in his own wife, Hughlings Jackson described the features of a seizure spreading from its origin in the prefrontal motor area. The so-called Jacksonian march manifests as a tonic-clonic seizure starting in the extremity and spreading to involve all muscle groups. The patient will deviate the eyes to the side opposite to the focus if area 8 of the prefrontal cortex is involved. Generalized spread will produce a loss of consciousness.

Hippocampal sclerosis results in damage, and therefore a seizure focus, in the mediotemporal areas. This produces a number of complex abnormal subjective experiences and bizarre motor behavior. An ictus confined to the mediotemporal area will produce context-inappropriate affective experience often associated with a rising epigastric discomfort and olfactory or gustatory hallucinations. The patient will often stare motionlessly and may also exhibit lip smacking or other bizarre orofacial movements.

Spread from the mediobasal temporal area to involve temporal neocortical areas may produce auditory hallucinations (Heschl's gyrus), visual hallucinations, or aphasia.

An ictal focus in a primary sensory cortex will produce unformed sensory experiences. Since the orbitofrontal lobe is a paralimbic association area, a seizure arising from this region will have autonomic manifestations.

746–750. The answers are: 746-C, 747-D, 748-G, 749-E, 750-B. (*Strub, pp 253–301.*) Lesions in the orbitomedial frontal lobes are characterized by stimulus-bound behavior and an inability to suppress limbic drives. Patients will therefore exhibit a lack of motivation and drive (abulia) if left to their own devices. However, in social situations they will fail to modulate their behavior and will act outside accepted social norms. They will be angered easily and may be involved in violent outbursts. They typically display a shallow facetiousness (witzelsucht) and disregard for the consequences of their actions.

Lesions in the inferoparietal lobule may produce a chronic confusional state. Since this area is considered to be a heteromodal association cortex, any small lesion of the area will have a profound influence on higher cognition and therefore behavior.

Temporolimbic epilepsy produces a classic constellation of symptoms including hyperreligiosity, hypergraphia, hyperviscosity (an inability to change the subject), a sense of personal importance, hyposexuality, and persistent dysphoria.

Discharging diencephalic lesions produce "rage attacks" consisting of brief, nonpurposeful, violent outbursts, which often include biting. These are often precipitated by hunger. Patients often exhibit other neuroendocrine abnormalities.

Left prefrontal lesions, particularly in the opercular area, usually produce a depressive disorder that usually responds to psychotropics. Right prefrontal lesions typically produce a "pseudohypomania" that is essentially an anosognosia (a blatant disregard of the gravity of a situation).

Bibliography

NEUROLOGY

Adams JH, Corsellis JAN, Duchen L: *Greenfield's Neuropathology,* 4th ed. New York, John Wiley, 1984.

Adams RD, Victor M: *Principles of Neurology,* 4th ed. New York, McGraw-Hill, 1989.

Balldessarini RJ, Frankenberg FR: Clozapine: A novel antipsychotic agent. *N Engl J Med* 324:746–754, 1991.

Carpenter MB: *Core Text of Neuroanatomy,* 3d ed. Baltimore, Williams & Wilkins, 1985.

Chusid JG: *Correlative Neuroanatomy and Functional Neurology,* 19th ed. Norwalk, CT, Appleton & Lange, 1985.

Cooper JR, Bloom FE, Roth RH: *The Biochemical Basis of Neuropharmacology,* 5th ed. New York, Oxford University Press, 1986.

Dalakos M, Wickman A, Sever J: AIDS and the nervous system. *JAMA* 261:2396–2399, 1989.

DeAngelis LM: Primary central nervous system lymphomas. *Neurology* 41:619–621, 1991.

Fischer HW, Ketonen L: *Radiographic Neuroanatomy: A Working Atlas.* New York, McGraw-Hill, 1991.

Fishman RA: *Cerebrospinal Fluid in Diseases of the Nervous System.* Philadelphia, WB Saunders, 1980.

Gilman AG, Rall TW, Nies AS, Taylor P: *Goodman and Gilman's The Pharmacological Basis of Therapeutics,* 8th ed. New York, Pergamon, 1990.

Gilman S, Newman SW: *Manter and Gatz's Essentials of Clinical Neuroanatomy and Neurophysiology,* 7th ed. Philadelphia, FA Davis, 1987.

Glaser JS: *Neuroophthalmology,* 2d ed. Philadelphia, JB Lippincott, 1990.

Goetz CG, Tanner CM, Klawans HL: Pharmacology of hallucinations induced by long-term drug therapy. *Am J Psychiatry* 139:494–497, 1982.

Jankovic J, Brin M: Therapeutic uses of botulinum toxin. *N Engl J Med* 324:1186–1194, 1991.

Jones HR, Siehert RG: Neurological manifestations of infective endocarditis. *Brain* 112:1295–1315, 1989.

Joynt RJ: *Clinical Neurology.* New York, Harper & Row, 1990.

Kandel ER, Schwartz JH: *Principles of Neural Science,* 2d ed. New York, Elsevier, 1985.

Kaplan HI, BJ Sadock: *Comprehensive Textbook of Psychiatry,* 5th ed. Baltimore, Williams & Wilkins, 1989.

Kaplan HI, BJ Sadock: *Synopsis of Psychiatry,* 6th ed. Baltimore, Williams & Wilkins, 1991.

Kelly JJ, Adelman LS, Beckman E, Bhan I: Polyneuropathies associated with IgM monoclonal gammopathies. *Arch Neurol* 45:1355–1359, 1988.

Langston JW, Irwin I: MPTP: Current concepts and controversies. *Adv Neurol* 9:485–507, 1986.

Logigian EL, Kaplan RF, Steere AC: Chronic neurologic manifestations of Lyme disease. *N Engl J Med* 323:1438–1443, 1990.

Mandell GL, Douglass RG Jr, Bennett JE: *Principles and Practice of Infectious Diseases,* 3d ed. New York, Churchill Livingstone, 1990.

McArthur JC: Neurologic manifestations of AIDS. *Medicine* 66:407–437, 1987.

McGeer PL, Eccles JC, McGeer EG: *Molecular Neurobiology of the Mammalian Brain,* 2d ed. Plenum, 1987.

Mesulam MM, Waxman SG, Geschwind N, Sabin T: Acute confusional states with right middle cerebral artery infarctions. *J Neurol Neurosurg Psychiatry* 39:84–89, 1986.

Meyers MG, Norris JW, Hackinski VC, et al: Cardiac sequelae of acute stroke. *Stroke* 13:838–842, 1982.

Musher DM, Hamill R, Baughn RE: Effect of human immunodeficiency virus (HIV) infection on the course of syphilis and on the response to treatment. *Ann Intern Med* 113:872–881, 1990.

Okazaki H: *Fundamentals of Neuropathology: Morphologic Basis of Neurologic Disorders,* 2d ed. New York, Igaku-Shoin, 1989.

Parkinson Study Group: Effects of deprenyl on the progression of disability in early Parkinson's disease. *N Engl J Med* 321:1364–1371, 1989.

Patten J: *Neurological Differential Diagnosis.* New York, Springer-Verlag, 1982.

Plum F, Posner JB: *The Diagnosis of Stupor and Coma,* 3d ed. Philadelphia, FA Davis, 1980.

Poirier J, Gray F, Escourolle RE: *Manual of Basic Neuropathology,* 3d ed. Philadelphia, WB Saunders, 1990.

Pruitt A, Rubin RH, Kerchmer AW, Duncan GW: Neurologic complications of bacterial endocarditis. *Medicine* 57:329–343, 1978.

Report of the Therapeutics and Technology Assessment Subcommittee of the American Academy of Neurology: Assessment: Positron emission tomography. *Neurology* 48:163–167, 1991.

Rowland LP: *Merritt's Textbook of Neurology,* 8th ed. Philadelphia, Lea & Febiger, 1989.

Siegel G, Agranoff B, Albers RW, Molinoff P: *Basic Neurochemistry,* 4th ed. New York, Raven, 1989.

Victor M, Adams RD, Collins GH: *The Wernicke-Korsakoff Syndrome and Related Neurologic Problems due to Alcohol and Malnutrition,* 2d ed. Philadelphia, FA Davis, 1989.

Weiger WA, Bear DM: An approach to the neurology of aggression. *J Psychiatr Res* 22:85–98, 1988.

PSYCHIATRY

Adams RD, Victor M: *Principles of Neurology,* 4th ed. New York, McGraw-Hill, 1989.

American Psychiatric Association (APA): *Diagnostic and Statistical Manual of Mental Disorders,* 3d ed, rev. (*DSM III-R*). Washington, DC, American Psychiatric Association, 1987.

American Psychiatric Association (APA)—Task Force Report: *Benzodiazepine: Dependence, Toxicity, Abuse.* Washington, DC, American Psychiatric Association, 1990.

American Psychiatric Association (APA): *Treatments of Psychiatric Disorders,* vols 1–3. Washington, DC, American Psychiatric Association, 1989.

American Psychiatric Press: *Review of Psychiatry,* vol 9. Washington, DC, American Psychiatric Press, 1990.

Davis K, Klar H, Coyle JT: *Foundations of Psychiatry.* Philadelphia, WB Saunders, 1991.

Hales RE, Frances AJ: *American Psychiatric Association Annual Review,* vol 6. Washington, DC, American Psychiatric Press, 1987.

Hollister LE, Csernansky JG: *Clinical Pharmacology of Psychotherapeutic Drugs,* 3d ed. New York, Churchill Livingstone, 1990.

Jenike MA: *Geriatric Psychiatry and Psychopharmacology.* Chicago, Year Book Medical, 1989.

Kaplan HI, Sadock BJ: *Comprehensive Textbook of Psychiatry,* 5th ed. Baltimore, Williams & Wilkins, 1989.

Kaufman DM: *Clinical Neurology for Psychiatrists,* 3d ed. Philadelphia, WB Saunders, 1990.

Lader M, Herrington R: *Biological Treatments in Psychiatry.* New York, Oxford University Press, 1990.

Physicians' Desk Reference (PDR). Oradell, NJ, Medical Economics, 1991.

Simon RI: *Clinical Psychiatry and the Law.* Washington, DC, American Psychiatric Press, 1987.

Strub RL, Black FW: *Neurobehavioral Disorders—A Clinical Approach.* Philadelphia, FA Davis, 1988.

Tasman A, Hales RE, Frances AJ: *Review of Psychiatry,* vol 8. Washington, DC, American Psychiatric Press, 1989.

Tasman A, Goldfinger SM, Kaufman CA: *Review of Psychiatry,* vol 9. Washington, DC, American Psychiatric Press, 1989.